MISCELLANEOUS WRITINGS

OF THE LATE

DR. MAGINN

EDITED BY

DR. SHELTON MACKENZIE

VOL. I.

The Odoherty Papers

William Maginn

Redfield, Publisher, N.Y.

THE

ODOHERTY PAPERS

BY THE LATE

WILLIAM MAGINN, LL.D.

ANNOTATED BY

DR. SHELTON MACKENZIE

EDITOR OF "SHEIL'S SKETCHES OF THE IRISH BAR"—"THE NOCTES AMBROSIANÆ," ETC.

IN TWO VOLUMES

VOL. I

REDFIELD
34 BEEKMAN STREET, NEW YORK
1855

STEREOTYPED BY C. C. SAVAGE,
13 Chambers Street, N. Y.

EDITOR'S PREFACE.

On William Maginn's death it was truly stated, by a writer in *Fraser's Magazine*, that he had "resembled Swift not merely in his wit, but in the utter carelessness with which he regarded the fate of the productions of his genius. If they served the purpose of the moment, whether it were to make a minister tremble or a lady smile, 'the Doctor' never troubled himself further about his thunder or his jest. They might be claimed by any passer-by, for no one ever contributed more to the fame of others or so completely disregarded his own. It is chiefly to this carelessness about all that more immediately affected him that we must ascribe the want of some one great work, whereby the Doctor might now be remembered. Though in a marked degree competent to bestow such a gift on the literary world, the natural discursiveness of his disposition induced him rather to find a ready vent for the superabundance of his learning and wit in the pages of the leading periodicals."

Maginn had what might be called a fatal facility of composition. The stores of his learning and knowledge were so vast that his memory ever found them exhaustless. The composition of a magazine-article, no matter what the subject, appeared to involve scarcely any thing more than the mere manual labour of putting it upon paper. He rarely had occasion to refer to authorities. He was a great reader, and what he once read he never forgot.

Few men were equal to him in conversation—though he was the reverse of a great talker. It was the variety of topics upon which he threw a light, and not the diffuseness of his remarks, which gave a proper idea of the wealth of his conversation. Meet him when you might, turn the discourse into whatever channels you pleased, Maginn was master of every subject—the most recondite as well as the most familiar.

Careless of his fame, and too fond of society (and its temptations) to devote himself steadily and continuously to any one work, he has left behind him but *disjecta membra poetæ.* He scattered—I might say wasted—his great powers on Magazines. All that he wrote was marked with originality and learning, wit and satire. They included a large range of subjects—poetry, politics, classics, antiquities, history, criticism, and fiction.

Under the *sobriquet* of MORGAN ODOHERTY, he first obtained a high reputation as a Magazine writer. The two volumes of "ODOHERTY PAPERS" which I now lay before the public, are principally taken from *Blackwood.* The remainder of this collection will include Maginn's Shakspere Papers, his Homeric Ballads, and other translations from the classics, his shorter prose stories, his miscellaneous poetry, and such of his Fraserian Papers as possess more than temporary interest. It may be well to add that most of the present volumes were published before Maginn had reached the age of thirty.

In the concluding portion of this collection of his Miscellaneous writings, I shall give a biography of Maginn, much more in detail than the Memoir which I wrote last year, for the closing volume of my edition of "THE NOCTES AMBROSIANÆ."

R. SHELTON MACKENZIE.

NEW YORK,
April 14, 1855.

EDITOR'S PREFACE.

On William Maginn's death it was truly stated, by a writer in *Fraser's Magazine*, that he had "resembled Swift not merely in his wit, but in the utter carelessness with which he regarded the fate of the productions of his genius. If they served the purpose of the moment, whether it were to make a minister tremble or a lady smile, 'the Doctor' never troubled himself further about his thunder or his jest. They might be claimed by any passer-by, for no one ever contributed more to the fame of others or so completely disregarded his own. It is chiefly to this carelessness about all that more immediately affected him that we must ascribe the want of some one great work, whereby the Doctor might now be remembered. Though in a marked degree competent to bestow such a gift on the literary world, the natural discursiveness of his disposition induced him rather to find a ready vent for the superabundance of his learning and wit in the pages of the leading periodicals."

Maginn had what might be called a fatal facility of composition. The stores of his learning and knowledge were so vast that his memory ever found them exhaustless. The composition of a magazine-article, no matter what the subject, appeared to involve scarcely any thing more than the mere manual labour of putting it upon paper. He rarely had occasion to refer to authorities. He was a great reader, and what he once read ho never forgot.

Few men were equal to him in conversation—though he was the reverse of a great talker. It was the variety of topics upon which he threw a light, and not the diffuseness of his remarks, which gave a proper idea of the wealth of his conversation. Meet him when you might, turn the discourse into whatever channels you pleased, Maginn was master of every subject—the most recondite as well as the most familiar.

Careless of his fame, and too fond of society (and its temptations) to devote himself steadily and continuously to any one work, he has left behind him but *disjecta membra poetæ.* He scattered—I might say wasted—his great powers on Magazines. All that he wrote was marked with originality and learning, wit and satire. They included a large range of subjects—poetry, politics, classics, antiquities, history, criticism, and fiction.

Under the *sobriquet* of MORGAN ODOHERTY, he first obtained a high reputation as a Magazine writer. The two volumes of "ODOHERTY PAPERS" which I now lay before the public, are principally taken from *Blackwood.* The remainder of this collection will include Maginn's Shakspere Papers, his Homeric Ballads, and other translations from the classics, his shorter prose stories, his miscellaneous poetry, and such of his Fraserian Papers as possess more than temporary interest. It may be well to add that most of the present volumes were published before Maginn had reached the age of thirty.

In the concluding portion of this collection of his Miscellaneous writings, I shall give a biography of Maginn, much more in detail than the Memoir which I wrote last year, for the closing volume of my edition of "THE NOCTES AMBROSIANÆ."

R. SHELTON MACKENZIE.

NEW YORK,
April 14, 1855.

CONTENTS OF VOLUME I.

MEMOIRS OF ENSIGN AND ADJUTANT ODOHERTY— PAGE.

Chapter I.—Early Life.—Enters the Army.—Epigram on a Dowager.—Tragedy of Euphemia.—Stanzas to Lady Gilhooly.—Ballad of Godolphin 1

Chapter II.—At the Battle of New Orleans.—Prisoner-at-War in America.—Love-passages with Mrs. M'Whirter.—Imitations of John Wilson's Poetry.—Chanson-a-boire.—Residence in Modern Athens. 14

Chapter III.—Acquaintance with the Ettrick Shepherd, Sir William Allan, &c.—Elegy in a Ball-Room.—Beppo Stanzas.—Laudation of the Nicotian Weed 27

Chapter IV.—Success in Edinburgh Society.—Songs.—Visit to Glasgow and Dublin.—Imitation of Monk Lewis.—Magazine Papers 46

Chapter V.—Christopher North's Guest in "The Tent."—Rencontre and Reconciliation with Mrs. M'Whirter.—Lecture on Whiggism.—Odoherty's Song.—The Powldoodies of Burran, a Bivalvicular Chant.—The Last of the Lady 71

NOTE FROM ODOHERTY 91

Odoherty's Garland 93

The Eve of St. Jerry 96

The Rime of the Auncient Waggonere 101

MAXIMS OF ODOHERTY 106

DON JUAN UNREAD 179

THE IRISHMAN AND THE LADY 183

HERE LET ME DINE 185

ANA 186

CHEVY CHASE; a Poem—Idem Latine Redditum 191

THE MAN IN THE BELL 205

PAGE.

The Lost (and Found) Memorandum Book........ 211
A Remedy for the Poor Laws........ 213
Diary........ 215
Love Song........ 216
The Somnambulatory Butcher........ 218
Ailie Mushat's Cairn........ 222
Japanese Poetry and Translation........ 223
Stanzas........ 225
Familiar Letter from the Adjutant........ 227
Imitation of Scott........ 232
Coleridge........ 235
Byron........ 236
Hogg........ 238
Wordsworth........ 238
.... 240
Inishowen........ 242
There's not a Joy that Life can give........ 242
'Tis in vain to complain........ 244
Chanson-a-Boire........ 244
Song of a Fallen Angel........ 245
Pococurante........ 246
An Hundred Years Hence........ 257
A Dozen Years Hence........ 259
The Pewter Quart........ 261
The Leather Bottle........ 264
The Black Jack........ 269
An Idyl on the Battle........ 277
A Twist-imony in Favour of Gin-Twist........ 289
Irish Songs........ 295
Cork is the Aiden for You, Love, and Me........ 305
English Songs........ 307
Lament for Lord Byron........ 319
Odoherty's Dirge........ 320
A Story without a Tail........ 321
Bob Burke's Duel with Ensign Brady........ 336
Drink........ 361
Crambambulee........ 362
Twenty-one Maxims to Marry by........ 363

DR. MAGINN'S

MISCELLANEOUS WRITINGS.

The Odoherty Papers.

SOME ACCOUNT OF THE LIFE AND WRITINGS OF ENSIGN AND ADJUTANT ODOHERTY, LATE OF THE 99th REGT.

CHAPTER I.

Odoherty's Debut.—His Progenitors and Education.—Obtains a Commission in the Militia.—Love-Passages with Augusta M'Craw.—A Ten-shot Duel.—Epigram on a Dowager.—Extract from an unpublished and uncommon Tragedy.—Stanzas to Lady Gilhooly.—Volunteers into the Line.—Voyage to Jamaica.—*Jeu d'Esprit.*—Too late for Embarkation.—Sent to Coventry by his Fellow-Officers.

If there is something painful to the feelings in the awful ceremonial of consigning a deceased friend to the grave, there is something equally consolatory to our affection in perpetuating the remembrance of his talents and virtues, and gathering for his grave a garland which shall long flourish green among the children of men. This may indeed be termed the last and highest proof of our regard, and it is this task which I am now about to discharge (I fear too inadequately) to my deceased friend, Ensign and Adjutant Odoherty, late of the 99th or King's Own Tipperary regiment.*

* In the deeply pathetic lyric—"most musical, most melancholy,"—called Jack Robinson (which may be sung, with a chorus, to that touching melody

In offering to the public some account of the life and writings of this gentleman, I have pleasure in believing that I am not intruding on their notice a person utterly unknown to them. His poems, which have appeared in various periodical publications, have excited a very large portion of the public curiosity and admiration; and when transplanted into the different volumes of the Annual Anthology, they have shone with undiminished lustre amid the blaze of the great poetical luminaries by which they were surrounded.*

The Sailors' Hornpipe), there are a few lines applicable to this case. A lady, rejoicing in the picturesque and euphonious name of Polly Grey, and who has "gone and done it," in the way of matrimony, with a male personage other than Mr. Robinson, to whom she had been engaged "three years ago, afore he went to sea," is accused of infidelity, and adroitly defends herself. Admitting that she had married another man, "because she could not wait," she — but we must quote her own words:—

> "For somebody one day came, and said
> As somebody else had someveres read,
> In some newspaper, as how you was dead,"—
> "I have not been dead at all," said Jack Robinson.

Odoherty's biographer appears in error, even as Polly Grey was, *in re* Jack Robinson, when he speaks of the ensign and adjutant as "deceased." This first portion of the biography appeared in *Blackwood's* Magazine, number eleven, for February, 1818, and in the course of the following year (as will subsequently be seen) Odoherty, like Jack Robinson, emphatically declared that he "had not been dead at all." As, in a case like this, the individual himself is generally supposed to be the best authority as to suspended or actual vitality, it is pretty evident that, albeit Odoherty be above mentioned as defunct, he is to be considered as actually alive — so far as the Magazine is concerned.— M.

* The Annual Anthology, which flourished some sixty or seventy years ago, when verse-writers were comparatively scarce in England, was a receptacle for compositions, bearing the brevet rank or courtesy title of Poetry, which, classed under the generic name of "little effusions," were usually collected from the mysterious portion of the newspapers called "Poets' corner." Now and then, by accident or luck, something readable was thus preserved, but the general character of the collection was so low that were a criminal given the choice between twelve months' labor at the oar, as a galley slave, and six months' perusal of the Anthology, the chance is that, at the end of the first fortnight, he would eagerly solicit the privilege of the galleys, as the lesser evil! The Annual Anthology, in fact, was a sort of poetic safety-valve, in its day, such as the Annuals have formed in our own, and its contents came under the general and generic terms "dull and decent."— M.

Never was there a man more imbued with the very soul and spirit of poetry than Ensign and Adjutant Odoherty. Cut off in the bloom of his years, ere the fair and lovely blossoms of his youth had time to ripen into the golden fruit by which the autumn of his days would have been beautified and adorned, he has deprived the literature of his country of one of its brightest ornaments, and left us to lament that youth, virtue, and talents, should afford no protection from the cruel hand of death.

Before proceeding to the biographical account of this extraordinary person, which it is my intention to give, I think it proper previously to state the very singular manner in which our friendship had its commencement. One evening, in the month of October, 1812, I had the misfortune, from some circumstances here unnecessary to mention, to be conveyed for a night's lodging to the watch-house in Dublin. I had there the good fortune to meet Mr. Odoherty, who was likewise a prisoner. He was seated on a wooden stool, before a table garnished with a great number of empty pots of porter.* He had a tobacco-pipe in his

* We beg leave to hint to our Irish correspondent, that if the *pots* were empty, they could scarcely be termed *pots of porter*.—BLACKWOOD. [And *I* beg leave to hint that, in the watch-house in Dublin, in 1812, such a liquid as *porter* was not at all likely to be in request. The drink of that region would inevitably be—whiskey punch. In 1812, very little malt liquor was used in Ireland. Most of what was made was exported to the British army then under Wellington in the peninsula, to the British West India islands, and to the East Indies. The soldiers drank it, of course, as if it were so much "mother's milk"—only a great deal stronger. In the West Indies, where the drought was great, the draughts were copious. In the East Indies, whenever what was called Cork porter and Fermoy ale happened to arrive, in anything like good condition, it brought a great price, and was imbibed freely. But, in those days, brewers had not arrived at the present certainty of making ale as drinkable on the banks of the Ganges as in London, Dublin, Cork, and Edinburgh, In 1812, London porter was scarcely exported to the East or West Indies: Edinburgh ale was not known much beyond the city of its birth; and the supplies were sent from the porter brewery of Beamish and Crawford, of Cork, and the ale brewery of Thomas Walker & Co., of Fermoy. The last-named concern has wholly ceased, but Cork city rejoices in Beamish and Crawford's porter brewery, whence it also taken one of its parliamentary representatives (1855), in the person of Frank Beamish. At present, the pale ale of Bass and Alsop—rival houses in the small English town of Burton-upon-Trent—is the favorite tipple in British India, where one man asks another to "take a glass

mouth, and was talking with great gallantry to two young ladies of a very interesting appearance, who had been brought there under similar circumstances to himself. There was a touching melancholy in the expression of his countenance, and a melting softness in his voice, which interested me extremely in his favor. With all that urbanity of manner by which he was distinguished, he asked me "to take a sneaker of his swipes." I accepted the invitation, and thus commenced a friendship which ended only with his life, and the fond remembrance of which shall cease only with mine.

Morgan Odoherty was born in the county of Kilkenny, in the year 1789. His father acted for many years as a drover to the Right Honorable Lord Ventry, at that period an eminent grazier;* and on that gentleman's being raised to the peerage, he

of Bass" with him, just as, elsewhere, he would invite him to take a glass of champagne. It is surprising that in Calcutta, Madras, or Bombay, some capitalist does not commence an ale and porter brewery, and go in to make a fortune thereby. Long after Odoherty's time, Guinness's Dublin porter came into note in rivalry with "London Stout." The story goes that Guinness had no great note until *the full body* of one particular brewing attracted the attention of those who *malt*. On cleaning out the vat, there were found the bones and part of the dress of one of the workmen, who had been missing for some weeks. Guinness, it is said, sang small about the matter, but to give his porter the required *body*, instead of boiling down a man, as before, substituted a side of beef, and has continued the ingredient from that time to this. So, after all, even a tee-totaller must admit that Guinness's porter is but a malted description of—*beef-tea!*—M.

* There is a trifling error of fact here. Lord Ventry never was "an eminent drover,"—nor anything half so useful. The family name is Mullins—a patronymic so ungenteel, that it was changed, by letters patent under Queen Victoria's signature (dated 24th February, 1841), to that of "De Moleyns," which, it was hoped, had somewhat of the Norman flavor, and sounded as if it had come down from the Conquest. The Mullins family pretend that they are relations of that Sir Richard Molyneaux, in Lancashire, who founded the ennobled house of Sefton; also that thence came the De Moleyns of Norfolk, descended from a baronial house of that name in Hants. The fact is a certain trooper called Colonel Mullins settled in Ireland, and bought estates (out of his plunder) in Ulster, which he exchanged for property in the "Kingdom of Kerry," and became a member of the Irish Parliament, in the reign of William III. A descendant of his was made a baronet in 1797, and raised to the peerage, as Baron Ventry, in July, 1800. A schoolfellow of mine, at Fermoy in Ireland, some thirty years ago, piqued himself so much on his noble birth that

succeeded to a very considerable portion of his business. He had certainly many opportunities of amassing wealth, but the truth is, he only provided *meat* for others, with the view of getting *drink* for himself. By his wife he had acquired a small property in the county of Carlow, which it was his intention to have kept as a provision for his family. His business, however, gradually decreased, and on the last settlement of his accounts, when he came to liquidate the claims of his creditors on his es-

he had written in all his school-books, "Frederick William Mullins, grandson of the Right Honorable Lord Ventry." As schoolboys are more or less democratic, such an aristocratical inscription as this was unanimously voted "most tolerable and not to be endured." Mullins was civilly requested to erase it, and, on his refusal, there was a solemn incremation of the whole of the books so inscribed. In later years, this Mullins sat in Parliament for Kerry, and was committed to Newgate, London, early in March, 1854, on the charge of uttering a forged power of attorney, and obtaining thereon the amount of fifteen hundred pounds sterling stock, &c., in the Bank of England, belonging to a person of the name of Simpson. Mrs. Lucy de Molyns, his wife, was likewise arrested, and committed on the same charge, but providing the necessary bail for her appearance at the next Central Criminal Court Sessions, she was liberated. Mr. de Molyns was unable to procure the extent of bail demanded (four thousand pounds sterling), and was in consequence conveyed to Newgate, where he died on March 16, 1854. An inquest was held, and a verdict of natural death recorded.—Apropos of the sneer, by Odoherty's biographer, at "an eminent grazier," it may be as well to state that this class of money makers usually accumulated large fortunes in Ireland. One of them, a Mr. Lyons, who lived at Croom in the county of Limerick, purchased vast landed estates, and pushed his sons forward, by his wealth, in the church, the army, and at the bar. Once upon a time (as the old story books say), he gave a splendid *dejeuner a la fourchette*, to which he invited the leading people of the county. Among them was the Lady Isabella Fitzgibbon, (sister of the Earl of Clare), who, affecting either fashionable airs or probably having had a good meal of beef-steaks, before she went out, neglected most of the delicacies of the table, and merely trifled with a lobster salad. Old Lyons, who had a great respect for the substantials, by which he had realized his money, turned round to her as she sat by his side, the picture of aristocratical nonchalance, and kindly said, "Ah, then, my lady, why don't you take some of the good beef and mutton, the chickens and the turkeys, and don't be filling your stomach with that *could* cabbage!" Lady Isabella almost fainted, but contrived to survive. She is yet alive, and unmarried, at that "certain age," which, Byron wickedly says, means "certainly aged." Such is the mournful result of neglecting wholesome fare, and "filling the stomach with *could* cabbage." Let it be a warning to her sex!—M.

tate, he found, to his astonishment, that he had long since *liquidated* his own. The discovery was fatal. The loss of his credit with the world he might have survived, but the loss of his credit with the *whiskey merchant* drove him to despair. He died in the year 1798, a melancholy monument of an ill-spent life.

Of his mother, Mr. Odoherty was ever in the habit of talking with gratitude and respect; and the manner in which she discharged the duties of her situation to himself and his three sisters, I have every reason to believe was highly exemplary. And with the exception of the circumstance of a posthumous child making its appearance about fourteen months after the death of her husband, there occurred nothing which could raise a doubt of her being the most virtuous of her sex. Being endowed with a considerable taste for letters, Mrs. Odoherty determined that her son should receive a *liberal* education, and accordingly sent him to a charity school in the neighborhood.

At this school, I have reason to believe, he remained about four years, when, by the interest of his uncle, Mr. Dennis Odoherty, butler to the Right Honorable Lord Muskerry,* he was received into his lordship's family as an under-domestic. In this noble family Ensign and Adjutant Odoherty soon became an universal favorite. The sweetness of his temper, the grace and vigor of his form, which certainly belonged more to the class of Hercules than the Apollo, rendered him the object of the fervent admiration of the whole female part of the family. Nor did he long remain in a menial situation. By the intercession of Lady Muskerry, he was appointed under-steward on the estate, and on his lordship's being appointed colonel of the Limerick militia in 1808, his first care was to bestow a pair of colors on Mr. Odoherty.

Never surely did a gift bestow more honor on the giver, and Lord Muskerry had the satisfaction of raising, to his proper sta-

* Baron Muskerry, of Springfield Castle, in the county of Limerick, Ireland, is the representative of a Mr. Deane, settled in Dromore, in the county of Cork, in the time of James I. A baronetcy was conferred on the then head of the family, in 1709, during the reign of Queen Anne, and an Irish peerage, in 1781, "when George III. was king." The first Lord Muskerry obtained his Limerick property by marriage with the heiress of the Fitzmaurice family.—M.

tion in society, a youth whose talents were destined, not only to do honor to the Limerick militia, but to his country and the world. In this situation, it is scarcely necessary to state, he was the very life and soul of society wherever he was quartered. Not a tea-party could be formed, not an excursion could be planned in the neighborhood, without Mr. Odoherty being included in it. In short he was like the *verb* in a sentence, quite impossible to be wanted. I have been informed by several officers of the regiment, that he was the greatest promoter of conviviality at the mess. His wine, to use their own expression, was never lost on him, and, toward the conclusion of the third bottle, he was always excessively amusing.

When quartered with his regiment at Ballinasloe, in the year 1809, he became smitten with the charms of a young lady of that city, who, from what I have heard of her person and temper, was all

> "That youthful poets fancy when they love."

Her father was a man of considerable wealth, and what is called middle-man, or agent to several of the noblemen and gentlemen of the country. Her name was Miss Augusta M'Craw, and her family were believed to be descended from the M'Craws of Inverness-shire, a house which yields to none in the pride of its descent, or the purity of its blood. Mr. M'Craw, indeed, used to dwell, with great complacency, on the exploits of an ancestor of the family, Sir John M'Craw, who flourished in the reign of James III., who not only defeated a Sir James M'Gregor, in a pitched battle, but actually kicked him round the lists, to the great amusement of the king and all his court. In this exercise, however, there is a tradition of his having dislocated his great toe, which ended in a whitlow, of which he died about three years afterward, leaving his fate as a lesson to his successors, of the consequences attending such unknightly behavior.

To this lady, as I already mentioned, Mr. Odoherty formed a most devoted attachment, and he accordingly made her an offer of his heart and hand. The young lady returned his attachment with sincerity, but her father and mother were most unaccountably averse to the connection. On stating to them the affection he entertained for their daughter, and soliciting their consent to its legal consummation, he was treated with the utmost indignity, and desired to quit the house immediately. On his remonstrating against this improper treatment, the brother of the lady attempted to pull him by the nose, and Mr. Odoherty retreated with the very proper resolution of demanding the satisfaction of a gentleman. He accordingly sent him a message the next day, and a meeting was the consequence.

On this occasion Ensign Odoherty behaved with all the coolness of the most experienced veteran. They fired nine shots each without effect, but, in the tenth round, Mr. Odoherty received a wound in the cheek, which carried off three of his jaw teeth, and entirely demolished one of his whiskers. On receiving the wound, he raised his hand to his face, and exclaimed with the greatest coolness, "a douce in the chops, egad." By this wound he was unfortunately ever afterward much disfigured, and was afflicted with a stiffness in the neck, from which he never recovered. Miss Augusta M'Craw was married, a short time afterward, to a lieutenant of artillery, and Mr. Odoherty very feelingly expressed his regret and sorrow on the occasion, by two odes on the inconstancy of women, which appeared in the Irish newspapers, and were afterward recorded in the Lady's Magazine for October, 1811.

Let it not be supposed, however, that, in the progress of the events which I have been relating, his poetical talents had remained dormant. Although we do not find, in his pieces of this period, the same lofty degree of excellence which was afterward so prominent in his more mature productions, yet they are all imbued with very considerable spirit and imagination. They had hitherto been generally rather of a light and amatory nature; but of his talents for satire, I believe the following epigram, on a certain amorous dowager, will afford not an unfavorable specimen:—

If a lover, sweet creature, should foolishly seek
  On thy face for the bloom of the rose,
Oh tell him, although it has died on thy cheek,
  He will find it at least on thy *nose*.

Sweet emblem of virtue! rely upon this,
  Should thy bosom be wantonly prest,
That if the rude ravisher gets but a kiss,
  He'll be ready to *fancy the rest*!

I also find, among his papers, an unfinished tragedy, which I conjecture, must have been composed about this time. It is entitled Euphemia, and, in my opinion, displays an uncommon degree of genius. I shall only extract part of one scene, which strikes me as being executed in the most masterly manner. The Princess Euphemia is represented as passing a sleepless night, in consequence of the imprisonment of her lover Don Carlos. Toward morning, she breaks out into the following impassioned reflections:—

Euphemia. Ah, 'tis a weary night! Alas, will sleep
Ne'er darken my poor day-lights! I have watched
The stars all rise and disappear again;
Capricorn, Orion, Venus, and the Bear:
I saw them each and all. And they are gone,
Yet not a wink for me. The blessed Moon
Has journeyed through the sky: I saw her rise
Above the distant hills, and gloriously
Decline beneath the waters. My poor head aches
Beyond endurance. I'll call on Beatrice,
And bid her bring me the all-potent draught
Left by Fernando the apothecary,
At his last visit. Beatrice! She sleeps
As sound as a top. What, ho, Beatrice!
Thou art indeed the laziest waiting maid
That ever cursed a princess. Beatrice!

Beatrice. Coming, your highness; give me time to throw
My night-gown o'er my shoulders, and to put
My flannel dicky on; 'tis mighty cold
At these hours of the morning.

Euphem. Beatrice.

Beat. I'm groping for my slippers; would you have me
Walk barefoot o'er the floors? Lord, I should catch
My death of cold.

Euphem. And must thy mistress, then, I say, must she
Endure the tortures of the damned, whilst thou
Art groping for thy slippers! Selfish wretch!
Learn, thou shalt come stark-naked at my bidding,
Or else pack up thy duds and hop the twig.

Beat. Oh, my lady, forgive me that I was so slow
In yielding due obedience. Pray, believe me,
It ne'er shall happen again. Oh, it would break
My very heart to leave so beautiful
And kind a mistress. Oh, forgive me!

Euphem. Well, well; I fear I was too hasty:

But want of sleep, and the fever of my blood,
Have soured my natural temper. Bring me the phial
Of physic left by that skilful leech Fernando,
With Laudanum on the label. It stands
Upon the dressing-table, close by the rouge
And the Olympian dew. No words. Evaporate.
Beat. I fly! [*exit.*
Euphem. (*sola.*) Alas, Don Carlos, mine own
Dear wedded husband! wedded! yes; wedded
In th' eye of Heaven, though not in that of man,
Which sees the forms of things, but least knows
That which is in the heart. Oh, can it be,
That some dull words, muttered by a parson
In a long drawling tone, can make a wife,
And not the——

Enter Beatrice.

Beat. Laudanum on the label; right:
Here, my lady, is the physic you require.
Euphem. Then pour me out one hundred drops and fifty,
With water in the glass, that I may quaff
Oblivion to my misery.
Beat. 'Tis done.
Euphem. (*drinks.*) My head turns round; it mounts into my brain.
I feel as if in paradise! My senses mock me:
Methinks I rest within thine arms, Don Carlos;
Can it be real? Pray, repeat that kiss!
I am thine own Euphemia. This is bliss
Too great for utterance. Oh, ye gods
If Hellespont and Greece! Alas, I faint.
[*faints.*

The heart of Mr. Odoherty was of the tenderest and most inflammable description, and he now formed an attachment to a lady Gilhooly, the rich widow of Sir Thomas Gilhooly, knight, who, on account of some private services to the state, was knighted during the lieutenancy of Lord Hardwicke.* His love to

* The third Earl of Hardwicke, grandson of the great Lord Chancellor Hardwicke, was born in 1757, was Lord Lieutenant of Ireland from 1801 to 1806, and died in 1834. His son, the present Earl (1854) has been a member of the British government (Tory) as postmaster general. During the viceroyalty of Lord Hardwicke (in May, 1804) Cobbett was tried for a libel in his *Register*, tending to bring the Viceroy and several Irish officials into contempt. For this he was fined five hundred pounds sterling. In the same month he was also tried and convicted for a libel on Mr. (the late Lord) Plunket, and had to pay another five hundred pounds damages. Up to that period Cobbett had

this lady was of the most modest and retiring nature, and he never ventured to make a personal declaration of his passion. He has commemorated it, however, in the following beautiful and pathetic stanzas: —

Oh, lady, in the laughing hours,
When time and joy go hand in hand;
When pleasure strews thy path with flowers,
And but to wish is to command;
When thousands swear, that to thy lips
A more than angel's voice is given,
And that thy jetty eyes eclipse
The bright, the blessed stars of heaven;
Might it not cast a trembling shade
Across the light of mirth and song,
To think that there is one, sweet *maid*,
That loved thee hopelessly and long;
That loved, yet never told his flame,
Although it burned his soul to madness;
That lov'd, yet never breathed thy name,
Even in his fondest dreams of gladness.
Though red my coat, yet pale my face,
Alas, 'tis love that made it so,
Thou only canst restore its grace,
And bid its wonted blush to glow.
Restore its blush! oh, I am wrong,
For here thine art were all in vain;
My face has ceased to blush so long,
I fear it ne'er can blush again!

This moving expression of passion appears to have produced no effect on the obdurate fair one, who was then fifty-four years of age, with nine children, and a large jointure, which would certainly have made a very convenient addition to the income of Mr. Odoherty. He now resolved on volunteering into the line.* He was unwilling that his services should be confined to

generally supported Pitt's Tory government, but these prosecutions, avowedly undertaken to silence him, only barbed his arrows against the Tory party. So, indirectly, Lord Hardwicke was the cause of Cobbett's becoming a democratic writer.— M.

* Volunteering from the militia into "the line" was generally in vogue during the last war between England and France. In the regular army of England, called "the line," commissions are mostly obtained by purchase only, whereas they might be got in the militia almost for the asking. It was a common practice, therefore, among those who were afflicted with what Johnson would

the comparatively inactive and inglorious duties of a militia officer, and he therefore determined to wield his sword, or, as he technically called it, his *spit*, wherever the cause of his country should demand it. He was soon after appointed to an ensigncy in the 44th regiment, then in the West Indies; and, on the 14th of August, 1814, he embarked at Dover in the schooner John Dory, Captain Godolphin, for Jamaica. He experienced a tedious passage, and they were unfortunate enough to fall in with an American privateer, from which, however, after a smart action, they had the good luck to escape.

The following *jeu d'esprit* gives so favorable a specimen of his talent for humor, that I can not refuse the reader the pleasure of submitting it to his perusal:—

Captain Godolphin was a very odd and stingy man,
Whose skipper was, as I'm assur'd, of a schooner-rigg'd West Indiaman;
The wind was fair, he went on board, and when he sail'd from Dover,
Says he, "this trip is but a joke, for now I'm half seas over!"

The captain's wife, she sail'd with him, this circumstance I heard of her,
Her brimstone breath, 'twas almost death to come within a yard of her;
With fiery nose, as red as rose, to tell no lies I'll stoop,
She looked just like an admiral with a lantern at his poop.

Her spirits sunk from eating junk, and as she was an epicure,
She swore a dish of dolphin fish would of her make a happy cure.
The captain's line, so strong and fine, had hooked a fish one day,
When his anxious wife *Godolphin* cried, and the dolphin swam away.

The wind was foul, the weather hot, between the tropics long she stewed,
The latitude was 5 or 6, 'bout 50 was the longitude,
When *Jack* the cook once spoilt the *sauce*, she thought it mighty odd,
But her husband bawl'd on deck, why, here's the Saucy Jack,* by God.

The captain sought his charming wife, and whispered to her private ear,
"My love, this night we'll have to fight a thumping Yankee privateer."
On this he took a glass of rum, by which he showed his sense;
Resolved that he would make at least a *spirited* defence.

---

call "impecuniosity" (or want of money), to become a militia officer, and thence volunteer into the line, for foreign service the result being a gratuitous appointment to a commission in some infantry regiment, on a vacancy by death or resignation. Some of the best officers in the British army thus obtained their first commissions. Odoherty, it seems was fired with a valorous desire thus cheaply to obtain the means of distinguishing himself in the field.—M.

* A celebrated American privateer.

The captain of the Saucy Jack, he was a dark and dingy man ;
Says he, " my ship must take, this trip, this schooner-rigg'd West Indianman.
Each at his gun, we'll show them fun, the decks are all in order:
But mind that every *lodger* here, must likewise be a *boarder*."

No, never was there warmer work, at least I rather think not,
With cannon, cutlass, grappling-iron, blunderbuss, and stink-pot.
The Yankee captain, boarding her, cried, either strike or drown;
Godolphin answered, " then I strike," and quickly knocked him down.

The remaining thirty verses of this poem, giving an account of the action and the subsequent voyage to Jamaica, of how Mrs. Godolphin was killed by a cannon ball lodging in her stomach, and how Captain Godolphin afterward died of the yellow fever, I do not think it necessary to insert. It is sufficient to say, they are fully equal to the preceding, and are distinguished by the same quaintness of imagination, and power of ludicrous expression.

On his arrival at Jamaica, he found it the rendezvous of the force destined for the attack of New Orleans, under the command of the brave though unfortunate Sir Edward Pakenham.* Of this force the 44th regiment formed a part, and the heart of Mr. Odoherty throbbed with delightful anticipation of the high destiny to which he felt himself called. A circumstance now occurred, however, which bid fair to cloud his prospects for ever. On the evening before the sailing of the armament for its destination, Mr. Odoherty had gone on shore. He there chanced to meet an old schoolfellow, who filled the situation of slave-driver or whipper-in to a neighboring plantation. This gentleman invited him to his house, and they spent the night in pouring forth the most liberal libations of new rum, which they drank fresh from the boilers. The consequence was, that next morning, on the sailing of the fleet, Mr. Odoherty was absent. His friend, the whipper-in, however, who was less drunk than his guest, had the good sense to foresee the consequences of his being left behind on so pressing an occasion. He hired a couple of negroes to row after the fleet, had Ensign Odoherty carried insensible to

* Major General Sir Edward Pakenham was killed at the battle of New Orleans, on the 8th of January, 1815. He was son of the second Lord Longford, brother-in-law of the Duke of Wellington, and had distinguished himself in the Peninsular war.—M.

the boat, and he was conveyed to his ship, as he himself humorously termed it, "as drunk as David's sow." The commanding officer immediately placed him under an arrest, and it was only on his expressing the most sincere contrition for his folly, joined with many promises of amendment, that he was again allowed to perform the duties of his situation. After this, few of the officers of the regiment thought proper to associate with him; and with the exception of some who had formerly been his companions in the militia, he was placed in Coventry by the whole corps.

CHAPTER II.

Odoherty at the Battle of New Orleans.—Disastrous Episode of the Snuff-Box. —A Prisoner-at-War in Boston.—Ode to the Whale off Long Island.—Residence in Philadelphia.—Intimacy with the Widow M'Whirter.—Return to England.—A Widow's Poetic Fulmination.—Imitation of Professor Wilson's Poetry.—Joins the 99th Foot.—Stanzas to his late Mess-mates.—Arrival at Edinburgh.—Popularity in "Auld Reekie."—The Dilettanti.—Ode to Bill Young, the Tavern-Keeper.

It is not my intention, in this chapter, to recapitulate the various calamities of the siege of New Orleans. That the armament was utterly inadequate to accomplish the object of the expedition, is now generally admitted. Fitted out for the express purpose of *besieging* one of the strongest and most formidable fortresses of America,* it was not only unprovided with a battering train, but without a single piece of heavy ordnance to assist in its reduction. Sir Edward Pakenham, therefore, on his arrival at Jamaica, found himself under the necessity of awaiting the tedious arrival of reinforcements from England, or of undertaking the expedition with the very inadequate means at his disposal. Listening rather to the suggestions of his gallantry than his pru-

* This second chapter, was published in *Blackwood* for March 1818.—Odoherty's biographer is rather wrong in speaking of New Orleans as "a fortress" to be besieged. General Jackson adroitly made his lines impregnable, by means of bold courage, riflemen, and cotton-bag defences.—M.

dence, he decided on the latter. If he erred in undertaking the expedition, it must be owned that he displayed the most consummate skill in the conduct of it.

On his arrival at New Orleans, he established himself immediately on the peninsula guarded by the fortress, and so vigorously did he push his operations, that on the third night he determined on giving the assault. The honor of heading the storming party was allotted to the 44th regiment, then under the command of the Honorable Lieutenant-Colonel Mullins, son to Lord Ventry, patron to our hero's father, and who did not at all congratulate himself, however, on his good fortune. The 44th regiment were driven back at the commencement of the attack; and on Sir Edward Pakenham's inquiring for the commanding officer, it was discovered that both he and Ensign Odoherty had remained in the rear. On search being made for them, Colonel Mullins was discovered under an ammunition wagon, and Ensign Odoherty was found in his tent, apparently very busy searching for his snuff-box, the loss of which, he solemnly declared, was the sole reason of his absence.*

In consequence of these circumstances, Colonel Mullins was brought to a court-martial, and dismissed the service; and such, most probably, would likewise have been the fate of Ensign Odoherty, had he not, by the most humble intercessions, pre-

* Lieutenant Colonel Mullins actually was in command of the 44th regiment of foot in the last American war. In the attack near Baltimore, September 12, 1814 (at which Major-General Ross was killed), Mullins commanded part of the right brigade, and was thanked, by Colonel Brooke, in his despatches "for the excellent order in which he led while charging the enemy in line." When the British attack was made on the lines of New Orleans, on the morning of the 8th of January, 1815, the 44th infantry were four hundred and twenty-seven strong. Mr. James Stuart (in a correspondence arising out of statements in his "Three years in North America") expressly states that the 44th regiment, "to whom was assigned the duty of being ready with scaling ladders and fascines, were not found at the appointed place," and that "a field officer was brought to trial on account of that mismanagement which it is said, most of all contributed to the deplorable result."—The defence was that the 44th were a mile and half in advance of the redoubt where lay the ladders and fascines, and that the Colonel's mistake was in not having brought them with him from the redoubt to the spot where he was ready, at the head of his regiment, like the rest, to advance to the attack, at the ascent of the signal rocket. This, if true, acquits Mullins of cowardice.—M.

vailed on the officers of the regiment to suppress their charges, on condition that he rid them of his presence, by an immediate exchange into another regiment. I am far from wishing to justify the line of conduct adopted in this instance by Mr. Odoherty, in yielding to the prejudices against his character which the officers of the regiment appear so gratuitously to have entertained. Knowing him, as I do, to have been as brave a man as ever pushed a bayonet to the throat of an enemy, I can not but sincerely regret that any change of circumstances should have occurred to give a different complexion to his character in the opinion of the world. But such regrets are useless. Who, when gazing on the brightness of the sun, can suppose his effulgence to be diminished, because, when viewed through a telescope, a few trifling spots are discernible on his disk!

Having entered into this arrangement, in order to effect his exchange, Mr. Odoherty took advantage of the sailing of the first ship to return to England, and accordingly embarked in the Beelzebub transport for that purpose. On their voyage home they encountered a severe storm when off the river Chesapeake, which broke the bobstay of the Beelzebub, and did considerable injury to her mainmast. To crown the misfortunes of this unlucky voyage, they were captured by the American frigate President, in latitude 35° 40′, longitude 27° 14′, and carried into Boston as prisoners-of-war. Mr. Odoherty bore his misfortunes with the greatest philosophy and calmness; and as a proof of the happy equanimity of his temper, I give the following extract from an extempore address to a whale, seen off Long Island on the 14th June, 1814:—*

Great king of the ocean, transcendent and grand
  Dost thou rest 'mid the waters so blue;
So vast is thy form, I am sure, on dry land,
  It would cover an acre or two.

Thou watery Colossus, how lovely the sight,
  When thou sailest majestic and slow,

* Considering that (as previously stated) Odoherty did not leave England until August, 1814, there appears a slight anachronism in making him see a whale off Long Island, on the preceding June. This is a poetic annihilation of "time and space," with a vengeance.—M.

And the sky and the ocean together unite
  Their splendor around thee to throw.

Or near to the pole, 'mid the elements' strife,
  Where the tempest the seaman appals,
Unmoved, like a Continent pregnant with life,
  Or rather a living St. Paul's.

Thee soon as the Greenlander fisherman sees,
  He plans thy destruction, odd rot him;
And often, before thou hast time to cry pease,
  He has whipped his harpoon in thy bottom.

Here unfortunately a hiatus occurs, which, I am sure, will be regretted by every lover of what is sublime in conception, grand in description, and beautiful in imagination. Odoherty is not the only author of high genius whose vivacity exceeded his perseverence. We may say of him what Voltaire said of Lord Bacon: "*Ce grand homme a commencé beaucoup de choses que personne ne peut jamais achever.*"

On his arrival at Boston, he received orders to proceed to Philadelphia, the station allotted for his residence by the American government. In this great city, the manly graces of his person, and the seductive elegance of his manners, gained him the notice and attention of all ranks. But, notwithstanding the kindness and hospitality which he experienced from his American friends, his pecuniary circumstances were by no means in the most flourishing condition. He found, to his astonishment, that American merchants, however kind and liberal in other respects, had a strange prejudice against discounting Irish bills; nor could any offers, however liberal, of an extraordinary percentage, reconcile their minds to the imaginary risk of the transaction. Under these circumstances, Mr. Odoherty was obliged to confine his expenses to his pay, a small part of which was advanced to him, with much liberality, by the British agent for prisoners-of-war in that city, to whose kindness he was, on several occasions, much indebted.

It was in Philadelphia that Ensign Odoherty had the misfortune to form a connection with a lady of the name of M'Whirter, who kept a well-known tavern and smoking-shop. Her husband had taken an active part in the rebellion of 1798 in Ireland, of which country he was a native, and had found it prudent to escape the consequences of his conduct by a flight to America. He accordingly repaired to Philadelphia, where he opened the "Goat in Armor" tavern and hotel, and soon after married a female emigrée from the Emerald Isle, an act which, I believe, he had only once occasion to repent. He died in a few years, and the "Goat in Armor" lost none of its reputation under the management of his widow.

In this house did Mr. Odoherty take up his residence on his arrival at Philadelphia; and it is almost needless to add, he soon made a complete conquest of the too susceptible heart of Mrs. M'Whirter. In the present difficulty of his pecuniary affairs, this circumstance afforded him too many advantages to be neglected or overlooked. Disgusting as she was in her person, vulgar in her manners, weak in her understanding, and unsuitable in years, he determined on espousing her. He accordingly made his proposals in form, and Mrs. M'Whirter was too much flattered with the idea of becoming an ensign's lady, not to swallow the bait with avidity.

They were privately married,* and continued to live together with tolerable harmony, until the peace of 1815 restored Mr. Odoherty once more to liberty. He was now heartily sick of the faded charms and uncultivated rudeness of his new wife, and accordingly determined once more to pursue the current of his fortune in another hemisphere. He accordingly possessed himself of as much ready money as he could conveniently lay his hands upon, and secretly embarked on board a ship, then on the point of sailing for England. The astonishment, rage, and grief, of his wife, at the discovery of his flight, may be more easily conceived than described. She has indeed embodied them all with the greatest fidelity, in an address to her husband, which, I have reason to believe, she composed immediately after his elopement. I shall only give the first verse, which possesses certainly much energy, if not elegance:—

* It will subsequently appear that this union was only a *mariage temporaire* — such as soldiers and sailors have the reputation of entering into at all places where they have more than three weeks' residence. It will be seen, by and by, that Mrs. M'Whirter was by no means the low, vulgar, and weak-minded woman here represented.—M.

"Confusion seize your lowsy sowl, ye nasty dirty varment,
Ye goes your ways, and leaves me here without the least preferment;
When you've drunk my gin, and robbed my till, and stolen all my pelf, ye
Sail away, and think no more on your wife at Philadelphy."

I shall certainly not presume to offer the delicate and refined reader any further specimen of this coarse and vulgar, but surely pathetic and feeling poem. Gray's "Bard" has been often and justly admired for the beautiful and unexpected abruptness of the opening stanza, the sudden vehemence of passion in which strange curses are imprecated on the head of the devoted monarch. It begins with the beautiful line,

"Ruin seize thee, ruthless king;"

but how inferior is this to the commencement of Mrs. Odoherty's poem, which I have just extracted. How emphatically it addresses itself to our feelings! How dreadful the curse which it invokes!

"Confusion seize your lowsy sowl!"

The blood runs cold at the monstrous imprecation—we feel an involuntary shuddering, such as comes on us when poring over the infernal cauldron of Macbeth, and listening to unearthly and hellish conjurations. Such are the proudest triumphs of the poet!

Mr. Odoherty arrived in England after a short and prosperous passage. The following piece was composed on sailing past Cape Trafalgar in the night. I mistake if it does not exhibit the strongest traces of powerful and wild imagination, and only leaves room to regret that, like most of his poetical effusions, it is unfinished. It reminds us of some of the best parts of John Wilson's Isle of Palms:—

Have you sailed on the breast of the deep,
When the winds had all silenced their breath,
And the waters were hushed in as holy a sleep,
And as calm, as the slumber of death.
When the yellow moon beaming on high,
Shone tranquilly bright on the wave,
And careered through the vast and impalpable sky,
Till she found in the ocean a grave,
And dying away by degrees on the sight,
The waters were clad in the mantle of night.

'Twould impart a delight to thy soul,
As I felt it imparted to mine,
And the draught of affliction that blackened my bowl
Grew bright as the silvery brine.
I carelessly lay on the deck,
And listened in silence to catch
The wonderful stories of battle or wreck
That were told by the men of the watch.
Sad stories of demons most deadly that be,
And of mermaids that rose from the depths of the sea.

Strange visions my fancy had filled,
I was wet with the dews of the night;
And I thought that the moon still continued to gild
The wave with a silvery light.
I sunk by degrees into sleep,
I thought of my friends who were far,
When a form seemed to glide o'er the face of the deep,
As bright as the evening star,
Ne'er rose there a spirit more lovely and fair,
Yet I trembled to think that a spirit was there.

Emerald green was her hair,
Braided with gems of the sea,
Her arm, like a meteor, she waved in the air,
And I knew that she beckoned on me.
She glanced upon me with her eyes,
How ineffably bright was their blaze;
I shrunk and I trembled with fear and surprise,
Yet still I continued to gaze;
But enchantingly sweet was the smile of her lip,
And I followed the vision and sprang from the ship.

'Mid the waves of the ocean I fell,
The dolphins were sporting around,
And many a triton was tuning the shell,
And extatic and wild was the sound;
There were thousands of fathoms above,
And thousands of fathoms below;
And we sunk to the caves where the sea lions rove,
And the topaz and emerald glow,
Where the diamond and sapphire eternally shed,
Their lustre around on the bones of the dead.

And well might their lustre be bright,
For they shone on the limbs of the brave,
Of those who had fought in the terrible fight,
And were buried at last in the wave.

In grottoes of coral they slept,
On white beds of pearl around;
And near them for ever the water snake crept,
And the sea lion guarded the ground,
While the dirge of the heroes by spirits was rung,
And solemn and wild were the strains that they sung.

Dirge.

Sweet is the slumber the mariners sleep,
Their bones are laid in the caves of the deep,
Far over their heads the tempests sweep,
That ne'er shall wake them more;
They died when raved the bloody fight,
And loud was the cannon's roar;
Their death was dark, their glory bright,
And they sunk to rise no more,
They sunk to rise no more.
But the loud wind past,
When they breathed their last,
And it carried their dying sigh
In a winding-sheet,
With a shot at their feet,
In coral caves they lie,
In coral caves they lie.
Or where the syren of the rocks
Lovely waves her sea-green locks,
Where the deadly breakers foam,
Found they an eternal home.

Horrid and long were the struggles of death,
Black was the night when they yielded their breath,
But not on the ocean, all buoyant and bloated,
The sport of the waters their white bodies floated,
For they were borne to coral caves,
Distant far beneath the waves,
And there on beds of pearl they sleep,
And far over their heads the tempests sweep,
That ne'er shall wake them more,
That ne'er shall wake them more.

On his arrival in England, he repaired immediately to London, and effected an exchange into the 99th, or King's Own Tipperary regiment, and set off immediately to join the depot then stationed in the Isle of Wight. In order to cover the reason of his leaving his former regiment, and to prevent the true cause of his exchange from becoming publicly known, he addressed the following stanzas to the officers of the 44th regiment, and took care to have them inserted in all the newspapers, with the signature of Morgan Odoherty. They are as follows:—

Come, push round the bottle; one glass ere we part
Must in sadness go round to the friends of my heart,
With whom many a bright hour of joy has gone by,
Whom with pleasure I met, whom I leave with a sigh.

Yes, the hours have gone by; like a bright sunny gleam,
In the dark sky of winter, they fled like a dream;
Yet when years shall have cast their dim shadows between,
I shall fondly remember the days that have been.

Come, push round the bottle; for ne'er shall the chain
That has bound us together be broken in twain,
And I'll drink, wheresoever my lot may be cast,
To the friends that I love, and the days that are past.

This ruse de guerre had the desired effect; for nobody could possibly suspect that the author of this sentimental and very feeling address had just been kicked out of the regiment by these very dear friends whom he thus pathetically lauds. Soon after his arrival at the depot of the 99th regiment, he was ordered to proceed on the recruiting service to Scotland, and arrived in Edinburgh in the summer of 1815.

Here new and unexpected honors awaited him. He had hitherto been a stranger to literary distinctions, and notwithstanding his writing in the different periodical publications attracted much of the public admiration, he had hitherto remained, in the more extended signification, of the word, absolutely unnoticed. This, however, was at length to cease; and though Mr. Odoherty was by birth an Irishman (to the shame of that country be it spoken), it was Scotland which first learned to appreciate and reward his merit.

Soon after his arrival at this metropolis, he was voted a member of the "Select Society."* Here he distinguished himself by

* The "Select" was a debating society in Scotland, much patronized by lawyers' clerks and gentlemen of the counter, who are a very argumentative people. In 1819, according to Peter's letters to his Kinsfolk (Lockhart's three-volume satire) besides The Speculative, of which Scott and Jeffrey had once been members, there were the following debating societies in Edinburgh—the Didactic, the Polemical, the Philomatic, the Dialectic, the Philathetic, the Select, the Select Forensic, and the Pantiseptral. The affectation

his eloquence in a very eminent degree; and as the gentlemen of this society seemed to pride themselves more on the quantity than the quality of their orations, and seemed to meet with much greater success in the multiplication of their words than in the multiplication of their ideas to correspond with them, Mr. Odoherty, from his natural volubility, soon succeeded in casting his rivals in the shade. In particular I am told he made a speech of four hours and a half, on the very new and interesting question of, Whether Brutus was justified in the assassination of Cæsar, which was carried in the affirmative by a majority of one, and may therefore be considered as being finally settled. He likewise made a long speech on the question of the propriety of early marriages, and clearly established, in a most pathetic and luminous oration, that Queen Elizabeth was by no means justified in the execution of Mary. It was impossible that these elaborate displays of the most extraordinary talent could long remain unnoticed.

In consequence of his giving a most clear and scientific description of a Roman frying-pan, found in the middle of a bog in the county of Kilkenny, he was immediately elected a member of the society of Scottish antiquaries, and read at their meetings several very interesting papers which were received by his brother antiquaries with the most grateful attention.*

of pedantic titles is not confined to Edinburgh. In the New York Tribune, of March 18, 1854, it is noticed and reproved in the following paragraph:—"We have received a report of certain proceedings in the *Kalokaigathian* Society of the University of Northern Pennsylvania, with a request that they should be published. The proceedings themselves are commendable, but the name of the society is not, and we must accordingly decline printing the report. Why should an innocent, and we trust even useful, literary association of respectable young Americans be loaded with an outlandish and old-fangled title like that? It is time that the boys were ashamed of Greek and Latin affections, to say the least." Probably youth cherishes an innate love for high-sounding words, just as colroed people are fond of bestowing polysyllabic names upon their children. Captain Marryat has an amusing anecdote, in one of his novels, of being asked by a black mother, in the West Indies, to give a grand name to her newly-born piccaninny. He delighted her, beyond measure, and infused envy into other maternal bosoms, by suggesting Chrononhotonthologos. After a little time, however, this sesquipedelian name, which baffled all nigger attempts to pronounce, settled down into the diminutive, *Chronny!*—M.

* The A. S. S. (or Antiquarian Society of Scotland) continues to flourish, and

He was likewise proposed a member of the Royal Society, and unfortunately black-balled. Candor induces me to state, for the credit of that learned body, that this rejection was not understood to proceed on the personal unfitness of Mr. Odoherty for the proposed honor, but was simply owing to the circumstances of several Irish members who had been recently chosen having bilked the Society of their fees, which made them unwilling to add to their number.* To make amends for this disappointment, the same week in which it occurred he was proposed in the Society of Dilettanti, and admitted by acclamation into that enlightened body.† The evenings which he spent at their

occasionally to publish old documents in which the bad spelling of departed and ignorant years is so scrupulously adhered to that few, even of the members, can do more than guess at the meaning. When Mr. Tytler produced his "History of Scotland" (unquestionably the best yet written), the A. S. S. violently denounced it and him, because, in quoting old documents, manuscript or printed, he used the spelling of the present day, so that history should be not a sealed volume, but a living letter, to the public. The rust of age, however it defaces the coin, is what the Scottish Antiquarians prize above the coin itself.—M.

* Until the resignation of its president, Sir James Hall, of Dunglass, (father of Captain Basil Hall, the author), the Royal Society of Edinburgh, which continues to flourish, had invariably elected a man of service for its head. Hall resigned in November, 1819, and Walter Scott, yielding to the strong and unanimous request of the body, consented to become its President. "His gentle skill was found effective," says Lockhart, "as long as he held the Chair, in maintaining and strengthening the tone of good feeling and good manners which alone can render the meetings of such a society either agreeable or useful." The Royal Society possesses a half-length portrait of Scott, painted in 1829, by Mr. John Graham, Scottish artist.—M.

† Lockhart mentions the very Abitri Elegantiarum, or Dilettanti Society, as holding their meetings [at Young's Tavern] "in one of the filthiest closes in the city of Edinburgh, braving with heroic courage, the risk of an impure baptism from the neighboring windows, at their entrance and exit, and drinking the memory of Michael Angelo, or Raphael, or Phidias, or Milton, in libations of whiskey-punch," and considers that the coarseness of such habits and propensities appears "utterly inconsistent with that delicacy of taste in other matters to which they make pretensions."—This was in 1819. Much of the implied censure was unmerited; for, as we happily learn from a poem called "The Mad Banker of Amsterdam," written under the *soubriquet* of William Wastle, of that Ilk, some of the most eminent men in Edinburgh were in fellowship in the Dilettanti. The principal member of the Dilettanti was David Bridges, who kept a clothier's shop in the High Street of Edinburgh. This place, and its occupant, are thus graphically described by Lockhart:—"On

meetings, in Young's Tavern, High street, were often mentioned by him as among the most radiant oases in the desert of his ex-

entering, one finds a very neat and tasteful-looking shop, well stocked with all the tempting diversities of broadcloth and bombazines, silk stockings, and spotted handkerchiefs. * * * After waiting a few minutes, the younger partner tips a sly wink across the counter, and beckons you to follow him through a narrow cut in its mahogany surface, into the unseen recesses of the establishment. A few steps downward, and in the dark, land you in a sort of cellar below the shop proper, and here by the dim and religious light which enters through one or two well-grated peeping-holes, your eyes soon discover enough of the furniture of the place to satisfy you, that you have at last reached the *Sanctum Sanctorum* of the Fine Arts. Plaster of Paris casts of the Head of Farnese Hercules—the Dancing Fawn—the Laocoon—and the Hermaphrodite, occupy conspicuous stations on the counter; one large table is entirely covered with a book of Canova's designs, Turner's Liber Studiorum, and such sort of manuals; and in those corners where the little light there is streams brightest, are placed, upon huge piles of corduroy and kerseymere, various wooden boxes, black, brown, and blue, wherein are locked up from all eyes, save those of the privileged and initiated frequenters of the scene, various pictures and sketches, chiefly by hiring artists, and presents to the proprietor. Mr. Bridges, when I asked him, on my first visit, what might be the contents of those mysterious receptacles, made answer in a true technico-Caledonian strain—'Oh, Dr. Morris, they're just a wheen *bits*—and,' (added he, with a most knowing compression of the lips,)—'let me tell you what, Dr. Morris, there's some no that ill *bits* amang them neither.'"—Bridges was secretary of the Dilettanti Society. John Wilson (Christopher North) was president. Among the members were Allan, the painter; John Gibson Lockhart; Doctor Schetky, a very clever amateur landscape-painter; Nicholson, a subject-artist, and then one of the best miniature-painters in Scotland; Baxter, another artist; Patrick Robertson, then commencing that course as a lawyer, which now (1854) he is finishing as a Scottish judge; Peter Hill, a well-known bookseller; and John Douglas, a lawyer; all of whom are hit off, or hit at, in William Wastle's already-mentioned poem.—*Ex.: gr.:*

They're pleased to call themselves **The Dilettanti**:
  The President's the first I chanced to show 'em;
He writes more malagrugrously than Dante,
  The City of the Plague's a shocking poem;
But yet he is a spirit light and jaunty,
  And jocular enough to those that know him.
To tell the truth, I think John Wilson shines
More o'er a bowl of punch than in his lines.

Wilson discussed, the tenor of my speech
  On to his Croupier-Secretary ran,
A person thoroughly qualified to teach
  The lingo of the Virtuoso clan,

istence. He composed a beautiful ode to the keeper of the tavern where they assemble, of which we can not at present quote more than the three opening stanzas:

Let Dandies to M'Culloch go,
And Ministers to Fortune's hall;
For Indians Oman's claret flow,
In John M'Phails let lawyers crow,

Pictures and prints alike within his reach.
— He is, in short, a most uncommon man;
The Painters view him with a fearful eye;
For me, I'm always mute when David's by.

The next that I enlarged upon was Allan,
That peerless master of the modern brush,
Born to restore a Muse from splendor fallen,
Born to see garlands of the Deathless Bush
(In spite of Envy's poisonous tendrils crawling)
Cling round his honored brow in glory's flush;
A famous fellow also o'er his toddy,
And, bating Artists, liked by everybody.

Then touched I off friend Lockhart (Gibson John),
So fond of jabbering about Tieck and Schlegel,
Klopstock and Wieland, Kant and Mendelsohn,
All High Dutch quacks, like Spurzheim or Feinagle.—
Him the Chaldee ycleped the Scorpion.—
The claws, but not the pinions, of the eagle,
Are Jack's: but though I do not mean to flatter,
Undoubtedly he has strong powers of satire.

Par nobile, the Schetkys next I hit,
— Gibson (who t'other day had changed his lot;)
The Master of St. Luke's, whom yonder Pit
With long *vivas* heard comic Liston quote.
Then Nicholson, to whom so oft I sit:
You've seen his etching, sure, of Walter Scott.
— Some half-a-dozen others I could name;
Among the rest was Baxter — yes — *lui-même.*

My tongue next glided to the praise of Pat,
Who loves not Robertson in Embro' city?
Dutch girls would call him Cupid, for he's fat,
Wears spectacles, is sly, and keen, and witty.
Next Peter Hill — you might be sure of that.
Next one, whom if you know not, more's the pity —
John Douglas — one of the true genuine tribe —
Mistake me not — our gentlemanly Scribe.

These places seem to me so so,
I love Bill Young's above them all.

One only rival, honest Bill,
Hast thou in Morgan's whim;
I mean Ben Waters, charming Ben,
Simplest and stupidest of men;
I take a tankard now and then,
And smoke a pipe with him.

Dear Ben! dear Bill! I love you both,
Between you oft my fancy wavers;
Thou, Bill, excell'st in sheepshead broth;
Thy porter-mugs are crowned with froth;
At Young's I listen, nothing loth,
To my dear Dilettanti shavers.
O scene of merriment and havers,
Of good rum-punch, and puns, and clavers,
And warbling sweet Elysian quavers!—
Who loves not Young's must be a Goth.*

CHAPTER III.

Odoherty's Acquaintance with and Stanzas to Hogg, the Ettrick Shepherd—Hogg's Lines to Odoherty—Allan, the Painter—"The Young Man of the West"—Elegy written in a Ball-room—New Version of "Young's Night Thoughts"—Lord Byron's Pathetic Invocation of "Sublime Tobacco," a Plagiarism from Odoherty.

THE Ode to Messrs. Young and Waters, with part of which we closed our last chapter of Mr. Odoherty's life,† has a merit

* M'Culloch, Fortune, Oman, M'Phail, Young, and Waters were respectively keepers of hotels and taverns in Edinburgh, in 1818.—M.

† This third chapter was published in *Blackwood's Magazine*, April 1818.—Part of it, I am persuaded, was interpolated in Edinburgh, because Maginn did not visit that city until 1821, and, therefore, could not have had the requisite local and personal knowledge with which the poems are imbued. Yet, some years later, in his famous "Maxims of Odoherty," certainly written by Maginn, the concluding stanzas on tobacco, as a

"Divine invention of the age of Bess,"

are especially and complacently alluded to as his own.—Mr. Gillies, in his "Memoirs of a Literary Veteran," states that the life of Odoherty was written by the late Captain Hamilton and was the first literary composition which is far from being common among modern lyrics—it expresses the habitual feelings of the author. The composer of an ode, in these times, is usually obliged to throw himself out of his own person, into that of some individual placed in a situation more picturesque than has fallen to his own share—he is obliged to dismiss all recollection of his own papered parlor and writing-desk, and to imagine himself, *pro tempore,* a burning Indian, a dying soldier, or a love-sick young lady, as it may happen. He thus loses that intense air of personal emotion, which forms the principal charm in the stern heroics of Pindar, the elegant drinking songs of Horace, the gay *chansons* of Deshoulieres, and the luxurious erotics of Tom Moore.* Odoherty wrote of

of one who subsequently obtained reputation by his "Youth and Manhood of Cyril Thornton," as a historian of the Peninsular War, and by his strange work, "Men and Manners in America." Without doubt, Hamilton could not have written the earlier portion of Odoherty's life in which there are so many allusions to Irish people. I believe that Maginn actually *did* write the greater part of Chapters III. and IV., and that the local hits were introduced by Hamilton and others.—Chapter IV., which did not appear until December, 1818, came out with a mystification in the form of an editorial note, as follows:—"The gentleman who drew up the two first notices of this life, having died of an apoplexy some time ago, the notice which appeared in March [April?], and the present one, are by a different hand." Yet, Chapter IV. was unquestionably written by Maginn! In *Blackwood's* notices to correspondents, in the number for April, 1818 (that in which Chapter III. appeared), the following was to be found, 'Memoirs of Roderic Milesius O'Donoghue, late of Tralee, county Kerry, Ireland, first cousin to Ensign and Adjutant Morgan Odoherty,' are received, and will follow the life of his illustrious kinsman, which we hope to conclude in a few more Numbers." This was one of Maginn's promises;—his intention was to write an autobiography of an Irish gentleman, and a very curious composition it would have been, had he seriously proceeded with it. But not a line of it was ever published—nor, perhaps, ever written.—M.

* It is scarcely necessary to do more than refer to three out of the four here-named. Pindar, the most famous lyric poet of Greece, was born about 540 B.C., and died in his 55th year. When the Lacedæmonians took Thebes, in Bœotia (of which he was a native), they spared the house of the poet, as also did Alexander the Great.—Horace, eminently the most elegant of all the Roman poets (such as we may fancy might be the result of a fusion of Pope and Moore, whereby philosophy, satire, and gaiety would be combined in one person), achieved a living popularity which Time has confirmed. He was born 65 B.C., and died in the year of Rome, 756, and 9 B.C., aged 56.—Moore, the poet of Ireland, truly designated by Shelley, as

"The sweetest lyrist of her saddest song,"

Young and Waters in his own person—the feelings which he has embodied in verse, are the daily, or rather nightly, visitants of his own bosom. If truth and nature form the chief excellence of poetry, our hero may take his place among the most favored children of the muse.

Those taverns were, however, far from being the scenes of mere merriment and punch-drinking. The bowl was seasoned with the conversation of associates, of whom it is sufficient to say, that they were indeed worthy to sit at the board with Ensign and Adjutant Odoherty. The writer of this has no personal knowledge of these distinguished persons, but from the letters and poems of the Ensign's, composed during his stay in Edinburgh, it is evident, that those upon whom he set most value, were the following gentlemen: James Hogg, Esq., the celebrated author of "The Queen's Wake," "Pilgrims of the Sun," "Mador of the Moor," and other well-known poems.*

was born in Dublin, on the 28th May, 1779 (as he states in the fragment of his Autobiography), and died at Sloperton Cottage, Wiltshire, England, on Feb. 26, 1852.—Beranger is, perhaps, the only modern song-writer, who can be named as a worthy rival. But the *chansons* of the French poets are rather to be read than sung, whereas Moore's are imbued with the true melody and sentiment of music.—Antoinette du Ligier Deshouliéres, a very versatile writer, and a handsome, accomplished, and witty woman, was born at Paris, in 1634; married a gentleman of family, and was on terms of friendship with the principal literati of the age. She produced numerous plays and operas—few of which were successful. Her Idyls, Eclogues, and Moral Reflections were more fortunate, and are still admired. She died, after twelve years of suffering, from a cancer in her breast, in 1694. It seems somewhat out of place to name Deshoulieres in the same sentence with Horace and Moore, as she was a more didactic and less sportive writer than either.—M.

* Beyond all doubt, James Hogg, commonly called "The Ettrick Shepherd," was as remarkable a literary phenomenon as ever lived. He has been compared with Burns,—but the latter had received the ordinary education of a Scottish peasant, could read and write correctly, besides having some knowledge of French; whereas, Hogg never received more than half a year's schooling, and that before he was seven years' old. Hogg was born on the 25th of January, 1772—the anniversary also of the natal day of Burns. His birth-place was an humble cottage on the banks of the small river Ettrick (a tributary of the Tweed), in one of the pleasant and secluded valleys in Selkirkshire, the most picturesque and mountainous district in the south of Scotland. His forefathers had been shepherds for many generations, and in this occupation James Hogg and his three brothers were brought up. Like nearly all

Of this great man Odoherty always wrote with rapture — take the following specimen: —

men who have eminently distinguished themselves, he had the advantage of having had a mother of more than ordinary intellect. Her memory was filled with traditionary song, and particularly with the old Border ballads, which she loved to repeat to her children — in a manner between chant and song — after her daily perusal, to them, of such portions of the Bible as she believed most likely to interest their minds and elevate their moral feelings. After a few months' attendance at school, Hogg was sent out into the world at the age of seven years, as an humble attendant on a few cows belonging to a neighboring farmer. In the winter months, when this occupation was intermitted, he tried to teach himself writing — but did not get beyond scrawling in a rude text-hand. To the last, even after practice had improved it, his caligraphy was imperfect and indecisive. Advancing in years, he became a shepherd, and was a careful and trustworthy one. At fourteen, when he had saved five shillings out of his wages, he bought an old violin, and taught himself to play. Next, he began to write verses — his mother encouraging his bias in that direction, and being the critic on his songs. Except the Bible, the life of Sir William Wallace, and Allan Ramsay's Gentle Shepherd, he had read nothing before his eighteenth year, when he became shepherd to Mr. Laidlaw, a Selkirkshire farmer, who allowed him the use of his library, which was rather extensive. He remained with Mr. Laidlaw from 1790 to 1800, and became a writer of songs about 1796 — the year of Burns's death. Then, and always, he used to compose and correct in his mind before writing it down upon a slate. He had never even heard of Burns, until a year after that poet's death, when Tam O'Shanter was repeated to him; — from that time the idea grew into his mind of trying to become a poet. William Laidlaw, his employer's son, encouraged him in writing poetry; and was himself eminently gifted, his beautiful lyric called "Lucy's Flittin," being an especial favorite with Sir Walter Scott. It was through Laidlaw that Scott's attention was drawn to Hogg. The result was a determination to "prent a book,"— his prose Essay on Sheep had previously won the premium given by the Highland Society. Hogg printed a volume of ballads — some of which, and particularly the song called "Donald MacDonald," became praised and popular. Introduced by Scott to Constable, the eminent Edinburgh publisher, in 1801, "The Mountain Bard" appeared; it consisted chiefly of pieces in the old ballad style, and though remarkable, from such a rude shepherd as Hogg then was, gave little promise of the excellence he soon after attained. He realized £300 by his book, and with this sum, which he considered immense, commenced sheep-farming, on his own account. After wasting all his money, and some years, in this speculation, he vainly attempted to resume his occupation as a shepherd — but his reputation of being a poet and a ruined farmer operated so much against him that he could not obtain employment. He was now (in 1810), over thirty-eight years old, and has truly confessed that he "knew no more of human life or manners than a child." Constable published another volume for him, called "The

While worldly men through stupid years
Without emotion jog,
Devoid of passions, hopes, and fears,
As senseless as a log—

Forest Minstrel," of which about a third was contributed by other writers. This book yielded him no profit. In September, 1810, Hogg commenced a sort of weekly periodical called "The Spy," which was given up at the end of twelve months. In 1813, he produced his "Queen's Wake,' consisting of a series of ballads, purporting to be sung for the amusement of the young Mary Queen of Scots, on her arrival from France at the ancient palace of Holyrood. The ballads were strung together in a poetic narrative, and the graceful purity of its style has seldom been equalled. The most popular poem in the "Queen's Wake," is that called "Kilmeny," a tale founded on the not uncommon Scottish tradition of a child being stolen by the fairies;—in artistical adaptation of language to ideas, in the mixture of simplicity and pathos, in fullness of melody and suitable management of the Doric dialect of Scotland, "Kilmeny" must rank as the best production of Hogg. In a very short time the "Queen's Wake" ran through three editions. On the failure of its publisher, it fell into the hands of Mr. Blackwood, and when that gentleman commenced his celebrated magazine, Hogg became one of its earliest contributors, and continued to write for it to the close of his life. The first draft of the famous *Chaldee Manuscript* (in which Constable and his literary friends were so much satirized, that it had to be withdrawn from the second and all future editions of the seventh number, from October, 1817,) was written by Hogg. His connection with *Blackwood's Magazine* introduced him to the friendship of Professor Wilson, Mr. Lockhart, and other literati of Edinburgh. Their repeated mention of him, in the "NOCTES AMBROSIANÆ," (in which they frequently made him an interlocutor,) unquestionably had great influence in winning celebrity for him. In later years, he complained of the liberties which the wits of "Blackwood" took with him, but he really was very proud of the association. Shortly after the appearance of the "Queen's Wake," in 1814, the late Duke of Buccleugh, fulfilling a desire of his late wife, and without any solicitation from the poet, presented him with the life-occupancy, free from rent, of the farm of Altrive Lake, in the wilds of Yarrow, which, as he gratefully says "gave me once more a habitation among my native moors and streams, where each face was that of a friend, and each house was a home, as well as residence for life to my aged father." In 1820, Hogg married, and having made a thousand pounds by his pen, took the farm of Mont-Benger, which adjoined his own, stocked it, and after several years' struggles, found himself without a shilling at the age of sixty. He continued to write, however, during and after his farming speculation. To name all his works would be to publish a long list. The most remarkable were the rustic tales entitled "Three Perils of Man," and "Three Perils of Woman," "Confessions of a Fanatic," "The Shepherd's Calendar" (which originally appeared in *Blackwood*), "Tales of the Wars of Montrose," "The Queer Book," and a great many short poems and stories contrib-

I much prefer my nights to spend,
  A happy ranting dog,
And see dull care his front unbend
  Before the smile of Hogg.

The life of man's a season drear,
  Immersed in mist and fog,
Until the star of wit appear,
  And set its clouds agog.
For me, I wish no brighter sky
  Than o'er a jug of grog,
When fancy kindles in the eye,
  The good gray eye of Hogg.

When Misery's car is at its speed,
  The glowing wheels to cog;
To make the heart where sorrows bleed
  Leap lightly like a frog;
Gay verdure o'er the crag to shower,
  And blossoms o'er the bog,
Wit's potent magic has the power,
  When thou dost wield it, Hogg!

In the escritoir of the Ensign, his executors found, among letters from the first literary characters of the day, many excellent ones from Mr. Hogg; and the following beautiful lines formed the postscript to that one in which he returned thanks to our poet for the above tribute to his own kindred genius:—

O hone, Odoherty!
  I canna weel tell what is wrang;
But oh, man, since you gaed frae me,
  The days are unco dull and lang.

---

uted to annuals and magazines. In 1820, a long narrative poem called "Queen Hynde," failed to win much attention, though it contained some of his best ballads. In 1831, Hogg was induced, by the success of the popular edition of the Waverley Novels, to re-issue the best of his own prose fictions in the new and attractive form. To negotiate for this purpose, in the best market, he visited London, where his reception was in the manner of an ovation. Early in 1832, appeared the first volume of "The Altrive Tales," but the failure of his publishers stopped the intended series. Soon after, he produced a volume of "Lay Sermons." He published a curiously characteristic life of Scott, which Lockhart has emphatically denounced as untrue and ungrateful. At last, on the 21st of November, 1835, aged sixty-three, he departed from this world. He left a widow and five children. In 1853, Mrs. Hogg received the tardy justice of being placed on the pension-list by the British Government.—M.

I try the paper and the sclate,
And pen, and cawk, and killivine;
But nothing can I write of late,
That even Girzzy ca's divine.
O hone, Odoherty!
O hone, Odoherty!
Oh weary fa' the fates' decree,
That garred the Captain part frae me.

O hone, Odoherty!
Come back, come back to Ettrick lake,
And ye sall hear, and ye sall see,
What I'se do for the Captain's sake.
I'll coff tobacco o' the best,
And pipes baith lang and short I'se gie;
And the toddy-stoup sall ne'er get rest,
Frae morn till night, 'tween you and me.
O hone, Odoherty!
O hone, Odoherty!
O welcome sall the moment be
That brings the Captain back to me.

Next to the Ettrick Shepherd, the member of the Dilettanti who shared most of Ensign Odoherty's confidence and affection was William Allan, Esq. This gentleman's genius as a painter does not require any notice on the present occasion. He has, we understand, done justice to his own feelings, and to his friend, by introducing a striking likeness of Odoherty's features into one of his principal pieces. Reader, the Cobler in the Press-gang is Odoherty! To Mr. Allan, Odoherty frequently addressed humorous epistles in verse. We prefer, however, to quote the following eulogy, which is written in the Adjutant's best serious manner:—

When wondering ages shall have rolled away,
And that be ancient which is new to-day;
When time has pour'd his warm and softening glow
O'er that pale virgin's* throbbing breast of snow,
And lent the settled majesty of years
To those grim Spahis, and those proud viziers;
From distant lands the ardent youth shall come
To gaze with admiration—breathless—dumb—
To fix his eyes, like orbs of marble, *there!*
And let his soul luxuriate in despair.

* Circassian Captive,

Posterity! ah, what's a name to thee!
What Raphael is, my Allan then shall be.*

As the writer of the present notice intends to publish in a separate form the poetical writings of Odoherty, with authentic portraits of his friends, it is not necessary to quote any more of these effusions now.† The pleasantry of the Ensign was always harmless, and his very satire was both dart and balsam. He never condescended to personalities, except in one solitary instance, in a song, entitled, "The Young Man of the West," composed upon Mr. James Grahame, the famous Anti-Malthusian philosopher. This song he used to sing with great humor, to the tune of "A Cobler there was," &c., but though frequently urged to do so, he never would print it; and on his own manuscript copy there is this note, "Let the Young Man of the West be destroyed," an injunction which has since been scrupulously complied with.‡

* Sir William Allan, an historical painter of much eminence, and long at the head of his profession in Scotland, was born in Edinburgh in 1782, and died at the same place in 1850. His predilection for art was manifested at an early age. While yet a young man, he visited Morocco, Greece, and Spain, in pursuit of works and subjects of art, and travelled through Russia, and Turkey, and various districts of the East. He returned to Edinburgh about 1816, and exhibited the results of his travel, observation, and genius. His best pictures at this time, for which he obtained high prices, were *The Sale of Circassian Captives to a Turkish Bashaw*, his *Jewish Family in Poland making merry before a Wedding*, and his *Slave Market at Constantinople.* Nor did he confine himself to foreign subjects. *The Press Gang* was the first in which he employed his pencil upon a domestic subject. After this came his *Murder of Archbishop Sharpe*, *Mary Queen of Scots and Rizzio*, *The Battle of Waterloo*, and a long array of others, most of which have become familiar to the public by means of engravings. In 1841, he succeeded Sir David Wilkie as President of the Royal Scottish Academy, and was knighted by Queen Victoria. He was an old and warm friend of Sir Walter Scott, and Lockhart devoted a large space in his "Peter's Letters to his Kinsfolk," published in 1819, to a description of Allan's studio, person, productions, and genius. Sir William Allan, who was never married, was a general favorite in society, from his unassuming manners, great store of anecdote, and large extent of observation on the countries he had traversed and the persons he had known.—M.

† This was one of the thousand promises which, in its early days, *Blackwood* was in the habit of making.—M.

‡ This James Grahame, a popular Whig lawyer in Glasgow, must not be confounded with his namesake, who commenced life as an advocate at the

During one of those brilliant evenings at the Dilettanti, which, says our bard in a letter to the present writer, "will for ever live in the memory of all who enjoyed them," the conversation ran upon the Italian improvisatori. Odoherty remarked, that the power which appeared to many so wonderful, was no way uncommon, and offered to recite, or write down *currente calamo*, a poem upon any given subject. The president proposed "An Elegy, by a young Lady in a Ball-room disappointed of a Partner," and the Adjutant wrote down the following twenty four-line stanzas in fifty-three minutes nineteen seconds by a stop-watch. Such an achievement throws the admirable Crichton into the shade:—

ELEGY WRITTEN IN A BALL-ROOM.

THE beaux are jogging on the pictured floor,
The belles responsive trip with lightsome heels;
While I, deserted, the cold pangs deplore,
Or breathe the wrath which slighted beauty feels.

When first I entered glad, with glad mamma,
The girls were ranged and clustered round us then;
Few beaux were there, those few with scorn I saw,
Unknowing Dandies that could come at ten.

My buoyant heart beat high with promised pleasure,
My dancing garland moved with airy grace;
Quick beat my active toe to Gow's gay measure,
And undissembled triumph wreathed my face.

Edinburgh bar, but being of a melancholy temperament, and a truly religious character, took holy orders in the Church of England, retired to a curacy near Durham, and died in 1811. His reputation as a poet rests upon his "Sabbath" of which and of him, Byron thus spoke in the English Bards, and Scotch Reviewers:—

"Lo! the Sabbath bard,
Sepulchral Grahame, pours his notes sublime
In mangled prose, nor e'en aspires to rhyme;
Breaks into blank the Gospel of St. Luke,
And boldly pilfers from the Pentateuch;
And, undisturbed by conscientious qualms,
Perverts the Prophets, and purloins the Psalms."

The Mr. Grahame whom Odoherty is stated to have satirized was a liberal in politics, an orator at public dinners and radical meetings, and a patron of (if not contributing to) the *Edinburgh Review*—any of which offences would have caused the wits of *Blackwood* to laugh at him.—M.

Fancy prospective took a proud survey
  Of all the coming glories of the night;
Even where I stood my legs began to play—
  So racers paw the turf e'er jockeys smite.

And "who shall be my partner first?" I said,
  As my thoughts glided o'er the coming beaux;
"Not Tom, nor Ned, nor Jack,"—I tossed my head,
  Nice grew my taste, and high my scorn arose.

"If Dicky asks me, I shall spit and sprain;
  When Sam approaches, headaches I will mention;
I'll freeze the colonel's heart with cold disdain;"
  Thus cruelly ran on my glib invention.

While yet my fancy revelled in her dreams,
  The sets are forming, and the fiddles scraping;
Gow's wakening chord a stirring prelude screams,
  The beaux are quizzing, and the misses gaping.

Beau after beau approaches, bows, and smiles,
  Quick to the dangler's arm springs glad ma'amselle;
Pair after pair augments the sparkling files,
  And full upon my ear "THE TRIUMPH" swells.

I flirt my fan in time with the mad fiddle,
  My eye pursues the dancers' motions flying;
Cross hands! Balancez! down and up the middle!
  To join the revel how my heart is dying.

One miss sits down all glowing from the dance,
  Another rises, and another yet;
Beaux upon belles, and belles on beaux advance,
  The tune unending, ever full the set.

At last a pause there comes—to Gow's keen hand
  The hurrying lackey hands the enlivening port;
The misses sip the ices where they stand,
  And gather vigor to renew the sport.

I round the room dispense a wistful glance,
  Wish Ned, or Dick, or Tom, would crave the honor;
I hear Sam whisper to Miss B., "Do—dance,"
  And launch a withering scowl of envy on her.

Sir Billy capers up to Lady Di;
  In vain I cough as gay Sir Billy passes;
The Major asks my sister—faint I sigh,
  "Well after this—the men are grown such asses!"

In vain! in vain! again the dancers mingle,
  With lazy eye I watch the busy scene,

Far on the pillowed sofa sad and single,
  Languid the attitude — but sharp the spleen.
"La! ma'am, how hot!"— "You're quite fatigued, I see;"
  "What a long dance!" — "And so you're come to town!"
Such casual whispers are addressed to me,
  But not one hint to lead the next set down.

The third, the fourth, the fifth, the sixth, are gone,
  And now the seventh — and yet I'm asked not once
When supper comes must I descend alone?
  Does Fate deny me my last prayer — a dunce?

Mamma supports me to the room for munching,
  There turkey's breast she crams, and wing of pullet;
I slobbering jelly, and hard nuts am crunching,
  And pouring tuns of trifle down my gullet.

No oeau invites me to a glass of sherry;
  Above me stops the salver of champaign;
While all the rest are tossing brimmers merry,
  I with cold water comfort my disdain.

Ye bucks of Edinburgh! ye tasteless creatures!
  Ye vapid Dandies! how I scorn you all! —
Green slender slips, with pale cheese-pairing features,
  And awkward, lumb'ring, red-faced boobies tall.

Strange compounds of the beau and the attorney!
  Raw lairds! and school-boys for a whisker shaving!
May injured beauty's glance of fury burn ye!
  I hate you — clowns and fools! —— but hah! — I'm raving!

We shall now take leave, for the present, of Odoherty and the Dilettanti Society, with an extract from his longest and latest poem, entitled "Young's Night Thoughts" (a humorous allusion to the before-mentioned celebrated tavern). Lively as this strain is, we can scarcely read it without tears; for it was, we repeat, the very last of his works here below. The following proem, copied by a female hand on hot-pressed gilt paper, is intended to explain the great leading object of the poem: —

There was a time when every sort of people
  Created, relished, and commended jokes;
But now a joker's stared at, like a steeple,
  By the majority of Christian folks.
Dulness has tanned her hide to thickness triple,
  And Observation sets one in the stocks,
When you've been known a comic song to sing,
Write notices, or any harmless thing.

This Edinburgh, Edina, or Dunedin —
('Cleped, in the Bailie's lingo, "the Good Town;"
But styled "Auld Reekie" by all Celts now treading
Her streets, bows, winds, lanes, crescents, up and down,
Her labyrinths of stairs and closes threading
On other people's business or their own —
Those bandy, broad-faced, rough-kneed, ragged laddies —
Those horney-fisted, those gill-swigging caddies.)

This Edinburgh some call Metropolis,
And Capital, and Athens of the North —
I know not what they mean.— I'm sure of this,—
Tho' she abounds in men of sense and worth,
Her staple and predominant qualities
Are ignorance, and nonsense, and so forth;
I don't like making use of a hard word,
But 'tis the merest *hum* I ever heard.

There's our Mackenzie; all with veneration
See him that Harley felt and Caustic drew:
There's Scott, the pride and darling of his nation,
Poet and cavalier, kind, generous, true.
There's Jeffrey, who has been the botheration
Of the whole world with his glib sharp Review,
And made most young Scots lawyers mad with whiggery —
There's Leslie, Stewart, Alison, and Gregory.*

---

* Henry Mackenzie, author of "The Man of Feeling," "The Man of the World," "Julia de Roubigné," numerous essays in "The Mirror," and "The Lounger," two tragedies, some translations from the German, was born at Edinburgh in 1745, and died in 1831, aged eighty-five.— Mr. Pitt made him Comptroller of the Taxes in Scotland, with a salary of eight hundred pounds sterling a year. In pathos and grace he has rarely been equalled as a writer of prose fiction. He was the life-long friend of Sir Walter Scott, and was one of the first to recognise and proclaim the genius of Burns. His character of Harley is beautifully drawn, and Scott, who dedicated Waverley to him, took occasion to say that his sketch of Colonel Caustic was admirable.— Of Sir Walter Scott it is not necessary to say more here than that he was born in 1771, died in 1832, aged sixty-one, and, by his writings has been the cause of more intellectual enjoyment than any author of his time.— Francis Jeffrey, who, by means of the *Edinburgh Review* (of which he was editor from October, 1802, when it was commenced, until 1829, when he became Dean of the Faculty of law) first raised British criticism into a science, was born in 1773, called to the Scottish bar in 1794, was made Lord Advocate of Scotland in 1830, entered Parliament, where he did not obtain anything like success, took his seat on the bench at Edinburgh, in 1834, as Lord Jeffrey, and died in 1850, in his seventieth year, leaving the highest reputation as a critic and lawyer, a polit-

But these and some few others being named,
  I don't remember one more great gun in her;
The remanent population can't be blamed,
  Because their chief concern in life's their dinner.
To give examples I should be ashamed,
  And people would cry, "Lord! that wicked sinner!"
(For all we gentry here are quite egg-shells,
We can't endure jokes that comes near "*oor-sells.*")

They say that knowledge is diffused and general,
  And taste and understanding are *so* common,
I'd rather see a sweep-boy suck a penny roll
  Than listen to a criticising woman.

---

cian and orator, a judge and a man of wit.—Sir John Leslie, born at Largo, in Scotland, in 1766, died in 1832. His parents were poor, but he obtained his education at the University of St. Andrews, and there laid the foundation of the scientific knowledge which, in 1805, caused his election to the Professorship of Mathematics in Edinburgh University. In 1819, on the death of Playfair, he exchanged this for the chair of philosophy. In 1832, he received the Guelphic order, and was knighted, but died the same year. He was author of many scientific works of great ability.—Dugald Stewart, born at Edinburgh in 1753, became Professor of Moral Philosophy in the university there, in 1785. The first volume of his "Philosophy of the Human Mind" appeared in 1792, and was followed by "Outlines of Moral Philosophy," and several other productions, including memoirs of Adam Smith, Dr. Robertson, and Dr. Reid. He died in 1828.—The Rev. Archibald Alison (father of Sir Archibald Alison, the historian) was born in 1757, at Edinburgh. He was a minister of the Church of England, and officiated as such, in his native city for many years. His "Sermons" are well written, but his literary reputation was established by the "Essay on the Nature and Principles of Taste," which has obtained extraordinary popularity. He died in 1839.—Several distinguished members of the family of Gregory have been attached by professorships, to the University of Edinburgh.—Dr. James Gregory, author of the "Treatise on Optics," in which he imparted his invention of the reflecting telescope, occupied the chair of Mathematics from 1674 to October, 1675, when he died. His nephew, David, after filling the same chair, was elected Savilian professor of Astronomy at Oxford, and died in 1710, after having produced several scientific works of merit.—Dr. John Gregory, who died in 1773, was Professor of Physic, and author of several works, of which the only one now cared for is his "Father's Legacy to his Daughters."—Dr. James Gregory, Professor of Medicine, produced a variety of eminent and useful professional works, died in 1821, and is the person alluded to in the poem. His son is now Professor of Chemistry in the University of Edinburgh, and has distinguished himself as a writer.—M.

And as for poetry, the time of dinner all,
  Thank God, I then have better things to do, man.—
Exceptions 'gainst the fair were coarse and shocking—
I've seen in breeches many a true blue stocking.

Blue stocking stands, in my vocabulary,
  For one that always chatters (sex is nothing)
About new books from June to January,
  And with re-echoed carpings moves your loathing
I like to see young people smart and airy,
  With well dressed hair and fashionable clothing,
Can't they discourse about ball, rout, or play,
And know reviewing's quite out of their way?

It strikes me as a thing exceeding stupid,
  This conversation about books, books, books,
When I was young, and sat midst damsels grouped,
  I talked of roses, zephyrs, gurgling brooks,
Venus, the Graces, Dian, Hymen, Cupid,
  Perilous glances, soul ubduing looks,
Slim tapering fingers, glossy clustering curls,
Diamonds and emeralds, cairngorms and pearls.

On Una that made sunshine in the shade,
  And Emily with eye of liquid jet,
And gentle Desdemona, and the maid
  That sleeps within the tomb of Capulet
Hearts love to ponder—would it not degrade
  Our notion of a nymph like Juliet,
To be informed that she had just read thro'
Last Number of the Edinburgh Review?

Leave ye to dominies and sticker stibblers,
  And all the sedentary generation,
The endless chitter-chatter about scribblers,
  And England's melancholy situation.
Let them be still the customary nibblers
  Of all that rule or edify the nation;
Leave off the corn-bill, and the law of libel,
And read the Pilgrim's Progress or your Bible.

From the poem itself we quote the following stanzas, without any remarks, convinced that their simple elegance and unaffected grace stand in no need of the critic's recommendations:—

I rose this morning about half past nine,
  At breakfast coffee I consumed *pour quatre*,
Unnumbered rolls enriched with marmalade fine,
  And little balls of butter dished in water,

Three eggs, two plateful of superb cold chine
  (Much recommended to make thin folks fatter);
And having thus my ballast stow'd on board,
Roamed forth to kill a day's time like a lord.

How I contrived to pass the whole forenoon,
  I can't remember though my life were on it;
I helped G. T. in jotting of a tune,*
  And hinted rhymes to G——s for a sonnet;†

---

* G. T. whom Lockhart speaks of as "old George Thompson, the friend of Burns," long held a lucrative appointment under the Crown at Edinburgh, and died there some two years ago. He possessed much musical taste, and published an excellent and well-known collection of Scottish Songs, to which, from 1792 to 1796 (when death removed the poet), Burns contributed a very considerable portion of the words. Thompson has been greatly blamed for his niggardly conduct towards Burns. The only voluntary payments he made, for the finest songs in the language, consisted of £5 sent to Burns in July, 1793, which the poet hesitated accepting, wishing that his contributions to Scottish Song should indeed be "a labor of love," and another £5 which Burns, driven, as he said, by "curst necessity," earnestly entreated as a loan, on July 12, 1796 — nine days before his death. Thompson sent the money, stating "it was the very sum I proposed sending." This £10, with a present of a worsted shawl to the poet's wife, was Thompson's only payment for sixty-two original songs expressly written for his collection by Burns, besides alterations of and additions to other songs, and suggestions, during five years, touching the music and other points. Burns would not have *asked* Thompson for money if, at the time, Poverty had not been sitting with her knees upon his hearth. It should be known, too, by all who have been induced to consider him a reckless, extravagant man, that, when he died, Robert Burns, "the glory and reproach of Scotland," owed no man a shilling. Thompson, who outlived him more than half a century, was "a prosperous gentleman" all his days. — M.

† Robert Pearce Gillies (whose "Memoirs of a Literary Veteran," were published in 1851), was a contributor to *Blackwood* from its commencement. His poem, "Childe Alarique," in 1813, attracted some attention. He had a knack at sonnet-writing, and was himself the subject of the sonnet by Wordsworth, in 1814, which concludes with the now-familiar lines

"A cheerful life is what the muses love,
A soaring spirit is their prime delight."

In 1835–6, Gillies contributed some very interesting "Recollections of Sir Walter Scott" to *Frazer's Magazine*, but his reputation will mainly rest on his *Blackwood* papers, called "Horæ Germanicæ," and "Horæ Danicæ," in which he may be said to have first introduced the best dramatic writings of Germany and Denmark to English and American readers. His knowledge of foreign literature, thus exhibited, obtained him the Editorship of the *Foreign Quarterly Review*, when first started in 1827. — M.

Called at the Knox's shop with Miss Balloon,
And heard her ipsa dixit on a bonnet;
Then washed my mouth with ices, tarts, and flummeries,
And ginger-beer and soda, at Montgomery's.*

Down Prince's Street I once or twice paraded,
And gazed upon these same eternal faces;
Those beardless beaux and bearded belles, those faded
And flashy silks, surtouts, pelisses, laces,
Those crowds of clerks, astride on hackneys jaded,
Prancing and capering with notorial grace;
Dreaming enthusiasts who indulge vain whimsies,
That they might pass in Bond Street or St. James's.†

I saw equestrian and pedestrian vanish
—One to a herring in his lonely shop.
And some of kind gregarious, and more clanish,
To club at Waters' for a mutton-chop;
Myself resolved for once my cares to banish,
And give the Cerberus of thought a sop,
Got Jack's, and Sam's, and Dick's, and Tom's consent,
And o'er the Mound to Billy Young's we went.‡

I am not nice, I care not what I dine on,
A sheep's head or beef-steak is all I wish;
Old Homer! how he loved the ερυθρον οινον
It is the glass that glorifies the dish.
The thing that I have always set my mind on
(A small foundation laid of fowl, flesh, fish)
Is out of bottle, pitcher, or punch-bowl,
To suck reviving solace to my soul.

---

* In 1818, Knox's mercery shop was in Prince's street, the Stewart's of Edinburgh. Montgomery's was in the same street—which, for its importance, and bustle of business, and being much frequented as a fashionable lounge, was something like Broadway in New York.—M.

† Bond-street and St. James's, where once beauty and rank, wealth and fashion used to congregate, have "fallen from their high estate," from the successful rivalry of Regent-street, now one of the richest and most popular thoroughfares of London.—M.

‡ The city of Edinburgh consists of the "Old town" and the "New town," separated by a valley. There is a passage from Prince's street, nearly opposite the Castle, into the ancient part of the city, over what is called "The Mound,"—on which now stands a splendid building, in which the Exhibitions of Painting and Sculpture take place. A little higher up, between the Mound and the North Bridge, is placed on that side of Prince's street, which is not built upon (to allow a view of the ancient city) a very magnificent monument of Scott, consisting of an ornamented cross, with a statue in the interior.—M.

Life's a dull dusty desert, waste and drear,
  With now and then an oasis between,
Where palm-trees rise, and fountains gushing clear
  Burst neath the shelter of that leafy screen;
Haste not your parting steps, when such appear,
  Repose, ye weary travellers, on the green.
Horace and Milton, Dante, Burns, and Schiller,
Dined at a tavern — when they had "the siller."

And ne'er did poet, epical or tragical,
  At Florence, London, Weimar, Rome, Maybole,
See time's dark lanthern glow with hues more magical
  Than I have witnessed in the Coffin-hole.
Praise of antiquity a bam and fudge I call,
  Ne'er past the present let my wishes roll;
A fig for all comparing, croaking grumblers,
Hear me, dear dimpling Billy, bring the tumblers.*

Let blank verse hero, or Spenserian rhymer,
  Treat Donna Musa with chateau-margout,
Chateau-la-fitte, Johannisberg, Hocheimer,
  In tall outlandish glasses green and blue,
Thanks to my stars, myself, a doggrel-chimer,
  Have nothing with such costly tastes to do;
My muse is always kindest when I court her
O'er whiskey-punch, gin-twist, strong beer, and porter.

And O, my pipe, though in these Dandy days
  Few love thee, fewer still their love confess,
Ne'er let me blush to celebrate thy praise,
  Divine invention of the age of Bess!
I for a moment interrupt my lays
  The tiny tube with loving lip to press,
I'll then come back with a reviving zest,
And give thee three more stanzas of my best.

(*I smoke.*)

Pipe! whether plain in fashion of Frey-herr,
  Or gaudy glittering in the taste of Boor,
Deep-darkened Meer-shaum or Ecume-de-mer,
  Or snowy clay of Gowda, light and pure.
Let different people different pipes prefer,
  Delft, horn, or catgut, long, short, older, newer,
Puff, every brother, as it likes him best,
De gustibus non disputandum est.

* The hostelrie kept by "Billy Young," in High-street, the old town of Edinburgh, was honored with the *sobriquet* of The Coffin-hole. — The select and classic gentlemen of the Dilettanti Society much affected the place, as has been already mentioned. — M.

Pipe! when I stuff into thee my canaster,
  With flower of camomile and leaf of rose,
And the calm rising fume comes fast and faster,
  Curling with balmy circles near my nose,
And all the while my dexter hand is master
  Of the full cup from Meux's vat that flows,
Heavens! all my brain a soft oblivion wraps
Of wafered letters and of single taps.

I've no objections to a good segar,
  A true Havana, smooth, and moist, and brown;*

---

* The reader may thank me for reminding him of some lines, by Lord Byron, on the same subject. They appeared in "The Island," written and published in 1823, exactly five years *after* the appearance of Odoherty's stanzas, (in April, 1818,) and, as Byron was a constant reader of *Blackwood's Magazine*, and much addicted to "cribbing" the ideas of others (as he confessed to Moore, which is done, more or less, by all clever writers — if they would only confess it!) it is very probable that he made free with Odoherty on this occasion. Byron's lines are,

"But here the herald of the self-same mouth
Come breathing o'er the aromatic South,
Not like a bed of violets on the gale,
But such as wafts its cloud o'er grog or ale,
Borne from a short frail pipe, which yet had blown
Its gentle odors over either zone,
And, puffed where'er winds rise or waters roll,
Had wafted smoke from Portsmouth to the Pole,
Opposed its vapor as the lightning flashed,
And reeked, mid mountain bellows, unabashed,
To Æolus a constant sacrifice,
Through every change of all the varying skies.
And what was he who bore it? — I may err,
But deem him sailor or philosopher.
Sublime tobacco! which from east to west
Cheers the tar's labor or the Turkman's rest;
Which on the Moslem's ottoman divides
His hours, and rivals opium and his brides;
Magnificent in Stamboul, but less grand,
Though not less loved, in Wapping or the Strand;
Divine in hookas, glorious in a pipe,
When tipped with amber, mellow, rich, and ripe;
Like other charmers, wooing the caress
More dazzlingly when daring in full dress;
Yet thy true lovers more admire by far
Thy naked beauties — Give me a cigar!

But then the smoke's too near the eye by far,
  And out of doors 'tis in a twinkling flown;
And somehow it sets all my teeth ajar,
  When to an inch or so we've smoked him down;
And if your leaf have got a straw within it,
You know 'tis like a cinder in a minute.

In priority of composition, Odoherty certainly takes precedence, and his stanzas anticipate the ideas expressed by Byron, on the subject of tobacco, which James I. and Charles Lamb have universally made illustrious. It is impossible, of course, to mention the Nicotian literature without thinking of Charles Lamb's lines, entitled "A Farewell to Tobacco," commencing,

"May the Babylonish curse
Strait confound my stammering verse,
If I can a passage see
In this word perplexity,
Or a fit expression find,
Or a language to my mind,
(Still the phrase is wide or scant)
To take leave of thee, GREAT PLANT!"

and, after subjecting the weed to an exquisite alternation of praise and abuse, concluding thus,

"For thy sake, TOBACCO, I,
Would do anything but die,
And but seek to extend my days
Long enough to sing thy praise,
But as she who once hath been
A king's consort, is a queen
Ever after, nor will bate
Any title of her state,
Though a widow, or divorced—
So I, from thy converse forced,
The old name and style retain,
A right Katherine of Spain;
And a seat, too, 'mongst the joys
Of the blest Tobacco Boys;
Where, though I, by sour physician
Am debarred the full fruition
Of thy favors, I may catch
Some collateral sweets, and match
Sidelong odors, that give life
Like glances from a neighbor's wife;
And still live in the by-places
And the suburbs of thy graces;
And in thy borders take delight,
An unconquered Canaanite."—M.

I have no doubt a long excursive hooker
  Suits well some lordly lounger of Bengal,
Who never writes, or looks into a book, or
  Does any thing with earnestness at all;
He sits, and his tobacco's in the nook, or
  Tended by some black heathen in the hall,
Lays up his legs, and thinks he does great things
If once in the half hour a puff he brings.

I rather follow in my smoking trim
  The example of Scots cottars and their wives
Who, while the evening air is warm and dim,
  In July sit beside their garden hives;
And, gazing all the while with wrinkles grim
  To see how the concern of honey thrives,
Empty before they've done a four-ounce bag
Of sailors' twist, or, what's less common—shag.

CHAPTER IV.*

Odoherty's Success in Edinburgh Society—Attends Lectures in the University—Remarks on Scottish Fashionables—Acts as Cicerone to the Austrian Archdukes—Specimens of his Songs—Visit to Glasgow and Honors from the University—A Tale of Terror!—Fragments: Abolition of the Pronoun I; Scandal; Blue-Stockings; Skull-Walls and the Catacombs.

THIS winter was indeed a memorable one in the life of Odoherty. Divided almost in equal proportions between the Old and the New Town of Edinburgh—the society of Hogg, Allan, and the Dilettanti, on the one hand, and that of the female and fashionable world on the other—and thus presenting to the active mind of the Ensign a perpetual succession, or rather alternation, of the richest viands—it produced the effects which might have been anticipated, and swelled considerably the bulk

* The gentleman who drew up the first two notices of this life, having died of an apoplexy some time ago, the notice which appeared in March, and the present one, are by a different hand. [The reader is advised to refer to, if he should have forgotten or passed over, the explanation of the above note in page 27.]—M.

of two portfolios, respectively set apart for the prose and verse compositions which, at this period of his career, our bard was so rapidly pouring forth to the admiration of his numerous friends and the public.

His morning hours were devoted to attend several courses of lectures in the University; for Odoherty was never weary of learning, and embraced with ardor every opportunity that was afforded him of increasing the stores of his literary acquisitions and accomplishments. His remarks upon the different lectures which he now attended, possess all his characteristic acuteness, and would have done honor to a more practised critic. But these we reserve for the separate publication of his works. To insert any mutilated fragments of them here would be an act of injustice to the illustrious Professors, Brown, Playfair, Leslie, Hope, Ritchie, &c., no less than to their distinguished disciple.*

* Dr. Thomas Brown, the immediate predecessor of the late John Wilson, as Professor of Moral Philosophy in the University of Edinburgh, was the son of a Scottish clergyman, and born in 1778. A pupil of Dugald Stewart, at the age of twenty he published Observations on the Zoonomia of Dr. Darwin (most of it written before he was eighteen), graduated as M.D. in 1803—published two volumes of poems in 1804—soon after brought out his Relation of Cause and Effect—and became Dugald Stewart's substitute in the chair of Moral Philosophy, in 1808–9, and Joint-Professor, in 1810. The Paradise of Coquettes, a poem of much merit, appeared in 1814. He died, at Brompton, near London, in April, 1820. His Lectures were given to the world after his death, and upon them chiefly rests his great reputation as a philosopher.—Professor John Playfair, the son of a Scottish minister, was born in 1748, educated at St. Andrew's, ordained for the church, early distinguished himself by his progress in science, succeeded to his father's parish in 1773, but eventually resigned it, and, after some time spent in travel and private tuition, was appointed Joint-Mathematical Professor, at Edinburgh University, in 1785—he had previously stood two unsuccessful contests, for a similar chair; at Aberdeen, when he was only eighteen, and at St. Andrew's when he was twenty-four. In 1805, resigning the mathematical chair, he was made Professor of Natural History, and died, in July, 1819, at Edinburgh. His acquirements, in literature and science, were very great. His writings embraced a vast variety of subjects—the most eminent among them are his Elements of Geometry, Illustrations of the Huttonian Theory, Outlines of Natural Philosophy, Dissertation on the Progress of Mathematical and Physical Science since the Revival of Letters in Europe (for the *Encyclopedia Britannica*), and a great number of articles for the *Edinburgh Review*, of which the best known are a masterly criticism on Madame de Staël's Corinne, and an account (in the eleventh volume of that periodical) of Laplace's Mecanique Celeste. This last article,

Great and illustrious as is the fame of these Philosophers, it is possible that the names of some of them may live in distant ages, chiefly because of their connexion with that of Odoherty. The Ensign may be to them what Xenophon has been to Socrates; he may be more, for it is possible that none of them may have a Plato.

The gay world of the northern metropolis, which, during this remarkable winter, was adorned by the graceful and ingenious Ensign, seems, we are constrained to observe, to have found less favor in his eyes than in those of most other visitors with whom we have had an opportunity of conversing. In one of those inimitable letters of his, addressed to the compiler of the present sketch, he comments with some little causticity on the incidents

if his best biographer be credited, there is no general account of the great facts and principles of astronomy so clear, comprehensive, and exact, nor half so beautiful and majestic in the composition. In that clever and caustic work, Peter's Letters to his Kinsfolk, Mr. Lockhart (as Doctor Morris) has paid high, eloquent, and merited homage to the genius of Brown, Playfair, and Leslie, and dwells with great *gusto* upon a trial of strength and agility which took place, about 1818, at Craig-crook, the country seat of Mr. Jeffrey, for which Playfair threw off his coat and waistcoat:—"With the exception of Leslie, they all jumped wonderfully; and Jeffrey was quite miraculous, considering his brevity of stride. But the greatest wonder of the whole was Mr. Playfair. He is also a short man, and he cannot be less than seventy, yet he took his stand with the assurance of an athletic, and positively beat every one of us—the very best of us, at least half a heel's breadth. I was quite thunderstruck, never having heard the least hint of his being so great a geometrician—in this sense of the word."—There were two Edinburgh lawyers of the name of Hope, at this time. One was Charles Hope, Lord President of the Court of Session, and (in 1819), Colonel of the Royal Blues, a foot regiment of Edinburgh volunteers. He was an upright judge, an eloquent speaker, a sound lawyer, and a strong tory. The other was John Hope, an intimate friend of Scott's, and the person referred to in the text. He was Dean of the Faculty of Advocates and Solicitor-General for Scotland, when he was thus mentioned in Scott's diary of December, 1825, "decidedly the most hopeful young man of his time: high connections, great talent, spirited ambition, a ready elocution, with a good voice and dignified manners, prompt and steady courage, vigilant and constant assiduity, popularity with the young men, and the good opinion of the old, will, if I mistake not, carry him as high as any man who has arisen here since the days of old Hal Dundas [the first Viscount Melville]."—John Hope fulfilled his high expectation. When I last saw him, in May, 1850, he was on the Scottish judicial bench as the Lord Justice Clerk, head of the chief criminal Court of Scotland.—M.

of several balls and routes which he had just attended. "The gayeties of Edinburgh," writes the Ensign, "are a bad and lame caricature of those of London. There is the same squeeze, the same heat, the same buzz; but, alas! the ease, the elegance, the non-chalance are awanting. In London, the different orders of society are so numerous that they keep themselves totally apart from each other; and the highest circles of fashion admit none as denizens except those who possess the hereditary claims of birth and fortune, or (as in my own case), those who are supposed to atone for their deficiencies in these respects, by extraordinary genius or merit.—Hence there are so few stones of the first, or even of the second, water, that recourse is necessarily had to far inferior gems—not unfrequently even to the transitory mimicries of *paste*. You shall see the lady of an attorney stowing away her bedsteads and basinstands, dismantling all her apartments, and turning her whole family topsy-turvy once in a season, in order that she may have the satisfaction of dispersing two hundred cards, with "*At home*" upon them. It is amusing enough to see with what laborious exertion, she and her daughters, sensible people that attend to domestic concerns, plain-work, &c., for three parts of the year, become for a few short weeks the awkward inapt copyists of their far less respectable betters. It is distressing to see the faded airs with which these good *Bourgeoises* endeavor to conceal their confusion in receiving the curtsy of a lady of quality, who comes to their houses only for the purpose of quizzing them in some corner, with some sarcastic younger brother," &c. The rest of the letter, consisting chiefly of rapturous descriptions of particular young ladies, is omitted from motives of delicacy. Two fair creatures, however, a most exquisite petite Blonde, and a superb sultana-like Brunette, who seem to have divided for several weeks the possession of the sensible heart of Odoherty, may receive, upon personal application to the publisher, several sonnets, elegies, &c., which are inscribed with their names in the above-mentioned portfolio of their departed admirer—faint and frail memorials of unripened affections—memorials over which they may now drop a tear of delightful pensiveness—which they may now press to the virgin bosom without a hope, and therefore, alas! without a blush.

About this period their Imperial Highnesses the Archdukes John and Lewis of Austria arrived in the Caledonian metropolis. Although they received every polite attention from the military, legal, and civic dignitaries of the place, these elevated personages were afflicted, notwithstanding, with considerable symptoms of ennui, in the course of the long evening which they spent at M'Culloch's, after returning from the pomps and festivities of the day.* It was then that their Highnesses, expressing some desire to partake of the more unceremonious and week-day society of the Northern Athens, various characters of singing, smoking, and scientific celebrity were introduced to their apartment, through the intervention of a gentleman in their suite. Among these, it is scarcely necessary to observe, was Odoherty. The Ensign, with that happy tact which a man of true genius carries into every situation of life, immediately perceived and caught the air, manner, &c.—in a word, whatever was best adapted for captivating the archiducal fancy. His proficiency in the German tongue, the only one which these princes spoke with much fluency, was not indeed great; but he made amends for this by the truly Germanic ferocity with which he smoked (for the Ensign was one of those who could send the cloud, *ad libitum*, through the ears and nostrils, as well as the mouth) by the unqualified admiration which he testified for the favorite imperial beverage of Giles' ale—but, above all, by the style of matchless excellence in which he sung some of his own songs, among which were the following:—

SONG I.

Confusion to routs and at homes,
To assemblies, and balls, and what not;
'Tis with pain e'er Odoherty roams
From the scenes of the pipe and the pot.
Your Dandies may call him a sot,
They never can call him a spoon;

* The Royal Hotel, Edinburgh, was kept by James M'Culloch, who literally resembled "a ton of flesh." His death took place on January 12, 1819, and is thus mentioned in a letter from Sir Walter Scott, "No news here but that the goodly hulk of conceit and tallow, which was called Macculloch, of the Royal Hotel, Prince's street, was put to bed dead-drunk on Wednesday night, and taken out the next morning dead-by-itself-dead."—M.

And Odoherty cares not a jot,
For he's sure you won't join in the tune.
With your pipes and your swipes,
And your herrings and tripes,
You never can join in the tune.

I'm a swapper, as every one knows,
In my pumps six feet three inches high;
'Tis no wonder your minikin beaux
Have a fancy to fight rather shy
Of a Gulliver chap such as I,
That could stride over troops of their tribes,
That had never occasion to buy
Either collars, or calves, or kibes.
My boot wrenches and pinches,
Though 'tis wide twenty inches,
And I don't bear my brass at my kibes.

When I see a fantastical hopper,
A trim little chip of the *ton*,
Not so thick as your Highness' pipe-stopper,
And scarcely, I take it, so long,
Swaddled prim and precise as a prong,
With his ribs running all down and up,
Says I, Does the creature belong
To the race of the ewe or the tup?
With their patches and their scratches,
And their plastered mustaches,
They are more of the ewe than the tup.

SONG II.

THAT nothing is perfect has frequently been
By the wisest philosophers stated untruly;
Which only can prove that they never had seen
The agreeable Lady Lucretia Gilhooly.
Where's the philosopher would not feel loss of her?
Whose bosom these bright sunny eyes would not thaw?
Although I'm a game one, these little highwaymen
Have rifled the heart of poor Major M'Craw.

Cook sail'd round the world, and Commodore Anson
The wonders he met with has noted down duly;
But Cook, nor yet Anson, could e'er light by chance on
A beauty like Lady Lucretia Gilhooly.
Let astronomer asses still peep through their glasses,
Then tell all the stars and the planets they saw;
Damn Georgium Sidus! We've Venus beside us,
And that is sufficient for Major M'Craw.

Delighted with this mirthful evening, the illustrious strangers, before breaking up, insisted that Odoherty, the principal source of its hilarity, should accompany them next day to the literary, mercantile, and manufacturing city of Glasgow. Here the Ensign was received in the most distinguished manner, not more on account of the company in which he travelled, than of the individual fame which had already found its way before him to the capital of St. Mungo.* The party put up at the Buck's Head, to the excellent hostess of which (Mrs. Jardine) the Ensign addressed a pathetic sonnet at parting.† At the dinner

* St. Mungo is the patron-saint of the City of Glasgow, and in the days of Papistry, the Cathedral (admirably described by Scott, in "Rob Roy," and by Lockhart, in the last volume of "Peter's Letters,") was dedicated to him. The city arms of Glasgow consist of the representation of a bay-tree, a bird, and a salmon with a ring in its mouth. Once upon a time (as the story-books used to say—for they have become utilitarian, scientific, sermonizing, and dull, of late years), there was an old gentleman of Glasgow with a young wife, of whom he was jealous, without cause. One day, as they were crossing what was then the only bridge over the Clyde, he annoyed her with inuendos which at once shocked and irritated her. Taking off her wedding ring, and appealing to an image of St. Mungo which stood in a niche on the bridge, she threw the circlet into the water, exclaiming that, if she were innocent, the good saint would prove it by restoring the ring. Some days after, having purchased a salmon for dinner, the old man happened to be in the kitchen when the cook was preparing it for the pot. The ring was found in the entrails of the fish, the husband confessed the injustice of his suspicions, the wife was happy in having her innocence thus established by a miracle, and, I dare say that, from that time forth, the husband was subdued and properly henpecked! The people of Glasgow, out of respect for his good deed, made Mungo their patron-saint, and the fish, holding a ring in his mouth, was forthwith added to their city's arms. So runs the story, at all events.—When Mrs. Siddons visited Glasgow, at the height of her fame, a piece of plate was presented to her on which were engraved the city-arms and this epigrammatic inscription:—

"Bays from our tree you cannot gather,
No branch of it deserves the name—
So take it all; call it a feather,
And place it in your cap of fame."—M.

† The Buck's-Head, in Glasgow, was a fine old-fashioned inn, between twenty and thirty years ago. Lockhart (in his Peter's Letters) taking the pseudo-Dr. Morris to this house, makes him say—"Both I and my horse were somewhat wearied with the journey, and the horns of a genuine Buck, proudly projecting over the gateway of the hotel to which I had been directed, were to me the most interesting features in the whole Trongate of Glasgow." It

given by the provost and magistrates, the Ensign attended in full puff, and was placed among the most illustrious guests, at the upper end of the table. He sung, he joked, he spoke; he

should be noticed that this Trongate is the principal business street in the Capital of the West, as Bailie Nicol Jarvie's fair city is called. In its glory, when Odoherty, Dr. Morris, and the Austrian princes, were guests of the Buck's-Head, that famous hostelrie was kept by a Mrs. Jardine, the Leviathan of landladies, of whom and of her house, Morris speaketh thus:—"A capital house. I begin to think our friend Tom's mode of choosing a hotel is not a bad one. His selection is generally regulated by the weight and dimensions of the different hosts, well judging that the landlord who exhibits the most unquestionable marks of good living in his own person, is the most likely to afford it to his guests. Upon this principle of choice, I apprehend the Buck's-Head is entitled to a preference over most houses of entertainment in the kingdom. The precise weight of Mrs. Jardine, the landlady, I certainly do not pretend to know, and certainly believe it to be something under that of the Durham Ox. But the size and rotundity of her person so greatly exceed the usual dimensions of the human frame, that were they subjected to that rule of arithmetic, entitled *Mensuration of Solids*, I am very sure the result would be something extraordinary. Her jollity and good humor, however, make her an universal favorite; and I can bear witness that her inmates have no cause to complain either of bad cheer or want of attention. I flatter myself I stand pretty well in her good graces; and, in consequence, am frequently invited to eat a *red herring* in the back parlor, and take a glass out of what she calls *her ain bottle*. The bottle contains not the worst stuff in the world, I assure you. It is excellent Burgundy, and the red herring commonly turns out to be a superb chop *en papilotte*."—The portly landlady of the Buck's-Head was by no means pleased with this notice of her ponderosity, and published a card in the newspapers, in which, to show that she was not as stout as Dr. Morris stated her to be, her weight was stated at *only* twenty-two stone, or *three hundred and eight pounds!*—The modest manner in which an excellent luncheon is designated as a mere trifle, is common in, and peculiar to Scotland. The first time I visited Edinburgh (one of the most picturesque cities in the world, and only eclipsed in beauty perhaps by Venice and Oxford), I was invited "just to step in about nine, and take an egg for supper." But I found that *the egg* was a sumptuous repast, in which Dee salmon, Edinburgh oysters, Finnan haddies (or haddocks), Fife crabs, brandered fowl, grouse-soup, beef collops, mutton chops, veal cutlets, and game *ad libitum* covered the table;—there were no eggs, however, except in the lobster salad. Apropos of chops, *en papillote*, as mentioned by Dr. Morris, I think he mistook the dish;—not mutton chops, but veal cutlets are cooked in paper. The process preserves the juices much better than Soyer's wasteful one of skewering three cutlets together, and roasting the mass by a clear red fire until the two outer pieces are burned, and then serving up the middle cutlet, which is untarnished by the fire, but done to a nicety. It is an was the *sine quâ non* of the meeting. At the collation prepared for the imperial party by the Professors of the University, he made himself equally agreeable; and indeed, upon both of these occasions, laid the foundations of several valuable friendships, which only terminated with his existence. Among his MSS. we have found a paper which purports to contain the words of a *programma* affixed to the gate of the college, on the morning preceding the visit of the Archdukes. We shall not hesitate to transcribe this fragment, although, from our ignorance of the style and ceremonial observed on similar occasions by the Scottish universities, we are not able to vouch for its authenticity. The Ensign kept his papers in much disorder—*seria mixta jocis*, as his Roman favorite expresses it.

Q. F. F. Q. S.

SENATUS Academicus Togatis et non Togatis Salutem dat.—Ab altissimo et potentissimo Principe Marchione de Douglas et Clydesdale, certiores facti quod eorum altitudines imperiales Archiduces Joannes et Ludovicus de Austria, hodie nos visitatione honorare intendunt, hasce regulas enunciare quomodo omnes se sunt gerere placuit nobis, et quicunque eas non volunt observare severrime puniti erunt postea.

1*mo*. Eorum altitudines imperiales Archiduces Joannes et Ludovicus de Austria capient frigidam collationem in aula priori cum principali et professoribus (cum togis suis) et quibusdam generosis hominibus ex urbe et vicinitate, et signifero Docherṫiade et alia sequela eorum circa horam meridianam, impensis Facultatis.

2. Studentes qui barbas habent tondeant et manus et facies lavent sicuti in die dominico.

3. Studentes omnes indusia nitida induant velut cum Dux Montis-Rosarum erat hic.

4. Studentes Theologici nigras braccas et vestes et pallia decentia induant quasi ministri.

old joke in Scotland (*conveyed* by Samuel Lover into his *Handy Andy*), that a gentleman who partook of salmon cutlets *en papillote*, and was asked how he liked them, answered that "The fish was very nice, but the skin rather tough!" He had actually contrived *to chew and swallow the thin tough paper in which the fish was cooked!*

5. Omnes studentes in casu sint videri per Archiduces et Marchiones et honorabiles personas qui cum iis sunt; et Hibernici et Montani supra omnia sibi oculum habeant et omnes pectantur.

6. Studentes duas lineas faciant decenter et cum quiete intra aulam priorem et aulam communem cum processio ambulat, et juniores ni rideant cum peregrinos vident.

7. In aula communi Professor * * * * * (name illegible) qui olim in Gallia fuit Francisce illis locutus erit nam Professor *** est mortuus.

8. Deinde Aliquis ex Physicis sermonem Anglicam pronunciabit et Principalis Latine precabitur.

9. Sine strepitu dismissi estotis cum omnia facta sunt.

It is to be regretted that several leaves are a-wanting in the Ensign's diary, which probably contained an account of the rest of the tour which he performed in company with the scions of the house of Hapsburg.* Their custom of smoking several

* These Archdukes of Austria were sons of the Emperor Leopold II. John, born in 1782, has achieved a name, and will be mentioned in history. In 1800, on the retirement of the Archduke Charles, his elder brother, father of the present Emperor (described by Napoleon as "the best general among the Austrians, though he has committed a thousand faults"), the Archduke John then but eighteen years old, was appointed to command the troops in the German Empire in the struggle with France, but did not remain in that position after the defeat at Hohenlinden, in December, 1800. Subsequently, after taking some part in the war and in the administration of state-affairs, he retired to Styria, where, from a strong taste for letters, he endeavored to elevate literature and art, by founding what continues to be an useful institution, the Johanneum at Grätz. Napoleon's return from Elba, in 1815, called him from his retirement. After the battle of Waterloo, the Archdukes John and Lewis made a tour through Great Britain and Ireland. My venerable friend, Doctor Francis, of New York, informs me that he was present in March, 1816, just before the Archdukes left London, when the President of the Royal Society of England (Sir Joseph Banks, the naturalist), admitted them as Fellows of that body, by virtue of a Royal Mandate, which dispensed with the formality and delay of their being proposed and ballotted for. When their names were called by him, each of the princes rose in his place, and acknowledged the compliment paid him. Returning to Austria in April, 1816, John fixed his summer residence in the old romantic castle of Thurnberg, where he led the unostentatious life of a country gentleman and man of letters, beloved by all classes, but especially the man of the people, but distrusted (for his liberality) by the Austrian government in 1828, he formed a morganatic marriage with the daughter of the postmaster of Aussee—who is said to have first attracted his atten-

pipes every evening after supper, took from him, it is not unlikely, the leisure that might have been necessary for composing a full narrative; but, however slight his *precis* might have been, its loss is to be regretted. The sketches of a master are of more value than the most elaborate works of secondary hands. The fragment of an Angelo surpasses the chef-d'œuvres of a West;—but, to return—at Dublin, the festivities with which the arrival of the party was celebrated, surpassed in splendor and variety, as might be expected, every thing that had been exhibited in the cities of Scotland. After spending several days in a round of gayeties, the Archdukes set sail for Liverpool. Odoherty, from the pressure of his professional engagements, found himself compelled to go no farther in the train of the princely travellers. The parting was one of those scenes which may be more easily imagined than described. Although the Ensign lingered a day or two in the midst of the most brilliant society of Dublin—although he spent his mornings with Philips,* and his evenings with Lady Morgan, his spirits did not soon recover their usual tone and elasticity. The state of gloom in which his mind was thus temporarily involved, extended no

tion by assuming the attire and actually performing the duty of a postillion, on one occasion when the Archduke was anxious to proceed and the regular postillions were all absent. The marriage was a happy one, and its offspring is the Count de Meran. In 1848, the tide of Revolution in Europe took the Archduke John from his beloved mountain home in Styria into the arena of action. He put an end (for the time) to a popular insurrection in Vienna, on March 13, by compelling Prince Metternich, long the virtual autocrat of Austria, to relinquish office and power, and retire into exile. Two months later, when the Emperor Ferdinand I., abandoned Vienna and went to Innspruck, John acted as his deputy in the capital, and endeavored to restore tranquillity. The German Assembly at Frankfort, considering him as a prince at once popular and independent, made him Regent of Germany, in June, 1848. He might have erected a throne for himself, on the ruins of the old feudalities, but was content with conservatively employing the vast powers intrusted to him as a reformer. In 1851, long after the Frankfort Assembly had been dispersed, and when despotism was re-established in Germany, John resigned his power, and retired into that private life which so much delighted him.—M.

* Of Charles Phillips, the Irish orator (in the very fulness of his fame, in 1818, when Maginn wrote this chapter), and of Lady Morgan, the well-known Irish writer, more extended notices shall be given by-and-bye, on a more suitable occasion than this mere mention of their names in the text.—M.

inconsiderable portion of its influence to his muse. We do not wish to extend this article beyond the allowable limit; but we must make room for a single specimen of the dark effusions which at this epoch flowed from the gay, the giddy, Odoherty.

THE ENGLISH SAILOR AND THE KING OF ACHEN'S DAUGHTER.

*A Tale of Terror.**

COME, listen Gentles all,
And Ladies unto me,
And you shall be told of a Sailor bold
As ever sail'd on Sea.

'Twas in the month of May,
Sixteen hundred sixty and four,
We sallied out, both fresh and stout,
In the good ship Swift-sure.

With wind and weather fair
We sail'd from Plymouth Sound,
And the Line we crossed, and the Cape we pass'd,
Being to China bound.

And we sail'd by Sunda Isles,
And Ternate and Tydore,
Till the wind it lagg'd, and our sails they flagg'd,
In sight of Achen's shore.

Becalm'd, days three times three,
We lay in th' burning sun;
Our Water we drank, and our Meat it stank,
And our Biscuits were well nigh done.

Oh! then 'twas an awful sight
Our Seamen for to behold,
Who t'other day were so fresh and gay,
And their hearts as stout as gold.

But now our hands they shook,
And our cheeks were yellow and lean—
Our faces all long, and our nerves unstrung,
And loose and squalid our skin.

And we walk'd up and down the deck
As long as our legs could bear us;

* This imitation of Monk Lewis's "Tales of Wonder," and of part of Coleridge's "Ancient Mariner," has something of the flavor of the quaint ballad, called "As I sailed, as I sailed," in which are recorded the piratical deeds and pendulous exit of Captain Kyd.—M.

And we thirsted all, but no rain would fall,
  And no dews arise to cheer us.

  But the red red Sun from the sky
  Lent his scorching beams all day,
Till our tongues, through drought, hung out of our mouth,
  And we had no voice to pray.

  And the hot hot air from the South
  Did lie on our lungs all night
As if the grim Devil, with his mouth full of evil,
  Had blown on our troubled Sprite.

  At last, so it happ'd one night,
  When we all in our hammocks lay,
Bereft of breath, and expecting death
  To come ere break of day.

  On a sudden a cooling breeze
  Shook the hammock where I was lain;
And then, by Heaven's grace, I felt on my face
  A drop of blessed rain.

  I open'd my half-closed eyes,
  And my mouth I open'd it wide
And I started with joy, from my hammock so high,
  And "A breeze, a breeze!" I cried.

  But no man heard me cry,
  And the breeze again fell down;
And a clap of Thunder, with fear and wonder
  Nigh cast me in a swound.

  I dared not look around,
  Till, by degrees grown bolder,
I saw a grim sprite, by the moon's pale light,
  Dim glimmering at my shoulder.

  He was drest in a Seamen's jacket,
  Wet trowsers, and dripping hose,
And an unfelt wind, I heard behind,
  That whistled among his clothes.

  I look'd at him by the light of the stars,
  I look'd by the light of the moon,
And I saw, though his face was cover'd with scars,
  John Jewkes, my Sister's Son.

  "Alas! John Jewkes," I cried,
  "Poor boy, what brings thee here?"
But nothing he said, but hung down his head,
  And made his bare scull appear.

Then I, by my grief grown bold,
To take his hand endeavor'd,
But his head he turned round, which a gaping wound
Had nigh from his shoulders sever'd.

He opened his mouth to speak,
Like a man with his last breath struggling,
And, before every word, in his throat was heard
A horrible misguggling.

At last, with a broken groan,
He gurgled, "Approach not me!
For the Fish have my head, and the Indians my blood,
'Tis only my Ghost you see.

"And dost thou not remember,
Three years ago to-day,
How at Aunt's we tarried, when Sister was married
To Farmer Robin, pray?

"Oh! then we were blythe and jolly,
But none of us all had seen,
While we sung and we laugh'd, and the stout ale quaff'd,
That our number was thirteen.

"And none of all the party,
At the head of the table, saw,
While our cares we drown'd, and the flagon went round,
Old Goody Martha Daw.

"But Martha she was there,
Though she never spake a word;
And by her sat her old black cat,
Though it never cried or purr'd.

"And she lean'd on her oaken crutch,
And a bundle of sticks she broke,
And her prayers backward mutter'd, and the Devil's words utter'd.
Though she never a word out spoke.

"'Twas on a Thursday morn,
That very day was se'nnight,
I ran to sweet Sue, to bid her adieu,
For I could not stay a minute.

"Then crying with words so tender,
She gave me a true lover's locket,
That I still might love her, forgetting her never—
So I put it in my pocket.

"And then we kiss'd and parted,
And knew not, all the while,

That Martha was nigh, on her broomstick so high,
Looking down with a devilish smile.

"So I went to sea again,
With my heart brim-full of Sue;
Though my mind misgave me, the salt waters would have me,
And I'd take my last adieu.

"We made a prosperous voyage
Till we came to this fatal coast,
When a storm it did rise, in seas and in skies,
That we gave ourselves up for lost.

"Our vessel it was stranded
All on the shoals of Achen,
And all then did die, save only I,
And I hardly saved my bacon.

"It happ'd that very hour,
The Black King walking by
Did see me sprawling, on hands and knees crawling,
And took to his palace hard by.

"And finding that I was
A likely lad for to see,
My bones well knit, and my joints well set,
And not above twenty-three,

"He made me his gardener boy,
To sow pease and potatoes,
To water his flowers, when there were no showers,
And cut his parsley and lettuce.

"Now it so fell out on a Sunday
(Which these Pagans never keep holy),
I was gathering rue, and thinking on Sue,
With a heart full of melancholy,

"When the King of Achen's Daughter
Did open her casement to see;
And, as she look'd round on the gooseberry ground,
Her eyes they lit upon me;

"And seeing me tall and slim,
And of shape right personable;
My skin so white, and so very unlike
The blacks at her Father's table,

"She took it into her head
(For so the Devil did move her),
That I in good sooth, was a comely youth,
And would make a gallant Lover.

"So she tripp'd from her chamber so high,
All in silks and satins clad,
And her gown it rustled, as down she bustled,
With steps like a Princess sad.

"Her shoes they were deck'd with pearls,
And her hair with diamonds glisten'd,
And her gimcracks and toys, they made such a noise,
My mouth water'd the while I listen'd.

"Then she tempted me with glances,
And with sugar'd words so tender,
(And tho' she was black, she was straight in the back,
And young, and tall, and slender—)

"But I my Love remember'd,
And the locket she did give me,
And resolv'd to be true to my darling Sue,
As she did ever believe me.

"Whereat the Princess wax'd
Both furious and angry,
And said, she was sure I had some Paramour
In kitchen or in laundry.

"And then, with a devilish grin,
She said, 'Give me your locket'—
But I damn'd her for a Witch, and a conjuring Bitch,
And kept it in my pocket.

"Howbeit, both day and night
She did torture and torment,
And said she, 'If you'll yield to me the field,
'I'll give thee thy heart's content.

"'But give me up the locket,
'And stay three months with me,
'And then, if the will remains with you still,
'I'll ship you off to sea."

"So I thought it the only way
To behold my lovely Sue,
And the thoughts of Old England, they made my heart tingle, and
I gave up the locket so true.

"Thereon she laugh'd outright
With a hellish grin, and I saw
That the Princess was gone, and in her room
There stood old Martha Daw.

"She was all astride a Broomstick,
And bid me get up behind;

So my wits being lost, the Broomstick I cross'd,
And away we flew, swift as the wind.

"But my head it soon turn'd giddy,
I reel'd and lost my balance,
So I tumbled over, like a perjur'd lover,
A warning to all gallants.

"And there where I tumbled down
The Indians found me lying;
My head they cut off, and my blood did quaff,
And set my flesh afrying.

"Hence, all ye English gallants,
A warning take by me,
Your true love's locket to keep in your pocket
Whenever you go to sea.

"And, oh dear uncle Thomas,
I come to give you warning,
As then 'twas my chance with Davy to dance,
'Twill be yours to-morrow morning.

"'Twas three years agone this night,
Three years gone clear and clean,
Since we sat down at Aunt's at the wedding to dance,
And our number was thirteen.

"Now I and sister Nan,
(Two of that fatal party)
Have both gone from Aunt's, with Davy to dance,
Tho' then we were hale and hearty.

"And, as we both have died,
(I speak it with grief and sorrow—)
At the end of each year, it now is clear
That you should die to-morrow.

"But if, good uncle Thomas,
You'll promise, and promise truly,
To plough the main for England again,
And perform my orders duly,

"Old Davy will allow you
Another year to live,
To visit your friends, and make up your odd ends,
And your enemies forgive.

"But friend, when you reach Old England,
To Laure'ston town you'll go,
And then to the Mayor, in open fair,
Impeach old Martha Daw.

"And next you'll see her hang'd
With the halter around her throat;
And, when void of life, with your clasp knife
The string of her apron cut.

"Then, if that you determine
My last desires to do,
In her left hand pocket, you'll find the locket,
And carry it to Sue."

The grisly Spectre thus
In mournful accents spoke,
By which time, being morning, he gave me no warning,
But vanish'd in sulphur and smoke.

Next day there sprang up a breeze,
And our ship began to tack,
And for fear of the Ghost, we left the coast,
And sail'd for England back.

And I being come home,
Did all his words pursue;
Old Martha likewise was hung at the 'size,
And I carried the locket to Sue.

And now, being tired of life,
I make up my mind to die;
But I thought this story I'd lay before ye,
For the good of Posterity.

Oh never then sit at table
When the number is thirteen;
And, lest witches be there, put salt in your beer,
And scrape your platters clean.

This "Tale of Terror" was composed at the express request of a distinguished female, nearly related (by marriage and genius) to its no less distinguished author.—In return, this matchless female christened a lovely and promising boy, of whom she was delivered, during the stay of the Ensign, after the name of Odoherty; an appellation, the ideas suggested by which, will be agreeable, or otherwise, to its bearer, according as he shall, in future years, inherit or not inherit, some portion of the genius in whose honor it was originally conferred. Of the various *genethliaca* composed upon the occasion, the most admired was the following:—

TO THE CHILD OF CORINNA!

Oh, boy! may the wit of thy mother awaking
  On thy dewy lip tremble, when years have gone by,
While the fire of Odoherty, fervidly breaking,
  In glances and gleams, may illume thy young eye.

Oh! then such a fulness of power shall be seen
  With the graces so blending, in union endearing,
That angels shall glide o'er the ocean green,
  To catch a bright glimpse of the glory of Erin!

Oh! sure such a vision of beauty and might,
  Commingling, in splendor, by him was exprest
The old Lydian sculptor, the delicate sprite,
  That in Venus' soft girdle his Hercules drest.

On his return to Edinburgh, we find the indefatigable mind of the Ensign earnestly engaged in laying the plan and preparing the materials for a weekly paper, upon the model of the Tatler, the Spectator, and the Saleroom.* His views in regard to this publication were never fully realised; but we have open before us, a drawer which contains a vast accumulation of notes and *esquisses* connected with it. We insert a few of the shortest in the meantime, and may perhaps quote a few dozens of them hereafter.

I.

THERE is nothing in this world more likely to produce a good understanding in families and neighborhoods, than a resolution to be immediately entered into by all the several members of the same, never again, from this time forward, upon any occasion or pretence whatever, in speech or writing, to use the monosyllable *I.* This will no doubt cause some trouble and incon-

* There is no need of characterizing the first two of these periodicals. *The Sale-Room* existed (it did not flourish) in 1817, and appropriately emanated, in Edinburgh, from the premises of John Ballantyne, who became an auctioneer after his ceasing to be Scott's publisher. The metrical essay called "The Sultan of Serendib, or the Search after Happiness," first appeared in *The Sale-Room,* with other contributions of less note from Scott's pen. It is a humorous poem on the old story of the Sultan, as a cure for low spirits, being ordered to wear the shirt of the happiest man in his dominions — of a gay and reckless Irishman being selected as the happiest — and of its turning out, when they had stripped him, to obtain the desiderated garment, that he did not possess, and therefore could not wear, one!—M.

veniences at first, especially to those who are not half so intimate with any other pronoun; but by the help of a small penalty, to be strictly levied upon every transgression, that will soon be got over, and this most wicked and pernicious monosyllable effectually banished from the world. The Golden Age will then re-descend on earth, and many other things will happen, of the particulars of which the curious reader may satisfy himself, by referring to Virgil's Eclogue. Among the most interesting circumstances of this great revolution, which, however, is not specified in the place referred to, will be the total abolition of both metallic and paper currency. *Money will be no more.* Those that have will give to those that want; and the redundant population will not, on having the matter properly explained to them, object to removing themselves by some convenient and gentle method of suicide, rendering war, famine, pestilence, and misery (so politely called by Mr. Malthus* by

* Thomas Robert Malthus, an English clergyman, was born in 1766, and died in 1835. In his "Essay on the Principle of Population," he contended that the Divine command to "increase and multiply" was a mandate for the destruction of human happiness, and that instead of its being better (as St. Paul has it) to "marry than burn," it is better to burn than marry! His anti-connubial system was founded on the hypothesis, that population increases in a geometrical, while provisions only increase in an arithmetical ratio. He argued, therefore, that an increase of people should always follow, and never precede, an increase in the produce of the soil. This reasoning (said Mr. Weyland, who refuted him), "when applied to a manufacturing society, appears to be tantamount to saying that an increase in the number of backs should always follow, and never precede, an increase in the manufacture of coats; whereas, surely a previous increase of wearers and consumers is absolutely necessary to the respective proportion of further food and raiment." When Byron said, "Without cash, Malthus tells us, take no wives," he hit off the gist of the Malthusian argument. In another part of "Don Juan," the poet, in very plain language, shows the difference between the theory and the practice of philosophy—

"And Malthus does the thing 'gainst which he writes"—

for not only did Malthus marry but actually had some ten or twelve children! His population-views were very unpopular, and may now be considered exploded. Adam Smith contended, in his Wealth of Nations, that it is *impossible* for the human race to multiply beyond the means of subsistence. M. T. Sadler, who answered Malthus, may be said to have proved this. Malthus insists that over population is to be dreaded—that, therefore, all parish assistance to children, both legitimate and illegitimate, should be legally prohibited—that it is the duty of the rich to withhold all increase of the comforts of the poor, lest it

the somewhat endearing term, *checks*), utterly unnecessary. Who would not wish to accelerate to mankind the approach of this blessed era? The simple and sure means are above stated; and if the world does not forthwith proceed to make itself happy, it can no longer shelter itself under the pretence of not knowing how to set about it.

II.

Of all the natural sciences, that of Scandal has been the most universally cultivated in every civilized country, and the most successfully in our own. Modern scandalographers have comprised it under two great divisions, open or direct scandal, and implied or indirect scandal.

Instances of the first are now less common in society than formerly. This perhaps arises more from an artificial refinement in our manners, than from any real refinement in our minds. There still exist many who would not hesitate, under favorable circumstances, to make use of the direct scandal; and there are many more who would not be ashamed to listen to it. But in all circles, whether public or private, there are, for the most part, three or four men and women, who are as different from the surrounding mass of starched neck-cloths and satin slips, "as red wine is from Rhenish." These humane and gentle beings check the growth of direct scandal, which, notwithstanding the fostering care of its vulgar disciples, is generally "no sooner blown than blasted." Being prevented from lifting its malignant head into the liberal air, it strikes downward, and, spreading its obscure ramifications under ground, gives rise to the indirect or implied scandal.

This is the more dangerous kind, in as far as it is more difficult to eradicate or guard against it. In polished society, where

should encourage them to marry—and, in the first edition of his book he had the following passage (so odious that he was compelled to expunge it in all subsequent publications):—"A man, who is born into a world already possessed, if he cannot get subsistence from his parents, and if society do not want his labor, has no claim of right to the smallest portion of food, and, in fact, has no business to be where he is. At Nature's mighty feast there is no vacant cover ready for him. She tells him to be gone, and will quickly execute her own orders!"—Such is Malthusian humanity and philosophy.—M.

it most frequently occurs, it has neither a local habitation nor a name. It is "an airy tongue, that syllables men's names," without pronouncing them distinctly; and the labor of the metaphysical chemist has been unequal to the discovery of any sure test for its detection. It is also, on that account, more fondly cherished by the disciples of the science, because the practical gratification arising from it is in consequence so much the greater. Thus a scandalous assertion, if made directly, can not be frequently repeated, because the mode of its expression admits of little variety; whereas your implied scandal is capable of being varied almost infinitely, and thus affords a pleasant and continued opportunity of showing off to advantage the ingenuity of the malicious man, without vexing the dull ear of the drowsy one. Under the name of personal talk, it may be regarded as constituting the essence of conversation in society at the present period.

III.

THERE are few subjects on which men differ so much as in regard to Blue Stockings. I believe that the majority of literary men look upon them as entirely useless. Yet a little reflection will serve us to show the unphilosophical nature of this opinion. There seems, indeed, to be a system of exclusive appropriation in literature, as well as in law, which cannot be too severely reprobated. A critic of the present day cannot hear a young woman make a harmless observation on poetry or politics without starting; which start, I am inclined to think, proceeds from affectation, considering how often he must have heard the same remark made on former occasions. Ought the female sex to be debarred from speaking nonsense on literary matters any more than the men? I think not. Even supposing that such privilege was not originally conferred by a law of nature, they have certainly acquired right to it by the long prescription. Besides, if common-place remarks were not daily and nightly rendered more common-place by continual repetition, even a man of original mind might run the hazard of occasionally so far forgetting himself and his subject, as to record an idea which, upon more mature deliberation, might be found to be no idea at all. This, I contend, is prevented by the judicious interference of the fair sex.

At the same time, "a highly polished understanding," in an ugly woman, is a thing rather to be deprecated than otherwise. A pretty girl may say what she chooses, and be "severe in youthful beauty" with impunity, for no one will interrupt her solely to criticise the color of her stockings; but I think that a plain one should reflect seriously before she "cultivates her mind assiduously."

IV.

ONE solitary death's head, all of a sudden grinning on us in our own bed-room, would be a much more trying sight than millions of skulls piled up into good large houses of three stories. Architecture of that kind is less impressive than could be imagined. There is a tolerable specimen of it at Mucruss Abbey, Killarney;* but the effect is indifferent. Skulls, somehow or other, do not build well. Perhaps they would look better in mortar. As they are arranged at Mucruss Abbey, they look like great clusters of the wax of the humble-bee; and after heavy rain, the effect of the water dripping from the jaw-bones and eye-holes is rather ludicrous than pathetic. They are all in the melting mood at one time, and apparently for no sufficient reason; while the extreme uniformity of their expression may, without much impropriety, be said to be quite monotonous. It may be questioned if a stranger, unacquainted with this order of architecture, would, at first sight, perceive the nature of its material. Perhaps he would, for a while, see the likeness of one or two skulls only, and wonder how they got there; till, by degrees, the whole end-wall would laughably break out, as it were, into a prodigious number of vacant faces, and wholly destroy the solemnity of that otherwise impressive religious edifice. Yet it is not to be thought that an Irishman could contemplate such a skullery with unmoved imagination. Where be all their brogue and all their bulls now! A silent gable-end of O'Donohues and Maggillicuddies! Walls with long arms—

* For a graphic account of Mucruss Abbey, at Killarney, including the array of skulls here mentioned, the reader is referred to Mrs. S. C. Hall's "Ireland," vol. i.—M.

but sans eyes, sans nose, sans ears, sans brains! A mockery of the live population of the county Kerry! A cairn of skulls erected over the dry bones of the buried independence of the south of Ireland! Yes, thanks to the genius of the Lake of Killarney, there is not here the skull of a single absentee.*

If the reader has ever been in the kingdom of Dahomey, he will remember the avenue leading up to the king's palace. For nearly a mile, it is lined on each side by a wall of skulls twenty feet high; and how nobly one comes at last on the skull palace! Yet the scene cloys on the spectator. One comes at last to be insensible to the likeness between the head on his own shoulders and those that compose the skull-work of the royal residence; and he might forget it entirely, were it not that he occasionally sees a loose skull replaced by a head belonging, the night before, to one of his friends. It is understood that the present king of Dahomey is about to remove these walls, and distribute the old materials through his kingdom, now greatly in want of inclosures. There is also some talk of taking down the ancestral palace itself, and of building another of fresh skulls. It is calculated that three hundred thousand adult skulls, and three hundred thousand infant ones, will be sufficient for a very handsome palace; and fifty thousand annually have been cheerfully subscribed for six years. It will be finished, most probably, about the same time with the college of Edinburgh; and report speaks highly of the beauty and grandeur of the elevation.

* It is a creditable fact that (with the exception of the Marquis of Lansdowne, an English peer) the principal landlords in the county of Kerry reside on their estates—and this in the teeth of J. R. M'Culloch, the political economist, who argues that Absenteeism really cannot injure a country, for that, though the rents may be sent to the landlord, even in China, and there expended by him, it is all the same in the end, as the money gets into circulation, and, by the good it thus confers, benefits the absentee landlord's tenants—remotely! If my Irish tenants pay me a thousand pounds a year, and that I spend none of that money among them—in exchange for the labor and food which they can supply to my exigencies—it is surely no consolation for them to know that I disburse it, in exchange for other food and labor, in America. But M'Culloch's doctrine is, that it makes *no* difference where the money is spent!—I have written this note, because Dr. Maginn felt a lively interest in this question of Absenteeism, and used to argue strongly against what Cobbett used to call "the feelosophy of M'Culloch."—M

From Mucruss and Dahomey the transition is easy and natural to the catacombs of Paris. They are on a larger scale, and consequently so much the less terrifying. One "skull by itself skull" may be no joking matter; but after remaining unmolested for a few minutes among some billions of pericraniums, we come to feel a sovereign contempt of the whole defunct world, and would not care a straw though a dozen of them were to jump down and attempt to kick our shins. One takes out a skull, and puts it back again into its place, just as one would a common book from the shelves of a library; and what is far worse, every skull is *verbatim et literatim* the same empty performance, and, not being bound in Russia leather, worm-eaten through and through. A man in the catacombs may indeed be said to be in a brown study.*

A night passed in a vaulted cell, with one or even two skeletons, especially if they were well known to have been able-bodied men when alive, might well occasion a cold sweat, and make the hair to stand on end. There would be something like equal terms there, one quick against two dead; and no man of spirit could refuse the encounter, though the odds were against him, guineas to pounds. A ring would have to be formed, the odd ghost-bottle holder and umpire. But in a populous Place of Skulls—a Craniopolis like the catacombs, containing so enormous an "inhabitation," that no regular census has ever been made—any accidental visitor might contrive, surely, to while away a few hours without much rational perturbation, and unless very much disposed indeed to pick a quarrel, might suffer the thigh-bones to lie at rest, as pieces of ornamental furniture, never intended to be wielded as weapons either of offensive or defensive warfare.

A night passed in a small, black, bleak, musty old church, not far from the catacombs, would be worse by far than the cat-

* This hint of a story was subsequently acted on, and a very powerful sketch, describing a Night in the Catacombs appeared, soon after, in *Blackwood.*—At present [1855], and for several years, there has not been any admission for visitors to the Catacombs of Paris, which, however, are by no means so interesting (from religious and historical associations) as the Catacombs of Rome, a reliable account of which, as illustrating the Church of the first three centuries, has been written by Dr. Kip, Missionary Bishop of California.—M.

acombs themselves. One would sit there full of the abstract image of skulls; and, beyond all doubt, several skulls would come trundling in during the course of the night. Of old, when a hero was dubbed knight, he sat up during the dark hours in a church, where an occasional ghost or two might touch him, when gliding by, with its icy fingers. It would have required but a small share of chivalrous feeling, to have kept watch in an intrenchment of skulls, seemingly impregnable. It asks more courage to fight the champion of an army in single combat, than to dash into the lines.

CHAPTER V.*

Visitors to the Tent—Dr. and Mrs. Magnus Oglethorpe—Their Reception by the Contributors—Mrs. M'Whirter, late of Philadelphia—The Lady Recognizes Odoherty—Amicable Relations Renewed—The Doctor's Lecture—His Lady's Popularity—Odoherty's Song—"The Powldoodies of Burran;" a M'Whirter Chant—The Last of the Widow.

THE toils of the day were now near a close, and the Editor with his Contributors were about to leave the Tent for an even-

* In order to gratify such readers as may take an interest in the personal history of Odoherty, I have here introduced, a little out of place and time, an account of his meeting, in Scotland, with his old flame, Mrs. M'Whirter, the fair Irish widow, whilom of Philadelphia. It will be seen, by reference to a preceding portion of his Life (p. 18), that Odoherty quitted this lady, without beat of drum, after they had lived together, for some time, on terms of the closest intimacy. This desertion took place about 1815. In *Blackwood's Magazine*, for September, 1819, is a pleasant and right merry account of a great meeting (in a capacious Tent on the Earl of Fife's moors, at the head of the river Dee, near Braemar, in Scotland,) of the Editor and the *elite* of his contributors. Of this band Odoherty was one, and greatly contributed by his eloquence, fun, learning, fishing, shooting, coursing, good temper, wit, punch-making, and punch-drinking, social fellowship, song-making, and song-singing, to the conviviality of the occasion. At the close of the first day's sport, speechmaking, singing, feasting, fumigating, and imbibing, the *rencontre* occurred, as narrated (no doubt by Odoherty's own pen), in what I have ventured to print as Chapter V. Odoherty's *liaison* with Mrs. M'Whirter is so frequently referred to, in the Noctes Ambrosianæ, and in different articles from Maginn's pen, that this conclusion of it appears indispensable.—M.

ing-walk along the Dee and its "bonny banks of blooming heather," to indulge the most delightful of all feelings, such, namely, as arise from the consciousness of having past our time in a way not only agreeable to ourselves, but useful to the whole of the wide-spread family of man, when John Mackay* came bouncing in upon us like a grasshopper, "Gots my life, here are twa unco landloupers cumin dirdin down the hill—the tane o' them a heech knock-kneed stravaiger wi' the breeks on, and the tither, ane o' the women-folk, as roun's she lang, in a green joseph, and a tappen o' feathers on her pow."

At the word "women-folk," each Contributor

"Sprang upwards like a pyramid of fire;"

and we had some difficulty in preventing a sally from the Tent. "Remember, gentlemen," quoth we, "that you are still under literary law—be seated." We ourselves, as master of the ceremonies, went out, and lo! we beheld two most extraordinary Itinerants.

The gentleman who was dressed in brown-once-black, had a sort of medico-theological exterior—which we afterward found to be representative of the inward man. He was very tall, and

* John Mackay flourished, in those days, as a caddy, in the city of Edinburgh. The caddies, a race of men peculiar to Auld Reekie, are described by Lockhart as a race "set apart, and destined *ab ovo*, for climbing stair-cases, and carrying messages." The stock originally came, and is re-inforced, from the rugged wilds of Lochaber and Braemar. Men accustomed to ascend the brow of Cairngorm and Ben-Nevis have the same light elastic spring up the many-staired-ascent of the tall houses of Edinburgh. Use and familiarity make them minutely familiar with every stair-case, every house, every family, and every individual in Edinburgh. In Smollett's Book of the Expedition of Humphrey Clinker their deeds are writ. Their own dialect is Gælic mingled with a barbarous *patois* which is a corruption of such English as is spoken in the East and Southeast of Scotland. They can take any quantity of snuff—high-dried Scotch snuff so strong that a pinch of it would make a stranger almost sneeze the roof off his head. They are active when at work, but luxuriate in laziness when off duty, smoking tobacco out of their pipes (such as, in Ireland, are classically called *dudheens*), lying at lazy-length on the pavement, in the sunny hours, or, in less propitious weather, playing whist (four-handed, three-handed, or double-dummy) with wofully-begrimed and greatly-worn cards. A few of them are curious in the noble game of Back-gammon, and have a scientific knowledge of its mysteries. To a man, they exult in strong drink, whether it be Scotch ale, or London porter, having a wholesome con-

in-kneed*—indeed, somewhat like Richmond the black† about the legs—the squint of his albino eyes was far from prepossessing—and stray tufts of his own white hair, here and there stole lankly down from beneath the up-curled edge of a brown caxon that crowned the apex of his organization. He seemed to have lost the roof of his mouth, and when he said to us, "You see before you Dr. Magnus Oglethorpe, itinerant lecturer on poetry, politics, oratory, and the belles letters," at each word, his tongue came away from the locum-tenens of his palate, with a bang, like a piece of wet leather from a stone, (called, by our Scottish children, "sookers," we forget the English name,) each syllable, indeed, standing quite per se, and not without difficulty to be drilled into companies or sentences.‡

But we are forgetting the lady. She was a short, fat, "dumpy woman"—quite a bundle of a body, as one may say—with smooth red cheeks, and little twinkling roguish eyes;—and when she returned our greeting, we were sensible of a slight ac-

tempt for such water bewitched as the embodied weakness brewed at, and bearing the name, of Prestonpans. They can imbibe any given quantity of strong whiskey—whatever name it bear, Islay, or Campbell-town, or Glenlivit, or Glen-Ury, which last is distilled at Ury, near Stonehaven, by Captain Barclay, the once famous pedestrian, who first walked a thousand miles in a thousand consecutive hours. Above all, the caddies are honest, bold, and faithful. The tribe is fast dying out in Edinburgh, where alone it ever flourished (the porters of Aberdeen, with their remarkable strength, being rather beasts of burthen than message-bearers), and the place which knew them will soon know them no more.—M.

* It was upon this gentleman that the celebrated punster of the West made that famous pun, "The Battle of the Pyrenees—(the pair o' knees)."—Ed.

† Richmond, the black, was a famed pugilist of former days, of whom particulars are given in one of the Odoherty articles called Boxiana.—M.

‡ In the year 1819, the epoch of this eventful story, Dr. Dionysius Lardner had not made his appearance as a public lecturer upon all earthly subjects; therefore, Dr. Magnus Oglethorpe, the American lecturer, cannot be taken or mistaken for him. I believe that the person intended to be ridiculed was the late John Thelwall, tried on a charge of high treason, in 1794 (with Hardy and others) and acquitted—chiefly owing to Erskine's eloquent defence. He afterward became a newspaper and magazine editor, and eventually subsided into a lecturer on oratory, poetry, and the belles lettres. I knew him, in 1830, when he was much advanced in life, and found him full of lively and learned conversation. He was once a great crony of Leigh Hunt.—M.

cent of Erin, which, we confess, up in life as we are, falls on the drum of our ear

"That's like a melody sweetly played in tune."

She was, as John Mackay had at some distance discovered, in a green riding habit, not, perhaps, much the worse, but certainly much the smoother for wear—and while her neat-turned ankles exhibited a pair of yellow laced boots which nearly reached the calf of her leg, on her head waved elegantly a plume of light-blue ostrich feathers. The colors altogether, both those of nature and of art, were splendid and harmonious, and the Shepherd,* whose honest face we by chance saw, (contrary to orders) peeping through a little chink of the Tent, whispered "Losh a day, gin there binna the queen o' the Fairies!"†

We requested the matchless pair to walk in—but Dr. Magnus, who was rather dusty, first got John Mackay to switch him behind and before, with a bunch of long heather, and we ourselves performed the same office, with the greatest delicacy tc the lady. The improvement on both was most striking and in stantaneous. The Doctor looked quite fresh and ready for a lecture—while the lady reminded us, so sleek, smooth, and beautiful, did she appear, of a hen after any little ruffling incident in a barn-yard.

We three entered the Tent—"Contributors! Dr. Magnus Oglethorpe and Lady on a lecturing tour through the Highlands."

In a moment twenty voices entreated the lady to be seated —Dr. Morris offered her a seat on his bed, which, being folded up, he now used as a chair or sopha—Wastle bowed to the antique carved oak arm-chair that had been sent from Mar-Lodge by the Thane—Tickler was lifting up from the ground an empty hamper to reach it across the table for her accommodation—Buller was ready with the top or bottom of the whiskey cask, and we ourselves insisted upon getting the honor of the fair burden to the Contributor's box. Seward kept looking at her through his quizzing glass‡—"deuced fine wumman by St. Jer-

* Hogg, of course.—All through *Blackwood*, when the "the shepherd" is named, it can and does only mean him of Ettrick.—M.

† In Scotland, and in some parts of Ireland, it is believed that green is the favorite color of fairies' garb.—M.

‡ Dr. Morris, the *nom de plume* under which Lockhart wrote the pleasant

icho! demme if she b'nt a fac-simile of Mary-Ann Clarke—only summat deeper in the fore-end—one of old Anacreon's βαθυκολποι."

Her curtsey was exceedingly graceful—when all of a sudden, casting her eyes on the Standard-Bearer who, contrary to his usual amenity toward the sex, stood sour and silent in a corner, she exclaimed, "By the powers, my own swate Morgan Odoherty," and jumping up upon the table, she nimbly picked her steps among jugs, glasses, and quechs, (upsetting alone Kempferhausen's ink horn over an ode to the moon) and in a moment was in the Adjutant's arms. Mrs. M'Whirter, the fair Irish widow whom the Ensign had loved in Philadelphia, stood confessed.

There clung she, like a mole, with her little paws to the Standard-bearer's sides—striving in vain to reach those beguiling lips, which he kept somewhat haughtily elevated about six feet three inches from the ground, leaving an unscaleable height of at least a yard between them and the mouth of the much flustered, deeply injured Mrs. M'Whirter. The widow, whose elegant taste is well known to the readers of *Blackwood*, exclaimed, in the words of Betty* (so she called him),

satire on men and manners, poetry and politics in Scotland, entitled Peter's Letters.—William Wastle of that Ilk, also an assumed name, under which appeared the many-cantoed poem called the Mad Banker of Amsterdam, and other lays in *Blackwood*.—In Buller of Brazen-nose, Oxford, was the late John Hughes, of Berks, England, author of an Itinerary of the Rhine, and a sworn friend of (Ingoldsby) Barham and Theodore Hook.—Harry Seward, of Christ-church, Cambridge, was another fictitious name, and the Mary Anne Clarke, to whom he compared Mrs. M'Whirter, was the clever, saucy, and unprincipled lady who lived with the Duke of York, for some years, as his mistress, until, in 1809, he was accused of awarding military preferments (as Commander-in-Chief) at her request to parties who paid her for the exercise of such influence. The fact of the disposal of preferments was proved, but the complicity of the Duke (a son of George III.), was not established. Mrs. Clarke, who died in 1851, was singularly acute. Many years after the Duke's trial, she was examined, as a witness, before Lord Ellenborough, Chief Justice of the King's Bench. To confuse or destroy her credibility, counsel asked "Under whose protection are you now?" With a bow and smile at the judge, she ingeniously and evasively replied, "Under Lord Ellenborough's."—He did protect her, on that appeal—from being subjected to such a line of questioning.—M.

* Dr. James Beattie, author of "The Minstrel," a poem, and several philosophical works, born in 1735; died 1803.—M.

"Ah! who can tell how hard it is to climb
The steep where love's proud temple shines afar!"

"Never mind the money—my dearest Morgan—Och! I have never known such another man as your sweet self since we parted at Philadelphia."

The Adjutant looked as if he had neither lost nor won—still gently but determinedly repelling the advances of the warm-hearted widow, whose face he thus kept, as it were, at arm's length. At last, with a countenance of imperturbable solemnity, worthy of a native of Ireland and a Contributor to *Blackwood,* he coolly said, "Why, Mr. Editor, the trick is a devilish good one, very well played, and knowingly kept up—but now that you gentlemen have all had your laugh against Odoherty, pray Mrs. Roundabout Fat-ribs, may I ask when you were last *bateing hemp*, and in what house of correction?"

"Och—you vile sadducee."

"I suspect," said Tickler, "that you yourself, my fair Mrs. M'Whirter, were the seducee, and the ensign the seducer."

"Why look ye," continued Odoherty, "if you are Molly M'Whirter, formerly of Philadelphia, you have the mark of a murphy (Hibernicé, potatoe) on your right side, just below the fifth rib—and of a shamrock, or as these English gentlemen would call it, a trefoil, between your shoulders behind, about half way down."

Here Mrs. M'Whirter lost all temper—and appealed to Dr. Magnus Oglethorpe, if Odoherty was not casting foul aspersions on her character. The doctor commenced an oration, with that extraordinary sort of utterance already hinted at, which quite upset the Adjutant's gravity—and the lady now seizing the "tempora mollia fandi," said, with a bewitching smile, "Come now my dearest Morgan, confess, confess!"

The Standard-bearer was overcome—and, kissing his old friend's cheek in the most respectful manner, he said, "I presume Mrs. M'Whirter is no more, and that I see before me the lady of Dr. Magnus Oglethorpe—in other words *Mrs. Dr.* Oglethorpe."*

* The Scottish ladies are fond, as the wives of Germany are, of shining in the reflected light of their husband's eminence. Thus, we have Mrs. Professor Ramsay at Glasgow, Mrs. Rector Buist at St. Andrew's, and even the

"Yes, Morgan, he is indeed my husband—come hither, Magnus, and shake hands with the Adjutant—this is the Mr. Odoherty, of whom you have heard me so often spake."

Nothing could be more delightful than this reconciliation. We again all took our seats—Dr. Magnus on our own left hand, and Mrs. Dr. Magnus on our right, close to whom sat and smiled, like another Mars, the invincible Standard-bearer. It was a high gratification to us now to find that Odoherty and Mrs. M'Whirter had never been united in matrimony. It was true that in America they had been tenderly attached to each other, but peculiar circumstances, some of which are alluded to in a memoir of the adjutant's life, in a former number of this Magazine,* had prevented their union, and soon after his return to Europe, the M'Whirter had bestowed her hand on a faithful suitor, whom she had formerly rejected, Dr. Magnus Oglethorpe, lecturer on poetry, politics, oratory, &c., a gentleman famous for removing impediments in the organs of speech, and who, after having instructed in public speaking some of the most distinguished orators in the House of Representatives, United States, had lately come over to Britain, to retard, by his precepts and his practice, the decline and fall of eloquence in our Island.

As we complimented the doctor on the magnificent object of his pedestrian tour, he volunteered a lecture on the spot, and in an instant—and springing up as nimbly upon the table as Sir Francis Burdett or Mr. John Hobhouse could have done,* the

Reverend Mrs. Tweedie at Edinburgh. I knew an old gentleman who had been Provost (or Mayor) of Aberdeen, and his wife was Mrs. Provost Milne. The Principal of Marischal College, some years ago, was Dr. Brown, a much henpecked husband, and his consort was appropriately called Mrs. *Principal* Brown. Nay, on the shore at Aberdeen, at a place called Foot-Dee, the spouse of a man who owned a small fishing-boat, had a little shed or shanty, where she retailed "strong waters," and her sign-board bore this legent:

A' SORTS SCOTS DRINK SELLED HERE.
WI' WEE DRAPS O' FOREIGN.
BY ME,
MRS. CAPTAIN SANDY SMITH.—M.

* See, previously, page 18, of this "o'er true tale." It is certain, either that the lady had been only too kind previously, or was tremendously libelled by the biographer of Morgan Odoherty.—M.

† Burdett and Hobhouse were the ultra-Radical leaders in 1818. In sixteen

American Demosthenes (who seemed still to have pebbles in his mouth, though far inland), thus opened it* and spake:

LECTURE ON WHIGGISM.

Ladies and Gentlemen: Fear is "Whiggism"—hatred is "Whiggism"—contempt, jealousy, remorse, wonder, despair, or madness, are all "Whiggism."

The miser when he hugs his gold—the savage who paints his idol with blood—the slave who worships a tyrant, or the tyrant who fancies himself a god—the vain, the ambitious, the proud, the choleric man—the coward, the beggar, all are "Whigs."

> "The 'Whig,' the lover, and the poet,
> Are of imagination all compact.
> One sees more devils than vast hell can hold—
> The madman."

"Whiggism" is strictly the language of *imagination*; and the imagination is that faculty which represents objects, not as they are in themselves, but as they are moulded, by *other* thoughts and feelings, into an infinite variety of shapes and combinations of power. This language is not the less true to nature, because it is false in point of *fact*, but so much the more true and *natural*, if it conveys the impression which the object under the *influence of passion* makes on the mind. Let an object, for instance, be presented in a state of agitation or fear, and the imagination will distort or magnify the object, and convert it into the likeness of whatever is most proper to encourage the fear.

Tragic "Whiggism," which is the most impassioned species of it, strives to carry on the feeling to the utmost point, by all

years after, Burdett declined into ultra-Toryism, in which he continued until 1844, when he died, aged seventy-four.—Hobhouse, after serving in the Grey, Melbourne, and Russell administrations, was called to the House of Lords, in 1851, by the title of Baron Broughton. It is curious to note how frequently those who profess extreme liberal opinions subside into moderates beneath the seductions of place and honors.—Is this confined to Europe?—M.

* The expression, "*Thus opened his mouth,*" is incorrect, for without a plate it would be impossible to show the manner in which Dr. Magnus opened his mouth.—C. North.

the force of comparison or contrast—loses the sense of present suffering in the imaginary exaggerations of it—exhausts the terror by an unlimited indulgence of it—*grapples with impossibilities in its desperate impatience of restraint.*

When Lear says of Edgar, nothing but the unkind "ministry" could have brought him to this—what a *bewildered* amazement, what a *wrench* of the imagination, that can not be brought to conceive of any other cause of misery than that which has bowed it down, and absorbs all other sorrow in its own! His sorrow, like a flood, supplies the sources of all other sorrow.

In regard to a certain Whig, of the unicorn species, we may say—How his passion lashes itself up, and swells and rages like a tide in its sounding course, when, in answer to the doubts expressed of his returning "temper," he says—

> "Never, *Iago*. Like to the Pontic Sea,
> Whose icy current and compulsive course
> Ne'er feels retiring ebb, but keeps due on
> To the Propontic and the Hellespont;
> Even so my 'frantic' thoughts, with violent pace,
> Shall ne'er look back, ne'er ebb to humble sense,
> Till that a capable and wide revenge
> Swallow them up."

The pleasure, however, derived from tragic "Whiggism," is not any thing peculiar to it as Whiggism, as a fictitious and fanciful thing. It is not an anomaly of the imagination. It has its source and ground-work in the common love of "power" and strong excitement. As Mr. Burke observes, people flock to "Whig meetings;" but if there were a public execution in the next street, the "house" would very soon be empty. It is not the difference between fiction and reality that solves the difficulty. Children are satisfied with stories of ghosts and witches. The grave politician drives a thriving trade of abuse and calumnies, poured out against those whom he makes his enemies for no other end than that he may live by them. The popular preacher makes less frequent mention of heaven than of hell. Oaths and nicknames are only a more vulgar sort of "Whiggism." We are as fond of indulging our violent passions as of reading a description of those of others. We are as prone to make a torment of our fears as to luxuriate in our hopes of "mischief." The love of power is as strong a principle in the mind as the love of pleasure. It is natural to hate as to love, to despise as to admire, to express our hatred or contempt as our love and admiration.

> "Masterless passion sways us to the mood
> Of what it likes or loathes."

Not that we like what we loathe, but we like to indulge our hatred and scorn of it (viz. Toryism), to dwell upon it—to exasperate our idea of it by every refinement of ingenuity and extravagance of illustration—to make it a bugbear to ourselves—to point it out to others in all the splendor of deformity—to embody it to the senses—to stigmatize it in words—to grapple with it in thought, in action—to sharpen our intellect—to arm our will against it—to know the worst we have to contend with, and to contend with it to the utmost.

Let who will strip nature of the colors and the shapes of "Whiggism," the "Whig" is not bound to do so; the impressions of common sense and strong imagination, that is, of passion and "temperance," can not be the same, and they must have a separate language to do justice to either. Objects must strike differently upon the mind, independently of what they are in themselves, so long as we have a different *interest* in them—as we see them in a different point of view, nearer or at a greater distance (morally or physically speaking), from novelty—from old acquaintance—from *our ignorance* of them—from our fear of their consequences—from contrast—from unexpected likeness; hence nothing but Whiggism *can* be agreeable to nature and truth.

This lecture gave universal satisfaction—but Dr. Magnus is a man of too much genius not to acknowledge unreservedly his obligations to other great men—and after our plaudits had expired, he informed us, that he claimed little other merit than that of having delivered the lecture according to the best rules and principles of oratory, for that the words were by his friend Mr. Hazlitt.* "In the original," said he, "Mr. Hazlitt employs

* This Lecture on Whiggism *is* a parody on the commencement of one of Hazlitt's articles on Poetry.—M.

the word 'Poetry,' which I have slightly changed into the word 'Whiggism,' and thus an excellent lecture on politics is procured, without the ingenious essayist having been at all aware of the ultimate meaning of his production. "As the lecture was but short, will you have another?"

"No—no—enough is as good as a feast," quod Odoherty—"perhaps," Mr. Editor, "if you request it, Mrs. Magnus will have the goodness to make tea."

There was not only much true politeness in this suggestion of the Adjutant, but a profound knowledge of the female character—and, accordingly, the *tea things* were not long of making their appearance, for in our Tent it was just sufficient to hint a wish, and that wish, whatever it might be, that moment was gratified. Mrs. Magnus, we observed, put in upward of thirty spoonfuls—being at the rate of two and a half for each Contributor,* and the lymph came out of the large silver tea-pot "a perfect tincture;" into his third and last cup of which each Contributor emptied a decent glass of whiskey; nor did the Lady of the Tent, any more than the Lady of the Lake, show any symptoms of distaste to the mountain dew. The conversation was indeed divine—and it was wonderful with what ease Mrs. Magnus conducted herself in so difficult a situation. She had a word or a smile for every one, and the Shepherd whispered to Tickler, just loud enough to be heard by those near the Contributor's Box, "sic a nice leddy wad just sute you or me to a hair, Mr. Tickler. Faith, thae blue ostrich plumbs wad astonish Davy Bryden, were he to see them hanging o'er the tea-pat at Eltrive-Lake, wi' a swurl." * * * * * *

* She was extravagant. The allowance, as defined by the most antique tea-drinkers is "one spoonful for each person present, and one extra *for the pot.*" Neither is mountain-dew the best corrective of the evil effects of the herb which cheers but doth not inebriate. A judicious addendum of old Jamaica is sometimes taken by anti-tea-totallers, with this intent.—In Ireland, among the poorer classes, nothing is considered more mean than the giving tea either weak or of an inferior quality An emigrant who had partaken of the hospitality of a neighbor's tea-and-turn-out (as they call it when supper does not follow) thus described the beverage:—"Faith, my dear, the tea was as weak as if you'd put a spoonful of bohea into the North River, up at the Palisades, and sup it up with a spoon, for the flavor, down in the Bay, right fornenst Staten Island!"—M.

Then the Bailie read an excellent new Song, which was applauded to "the very echo" by all but Mrs. Magnus, who was too polite to say anything derogatory to Bailie Jarvie's genius. Indeed she no doubt admired that genius, but the subject did not seem to interest her. "My dear Mr. Odoherty" (for they treated each other with infinite respect), "will you give us something amatory?"

"I gives my vice, too, for something hamatory," pertly enough whiffled Mr. Tims; — when the Standard-bearer, after humming a few notes, and taking the altitude from the pitch-key of Tickler (which he carries about with him as certainly as a parson carries a corkscrew), went off in noble style with the following song, his eyes all the while turned toward Mrs. Magnus Oglethorpe, whose twinklers emanated still but eloquent responses not to be misunderstood.

INCONSTANCY; A SONG TO MRS. M'WHIRTER.

By Mr. Odoherty.

"Ye fleeces of gold amidst crimson enroll'd
  That sleep in the calm western sky,
Lovely relics of day float — ah! float not away!
  Are ye gone? then, ye beauties, good-bye!"
It was thus the fair maid I had loved would have staid
  The last gleamings of passion in me;
But the orb's fiery glow in the soft wave below
  Had been cooled — and the thing could not be.

While thro' deserts you rove, if you find a green grove
  Where the dark branches overhead meet,
There repose you a while from the heat and the toil,
  And be thankful the shade is so sweet;
But if long you remain it is odds but the rain
  Or the wind 'mong the leaves may be stirring,
They will strip the boughs bare — you're a fool to stay there —
  Change the scene without further demurring.

If a rich-laden tree in your wanderings you see
  With the ripe fruit all glowing and swelling,
Take your fill as you pass — if you don't you're an ass,
  But I daresay you don't need my telling —
'Twould be just as great fooling to come back for more pulling,

When a week or two more shall have gone,
These firm plums very rapidly, they will taste very vapidly,
—By good luck we'll have pears coming on!

All around Nature's range is from changes to changes,
And in change all her charming is centered—
When you step from the stream where you've bathed, 'twere a dream
To suppose't the same stream that you entered;
Each clear crystal wave just a passing kiss gave,
And kept rolling away to the sea—
So the love-stricken slave for a moment may rave,
But ere long oh! how distant he'll be?

Why—tis only in name, you, e'en you, are the same
With the SHE that inspired my devotion,
Every bit of the lip that I lov'd so to sip
Has been changed in the general commotion—
Even these soft gleaming eyes that awaked my young sighs
Have been altered a thousand times over;
Why? Oh! why then complain that so short was your reign?
Must all Nature go round but your lover?

The tears flowed in torrents, from the blue eyes of Mrs. Magnus, during the whole of this song; and when Mr. Tims, who was now extremely inebriated, (he has since apologised to us for his behavior, and assured us, that when tipsey on tea he is always quite beyond himself,) vehemently cried, "Hangcore! hangcore!" the gross impropriety of such unfeeling conduct was felt by Mr. Seward, who offered, if agreeable to us, to turn him out of the Tent; but Tims became more reasonable upon this, and asked permission to go to bed; which being granted, his friend Price* assisted the small cit to *lay* down, and in a few minutes, we think, unless we were deceived, that we faintly heard something like his own thin tiny little snore.

Mrs. Magnus soon recovered her cheerfulness; for being, with all her vivacity, subject to frequent but short fits of absence, she every now and then, no doubt without knowing what she was about, filled up her tea-cup, not from the silver tea-pot, but from a magisterial-looking bottle of whiskey, which then, and indeed

* Mr. Price, who figures as "a nephy of the late Sir Charles Price, that was o' Lunnun," was introduced as a metropolitan dandy, rejoicing in those days in swallow-tailed coats, tightly-laced stays, tall hats, high shirt-collars, and wide trousers, exaggerated with immense full plaits over the hips.—M.

at all times, stood on our table. She now volunteered a song of her own composition; and after fingering away in the most rapid style of manipulation on the edge of the table, as if upon her own spinnet in Philadelphia, she too took the key from Tickler's ready instrument, and chanted in recitativo what follows — an anomolous kind of poetry.

CHANT. — BY MRS. M'WHIRTER.

Tune — *The Powldoodies of Burran.*

I WONDER what the mischief was in me when a bit of my music I proffered ye!
How could any woman sing a good song when she's just parting with Morgan
Odoherty?
A poor body, I think, would have more occasion for a comfortable quiet can,
To keep up her spirits in taking lave of so nate a young man —
Besides, as for me, I'm not an orator like Bushe, Plunket, Grattan, or Curran,*
So I can only hum a few words to the old chant of the Powldoodies of Burran.
Chorus — Oh! the Powldoodies of Burran,
The green green Powldoodies of Burran,
The green Powldoodies, the clean Powldoodies,
The gaping Powldoodies of Burran.†

---

* Charles Kendal Bushe, Chief-Justice of Ireland; William Conyngham Plunket, Lord Chancellor, from 1830 to 1841; Henry Grattan, the eloquent patriot of 1783; and John Philpot Curran, "over whose ashes," to use his own words, "the most precious tears of Ireland have been shed."—M.

† There is a fashion in everything — even in oysters. The fashion is perpetually shifting and changing. Twenty years ago, the run was on brown Duff Gordon sherry: — now it has veered round to Amontillado. Then, we used to luxuriate in what was called Comet-brand champaigne — now we descend to a substitute which probably derives its name (*Head-sick*) from its effects on the corporeal system. Formerly, gentlemen strutted about in blue swallow-tail-coats, bag-trousers, one-button waistcoats, hugely-frilled shirts, high and rigid collars, and tall stocks — now their attire is wholly different. Then, ladies looked absurd in short petticoats, shoulder-of-mutton (*en gigot*) sleeves, exaggerated bustles, low-bodies, uncovered shoulders, and a plentitude of cork-screw curls — now, their dresses must sweep the pavement, their *crinolins* are subdued, their dresses cover their shoulders, and their hair is "fixed" either in braids, like Queen Victoria's, or brushed back off the forehead, in the amiable ambition of making a pretty woman look like a buy-a-broom girl from Bavaria — bold and brazen. In other days, when Mozart and Rossini ruled the roast, the music of the Italian opera was composed somewhat on the principle of being an accompaniment to the singers — a sort of undercurrent to the waves of their magic melody. Now, with Donizetti and Verdi in favor, the music is to drown

I remember a saying of my Lord Norbury, that excellent Judge,
Says he, never believe what a man says to ye, Molly, for believe me 'tis all fudge;
He said it sitting on the Bench before the whole Grand Jury of Tipperary,
If I had minded it, I had been the better on't, as sure as my name's Mary:

---

the voice; the singers have to roar in opposition to the crash of a crowd of wind instruments; ophecleides, trumpets, bassoons, violincellos, and mammoth-drums play the mischief with the human tympanum; and noise wins the day against melody and sentiment. As wines, dress, music, and other condiments, so has it been with—oysters! In Ireland, at least, Fashion has affected the popularity of bivalves. Ireland, fortunate and wealthy in all natural productions, especially rejoices in a general and generous supply of a species of oysters called "The Powldoodies of Burran," which are commemorated in this chant of Mrs. M'Whirter's. The Powldoodies are a small oyster (about the size of a silver dollar or five-franc piece, or English crown), with a delicate black beard, and a flavor which may be imagined but cannot be described. Those visiters to Paris who (at the restaurant called Les Frères Provincaux, in the Palais Royal) have commenced a dinner with the usual half dozen Ostend oysters, small but savory and appetizing (particularly when washed down with chablis), and wished, in their delight, that the said Ostends were just double their actual size, may take my word for it that the Powldoodies are exactly what they sighed for. But every thing has its day, in this world of chance and change. Powldoodies went out of fashion, and Carlingford oysters came in. After a time, these, also, ceased to be the *ton*. Then, from the county of Clare, all the way across the island, we received the Burton-Bindon oysters, which, unquestionably, are among the natural riches of Ireland. They have been some years in favor, and are not likely to be superseded in a hurry. Any lover of bivalves, who may think it worth his while to make a voyage to Ireland for the sake of fully enjoying the luxury, would do well to land on the coast of Clare, to try the Burton-Bindons; thence coast along into what was called Cove and now is Queenstown, to partake of the Cork Harbor oysters, as large as the largest Prince's Bays, and delicate in flavor as—the dewy kiss from a maiden's lips when she first confesses to a mutual passion. Thence up the Irish sea, touching on the shores of Wexford and Wicklow, for other, but less known varieties of the beloved piscine delicacy. Forward to the beds whereupon repose the luscious Carrickfergusites, the Malahides, and the delightful "natives" of Carlingford. The whole tour of Ireland may thus be advantageously made, for there be oysters on nearly every part of the coast, but the leading resting-places are such as are here named. It may be right to add, as I am upon this important subject, that in Ireland, oysters are rarely stewed, never fried, and only occasionally scolloped. They are invariably taken raw, each man having a hundred, or so, placed before him, with a coarse towel to protect his hand, while he opens the oyster with a short stumpy knife. The art of opening (consisting in employing skill rather than force, so that even a lady (who is up to the knack) can open oysters as fast as a man,) is the result

I would have paid not the smallest attention, ye good-for-nothing elf ye,
To the fine speeches that took me off my feet in the swate city Philadelphy.
Oh! the Powldoodies of Burran, &c., &c.

---

of practice. Those who like to preserve the fish in the deeper shell, so as to retain the juice, open the oyster at the hinge, by a short sharp jerk of the knife. When a man has disposed of half a dozen score of oysters in the natural way (with a couple of pots of Guinness's to assist him), and yet feels a void in the inner man, he finishes off another score or two, by putting them to roast between the bars—the chief pleasure then consisting in "dallying with danger on life's troubled sea" (a line, by the way, from a sentimental sonnet of my own), by risking the burning of his fingers in taking the nearly red-hot roasters off the fire. To assist the digestion of roasted oysters, it is improving to imbibe a *dandy* (half a wine-glass full) of neat whiskey to every fifteen oysters. Six score, or a hundred-and-twenty moderate sized oysters is considered a fair (Irish) allowance for a gentleman, before he enters upon such substantialities of a supper as rump-steaks, salmon-cutlets, sweetbreads, lobster-salads, game, and that crowning glory of the feast—some ripe Stilton (about the size of a piece of chalk) washed down with one tall glass of stunning Edinburgh ale! After such a supper, a man may safely commence to "make a night of it," secure in the certainty of having laid a good foundation in the stomach for the drink to rest upon. N. B.—Should the sitting be prolonged until 5 A. M., exhausted Nature may have her strength somewhat renewed, by a deviled turkey's leg or so. Eschew grilled gizzards, as indigestible. Avoid the pleasant and unwholesome iniquity yclept Welsh Rabbit, but if you *will* have one (and I own that I am rather fond of it, myself), imbue the cook with the twenty-eighth of the "Maxims of Odoherty," which treats on toasted cheese for supper. Stick to one description of drink; after supper it is infantile to mix your liquors. By way of a fillip to the appetite (but Irishmen seldom require it) a man may sometimes, in advance of the regular "devils," take devilled biscuit or dittoed back-bone of mackerel. Prepare them thus:—Moderately cover biscuit or back-bone with butter; sprinkle with cayenne and fine salt; put into the oven to crisp; take out in an hour, when browned and crisped; nibble occasionally, and take my word for it, you will not be deficient in the way of thirst.—Speaking of oysters, we must refer the curious reader to No. XVIII. of the Noctes Ambrosianæ, in which Odoherty speaks critically on the bivalves of Ireland. He lauds the Carlingford ("small, but of a particularly fine flavor"), also the Bland oysters of Kerry, so called from the family who owned the particular bed on which they multiplied, as well as the gigantic from Cork Harbor. "The large oyster," said he, "is like your large beauty—melting, luxurious, and soul-soothing. The small like your small beauties—piquant, savory, and soul-awakening." He added (the prevalent opinion, across the water,) that good oysters should taste like a copper half-penny! The Irish mode of doing roasted oysters was this:—Put them between the bars, take them out when roasted, put a hazel-nut size of butter

By the same rule, says my dear Mr. Bushe, one night when I was sitting beside Mausey,
"Molly, love," says he, "if you go on at this rate, you've no idea what bad luck it will cause ye;
You may go on very merrily for a while, but you'll see what will come on't,
When to answer for all your misdeeds, at the last you are summoned;
Do you fancy a young woman can proceed in this sad lightheaded way,
And not suffer in the long run, tho' manetime she may merrily say,
Oh! the Powldoodies of Burran, &c., &c.

But I'm sure there's plenty of other people that's very near as bad as me.
Yes, and I will make bould to affirm it in the very tiptopsomest degree;
Only they're rather more cunning concealing on't, tho' they meet with their fops
Every now and then, by the mass, about four o'clock in their Milliner's shops;
In our own pretty Dame street I've seen it—the fine Lady comes commonly first,
And then comes her beau on pretence of a watch-ribbon, or the like I purtest.
Oh! the Powldoodies of Burran, &c., &c.

But as for me, I could not withstand him, 'tis the beautiful dear Ensign I mean,
When he came into the Shining Daisy* with his milkwhite smallclothes so clean,
With his epaulette shining on his shoulder, and his golden gorget at his breast,
And his long silken sash so genteely twisted many times round about his neat waist;
His black gaiters that were so tight, and reached up to a little below his knee,
And shewed so well the prettiest calf e'er an Irish lass had the good luck to see.
Oh! the Powldoodies of Burran, &c., &c.

His eyes were like a flaming coal-fire, all so black and yet so bright,
Or like a star shining clearly in the middle of the dark heaven at night,
And the white of them was not white, but a sort of charming hue,
Like a morning sky, or skimmed milk, of a delicate sweet blue;
But when he whispered sweetly, then his eyes were so soft and dim,
That it would have been a heart of brass not to have pity upon him,
Oh! the Powldoodies of Burran, &c., &c

---

under the oyster in its deep shell, which melts it, as a young woman melts beneath the warm influence of love, then shred your eschalot gently into it, shower in your cayenne, add a little salt, and it is a mouthful for an Editor.—M.

* The *Shining Daisy* was the sign of Mrs. M'Whirter's chop-house at Philadelphia—Sir Daniel Donelly hoisted the same sign over his booth the other day at Donnybrook fair.—EDITOR. [Sir Daniel, an Irish pugilist, of whose life and death a full account was subsequently written by Maginn—as will be seen, and may be read, anon.—M.]

And yet now you see he's left me like a pair of old boots or shoes,
And makes love to all the handsome ladies, for ne'er a one of them can refuse;
Through America and sweet Ireland, and Bath and London City,
For he must always be running after something that's new and pretty,
Playing the devil's own delights in Holland, Spain, Portugal, and France,
And here too in the cold Scotch mountains, where I've met with him by very chance. Oh! the Powldoodies of Burran, &c., &c.

When he first ran off and deserted me, I thought my heart was plucked away,
Such a tugging in my breast, I did not sleep a wink till peep of day—
May I be a sinner if I ever bowed but for a moment my eye-lid,
Tossing round about from side to side in the middle of my bid.
One minute kicking off all the three blankets, the sheets, and the counterpane,
And then stuffing them up over my head like a body beside myself again.
Oh! the Powldoodies of Burran, &c., &c.

Says I to myself, I'll repeat over the whole of the Pater Noster, Ave-Maria, and Creed,
If I don't fall over into a doze e'er I'm done with them 'twill be a very uncommon thing indeed;
But, would you believe it? I was quite lively when I came down to the Amen,
And it was always just as bad tho' I repeated them twenty times over and over again;
I also tried counting of a thousand, but still found myself broad awake,
With a cursed pain in the fore part of my head, all for my dear sweet Ensign Odoherty's sake. Oh! the Powldoodies of Burran, &c., &c.

But, to cut a long story short, I was in a high fever when I woke in the morning,
Whereby all women in my situation should take profit and warning;
And Doctor Oglethorpe he was sent for, and he ordered me on no account to rise,
But to lie still and have the whole of my back covered over with Spanish flies;
He also gave me leeches and salts, castor oil, and the balsam capivi,
Till I was brought down to a mere shadow, and so pale that the sight would have grieved ye. Oh! the Powldoodies of Burran, &c., &c.

But in the course of a few days more I began to stump a little about,
And by the blessing of air and exercise, I grew every day more and more stout;
And in a week or two I recovered my twist, and could play a capital knife and fork,
Being not in the least particular whether it was beef, veal, lamb, mutton, or pork;
But of all the things in the world, for I was always my father's own true daughter,
I liked best to dine on fried tripes, and wash it down with a little hot brandy and water. Oh! the Powldoodies of Burran, &c., &c.

If I had the least bit of genius for poems, I could make some very nice songs,
On the cruelties of some people's sweethearts, and some people's sufferings and wrongs;

For he was master, I'm sure, of my house, and there was nothing at all at all
In the whole of the Shining Daisy for which he could not just ring the bell
and call;
We kept always a good larder of pigeon pyes, hung beef, ham, and cowheel,
And we would have got anything to please him that we could either beg, borrow, or steal. Oh! the Powldoodies of Burran, &c., &c.

And at night when we might be taking our noggin in the little back-room,
I thought myself as sure of my charmer as if he had gone to church my bridegroom;
But I need not deep harping on that string and ripping up of the same old sore,
He went off in the twinkling of a bed-post, and I never heard tell of him no more,
So I married the great Doctor Oglethorpe, who had been my admirer all along,
And we had some scolloped Powldoodies for supper; and every crature joined in the old song, Oh! the Powldoodies of Burran, &c., &c.

Some people eats their Powldoodies quite neat just as they came out of the sea,
But with a little black pepper and vinegar some other people's stomachs better agree;
Young ladies are very fond of oyster pates, and young gentlemen of oyster broth,
But I think I know a bit of pasture that is far better than them both:
For whenever we want to be comfortable says I to the Doctor—my dear man,
Let's have a few scolloped Powldoodies, and a bit of tripe fried in the pan,
Chorus—Oh! the Powldoodies of Burran,
The green green Powldoodies of Burran,
The green Powldoodies, the clean Powldoodies,
The gaping Powldoodies of Burran.

After Mrs. Magnus had received those plaudits from the Tent due to this exhibition of native genius, the learned Doctor somewhat anxiously asked us what sort of accommodation we had for him and his lady during the night? We told him that the Tent slept twenty easily, and that a few more could be stowed away between the interstices. "But give yourself no uneasiness, Dr. Magnus, on that score; we are aware of the awkwardness of a lady passing the night with so many Contributors, and of the censoriousness of the world, many people in which seem determined, Doctor, to put an unfavorable construction on every thing we do or say. Besides, your excellent lady might find our Tent like the Black Bull Inn of Edinburgh, as it was twenty years ago, when Dr. Morris first visited it, 'crowded, noisy, shabby, and uncomfortable.' Now the inn at Braemar is a most capital one, where the young ladies of the family will pay every attention to Mrs. Magnus. We have already despatched a special messenger for Dr. Morris' shandrydan,* and as it is a fine moonlight night, you can trundle yourselves down to bed in a jiffey."

The sound of the shandrydan comfirmed our words, and we all attended Mrs. Magnus and her husband to the road, to see them safely mounted. Our readers have all seen Peter's shandrydan — a smart, suug, safe, smooth, roomy, easy-going concern that carries you over the stones as if you were on turf; and where, may we ask, will you see a more compact nimble little horse than Peter's horse, Scrub — with feet as steady as clock-work, and a mouth that carries his bit with a singular union of force aud tenderness?

"I fear that I cannot guide this vehicle along Highland roads," said Dr. Magnus; "and I suspect that steed is given to starting, from the manner in which he keeps rearing his head about, and pawing the ground like a mad bull. My dear, it would be flying in the face of Providence to ascend the steps of that shandrydan."

While the orator was thus expressing his trepidation, the Standard-bearer handed Mrs. Magnus forward, who, with her nodding plumes, leapt lightly up beneath the giant strength of his warlike arm, and took her seat with an air of perfect composure and dignity; while Odoherty, adjusting the reins with the skill of a Lade or Buxton, and elevating his dexter hand that held them and the whip in its gnostic grasp, caught hold of the rail of the shandrydan with his left, and flung himself, as it were, to the fair side of her who had once been the mistress of his youthful heart, but for whom he now retained only the most respectful affection.

"Mount up behind, Dr. Magnus," cried the Adjutant, somewhat impatiently; "your feet will not be more than six inches

* The shandrydan, in which (*vide* Peter's Letters) Dr. Morris drove into Edinburgh, when commencing his great visit, was a rather high one-horse and two-wheeled gig, capable of holding two persons. The frontispiece to vol. i. of the famous Letters is enriched with a vignette showing the Doctor and his man in this vehicle, which he describes as "positively the very best vehicle in existence. The lightness of the gig — the capacity of the chariot — and the stylishness of the car — it is a wonderful combination of excellencies." — M.

from the ground, so that in case of any disaster, you can drop off like a ripe pease-cod—mount, I say, Doctor, mount."

The Doctor did so; and the Standard-bearer, giving a blast on Wastle's bugle, and cutting the thin air with his thong several yards beyond Scrub's nose, away went the shandrydan, while the mountains of the Dee echoed again to the rattling of its wheels.

NOTE FROM MR. ODOHERTY.

MY DEAR EDITOR,

The report of my death—a report originally created by the malevolence of a fiend—has, I am sorry to observe, gained considerable currency through the inadvertence of you—a friend. Had my body been really consigned to the dust, you should have received intelligence of that event, not from the casual whispers of a stranger, but from the affectionate bequest of a sincere admirer; for, sir, I may as well mention the fact, that by a holograph codicil to my last will and testament, I have constituted you sole tutor and curator of all my MSS.; thus providing, in case of accidents, for these my intellectual offspring, the care of a guardian, who, I am well aware, would superintend, with a father's eye, the mode of their introduction into public life.

I flatter myself, however, that you will not hear with indifference, of my being still in a condition to fulfil this office in propriâ personâ. On some future occasion I shall describe to your readers, in, I hope, no uninteresting strains, the strange vicissitudes of my fate during the last two years: among these not the least amusing will be the narrative of those very peculiar circumstances which have induced me to lie *perdue*, a listener to no less than two succeeding historians of my life, supposed to be terminated—and eulogists of my genius, no less falsely supposed to have been swallowed up in the great vortex of animation. But of all this anon.

I inclose, in the mean time, as the first offerings of my re-acknowledged existence, three several productions of my muse. The first (the Garland) was composed by me a few weeks ago on the following occasion.

I happened to be in Hawick at the moment when the celebrated Giantess, Mrs. Cook, passed through that town on her way from the South. Animated with that rightful spirit of curiosity which has been pronounced to be the mother of all knowledge, I immediately hastened to wait upon her. The vast stature of this remarkable woman—her strength (for, with a single squeeze, she had well nigh crushed my fingers to dust), the symmetry of her figure—but above all, the soft elegance of her features—these united attractions were more than sufficient to make a deep impression on the mind of one who has never professed himself to be "a stoic of the woods." After spending a comfortable evening at Mrs. Brown's, I set out for Eltrive, the seat of my friend Mr. Hogg, and, in the course of the walk, composed the following lines, which I soon afterward sent to Mrs. Cook. It is proper to mention, that the fair daughter of Anak enclosed to me, in return, a ticket of free admission for the season—of which I shall certainly very frequently avail myself after my arrival in Edinburgh.

The other two poems, the Eve of St. Jerry, and the Rime of the Auncient Waggonere, were composed by me many years ago. The reader will at once detect the resemblance which they bear to two well-known and justly celebrated pieces of Scott and Coleridge. This resemblance, in justice to myself, is the fruit of their imitation—not of mine. I remember reciting the Eve of St. Jerry about the year 1795 to Mr. Scott,* then a very young man; but as I have not had the pleasure of seeing Mr. Coleridge, although I have often wished to do so, and hold his genius in the highest estimation, I am more at a loss to account for

* There is an anachronism here.—Odoherty's biographer (*vide* chap. i. p. 4) fixes 1789 as the date of the Ensign's birth, whereas, as we shall presently see, it was in 1780. Consequently, he must have written and recited his poem at the age of *six*. This is about as strong an instance of precocious talent as we have on record.—Scott's poem, "The Eve of St. John," was written in 1799, at the age of twenty-eight. The "The Rhyme of the Ancient Mariner" was one of Coleridge's earliest performances.—M.

the accurate idea he seems to have possessed of my production, unless, indeed, I may have casually dropt a copy of the MS. in some bookseller's shop in Bristol, where he may have found it. Meantime, I remain, Dear Editor, your affectionate servant,

MORGAN ODOHERTY.

ELTRIVE LAKE, *Feb. 29th*, 1819.

ODOHERTY'S GARLAND.

IN HONOR OF MRS. COOK, *THE GREAT.*

LET the Emerald Isle make O'Brien her boast,*
And let Yorkshire be proud of her "strapping young man,"†
But London, gay London, should glory the most,

* Charles O'Brien, the person here alluded to, measured exactly eight feet two inches in his pumps. His countenance was comely, and his chest well formed, but, like the "Mulier Formosa" of Horace's Satire, or (what may be considered as a more appropriate illustration) like the idol of the Philistines, he was very awkwardly shaped in the lower extremities. He made a practice of selling successively to many gentlemen of the medical profession, the reversion of his enormous carcase. It is said that one of these bargains—viz. that contracted between him and the celebrated Liston of Edinburgh, was reduced to a strictly legal shape. It is well known that, according to the forms of Scots law, nothing but moveables can be conveyed by *testament*—every other species of property requires to be transferred by a deed *inter vivos.* The acute northern anatomist, doubting whether any court of law would have been inclined to class O'Brien's body among *moveables*, insisted that the giant should vest the *fee* of the said body in him (the surgeon), saving and retaining to himself (the giant), a right of usufruct or liferent. We have not heard by what *symbol* the Dr. completed his infeftment. [The skeleton of O'Brien, the Irish giant, is preserved in the Museum of Trinity College, Dublin.—M.]

† The "strapping young man" was the late Thomas Higgins, on occasion of whose death was composed a poetical dialogue, formerly alluded to in *Blackwood's Magazine.*

TRAVELLER.

Why! I was told you woollen-weavers here
Were starved outright for lack of all employment;
But I perceive a very different cheer.
Your looms are rattling all in full enjoyment.

INHABITANTS.

Oh! those that told you so, sir, told you right;
We were indeed a woful famish'd crowd;
But now the case is altered clean and white,
We have got the making of the Giant's Shroud.

She has reared Mrs. Cook,* let them match her who can;
This female Goliah† is thicker and higher
Than Italian Belzoni,‡ or Highlandman Sam.
Yet the terrible creature is pretty in feature,
And her smile is as soft as a dove or a lamb.

---

* Mrs. Cook, the largest of female mortals, was commonly called "The Gentle Giantess." She was married to a gentleman the crown of whose head was only on a level with her girdle. Great was the contrast between his five feet nothing and her six feet six. As a true historian, I am compelled to state that Mr. Cook was accustomed (particularly after his ninth tumbler of punch) to exercise on the person of his gigantic Dulcinea the marital rights which the law of England intrusts to a husband — of moderately correcting his better half with a stick not exceeding the thickness of a man's thumb. This was publicly enunciated, at Stafford assizes, by Sir Francis Buller, one of the Justices of the Court of Common Pleas. The indignant wives of Stafford sent him a round-robin, inquiring the dimensions of *his* thumb. It is particularly note-worthy that Buller himself, married early, had the reputation of being eminently henpecked! The great Mrs. Cook, magnanimous in her bulk and strength, complacently submitted to the *striking* proofs of her small husband's regard. Once, she resisted — but gently, as became her majestic nature — and raising Mr. Cook from the ground, with one hand, carefully deposited him, on his legs, upon the chimney-piece, whence she did not allow him to be taken until he had promised better conduct in future. It is a singular thing, and might be cited as an instance of the compensating principle of nature, that small men are extremely fond of possessing exceedingly lofty wives, and that giantesses do affect small-statured men. For my own part, while I own that, after all, it may not be very unpleasant for a tall man to bend down and salute a *petite* lady-love, I confess that, were I a giantess, I do not think I could much like a lover so short that, in order to kiss me, he must mount on a table to get on a level with my lips. Mrs. C. did not long survive the visit of the illustrious Odoherty. Young in years, but stupendous in bulk, she returned to mother-earth before she was thirty years old.—M.

† *Goliah*, Cocknicé, *Goliar*.

"I don't defend that rhyme, 'tis very bad,
Tho' us'd by Hunt and Keats, and all that squad."—WASTLE.

‡ John Baptiste Belzoni, born at Padua, in 1780, emigrated to England in 1803, and, falling into pecuniary difficulties, obtained his living by displaying feats of strength and activity, at Astley's Amphitheatre, in London, for which his colossal stature and extraordinary muscular powers eminently qualified him. At that time he was only twenty-four years old, but was six feet seven inches high, and used to walk across the stage with two-and-twenty persons attached by straps to different parts of his body. In 1812 he exhibited in Lisbon and Malta. Thence he went to Egypt, to construct a hydraulic machine for the Pacha. In June, 1815, he undertook an expedition to Thebes to remove an

When she opens her eyelids she dazzles you quite
  With the vast flood of splendor that flashes around;
Old Ajax, ambitious to perish in light,*
  In one glance of her glory perdition had found.
Both in verse and in prose, to the bud of a rose,
  Sweet lips have been likened by amorous beau;
But her lips may be said to be like a rose-bed
  Their fragrance so full is, so broad is their glow.

The similitudes used in king Solomon's book,
  In laudation of some little Jewess of old,
If we only suppose them devised for the Cook,
  Would appear the reverse of improper or bold.
There is many a tree that is shorter than she,
  In particular that on which Johnston was swung,
Had the rope been about her huge arm, there's no doubt,
  That the friend of the Scotsman at once had been hung,†

The cedars that grew upon Lebanon hill,
  And the towers of Damascus might well be applied,
With imperfect ideas the fancy to fill,
  Of the monstrous perfections of Cook's pretty bride.
Oh! if one of the name be immortal in fame,
  Because round the wide globe he adventured to roam,
Mr. Cook, I don't see why yourself should not be
  As illustrious as he without stirring from home!

QUOTH ODOHERTY.

---

enormous bust, called "the Younger Memnon," which he succeeded in doing, and sent it to England; it is now in the British Museum, with a variety of other ancient sculptures discovered and transmitted by him. Pursuing his travels and researches, during which he made many discoveries highly valuable to the antiquarian and historian, Belzoni crowned his exploits by discovering a vast and magnificent tomb near Thebes (a representation of which he subsequently exhibited in London), and by penetrating into the interior of the second great pyramid of Ghizeh, which had previously been believed to consist of one solid mass. Returning to England in 1820, he published a narrative of his operations, returned to Africa in 1822, and died at Gato, on his way to Houssa and Timbuctoo, in December, 1823. He was accompanied, in all his expeditions but the last, by his wife, whom he married in England in 1803. She was, for a woman, as prodigious in size and strength as Belzoni was for a man, and much assisted him in his researches.—M.

* An allusion to the prayer of this great Greek hero in Homer—
"Εν φαει και ολεσσον."—M. O.

† Blackwood's contributors let no opportunity slip of attacking their Whig opponents—hence the frequent hits at "The Scotsman," a liberal paper in Edinburgh, then edited by J. R. M'Culloch, the political economist.—M.

THE EVE OF ST. JERRY.

[THE reader will learn with astonishment that I composed the two following ballads in the fourteenth year of my age, i. e. A. D. 1780. I doubt if either Milton or Pope rivalled this precocity of genius.—M. O.]

DICK GOSSIP the barber arose with the cock,
And pull'd his breeches on;
Down the staircase of wood, as fast as he could,
The valiant shaver ran.

He went not to the country forth
To shave or frizzle hair;
Nor to join in the battle to be fought
At Canterbury fair.

Yet his hat was fiercely cocked, and his razors in his pocket,
And his torturing irons he bore;
A staff of crab-tree in his hand had he,
Full five feet long and more.

The barber return'd in three days space,
And blistered were his feet;
And sad and peevish were his looks,
As he turn'd the corner street.

He came not from where Canterbury
Ran ankle-deep in blood;
Where butcher Jem, and his comrades grim,
The shaving tribe withstood.

Yet were his eyes bruis'd black and blue;
His cravat twisted and tore;
His razors were with gore imbued—
But it was not professional gore.*

He halted at the painted pole,
Full loudly did he rap,
And whistled on his shaving boy,
Whose name was Johnny Strap.

Come hither, come hither, young tickle-beard,
And mind that you tell me true,

* We have no wish to injure the reputation of this gentleman; but, from the above stanza, it is evident that his hand was liable to tremor, whether from natural nervous debility, or the effect of brandy, we cannot take upon us to determine.—M. OD.

For these three long days that I've been away,
  What did Mrs. Gossip do?

When the clock struck eight, Mrs. Gossip went straight,
  In spite of the pattering rain,
Without stay or stop to the butcher's shop,
  That lives in Cleaver-lane.

I watch'd her steps, and secret came
  Where she sat upon a chair.
No person was in the butcher's shop—
  The devil a soul was there.

The second night I 'spy'd a light
  As I went up the strand,
'Twas she who ran, with pattens on,
  And a lanthern in her hand:

She laid it down upon a bench,
  And shook her wet attire;
And drew in the elbow chair, to warm
  Her toes before the fire.

In the twinkling of a walking stick,*
  A greasy butcher came,
And with a pair of bellows, he
  Blew up the dying flame.

And many a word the butcher spoke
  To Mrs. Gossip there,
But the rain fell fast, and it blew such a blast,
  That I could not tell what they were.

The third night there the sky was fair,
  There neither was wind nor rain;
And again I watch'd the secret pair
  At the shop in Cleaver-lane.

And I heard her say, "Dick Gossip's away,
  So we'll be blithe and merry,
And the bolts I'll undo, sweet butcher to you,
  On the eve of good St. Jerry."†

"I can not come, I must not come"—
  "For shame, faint hearted snarler,
Must I then moan, and sit alone,
  In Dicky Gossip's parlor.

---

* From this line, it is to be inferred, that the oaken saplings of our ancestors rivalled in elasticity the bamboo canes of our modern dandies.—M. OD.

† We have in vain scrutinized the kalendar for the name of this saint.—OD.

"The dog shall not tear you, and Strap* shall not hear you,
And blankets I'll spread on the stair;
By the blood-red sherry,† and holy St. Jerry,
I conjure thee sweet butcher be there."

"Tho' the dog should not tear me, and Strap should not hear me.
And blankets be spread on the stair,
Yet there's Mr. Parrot, who sleeps in the garret,
To my footsteps he could swear."—

"Fear not, Mr. Parrot, who sleeps in the garret,
For to Hampstead the way he has ta'en;
An inquest to hold, as I have been told,
On the corpse of a butcher that's slain."

He turned him around, and grimly he frown'd,
And he laugh'd right scornfully,
"The inquest that's held, on the man that's been killed,
May as well be held on me.

"At the lone midnight hour, when hobgoblins have power,
In thy chamber I'll appear;"—
With that he was gone, and your wife left alone,
And I came running here."—

Then changed I trow, was the barber's brow,
From the chalk to the beet-root red,
"Now tell me the mien of the butcher thou'st seen,
By Mambrino I'll smite off his head."

---

* After his master's misfortune, this gentleman settled in the north, and was the great grand-father of that Strap, so honorably noticed by Smollet. [In Roderick Random.—M.]

† This valuable species of wine is unfortunately for modern epicures now unknown. [Any wine-merchant who is up to his business, could produce blood-red sherry, or any other species of drink, at four-and-twenty hours' notice. George IV. had a favorite wine of which a large supply was laid in. He capriciously took a fancy to some other tap and the members of his household drank up *the* wine. It pleased the King, one day at lunch, to announce that, at a grand dinner that evening, he would sport the neglected wine. His butler was at his wits-ends, and sent for a wine-merchant to whom he told his story. "Any of the wine left?" asked the vintner. A solitary bottle was found. "Very good," said he, "tell me the exact hour you will want this fancy wine and I shall give you a supply." The dinner took place, the favorite wine was called for, was drank, was praised. The wine-merchant had fabricated the wine, and thus saved the credit of his friend, the butler. This anecdote was given in evidence, in 1852, before a committee of the House of Commons appointed to investigate the subject of the duties on wine. I had previously heard it, twenty years before, from the King's butler, Mr. Valimi.—M.

"On the point of his nose, which was like a red rose,
Was a wart of enormous size;
And he made a great vaporing with a blue and white apron,
And red stockings roll'd up to his thighs."*

"Thou liest, thou liest, young Johnny Strap,
It is all a fib you tell,
For the butcher was taken, as dead as bacon,
From the bottom of Carisbrook well."

"My master attend, and I'll be your friend,
I don't value madam a button;
But I heard Mistress say, don't leave, I pray,
Sweet Timothy Slaughter-mutton."

He ope'd the shop door, the counter he jump'd o'er,
And overturned Strap,
Then bolted up the stair, where he found his lady fair,
With the Kitten on her lap.

"Now hail, now hail, thou lady bright,—
Now hail, thou barber trim,
What news from Canterbury fight,
What news from bloody Jem?"†

"Canterbury is red with gore,
For many a barber fell;
And the mayor has charg'd us for evermore,
To watch the butcher's well."—

Mrs. Gossip blush'd, and her cheek was flush'd,
But the barber shook his head;
And having observed that the night was cold,
He tumbled into bed.

Mrs. Gossip lay and mourn'd, and Dicky toss'd and turn'd;
And he mutter'd while half asleep,
The stone is large and round, and the halter tight and sound,
And the well thirty fathoms deep.

The gloomy dome of St. Paul's struck three,
The morning began to blink,
And Gossip slept, as if his wife
Had put laudanum in his drink.

---

* This was no doubt a bold and masterly attempt of the butcher to imitate plush breeches.—M. OD.

† It is astonishing that Hume and other historians make no mention of this bloody encounter, which threatened to exterminate the whole shaving generation; or, at least, scatter them like the twelve tribes of Israel.—M. OD.

Mrs. Gossip drew wide the curtains aside,
The candle had burn'd to the socket,
And lo! Timothy stood, all cover'd with blood,
With his right hand in his pocket.

"Dear Slaughter-mutton, away," she cried,
"I pray thee do not stop"—
"Mrs. Gossip, I know, who sleeps by thy side,
But he sleeps as sound as a top.

"Near Carisbrook well I lately fell
Beneath a barber's knife;
The coroner's inquest was held on me—
But it did not restore me to life.*

"By thy husband's hand, was I foully slain,
He threw me into the well,
And my sprite in the shop, in Cleaver-lane,
For a season is doom'd to dwell."—

Love master'd fear—"What brings thee here?"
The Love-sick matron said,—
"Is thy fair carcase gone to pot?"—
The goblin shook his head.

"I slaughter'd sheep, and slaughter'd was,
And for breaking the marriage band,
My flesh and bones go to David Jones†—
But let us first shake hands."

He laid his left fist, on an oaken chest,
And, as she cried—"don't burn us;"
With the other he grasp'd her by the nose,
And scorch'd her like a furnace.

There is a felon in Newgate jail,
Who dreads the next assize;
A woman doth dwell, in Bedlam cell,
With a patch between her eyes.

The woman who dwells in Bedlam cell,
Whose reason is not worth a button,
Is the wife of the barber in Newgate jail,
Who slaughter'd Slaughter-mutton.

---

* It seems to us an unconscionable expectation of the butcher, that the inquest of the coroner was to restore the "vis vitæ." M. OD.

† Apparently one of the slang names for the "hangman of creation," omitted by Burns in his address to that celebrated personage. [It is somewhat surprising for Odoherty not to know that Davy Jones is the Azrael, of Death-Angel of Sailors. In their terse phraseology, "going to Davy Jones's locker" intimates a departure from this mortal life.—M.]

THE RIME OF THE AUNCIENT WAGGONERE.

IN FOUR PARTS.

Part First.

An auncient waggonere stoppeth ane tailore going to a wedding, whereat he hath been appointed to be best manne, and to take a hand in the casting of the slippere.

It is an auncient Waggonere,*
  And hee stoppeth one of nine:—
"Now wherefore dost thou grip me soe
  With that horny fist of thine?"

The waggonere in mood for chat, and admits of no excuse.

"The bridegroom's doors are opened wide,
  And thither I must walke;
Soe, by youre leave, I must be gone,
  I have noe time for talke!"

The tailore seized with the ague.

Hee holds him with his horny fist—
  "There was a wain," quothe hee,
"Hold offe thou raggamouffine tykke,"—
  Eftsoones his fist dropped hee.

He listeneth like a three years and a half child.

Hee satte him downe upon a stone,
  With ruefulle looks of feare;
And thus began this tippyse manne,
  The red nosed waggonere.

The appetite of the tailore whetted by the smell of cabbage.

"The waine is fulle, the horses pulle,
  Merrilye did we trotte
Alonge the bridge, alonge the road,
  A jolly crewe I wotte;"——
And here the tailore smotte his breaste,
  He smelte the cabbage potte!

The waggonere, in talking anent Boreas, maketh bad orthographye.

"The nighte was darke, like Noe's arke,
  Oure waggone moved alonge;
The hail pour'd faste, loude roared the blaste,
  Yet stille we moved alonge;
And sung in chorus, 'Cease loud Borus,'
  A very charminge songe.

Their mirthe interrupted.

"'Bravoe, bravissimoe,' I cried,
  The sounde was quite elatinge;
But, in a trice, upon the ice,
  We hearde the horses skaitinge.

And the passengers exercise themselves in the pleasant art of swiminge, as doeth also their prog, to witte, great store of colde roasted beef; item, ane beefstake pye; item, viii choppines of usquebaugh.

"The ice was here, the ice was there,
  It was a dismale mattere,
To see the cargoe, one by one,
  Flounderinge in the wattere!

---

* The Rhyme of the Ancient Mariner is so well known that extracts, for the sake of comparison with the parody, are unnecessary.—M.

"With rout and roare, we reached the shore,
And never a soul did sinke;
But in the rivere, gone for evere,
Swum our meate and drinke.

The waggonere hailethe ane goose, with ane novel salutatione.

"At lengthe we spied a goode grey goose,
Thorough the snow it came;
And with the butte ende of my whippe,
I hailed it in Goddhis name.

"It staggered as it had been drunke,
So dexterous was it hitte;
Of brokene boughs we made a fire,
Thomme Loncheone roasted itte."—

The tailore impatient to be gone, but is forcibly persuaded to remain.

"Be done, thou tipsye waggonere,
"To the feaste I must awaye."——
The waggonere seized him bye the coatte,
And forced him there to staye,
Begginge, in gentlemanlie style,
Butte halfe ane hour's delaye.

THE RIME OF THE AUNCIENT WAGGONERE.

Part Second.

The waggonere's bowels yearn towards the sunne.

"THE crimson sunne was rising o'ere
The verge of the horizon;
Upon my worde, as faire a sunne
As ever I clapped eyes onne.

The passengers throwe the blame of the goose massacre on the innocent waggonere.

"'Twill bee ane comfortable thinge,"
The mutinous crewe 'gan crye;
"'Twill be an comfortable thinge,
Within the jaile to lye;
Ah! execrable wretche," saide they,
"Thatte caused the goose to die!

The sunne sufferes ane artificial eclipse, and horror follows, the same not being mentioned in the Belfaste Almanacke.

"The day was drawing near itte's close,
The sunne was well nighe settinge;
When lo! it seemed as iffe his face
Was veiled with fringe-warke-nettinge.

Various hypotheses on the subject, frome which the passengeres draw wronge conclusions.

"Somme saide itte was ane apple tree,
Laden with goodlye fruite,
Somme swore itte was ane foreigne birde,
Some said it was ane brute;
Alas! it was ane bumbailiffe,
Riding in pursuite!

"A hue and crye sterte uppe behind,
Whilke smote oure ears like thunder,
Within the waggone there was drede,
Astonishmente and wonder.

Ane lovelye sound ariseth; ittes effects described.

"One after one, the rascalls rann,
And from the carre did jump;
One after one, one after one,
They felle with heavy thump.

The passengers throw somersets.

"Six miles ane houre theye offe did scoure,
Like shippes on ane stormye ocean,
Theire garments flappinge in the winde,
With ane shorte uneasy motion.

"Their bodies with their legs did flye,
Theye fled withe feare and glyffe;
Why star'st thoue soe?—With one goode blow,
I felled the bumbailiffe!"

The waggonere complimenteth the bumbailiffe with ane Mendoza.

THE RIME OF THE AUNCIENT WAGGONERE.

Part Third.

"I FEARE thee, auncient waggonere,
I feare thy hornye fiste,
For itte is stained with gooses gore,
And bailiffe's blood, I wist.

"I fear to gette ane fisticuffe
From thy leathern knuckles brown;
With that the tailore strove to ryse—
The waggonere thrusts him down.

The tailore meeteth Corporal Feare.

"'Thou craven, if thou mov'st a limbe,
I'll give thee cause for feare;'—
And thus went on, that tipsye man,
The red-billed waggonere.

"The bumbailiffe so beautifull!
Declared itte was no joke,
For, to his knowledge, both his legs,
And fifteen ribbes were broke.

The bailiffe complaineth of considerable derangement of his animal economye.

"The lighte was gone, the nighte came on,
Ane hundrede lantherns sheen,
Glimmerred upon the kinge's highwaye,
Ane lovelye sighte I ween.

Policemen with their lanthernes, pursue the waggonere.

"'Is it he,' quoth one, 'is this the manne,
I'll laye the rascalle stiffe;'—
With cruel stroke the beak he broke
Of the harmless bumbailiffe.

Steppeth 20 feete in imitatione of the Admirable Crichtoun.

"The threatening of the saucye rogue
No more I coulde abide.
Advancing forthe my goode right legge,
Three paces and a stride,
I sent my lefte foot dexterously
Seven inches thro' his side.

Complaineth of foul play, and falleth down in ane trance.

"Up came the seconde from the vanne;
We had scarcely fought a round,
When some one smote me from behinde,
And I fell down in a swound:

One acteth the parte of Job's comforter.

"And when my head began to clear,
I heard the yemering crew—
Quoth one, 'this man hath penance done,
And penance more shall do.'"

THE RIME OF THE AUNCIENT WAGGONERE.

Part Fourth.

The waggonere maketh ane shrewd observation.

"Oh! Freedom is a glorious thing!—
And tailore, by the bye,
I'd rather in a halter swing,
Than in a dungeon lie.

The waggonere tickleth the spleen of the jailor, who daunces ane Fadango.

"The jailore came to bring me foode,
Forget it will I never,
How he turned up the white o' his eye,
When I stuck him in the liver.

Rejoicethe in the fragrance of the aire.

"His threade of life was snapt; once more
I reached the open streete;
The people sung out 'Gardyloo'
As I ran down the streete.
Methought the blessed air of heaven
Never smelte so sweete.

Dreadeth Shoan Dhu, the corporal of the guarde.

"Once more upon the broad highwaye,
I walked with feare and drede;
And every fifteen steppes I tooke
I turned about my heade,
For feare the corporal of the guarde
Might close behind me trede!

"Behold upon the western wave,
  Setteth the broad bright sunne;
So I must onward, as I have
  Full fifteen miles to runne;—

"And should the bailliffes hither come
  To aske whilke waye I've gone,
Tell them I took the othere road,
  Said hee, and trotted onne."

The waggonere taketh leave of the tailore,

The tailore rushed into the roome,
  O'erturning three or foure;
Fractured his skulle against the walle,
  And worde spake never more!!

to whome ane small accidente happeneth. Whereupon followeth the morale very proper to be had in minde by all members of the Dilettanti Society when they come over the bridge at these houres. Wherefore let them take heed and not lay blame where it lyeth nott.

Morale.

Such is the fate of foolish men,
  The danger all may see,
Of those, who list to waggonere,
  And keepe bad companye.

Maxims of ODoherty.*

Introduction.

I HAVE often thought that the world loses much valuable information from the laziness or diffidence of people, who have it in their power to communicate facts and observations resulting from their own experience, and yet neglect doing so. The idlest or most unobservant has seen, heard, or thought something, which might conduce to the general stock of knowledge. A single remark may throw light on a doubtful or a knotty point—a solitary fact, observed by a careless individual, and which may have escaped the notice of other observers, however acute, may suffice to upset, or to establish, a theory.

For my part, my life has been abundantly checkered. I have mixed in society of all kinds, high and low. I have read much, wrote much, and thought a little;—very little, it is true, but still, more than nine tenths of people who write books. I am still in the prime of my life, and, I believe, in the vigor of my intellect. I intend, therefore, to write down as they occur to me,

* The Maxims of Odoherty appeared in *Blackwood's Magazine*, in 1824, shortly after Dr. Maginn had changed his residence from Cork to London. They were very popular, nearly all the provincial journals quoting largely from them. No. I. appeared in May, No. II. in June, and No. III. in September, 1824. They were collected and published, in book form, by Messrs. Blackwood, in 1849—seven years after Maginn's death. The strong common sense, mingled with shrewdness and keen knowledge of the world, which characterize them, has rarely been rivalled. The late Dr. Macnish attempted it, in his "Book of Aphorisms" (annotated, very ludicrously, by Maginn), but by no means "hit the white." Maginn was fond of referring to and quoting from his "Maxims," not only in subsequent articles, but in conversation.—M.

without binding myself to any order, whether expressed or understood, any general reflections that may occur on men and manners, on the modes of thought and action, on the hopes, fears, wishes, doubts, loves, and hatreds, of mankind. It is probable that what I shall write will not be worth reading. I can not help that. All my bargain is, that I shall give genuine reflection, and narrate nothing but what I have seen and heard.

I was one day in the Salopian Coffeehouse, near Charing-Cross,* taking a bowl of ox-tail soup, when a venerable and imposing-looking gentleman came in. The coffee-room of that house is small, and it so happened that every box was occupied—that is, had a gentleman or two in it. The elderly gentleman looked about a little confused, and every body in the room gazed at him, without offering him a share of any table. Such is the politeness and affability of the English. I instantly rose, and requested him to be seated opposite me. He complied with a bow; and, after he had ordered what he wanted, we fell into conversation. He was a thoughtful man, who delivered his sentences in a weighty and well-considered style. He did not say much, but what he did say was marked with the impress of thought. I found, indeed, that he was a man of only one reflection; but that was a great one. He cast his eye solemnly over the morning paper, which happened to contain the announcement of many bankruptcies. This struck the key-note of his one reflection. "Sir," said he to me, laying down the paper, and taking his spoon cautiously between his fingers, without making any attempt to lift it to his mouth, "Sir, I have now lived in this world sixty-three years, through at least forty of which I have not been a careless or inattentive spectator of what has been passing around me; and I have uniformly found, when a man lives annually on a sum *less* than his year's income—say, five hundred, or five thousand, or five hundred thousand pounds—for the sum makes no difference—that *that* man's accounts are

* A celebrated coffeehouse, close to Drummond's Bank, which still maintains its reputation. When Dr. Buckland, the geologist, now Dean of Westminster, was Canon of Christ's Church, Oxford, used to visit London, he invariably lived at the Salopian, and his example induced many of "the dons" of Oxford to frequent the house.—M.

clear at the end of the twelvemonth, and that he does not run into debt. On the contrary, I have uniformly found, when a man lives annually on a sum *more* than his year's income—say, five hundred, five thousand, or five hundred thousand pounds—for the sum makes no difference—that *that* man's accounts are liable, at the end of the twelvemonth, to get into confusion, and that it must end by his running into debt. Believe me, sir, that such is the result of my forty and odd years' experience in the world."

The oracular gravity in which this sentence was delivered—for he paused between every word, I might say between every syllable, and kept the uplifted spoon all the time in suspense between the plate of mulligatawny and his lip, which did not receive the savoury contents until the last syllable died away—struck me with peculiar emphasis, and I puzzled my brain to draw out, if possible, something equally profound to give in return. Accordingly, after looking straight across at him for a minute, with my head firmly imbedded on my hands, while my elbows rested on the table, I addressed him thus: "Sir," said I, "I have only lived thirty-three years in the world, and can not, of course, boast of the vast experience which you have had; neither have my reasoning faculties been exerted so laboriously as yours appear to have been; but from twenty years' consideration, I can assure you that I have observed it as a general rule, admitting of no exception, and thereby in itself forming an exception to a general rule, that if a man walks through Piccadilly, or the Strand, or Oxford street—for the street makes no difference, provided it be of sufficient length—without an umbrella or other defence against a shower, during a heavy fall of rain, he is inevitably wet; while, on the contrary, if a man walks through Piccadilly, or the Strand, or Oxford street—for the street makes no difference—during fine dry weather, he runs no chance whatever of being wet to the skin. Believe me, sir, that such is the result of my twenty and odd years' experience in the world."

The elderly gentleman had by this time finished his soup. "Sir," said he, "I agree with you. I like to hear rational conversation. Be so good as to give me your card. Here is mine.

name an early day to dine with me. Waiter, what's to pay? Will you, sir, try my snuff? I take thirty-seven. I wish you, sir, a good morning." So saying, he quitted the box, leaving me to ruminate upon the discovery made by a man who had lived sixty-three years in the world, and had observed its ways for forty and odd years of that period. I thought with myself, that I, too, if I set about it seriously to reflect, might perhaps come to something as striking and original; and have accordingly set about this little work, which I dedicate to your kindness, gentle reader. If from it you can extract even one observation conducive toward making you a better or a happier man, the end has been answered which was proposed to himself by,

Gentle reader,

Your most obedient and

Very humble servant,

MORGAN ODOHERTY.

SALOPIAN, *May* 1, 1824, *P. T. T.*

Maxim First.

IF you intend to drink much *after* dinner, never drink much *at* dinner, and particularly avoid mixing wines. If you begin with Sauterne, for example, stick to Sauterne, though, on the whole, red wines are best. Avoid malt liquor most cautiously; for nothing is so apt to get into the head unawares, or, what is almost as bad, to fill the stomach with wind. Champagne, on the latter account, is bad. Port, three glasses at dinner—claret, three bottles after: behold the fair proportion, and the most excellent wines.

Maxim Second.

IT is laid down in fashionable life, that you must drink champagne after white cheeses—water after red. This is mere nonsense. The best thing to be drunk after cheese is strong ale, for the taste is more coherent. We should always take our ideas of those things from the most constant practitioners. Now, you never hear of a drayman, who lives almost entirely on bread and cheese, thinking of washing it down with water, far less with champagne.* He knows what is better. As for champagne, there is a reason against drinking it after cheese, which I could give if it were cleanly. It is not so, and therefore I am silent concerning it; but it is true.

N. B.—According to apophthegm the first, ale is to be avoided in case a wet night is expected—as should cheese also. I recommend ale only when there is no chance of a man's getting a skinful.

Maxim Third.

A PUNSTER, during dinner, is a most inconvenient animal. He should, therefore, be immediately discomfited. The art of discomfiting a punster is this: Pretend to be deaf; and after he has committed his pun, and just before he expects people to laugh at it, beg his pardon, and request him to repeat it again. After you have made him do this three times, say, O! that is a pun, I believe. I never knew a punster venture a third exhibition under similar treatment. It requires a little nicety, so as to make him repeat it in proper time. If well done, the company laugh at the punster, and then he is ruined for ever.

Maxim Fourth.

A FINE singer, after dinner, is a still greater bore, for he stops the wine. This we pardon in a slang or drinking song, for such things serve as shoeing-horns to draw on more bottles, by jollifying your host; so that, though the supply may be slow, it is more copious in the end; but a fine-song-singer only serves to put people in mind of tea. You, therefore, not only lose the circulation of the bottle while he is getting through his crotchets and quavers, but he actually tends to cut off the final supply. He, then, by all means is to be discouraged. These fellows are are always most insufferably conceited, so that it is not very easy to keep them down—but it is possible, nevertheless. One

* How could a drayman obtain champagne?—M.

of the best rules is, as soon as he has sung the first verse, and while he is taking breath for the second, applaud him most vociferously, as if all was over; and say to the gentleman farthest from you at table, that you admire the conclusion of this song very much. It is ten to one but his musical pride will take affront, and he will refuse to sing any more, saying or muttering something savage about your want of taste or politeness; for that, of course, you will not care three straws, having extinguished him. If the company press him to go on, you are safe, for he will then decidedly grow restive, to show his importance, and you will escape his songs for the rest of the evening.

Or, after he has really done, and is sucking in the bravo of the people at table, stretch across to him and say, You sung that very well, Mr. a-a-a, very well indeed, but did you *not* (laying a most decided emphasis upon the *not*), did you *not* hear Mr. Incledon, or Mr. Braham (or anybody else whom you think most annoying to him) sing in some play, pantomime, or something? When he answers, No, in a pert, snappish style—for all these people are asses—resume your most erect posture, and say quite audibly to your next neighbor—*So I thought.* This twice repeated is a dose.

Maxim Fifth.

BROUGHAM the politician is to be hated, but not so every Brougham. In this apophthegm I particularly have an eye to John Waugh Brougham, Esq., wine-merchant, or οινοῶωλος, in the court of the Pnyx, Athens, and partner of Samuel Anderson, Esq.—a man for whom I have a particular regard. This Mr. Brougham* has had the merit of re-introducing among the

* This Mr. Brougham was a brother of Henry Brougham, Lord Chancellor of England from 1830 to 1834. The firm of Anderson and Brougham were unfortunate as wine merchants. When Lord Brougham had the opportunity (his brother had died in the meantime), he appointed Mr. Anderson to the lucrative office of Registrar of the Court of Chancery, a post which he occupied until his death, four years ago. Anderson is mentioned in the famous Chaldee Manuscript of *Blackwood's Magazine*, in the following verse: "And in the fourth band I saw the face of Samuel which is a mason, who is clothed in glorious apparel, and his face was as the face of the moon shining in the north-

αὐτοχθονες of Attica the custom of drinking *Vin de Bordeaux* from the tap — a custom which, more especially in hot weather, is deserving of much commendation and diligent observance. One gets the tipple much cheaper in this way; and I have found, by personal experience, that the headache, of which copious potation of this potable is productive, yields at once to a dose of the Seidlitz, whereas that arising from old-bottled claret not unfrequently requires a touch of the Glauber — an offensive salt, acting harshly and ungenteelly upon the inner Adam.

Maxim Sixth.

A WHIG is an ass.*

Maxim Seventh.

TAP claret tastes best out of a pewter pot. There is something solemn and affecting in these renewals of the antique observances of the symposium. I never was so pleasantly situated as the first time I saw on the board of friend Francis Jeffrey, Esq., editor of a periodical work published in Athens, a man for whom I have a particular regard, an array of these venerable concerns, inscribed "More Majorum." Mr. Hallam furnished the classic motto to Mr. Jeffrey, who is himself as ignorant of Latin as Mr. Cobbett; for he understood the meaning to be, "more in the jorum," until Mr. Pillans expounded to him the real meaning of Mr. Hallam.†

west." This was in 1817. In No. LXV. of the "Noctes Ambrosianæ" (May 1834) Anderson is introduced as one of North's guests, under the name of "Registrar Sam," and, whether in conversation, singing, or translating from the Greek — is made to keep up the ball agreeably and cleverly, with Old Kit, Hogg, and Tickler.—M.

* This was the constant assertion of Blackwood.—M.

† Lord Jeffrey (born in 1773 and died in 1850) edited the *Edinburgh Review* for nearly thirty years, and exercised great influence on the public mind, in literature and politics, as a critic and partisan. Under him, the *Review* was the organ and champion of the Whig party in Great Britain, from the premiership of Pitt, in 1802, to that of Wellington, in 1829. In parliament, which he entered at the age of 63, Jeffrey completely failed. In 1834, he was made a Scottish Judge, in which capacity he gave general satisfaction. — Mr

Maxim Eighth.

A STORY-TELLER is so often a mighty pleasant fellow, that it may be deemed a difficult matter to decide whether he ought to be stopped or not. In case, however, that it be required, far the best way of doing it is this: After he has discharged his first tale, say across, to some confederate (for this method requires confederates, like some jugglers' tricks), *Number one.* As soon as he has told a second, in like manner say, *Number two.* Perhaps he may perceive it, and if so, he stops: if not, the very moment his third story is told, laugh out quite loud, and cry to your friend, "I trouble you for the sovereign. You see I was right, when I betted that he would tell these three stories exactly in that order, in the first twenty minutes after his arrival in the room." Depend on it he is mum after that.

Maxim Ninth.

IF your host is curious in wines, he deserves much encouragement, for the mere operation of tasting seven or eight kinds of wine, goes far toward pouching for you an additional bottle However, it may happen that he is becoming a bore by bamming you with stuff of wine, which he says is sherry of God knows how long, or hock of the days of Noah, and it all the while the rinsing of wine-tubs. That must be put down with the utmost severity. Good manners will not permit you to tell him the truth, and rebel at once under such unworthy treatment; but if you wear a stiff collar, *à la George Quatre,** much may be done by turning your head round on the top of the vertebræ, and asking him in the most cognoscenti style, "Pray, sir,

Hallam, the historian of the Middle Ages, is one of the best classical scholars in England. Byron's satire mentioned him as

"Classic Hallam, much renowned for Greek,"

and was personally severe on "paltry Pillars," who has long been Professor of Latin in the University of Edinburgh.—M.

* The high black stock, worn during the first five-and-thirty years of the present century, was introduced by George IV., when Prince of Wales, to hide the marks of scrofula on his neck and the lower part of his face.—M.

have you ever tasted sheeraz,* the favourite wine of Hafiz, you know?"—Perhaps he may have tasted it, and thereby defeat you by saying so; in which case you must immediately make a double reserve by adding—"For it always puts me in mind of that famous Chinese wine that they make at Yang-poo-tchoo-foo-nim-pang, which strikes me to be most delicious drinking." If you beat him this way two or three times, by mentioning wines he never heard of, [and in order to make quite sure of that, it will be best to mention those which never were in existence,] you will out-crow him in the opinion of the company, and he, finding his popularity declining, will not go on with any further display.

Maxim Tenth.

On the subject of the last apophthegm, it must be remarked, that you should know that the most famous Rhenish is made at Johannisberg, a very small farm—so small, that every drop made on it is consumed by the proprietor, Prince Metternich, or given away to crowned heads.† You can always dumfound any

* Respecting this wine, an amusing anecdote is related in Lockhart's Life of Scott. Sir John Malcolm, alike distinguished as a diplomatist, soldier, and man of letters, who had been British Minister at the Court of Persia, sent Sir Walter a butt of sheeraz, from Ispahan. Some years after, at Abbotsford, it was mentioned that such a wine had been received, and some of it was ordered up, Scott remarking that *he* had no recollection of any thing extraordinary in the flavor or appearance of the wine. It turned out that it had been bottled and binned as *Sherry!* As every body has not "tasted sheeraz, the favorite wine of Hafiz," the poet, and as I have (it was brought over by the late Admiral Ranier, and had been forty-six years in bottle when it reached my lips), I beg to say that it resembles Madeira in color, and in taste is a cross between the best quality of that fine wine, and the most delicate Sherry.—M.

† This is not exactly the case. The castle of Johannisberg is situated on a hill in the Rheingau. The estate is famous for its Rhenish wines, the best quality of which is made on the castle-hill itself. Napoleon presented castle and vineyards to Marshal Kellermann, in 1807. They were reclaimed, in 1814, by the Emperor of Austria, who gave them to his prime Minister, Prince Metternich, in 1816, on condition of receiving a tenth of the annual produce. The sixty acres of this land yield about 32,500 bottles—but, in favorable vintage years this quantity has been doubled. This is the *best* wine, for an inferior quality is also produced in the same locality. The price is very high—some of the older Johannisberg has been sold at the rate of $15 to $20 a bottle—but the

panegyrist of his Rhine wine, by mentioning this circumstance. "Ay, ay," you may say, "it is pretty passable stuff, but it is *not* Johannisberg. I lived three years in that part of the country, and I flatter myself I am a judge."

Maxim Eleventh.

THE reverend Edward Irving, a man for whom I have a particular regard, is nevertheless a quack.* I never saw so horrible a squint—gestures so uncouth, a "tottle of the whole" so abominable. He is a dandy about his hair and his shirt-collar. He is no more an orator than his countryman Joseph† is a philosopher. Set down as maxim the eleventh, that every popular preacher is a goose.

Maxim Twelfth.

THE work "De Tribus Impostoribus" never had any exist-

cultivation of this particular vineyard is so expensive and the cost of manufacture so dear (from the great care required), that the profit is by no means large. Johannisberg *can* be purchased, but at a costly price. It may simply be described as the finest Rhenish in the world. When the cork is drawn, the aromatic perfume from the wine literally pervades the atmosphere. Of course, ice should never go near it.—M.

* If not actually "a quack," the Rev. Edward Irving, during his early popularity as a preacher in London, had many very quackish ways. He was born in 1792, and, as Minister of the Scottish Church, became assistant to Dr. Chalmers, then of St. John's Church, Glasgow. In 1823, he was engaged as preacher to the Caledonian Asylum, in Hatton Garden, London. Here the novelty of his style and manner, and the striking peculiarity of his personal appearance (he was tall and slight, with long dark hair parted on his forehead and falling in curls on his shoulders, to say nothing of a decided obliquity of vision) immediately made him popular. His sermons, when published, were simply clever—so much did they owe to his peculiar delivery. In 1827–'30, Irving's religious opinions became so eccentric (he had taken up with "prophecy" and "the gift of tongues") that he was formally deposed from the Ministry, by the Scottish Church, on the proven charge of heresy. He died in December, 1834, of premature old age. Theodore Hook squibbed him as "Dr. Squintem"—but the nickname, poor as it was, was not even original, as Foote had applied it, long before, to the Rev. George Whitefield, the preacher.—M.

† Joseph Hume was "Father of the House," as the oldest member of the House of Commons. He was born in 1778 and died Feb. 20, 1855.—M.

ence.* — Well, be it so — I intend to supply this deficiency soon, and my trio shall consist of Neddy Irving, Joe Hume, and The Writer Tam.† Three men for whom I have a particular regard.

Maxim Thirteenth.

POETRY does not sell again in England for thirty years to come. Mark my words. No poetry sells at present, except Scott's and Byron's, and these not much. None of even their later poems have sold. Halidon Hill, Don Juan, &c. &c. are examples of what I mean. Wordsworth's poetry never sold: ditto Southey's: ditto even Coleridge's, which is worth them both put together: ditto John Wilson's: ditto Lamb's: ditto Lloyd's: ditto Miss Baillie's: ditto Rogers'; ditto Cottle's, of whom Canning singeth: —

> "Great Cottle, not HE whom the ALFRED made famous,
> But JOSEPH, of BRISTOL — the BROTHER of AMOS."

There was a pause in poetry-reading from the time of Pope till the time of Goldsmith. Again, there was a dead stop between Goldy and the appearance of the Scots Minstrelsy. We have now got enough to keep our fancy from starvation for thirty or forty years to come. I hate repletion.

Maxim Fourteenth.

POETRY is like claret, one enjoys it only when it is very new,‡ or when it is very old.

Maxim Fifteenth.

IF you want good porter in London, you must always inquire where there is a stand of coal-heavers. The gentlemen of the

* The three personages whose merits were discussed in a book which (Odoherty says) "never had any existence" were Moses, Jesus Christ, and Mahomet. — M.

† By "the Writer Tam" was indicated Thomas Campbell the poet, who, at this time, was editor of the *New Monthly Magazine.* — M.

‡ Very old claret is rarely equal to expectation. Very new, when the wine is really good, is admirable tipple, if drawn out of the hogshead, in a cellar where the temperature is even. — M.

press have voted porter ungenteel of late, after the manner of the Tenth.* They deal chiefly in gin and water, at threepence sterling the tumbler; and their chief resorts are the Wrekin, and Offley's Burton ale-house, near Covent-Garden, where He of the Trombone† and I have occasionally amused ourselves contemplating their orgies. The Finish is a place where they may also be seen now and then—I mean the upper ranks. The Cyder Cellar I do not admire—nor the Eccentric neither—but *chacun à son gout.*

Maxim Sixteenth.

THE Londoners have got a great start of the provincials, Irish, Scotch, Yorkshire, &c., in the matter of dinner hours. I consider five or even six o'clock, as too early for a man deeply engaged in business. By dining at seven or eight, one gains a whole hour or two of sobriety, for the purpose of transacting the more serious affairs of life. In other words, no man can do anything but drink after dinner;‡ and thus it follows that the later one dines, the less does one's drinking break in upon that valuable concern, time, of which, whatever may be the case with others, I, for one, have always had more than of money. A man, however busy, who sits down to dinner as eight strikes, may say to himself with a placid conscience—Come, fair play is a jewel—the day is over—nothing but boozing until bed-time.

Maxim Seventeenth.

JOHN MURRAY is a first-rate fellow in his way, but he should not publish so many baddish books, written by gentlemen and ladies, who have no merit except that of figuring in the elegant

* The Tenth Hussars, a regiment which, by the intolerable puppyism of its officers, became excessively unpopular in Dublin in 1822–'3.—M.

† "He of the Trombone" was Mordecai Mullion, one of the occasional guests at "THE NOCTES" (where he figured as North's secretary) and wholly a fictitious personage.—M.

‡ In England, this habit of drinking after dinner has very much declined, since the first publication of these Maxims. At present, a man would be very oddly regarded who would seriously say, at 8 P. M., "the day is over—nothing but boozing until bed-time."—M.

coteries of May-fair. There seems to me to be no greater impertinence than that of a man of fashion pretending to understand the real feelings of man. A Byron, or so, appears once in a hundred years or so, perhaps; but then even Byron was always a *roué*, and had seen the froth foam over the side of many a pewter pot, ere he attempted to sing Childe Harold's melancholious moods. A man has no conception of the true sentimental sadness of the poetic mind, unless he has been blind-drunk once and again, mixing tears with toddy, and the heigho with the hiccup. What can these dandies know who have never even spent a cool morning in The Shades? No good poetry was ever written by a character in silk stockings. Hogg writes in corduroy breeches and top-boots: Coleridge in black breeches and gray worsteds: Sir Walter in rig-and-furrows: Tom Moore in Connemaras, all his good songs—Lalla Rookh, I opine, in economy-silks: Tom Campbell wrote his old affairs bareheaded and without breeches—Ritter Bann, on the contrary, smells of natty stocking pantaloons, and a scratch wig: Lord Byron wears cossacks in spite of Almacks: Allan Cunningham sports a leathern apron: William Wordsworth rejoices in velveteens: and Willison Glass the same.* It is long since I have seen Dr. Southey, but I understand he has adopted the present fashion of green silk stockings with gold clocks: Barry Cornwall wears a tawny waistcoat of beggar's velvet, with silver frogs, and a sham platina chain twisted through two button holes. Leigh Hunt's yellow breeches are well known:†—So are my own Wellingtons, for that matter.

Maxim Eighteenth.

LORD BYRON recommends hock and soda-water in the crop-sickness. My own opinion is in favor of five drops of laudanum,

* Willison Glass kept a small public-house in Edinburgh, wherein he composed punch and poetry—of which the former was by far the best. In September, 1819, Wilson introduced him into the article "Christopher in the Tent," which preceded the first appearance of THE NOCTES, in March, 1822.—M.

† Leigh Hunt was educated at Christ's Hospital, London, where the costume (the same as when the school was endowed by its founder, Edward VI.) consists of a long gown of blue cloth, with yellow hose and breeches.—M.

and a teaspoonful of vinegar, in a tumbler of fair spring water. Try this: although much may also be said in praise of that maxim which Fielding has inserted in one of his plays—the Covent-Garden Tragedy, I think,—videlicet, that "the most grateful of all drinks

'Cool small-beer unto the waking drunkard."

Maxim Nineteenth.

NOTHING can be more proper than the late parliamentary grant of half a million for the building of new churches.

Maxim Twentieth.

WHAT I said in Maxim Third, of stopping punsters, must be understood with reservation. Puns are frequently provocative. One day, after dinner with a Nabob, he was giving us Madeira—

London—East India—picked—particular,

then a second thought struck him, and he remembered that he had a few flasks of Constantia in the house, and he produced *one*. He gave us just a glass a-piece. We became clamorous for another, but the old qui-hi was firm in refusal. "Well, well," said Sydney Smith, a man for whom I have a particular regard, "since we can't double the Cape, we must e'en go back to Madeira." We all laughed—our host most of all—and he too, luckily, had his joke. "Be of Good Hope, you shall double it;" at which we all laughed still more immoderately, and drank the second flask.

Maxim Twenty-first.

WHAT stuff in Mrs. Hemans, Miss Porden,* &c. &c., to be writing plays and epics! There is no such thing as female genius. The only good things that women have written, are

* Eleanor Anne Porden, born in 1795, wrote a poem called "The Veils," at the age of seventeen. Her next was "The Arctic Expedition," which introduced her to Captain (the late Sir John) Franklin, whom she married. Her last and principal work was the epic of "Cœur de Lion." She died in 1825, a few days after her husband had sailed from England on his second Arctic Expedition.—M.

Sappho's Ode upon Phaon, and Madame de Stael's Corinne; and of these two good things the inspiration is simply and entirely that one glorious feeling, in which, and in which alone, woman is the equal of man.

Maxim Twenty-second.

THERE is a kind of mythological jacobitism going just now which I cannot patronise. You see Barry Cornwall, and other great poets of his calibre, running down Jupiter and the existing dynasty very much, and bringing up old Saturn and the Titans. This they do in order to show off learning and depth, but they know nothing after all of the sky gods. I have long had an idea of writing a dithyrambic in order to show these fellows how to touch off mythology. Here is a sample—

Come to the meeting, there's drinking and eating,
  Plenty and famous, your bellies to cram;
Jupiter Ammon, with gills red as salmon,
  Twists round his eyebrows the horns of a ram.

Juno the she-cock has harnessed her peacock,
  Warming the way with a drop of a dram;
Phœbus Apollo in order will follow,
  Lighting the road with his old patent flam.

Cuckoldy Vulcan, dispatching a full can,
  Limps to the banquet on tottering ham;
Venus her sparrows, and Cupid his arrows,
  Sport on th' occasion — fine infant and dam.

Mars, in full armour, to follow his charmer,
  Looks as ferocious as Highlander Sam;
Jocus and Comus ride tandem with Momus,
  Cheering the road with gibe, banter, and bam.

Madam Latona, the old Roba Bona,
  Simpering as mild as a fawn or a lamb,
Drives with Aurora the red-nosed Signora,
  With fingers as rosy as raspberry jam.

There is real mythology for you!

Maxim Twenty-third.

THE English really are, after all, a mighty 'cute people. I never went anywhere when I was first imported, that they did not find me out to be an Irishman, the moment I opened my mouth. And how think ye? Because I used at first to call always for a *pot* of porter; whereas, in England, they never drink more than a pint at a draught.

Maxim Twenty-fourth.

I do not agree with Doctor Adam Clarke's translation of כחדוי, in Genesis.* I think it must mean a serpent, not an ou-rang-outang. Bellamy's Ophion is, however, a weak work, which does not answer Clarke, for whom he is evidently no match on the score of learning. There is, after all, no antipathy between serpents and men naturally, as is proved by the late experiments of Monsieur Neille in America.

Maxim Twenty-fifth.

A man saving his wine must be cut up savagely. Those who wish to keep their expensive wines pretend they do not like them. You meet people occasionally who tell you it is bad taste to give champagne at dinner — at least in *their* opinion — Port and Teneriffe being such superior drinking. Some, again, patronise Cape Madeira, and tell you that the *smack* is very agreeable — adding sometimes, in a candid and patriotic tone, that even if it were not, it would become *us* to try to bring it into fashion, it being the only wine grown in his Majesty's dominions.

In Ireland and Scotland they always smuggle in the tumblers or the bowl. Now, I hold that if punch was raised by taxation or otherwise, (but Jupiter Ammon avert the day!) to a guinea a-bottle, every body would think it the balmiest, sweetest, dearest, and most splendid of fluids — a fluid to which King Burgundy or Emperor Tokay themselves should hide their diminished heads, and it is, consequently, a liquor which I quaff most joyously — but *never* when I think it brought in from any other motive than mere affection to itself. I remember dining one day with Lord ——, (I spare his name,)† in the south of Ire-

* *Vide* Maxim LXXXI. — M.

† The peer was Viscount Doneraile, of Doneraile House, County of Cork, who died in March, 1854, and was what the Irish call "a *near* man" — i. e.,

land, and my friend Charley Crofts was also of the party. The claret went lazily round the table, and his lordship's toad-eaters hinted that they preferred punch, and called for hot water. My lord gave in, after a humbug show of resistance, and whisky punch was in a few minutes the order of the night. Charley, however, to the annoyance of the host, kept swilling away at the claret, on which Lord —— lost all patience, and said to him, "Charley, you are missing quite a treat—this punch is so excellent."—"Thank ye, my lord," said Charley; "I am a plain man, who does not want trates—I am no epicure, so I stick to the claret."

Maxim Twenty-sixth.

WHEN a man is drunk, it is no matter upon what he has got drunk.*

> He sucks with equal throat, as up to all,
> Tokay from Hungary, or beer the small. POPE.

Maxim Twenty-seventh.

THE great superiority of Blackwood's Magazine over all other works of our time is, that one *can* be allowed to speak one's mind there. There never yet was one word of genuine unsophisticated truth in the Edinburgh, the Quarterly, or indeed in any other of the Periodicals—in relation, I mean, to any thing that can be called opinion or sentiment. All is conventional mystification, except in Ebony, the jewel, alone. Here alone can a man tell smack out that he is a Tory, an Orangeman, a Radical, a Catholic, anything he pleases to be, to the backbone. No necessity for conciliatory mincing and paring away of one's own intellect. I love whisky punch; I say so. I ad-

a mean and saving man. Charley Crofts, the actual hero of this anecdote, was a decayed *Squireen*, who had once been in good circumstances, and was a welcome guest at the tables of those who had known his more prosperous days. Such a mixture of shrewdness and blunders, simplicity and wit has rarely existed—even in Ireland. But he deserves a separate and full-length sketch, and may have it one of these days, perhaps.—M.

* The orthodoxy of this aphorism is very questionable. Let a man get drunk on mixed liquors, and his stomach will be out of order next day. Not so, with rare exceptions, if he imbibe only one fluid and stick to that.—M.

mire Wordsworth and Don Juan; I say so. Southey is a humbug; well, let it be said distinctly. Tom Campbell is in his dotage; why conceal a *fact* like this? I scorn all paltering with the public — I hate all shuffling, equivocating, trick, stuff, nonsense. I write in Blackwood, because there Morgan ODoherty can be Morgan ODoherty. If I wrote in the Quarterly, I should be bothered partly with, and partly without, being conscious of it, with a hampering, binding, fettering, nullifying sort of notion, that I must make myself, *pro tempore*, a bit of a Gifford* — and so of every thing else.

Maxim Twenty-eighth.

MUCH is to be said in favour of toasted cheese for supper. It is the cant to say, that Welsh rabbit is heavy eating.† I know this; but have I really found it to be so in my own case? Certainly not. I like it best in the genuine Welsh way, however — that is, the toasted bread buttered on both sides profusely, then a layer of cold roast beef, with mustard and horse-radish, and then, on the top of all, the superstratum of Cheshire *thoroughly* saturated, while in the process of toasting, with cwrw,‡ or, in its absence, genuine porter, black pepper, and shallot vinegar. I peril myself upon the assertion, that this is not a heavy supper for a man who has been busy all day till dinner, in reading, writing, walking, or riding — who has occupied himself between dinner and supper in the discussion of a bottle or two of sound wine, or any equivalent — and who proposes to swallow at least three tumblers of something hot, ere he resigns himself to the embrace of Somnus. With these provisoes, I recommend toasted cheese for supper. And I bet half-a-crown that Kitchener|| coincides with me as to this.

* William Gifford, who was editor of the *Quarterly Review*, from its establishment in 1809 until 1824. — M.

† Are heavy suppers injurious? Does not the process of digestion quietly proceed in sleep? — M.

‡ Cwrw, pronounced *croo*, is the name of ale, in Wales. — M.

|| Dr. William Kitchener (born in 1775, died in 1827), wrote "The Cook's Oracle" and other works, through all of which ran a vein of eccentricity. He was eminently social, and, at his hospitable table, entertained his friends with the fruits of his gastronomic and culinary practice and precept. — M.

Maxims of O'Doherty.

PART THE SECOND.

Introduction.

GENTLE READER,

FEW pieces of cant are more common than that which consists in re-echoing the old and ridiculous cry of "variety is charming;" "*toujours perdrix,*" &c. &c. &c. I deny the fact. I want no variety. Let things be really good, and I, for one, am in no danger of wearying of them. For example, to rise every day about half after nine — eat a couple of eggs and muffins, and drink some cups of genuine, sound, clear coffee — then to smoke a cigar or so — read the Chronicle* — skim a few volumes of some first-rate new novel, or perhaps pen a libel or two in a light sketchy vein — then to take a bowl of strong, rich, invigorating soup — then to get on horseback, and ride seven or eight miles, paying a visit to some amiable, well-bred, accomplished young lady, in the course of it, and chattering away an hour with her,

> "Sporting with Amaryllis in the shade,
> Or with the tangles of Neæra's hair,"

as Milton expresses it — then to take a hot-bath, and dress — then to sit down to a plain substantial dinner, in company with a select party of real good, honest, jolly Tories — and to spend the rest of the evening with them over a pitcher of cool Chateau-Margot,

* In 1824, The *Morning Chronicle,* which Mr. James Perry, its late proprietor, had raised into great popularity, was read by Whig and Tory, as the metropolitan organ of the liberal party. — M.

singing, laughing, speechifying, blending wit and wisdom, and winding up the whole with a devil and a tumbler or two of hot rum-punch.—This, repeated day after day, week after week, month after month, and year after year, may perhaps appear, to some people, a picture pregnant with ideas of the most sickening and disgusting monotony. Not so with me, however. I am a plain man. I could lead this dull course of uniform unvaried existence for the whole period of the Millenium. Indeed I mean to do so.

Hoping that you, benevolent reader, after weighing matters with yourself in calm contemplation for a few minutes, may be satisfied that the view I have taken is the right one—I now venture to submit to your friendly notice a small additional slice of the same genuine honest cut-and-come-again dish, to which I recently had the honor of introducing you. Do not, therefore, turn up your nose in fashionable fastidiousness; but mix your grog, light your pipe, and—laying out your dexter leg before you in a comfortable manner upon a well-padded chair, or sofa, or footstool, (for the stuffing of the cushion, not the form of the furniture, is the point of real importance,) and, above all, take particular care that your cravat, braces, waistband, &c. &c. &c., be duly relaxed—proceed, I say, with an easy body, and a well-disposed, humble, and meditative mind, to cast your eye over a few more of those "pebbles," (to use a fine expression of the immortal Burke,) which have been rounded and polished by long tossing about in the mighty ocean of the intellect of,

Gentle reader,

Your most devoted servant,

MORGAN ODOHERTY.

BLUE POSTS, *June* 19, 1824

Maxim Twenty-ninth.

WHENEVER there is any sort of shadow of doubt as to the politics of an individual, that individual has reason to be ashamed of his politics—in other words, he is a WHIG. A Tory always deals above board.* Your Whig, on the other hand, particularly your Whigling, or young Whig, may have, and in point of fact, very often has, his private reasons for wishing to keep the stain of which he is conscious as much in the shade as may be. It is wonderful how soon such characters make up their minds when they are once fairly settled in a good thing.

Maxim Thirtieth.

HOCK cannot be too much, claret cannot be too little, iced. Indeed, I have my doubts whether any red wine should ever see the ice-pail at all. Burgundy, unquestionably, never should; and I am inclined to think, that with regard to hermitage, claret, &c., it is *always* quite sufficient to wrap a wet towel (or perhaps a wisp of wet straw is better still) about the bottle, and put it in the draft of a shady window for a couple of hours before enjoyment. I do not mention port, because that is a winter wine.†

Maxim Thirty-first.

IN whatever country one is, one should choose the dishes of the country.‡ Every really national dish is good—at least, I never yet met with one that did not gratify my appetite. The Turkish pilaws are most excellent—but the so-called French

* In those days, when Toryism had been "Lord of th' ascendant" for forty years—with a brief interregnum for the few months that Fox and "All the Talents" has obtained office—it was the fashion for Tory writers to laud their own party, its leaders, its principles, and its members, as exclusively national, honest, conservative, and respectable. From his earliest start in life, Dr. Maginn was a Tory. Under the Magazine *sobriquet* of Sir Morgan Odoherty, he was more particularly Conservative in his professions.—M.

† That "hock can not be too much iced" is an assertion not sustained by fact. As a summer wine, hock should be kept *cool*, but not artificially *cold*. Drinking it out of green glasses is intended to carry out the idea of coolness. Red wine—claret, port, hermitage, &c.—should be rather *warm* than *cold*. Hock is utterly ruined by being put into the ice-pail. There is nothing more absurd than icing the Rhenish wines—it is a needless painting of the lily.—M.

‡ Of course—but with exceptions. A plain man (like Charley Crofts) and "not fond of trates," could willingly dispense with an *entremet* of seal-fat or whale-blubber, which is one of the national dishes of the Esquimaux.—M.

cookery of Pera is execrable.* In like manner, roast beef with Yorkshire pudding is always a prime feast in England, while John Bull's *Fricandeaux soufflés*, &c., are decidedly anathema. What a horror, again, is a *Bifstick* of the Palais Royal! On the same principle—(for all the fine arts follow exactly the same principles)—on the same principle it is, that while Principal Robertson, Dugald Stewart, Dr. Thomas Brown, and all the other would-be-English writers of Scotland,† have long since been voted tame, insipid, and tasteless diet, the real haggis-bag of a Robert Burns keeps, and must always keep, its place.

Maxim Thirty-second.

NEVER take lobster-sauce to salmon; it is mere painting of the lily, or, I should rather say, of the rose. The only true sauce for salmon is vinegar, mustard, Cayenne pepper, and parsley. Try this *once*, my dear Dr. Kitchener, and I have no hesitation in betting three tenpennies‡ that you will never depart from it again while the breath of gastronomy is in your nostrils. As for the lobster, either make soup of him, or eat him cold (with cucumber) at supper.||

Maxim Thirty-third.

I TALKED in the last maxim of cold lobster for supper; but this requires explanation. If by accident you have dined in a quiet way, and deferred for once the main business of existence until the night, then eat cold lobsters, cold beef, or cold any

* The French cookery in all parts of the Ottoman Empire *is* execrable. But the Turkish dishes are good. With hunger for sauce, the *pilau* is acceptable, and a platter of *kabobs* by no means to be treated lightly, with or without hunger, especially when followed by fine Mocha and a *chibouque*.—M.

† There is something particularly cool in Odoherty's thus, in a Scotch magazine, affecting to speak contemptuously of Robertson, Stewart, and Brown—writers of whom Scotland is proud, and with reason.—M.

‡ In 1824, part of the silver coinage of Ireland consisted of Bank Tokens, of tenpence and fivepence respectively. They were called *tenpennies* and *fivepennies*. In 1825, these coins were withdrawn, and the Irish assimilated to the British, or as Paddy called it, the "Breeches money."—M.

|| Of lobster-salad, Odoherty appears to have had no knowledge! Wonderful ignorance in a gourmand.—M.

thing you like for supper; but in the ordinary case, when a man has already got his two bottles, or perhaps three under his belt, depend on it, the supper of that man should be hot—hot—hot—

"Nunquam aliud Natura, aliud Sapientia docet."

Such is my simple view of the matter; but a friend at my elbow, who is always for refining on things, says, that the philosophical rule is this—"When you have been drinking cold wine or cold punch, your supper ought to be a devil, or at least something partaking of the devil character; and, on the other hand, when you have been swallowing mulled wine, or hot punch, or hot toddy, something cold, with vinegar, salad, &c., should form the supper."—I have given you my friend's theory in his own words.—If men of sense would but communicate the results of their different experiments to the public, we should soon have abundant *data* for the settlement of all these disputes.

Maxim Thirty-fourth.

It is a common thing to hear big wigs prosing against *drinking*, as "a principal source of the evil that we see in this world." I heard a very big wig say so myself the other day from the bench, and we have all heard the same cant, *ad nauseam usque*, from the pulpit. There cannot, however, be a more egregious mistake. Had Voltaire, Robespierre, Buonaparte, Talleyrand, &c., been all a set of jolly, boozing lads, what a mass of sin and horror, of blasphemy, uproar, blood-thirsty revolution, wars, battles, sieges, butcherings, ravishings, &c. &c. &c., in France, Germany, Egypt, Spain, Sicily, Syria, North America, Portugal, &c., had been spared within the last twenty or thirty years! Had Mahomet been a comfortable, social good fellow, devotedly fond of his pipe and pot, would not the world have avoided the whole of the humbug of Islamism?—a superstition, reader, that has chained up and degraded the intellect of man in so many of the finest districts of the globe, during the space of so many long centuries. Is it not manifest, that if Southey had been a greater dealer in quarts, his trade would have been more limited as to quartos?—It is clear, then, that loyalty, religion, and literature, have had occasion, one and all of them, to bemoan not the wine-sop, but the milk-sop, propensities of their most deadly foes.

Maxim Thirty-fifth.

IN making our estimate of a man's character, we should always lay entirely out of view whatever has any connexion with "the womankind." In fact, we all are, or have been, or shall be,—or, if this be too much, we all at least might, could, would, or should be,—Fools, *quoad hoc*. I wish this were the worst of it—but enough.

Maxim Thirty-sixth.

THE next best thing to a really good woman, is a really good-natured one.

Maxim Thirty-seventh.

THE next worst thing to a really bad man, (in other words *a knave*,) is a really good-natured one, (in other words, *a fool*.)

Maxim Thirty-eighth.

A FOOL admires likeness to himself; but, except in the case of fools, people fall in love with something unlike themselves—a tall man with a short woman—a little man with a strapper—fair people with dark—and so on.*

Maxim Thirty-ninth.

A MARRIED woman commonly falls in love with a man as unlike her husband as is possible—but a widow very often marries a man extremely resembling the defunct. The reason is obvious.

Maxim Fortieth.

YOU may always ascertain whether you are in a city or a village, by finding out whether the inhabitants do or do not

* Shakspere had been beforehand in this remark.—M.

care for, or speak about, ANY THING three days after it has happened.

Maxim Forty-first.

THERE are four kinds of men — the Whig who has always been a Whig — the Tory who has once been a Whig — the Whig who has once been a Tory — and the Tory who has always been a Tory. Of these I drink willingly only with the last, — considering the *first* as a fool, the *second* as a knave, and the *third* as both a fool and a knave; but if I must choose among the others, give me the mere fool.

Maxim Forty-second.

NEVER boozify a second time with the man whom you have seen misbehave himself in his cups. I have seen a great deal of life, and I stake myself upon the assertion, that no man ever says or does that brutal thing when drunk, which he would not also say or do when sober, *if he durst.**

Maxim Forty-third

IN literature and in love we generally begin in bad taste. I myself wrote very pompous verses at twenty, and my first flame was a flaunting, airy, artificial attitudiniser, several years older than myself. By means of experience, we educate our imagination, and become sensible to the charm of the simple and the unaffected, both in belles and belles-lettres. Your septuagenarian of accomplished taste discards epithets with religious scrupulosity, and prefers an innocent blushing maiden of sixteen to all the blazing duchesses of St. James's.

Maxim Forty-fourth.

NOTHING is more disgusting than the *coram publico* endearments in which new-married people so frequently indulge themselves. The thing is obviously indecent; but this I could over-

* In the hundred and thirty-fourth Maxim, however, Odoherty contradicts this assertion. — M.

look, were it not also the perfection of folly and imbecility. No wise man counts his coin in the presence of those who, for aught he knows, may be thieves—and no good sportsman permits the *pup* to do that for which the dog must be corrected.

Maxim Forty-fifth.

A HUSBAND should be very attentive to his wife until the first child is born. After that she can amuse herself at home, while he resumes his jolly habits.

Maxim Forty-sixth.

NEVER believe in the intellect of a Whig merely because you hear all the Whigs trumpet him—nay, hold fast your faith that he is a dunderhead, even although the Pluckless pipe symphonious. This is, you will please to observe, merely a plain English version of that good old *adagium:*

> "Mille licet cyphris cyphrarum millia jugas,
> Nil præter magnum conficies nihilum."

Maxim Forty-seventh.

THERE are two methods of mail-coach travelling—the generous and the sparing. I have tried both, and give my voice decidedly for the former. It is all stuff that you hear about eating and drinking plentifully inducing fever, &c. &c., during a long journey. Eating and drinking copiously produce nothing, mind and body being well regulated, but sleepiness—and I know no place where that inclination may be indulged less reprehensibly than in a mail-coach, for at least sixteen hours out of the four-and twenty. In travelling, I make a point to eat whenever I can sit down, and to drink (ale) whenever the coach stops.*

* There is nothing like bringing figures of arithmetic to bear upon figures of speech. In 1824, before railways were in England, the mail-coaches travelled at the rate of twelve miles an hour, and changed horses every eight or nine miles. Take the latter as the average, and, in the sixteen hours of which Odoherty speaks, the coach would have stopped twenty-one times. *Argal*—so many pints of ale to be drank in that period!—M.

As for the interim, when I can neither eat nor drink, I smoke if upon deck, and snuff if inside.

N. B. Of course, I mean when there is no opportunity of flirtation.

Maxim Forty-eighth.

If you meet with a pleasant fellow in a stage-coach, dine and get drunk with him, and, still holding him to be a pleasant fellow, hear from his own lips just at parting that he is a *Whig*—do not change your opinion of the man. Depend on it he is quizzing you.

Maxim Forty-ninth.

Show me the young lady that runs after preachers—and I will show you one who has no particular aversion to men.

Maxim Fiftieth.

There are only three liquors that harmonise with smoking—beer—coffee—and hock. Cigars altogether destroy the flavour of claret, and indeed of all red wines, except *Auchmanshaüser;* which, in case you are not knowing in such matters, is the produce of the Burgundy grape transplanted to the banks of the Rhine—a wine for which I have a particular regard.

Maxim Fifty-first.

He whose friendship is worth having, must hate and be hated.

Maxim Fifty-second.

Your highly popular young lady seldom—I believe I might say *never*—inspires a true, deep, soul-filling passion. I cannot suppose Juliet d'Etagne to have been a favourite partner in a ball-room. She could not take the trouble to smile upon so many fops.

Maxim Fifty-third.

THE intensely amorous temperament in a young girl never fails to stamp melancholy on her eye-lid. The lively, rattling, giggling romp, may be capable of a love of her own kind—but never the true luxury of the passion.

Maxim Fifty-fourth.

NO fool can be in love.—N. B. It has already been laid down, that all good-natured *men* are fools.

Maxim Fifty-fifth.

NOTHING is more over-rated, in common parlance at least, than the influence of personal handsomeness in men.* For my part, I can easily imagine a woman (I mean one really worth being loved by) falling in love with a Balfour of Burleigh, but I cannot say the same thing as to a young Milnwood. A real Rebecca would, I also think, have been more likely to fall in love with the Templar than with Ivanhoe; but these, I believe, were both handsome fellows in their several styles. The converse of all this applies to the case of women. Rousseau did not dare to let the small-pox permanently injure the beauty of his Heloise. One would have closed the book had he destroyed the *sine quâ non* of all romance.

Maxim Fifty-sixth.

WHENEVER you see a book frequently advertised, you may be pretty sure it is a bad one. If you see a *puff* quoted in the advertisements, you may be quite sure.

Maxim Fifty-seventh.

EMPLOY but one tradesman of the same trade, and let him be the *first* man in his line. He has the best materials, and can

* Curran, the Irish orator, who was particularly unhandsome, was wont to say (what John Wilkes, who squinted, had said before him) that give him half an hour the start in the society of a fine woman, and he would not care for the rivalry of an Adonis. What are called *pretty* men are not generally acceptable to the fair sex—these popinjays too much resemble themselves.—M.

give the best tick; and one long bill is, at all times, a mere trifle on a man's mind, compared with three short ones.

Maxim Fifty-eighth.

I CANNOT very well tell the reason, but such is the fact,—the best boots and shoes are made at York. I mean as to the quality of the leather.*

Maxim Fifty-ninth.

BE on your guard when you hear a young lady speak slightingly of a young gentleman with whom she has any sort of acquaintance. She is probably in love with him, and will be sure to remember what you say after she is married. But if you have been heedless enough to follow her lead, and abuse him, you must make the best of it. If you have great face, go boldly at one, and, drawing her into a corner, say, "Aha! do you remember a certain conversation we had? Did you think I was not up to your tricks all the time?" Or, better still, take the *bull* by the horns, and say, "So ho! you lucky dog. I could have prophesied this long ago. She and I were always at you when we met: she thought I did not see through the affair. Poor girl! she was desperately in for it, to be sure. By Jupiter, what a fortunate fellow you have been!" &c. &c. &c. Or, best of all, follow my own plan—*i. e.* don't call till the honeymoon is over.

Maxim Sixtieth.

IT is the prevailing humbug for authors to abstain from putting their names on their title-pages; and well may I call this a humbug, since of every book that ever attracts the smallest attention, the author is instantly just as well known as if he had clapt his portrait to the beginning of it. This nonsense sometimes annoys me; and I have a never-failing method. My way is this: I do not, as other people do, utter modest, mincing little

* This was before, by the reduction of the high protective duty, French leather had come into general use in England.—M.

compliments, in hopes of seeing the culprit blush, and thereby betray himself. This is much too pretty treatment for a man guilty of playing upon the public; and, besides, few of them *can* blush. I pretend the most perfect ignorance of the prevailing, and, of course, just suspicion; and the moment the work is mentioned, I begin to abuse it up hill and down dale. The company tip me the wink, nod, frown in abundance — no matter. On I go, *mordicus*, and one of two things is the result, viz. — either the anonymous hero waxeth wroth, and in that case the cat is out of the poke for ever and a day; or he takes it in good part, keeping his countenance with perfect composure; and then it is *proved* that he is really a sensible fellow, and by consequence really has a right to follow his own fancies, however ridiculous.

Maxim Sixty-first.

LORD BYRON* observes, that the daily necessity of shaving imposed upon the European male, places him on a level, as to misery, with the sex to whose share the occasional botheration of parturition has fallen. I quite agree with his lordship: and in order to diminish, as far as in me lies, the pains of my species, I hereby lay down the result of my experience in abrasion. If I had ever lain-in, I would have done my best for the ladies too. But to proceed: First, then, buy your razors at PAGET'S — a queer, dark-looking, little shop in Piccadilly, a few doors eastward from the head of St. James's Street. He is a decent, shrewd, intelligent old man — makes the best blades in Europe — tempers every one of them with his own hand — and would sooner cut his throat than give you a second-rate article. Secondly, In stropping your razor, (and a piece of plain buff leather is by far the best strop,) play *from* you, not *towards* you. Thirdly, Anoint your beard over night, if the skin be in any degree hard or dry, or out of repair, with cold cream, or, better still, with bear's grease. Fourthly, Whether you have anointed or not, wash your face carefully and copiously before shaving, for the chief difficulty almost always arises from dust, perspiration &c., clogging the roots of the beard. Fifthly, Let your

* Rabelais said so, some time before Don Juan appeared. — C. N.

soap be the Pasta di Castagna. Sixthly, Let your brush be a *full* one of *camel's* hair. Seventhly, In spite of Sir John Sinclair, always use hot water—boiling water. These are the seven golden rules.

N. B. Use the strop again after you have done shaving, and get old Paget, if possible to give you a lesson in setting your razors. If you cannot manage, send them to him to be set—ay, even if you live five hundred miles from London.* People send to town about their coats, boots, &c., but what are all these things to the real comfort of a man, compared with a good razor?

Maxim Sixty-second.

ASS-MILK, they say, tastes exceedingly like woman's. No wonder.

Maxim Sixty-third.

A SMOKER should take as much care about his cigars as a wine-bibber does of his cellar, yet most of them are exceedingly remiss and negligent. The rules are as follows: First, keep a large stock—for good tobacco improves very much by time—say enough for two years' consumption. Secondly, keep them in the coolest place you have, provided it be perfectly dry; for a cigar that is once wet is useless and irreclaimable. Thirdly, keep them *always* in air-tight cannisters—for the common wooden boxes play the devil.

N. B. The tobacco laws are the greatest opprobrium of the British code. We laid those most extravagant duties on tobacco at the time when North America was a part of our own empire, and we still retain them in spite of rhyme and reason. One consequence is, that every *gentleman* who smokes, smuggles; for the duty on manufactured tobacco amounts to a prohibition—it is, I think, no less than eighteen shillings per pound†—and

* This notice of Paget was literally the making of that razor-maker and razor-setter. Immediately after it appeared there was such a rush to the "queer, dark-looking, little shop in Piccadilly," that Paget had great difficulty in meeting the greatly augmented demand for his razors.—M.

† The present duty (in 1855) is a trifle less than what is mentioned here.

what is a pound of cigars? Why does not the Duke of Sussex speak up in the House of Lords? "I like King George, but I can't afford to pay duties," quoth Nanty Ewart;* and I quite agree with the inimitable Nanty.

Maxim Sixty-fourth.

No cigar-smoker ever committed suicide.

Maxim Sixty-fifth.

In making hot toddy, or hot punch, you must put in the spirits before the water: in cold punch, grog, &c., the other way. Let Dr. Hope explain the reason. I state facts.

Maxim Sixty-sixth.

The safety of women consists in one circumstance: Men do not possess at the same time the knowledge of thirty-five and the blood of seventeen.

Maxim Sixty-seventh.

The extreme instance of the *bathos* is this: Any modern sermon *after* the Litany of the Church of England.

Maxim Sixty-eighth.

The finest of all times for flirting is a wedding. They are all agog, poor things!

Maxim Sixty-ninth.

To me there is nothing very stare-worthy in the licentiousness of a few empresses, queens, &c., of whom we have all heard so much. After all, these elevated females only thought themselves the equals of common men.

You can not have a pound of imported cigars in England without paying a duty of eight shillings and sixpence (a trifle over $2) and the mere duty on the unmanufactured or leaf tobacco is two shillings and nine pence a pound.— M.

* In Scott's "Redgauntlet." — M.

Maxim Seventieth.

If prudes were as pure as they would have us believe, they would not rail so bitterly as they do. We do not thoroughly hate that which we do not thoroughly understand.

Maxim Seventy-first.

(Composed after six months' residence in Athens.)

John Brougham for bordeaux,
  Robert Cockburn for champagne,
John Ferguson for hocks,
  Cay for Sherris sack of Spain.

Phin for rod, pirn, and hooks,
  Dunn for congé and salaam,
Bailie Blackwood for books,
  Macvey Napier for balaam.*

Sir Walter for fables,
  Peter Robertson for speeches,
Mr. Trotter for tables,
  Mr. Bridges for breeches.†

Gall for coaches and gigs,
  Steele for ices and jam,
Mr. Urquhart for wigs,
  Mr. Jeffrey for bam.

Lord Morton for the zebra,
  Billy Allan for the brush,
Johnny Leslie for the Hebrew,‡
  And myself for a blush.

---

* Macvey Napier, who died in 1847, was Editor of the *Edinburgh Review*, and the *Encyclopædia Britannica*, after these rhymes appeared. — M.

† "Peter" Robertson's real Christian name was Patrick. He died early in 1855,) one of the Scotch judges. Trotter was the leading upholsterer of Edinburgh in 1824. David Brydges — mentioned in a previous notice — was at once clothier and fine-arts connoisseur. — M.

‡ The Earl of Morton had endeavored to acclimatize the zebra in Scotland. Sir William Allan, the painter, was President of the Royal Scottish Academy, when he died in 1850. There was an ancient feud between Sir John Leslie, the Professor in Edinburgh University, and Maginn — one of the latter's earliest articles in *Blackwood* was an exposure of Leslie's ignorance of the Hebrew language, which he had attempted to criticize. — M.

Maxim Seventy-second.

PEOPLE may talk as they like, but, after all, London is London. Now, somebody will say, here is a foolish tautology—does not everybody know that? Hooly and fairly, my friend—it is ten to one if *you* know it. If you were asked what are the fine things of London?—what is it that gives it its metropolitan and decidedly superior character? You would say Parliament—St. James's—Carlton House—the Parks—Almack's—White's—Brookes's—Crockford's—Boodle's—Regent Street—the Theatres—the Dioramas—the Naturoramas—the fiddle-de-devils. Not one of these is in London, except perhaps the last, for I do not well know what that is—but London itself—the city inside Temple-bar, is the place for a philosopher.

> Houses of lath may flourish or may fade,
> Bob Nash may make them as Bob Nash has made.

But can Bob Nash (*quem honoris causâ nomino*) create the glories of Cockney-land? Can he build a Watling Street—narrow, dirty, irregular, it is true, but still a Roman way, trod by proud Prætors, and still to be walked over by you or me, in the same form as it was trampled by the "hobnail" of the legionary soldier, who did service at Pharsalia? What is London Stone, a black lump in a hole of the wall of a paltry church, (the London Stone Coffee-house opposite is a very fair concern,) but a Roman milliarium, laid down there, for any thing you know to the contrary, by Julius Agricola, who discovered Scotland, and was the friend of Cornelius Tacitus, according to the rules enacted by the roadmeters of old Appius Claudius? But I must not go on with the recollection of London. Curse on the Cockney school of scribblers—they, who know nothing, have, by writing in praise of Augusta Trinobantum, (I use this word on purpose, in order to conceal from them what I mean,) made us sick of the subject. I, therefore, have barely adverted to the Roman times, for luckily they have not had the audacity to pretend to any acquaintance with such a period.

The Court—Why, to be sure, it contains the King, whom, as a Tory, I reverence as an integral portion of the State—I hate to hear him called the Chief Magistrate, as if he was but an upper sort of Lord Waithman* — and whom as a man I regard — but my attachment is constitutional, and in the present case personal, and not local. The same may be said of Parliament. As for the clubs, why, they are but knots of humdrum people after all, out of all which you could not shake five wits. The Almackites are asses — the theatres stuff — the fashionables nothing. In money — in comfort — in cookery — in antiquity — in undying subjects for quizzification — in pretty Jewesses — as Spenser says, F. Q. B. I. C. v. St. xxi.

> ——Jewessa, sunny bright,
> Adorn'd with gold and jewels shinning cleare —

London proper I back against Southwark and Westminster, including all the adjacent *hams*, and *steads*, and *tons*, and *wells*. Where can we find the match for the Albion, in Aldergate Street,† as thou goest from St. Martin-le-Grand to the territory of Goswell Street, in the whole world, take the world either ways, from Melville Island to Van Dieman's Land, or from Yeddo in the Island of Japan, to Iveragh in the kingdom of Kerry, and back again? Nowhere!

But I am straying from my cups.

> Retournons, dist Grand Gousier, à nostre propous.
> Quel? dist Gargantua.

Why, punch-making.

Maxim Seventy-third.

In making 'rack punch, you ought to put two glasses of rum to three of arrack. A good deal of sugar is required; but sweetening, after all, must be left to taste. Kitchener is frequently absurd, when he prescribes by weight and measure for such things. Lemons and limes are also matter of palate, but two lemons is enough for the above quantity: put then an equal quantity of water — *i. e.* not five but *six* glasses, to allow

* Robert Waithman, draper and Alderman of London, of which he had been Lord Mayor, and for which he sat in Parliament, was a well-meaning, liberal, uneducated man who was greatly ridiculed, for his intense cockneyism, by Theodore Hook, Dr. Maginn, and the rest of the Tory wits. — M.

† The Albion retains its character as a first-class dining-hotel. Most of the trade dinners of the London booksellers are held therein. — M.

for the lemon juice,—and you have a very pretty three tumblers of punch. Mix in a jug. If you are afraid of headaches —for, as Xenophon says of another kind of Eastern tipple, 'rack punch is κεφαλαλγες—put *twice* as much water as spirits.* I, however, never used it that way for my own private drinking.

Maxim Seventy-fourth.

THE controversy respecting the fit liquor for punch is far from being set at rest. As some folk mention Dr. Kitchener, I may as well at once dispose of him. In his 477th nostrum, he professes to give you a receipt for making lemonade in a minute, and he commences by bidding you to mix essence of lemon-peel *by degrees* with capillaire. How that is to be done in a minute passes my comprehension. But, waiving this, he proceeds to describe the process of acid-making, and then, in the coolest and most audacious way in the world, bids you put a spoonful of it into a pint of water, which will produce a very agreeable sherbet, "the addition of rum or brandy (quoth our hero) will convert this into PUNCH DIRECTLY." What a pretty way of doing business this is! It is just as much as if I were to say, get a flint—the addition of a stock, lock, and barrel, to which will convert it into a GUN DIRECTLY. Why, the spirits were first to be considered.

Maxim Seventy-fifth.

BRANDY I do not think good punch. The lemon does not blandly amalgamate, and sugar hurts the vinous flavour. Nor is it over good as grog. I recommend brandy to be used as a dram solely. In drinking claret, when that cold wine begins, as it will do, to chill the stomach, a glass of brandy after every four glasses of claret corrects the frigidity.

N. B.—Brandy, and indeed all other drams, should be taken at one sup, no matter how large the glass may be. The old

* This receipt differs materially from Father Tom Maguire's, as given by him to the Pope in the Vatican:—"First put in the spirits, then add the sugar, and every drop of water after that spoils the punch."—M.

rule of "never to make two bites of a cherry," applies with peculiar emphasis to cherry brandy.

Maxim Seventy-sixth.

RUM is the liquor consecrate to grog.* Half and half is the fair proportion. Grog should never be stirred with a spoon, but immediately drunk as soon as the rum has been poured in. Rum punch is apt to be heavy on the stomach — and, unless very old, it has not peculiar merit as a dram. The American pineapple rum is fine drinking, and I wonder it is not introduced into this country. In my last Maxims, I omitted to panegyrise the peach brandy of our Transatlantic brethren — an omission which I beg leave here to correct.†

Maxim Seventy-seventh.

THE pursers on board ships water the rum too much. You hear fools in Parliament, and elsewhere, prating about the evils of impressment: but the real grievances of the navy are left untouched. Croker should take this up, for it would make him extensively popular.‡

Maxim Seventy-eighth.

SHRUB is decidedly a pleasant drink, particularly in the morning. It is, however, expensive. Sheridan used to say it was better to drink champagne out of economy; for, said he, your brains get addled with a single flask of champagne, whereas you drink rum shrub all night before you are properly drunk. Sheridan *was* a great man.

* *Grog*, in the purely English acceptation of the term, means spirits taken in *cold* water. — M.

† Odoherty must have been particularly fortunate if he found any peach brandy worth drinking or panegyrising. Evidently, he only knew the liquor by name. — M.

‡ In 1824, and until the break-up of the Wellington Cabinet in November, 1830, John Wilson Croker, editor of Boswell's Johnson, and a principal contributor to the *Quarterly Review*, was Secretary to the Admiralty, in London. — M.

Maxim Seventy-ninth.

As for arrack — I can't say I like it. You would bam the first Mull or Qui-hi of them all, by infusing a couple of scruples of the flowers of benjamin in a bottle of rum. You would see him snuffing it up his nose, and swearing that he would know its fragrance at the distance of a parasang. The flowers of benjamin cost about twopence. The best place for 'rack is Vauxhall; but I suspect they run this hum on you. At Tom's, in Cornhill, you get it genuine.

Maxim Eightieth.

Of Tom's, thus casually presented to my mind, let me indulge in the recollection.* Coffee-house, redolent of cash, what magnificent associations of ideas do you not create! By you for generations has rolled the never-ceasing flow of wealth — the chink of money, since the memory of man, has not been checked within your hearing. Yet, with the *insouciance* of a sublime philosophy, your cooks and waiters have never turned away from their works of gastrosophy, to think of the neighboring millions. How superb is your real turtle-soup — how peppery your mullagatawny — how particular your Madeira! Depend upon it, the places for dining in are the city taverns or coffee-houses. You have not, to be sure, a skip-jack monkey hopping behind your chair — you have no flaring mirror *glowering* out on you in all the majesty of a deep gilt frame — you have no marble chimney-pieces, pleasant to look at, but all telling accursedly against you in the bill. Instead of them, you have steady-going waiters, all duly impressed with the dead certainty of their working up gradually to be tavern-keepers themselves — thence men of potency in the ward — in time merchants of some degree — aldermen in due course, perhaps — and perhaps the vista presented to their mental optics is gilded at the end by the august chain of Lord Mayor. They bow to you for a penny, while a jacka-

* Tom's, which is not *in* but very *near* Cornhill, was and is a famous restaurant. The prices, it is true, were high, but the articles supplied were the very best of their kind. — M.

napes at the West End would toss up his nose at half-a-crown. The prudence of their visitors makes them prudent themselves. The eastern pence are hoarded, while the western two-and-six-pennies are flung to the winds, after the thousands of dandies who have bestowed them. Then their boxes are dark and dingy — but warm and cozy. A clock ticks audibly to remind you of the necessity of keeping good hours, even in the midst of revelry. Even if a man gets muzzy in one of them, it is a sober intoxication — you are thinking of profit and loss in the meanderings of your intellect — and you retire to rest to dream of the necessity of industry and attention.

Maxim Eighty-first.

WHEN you write any outlandish lingo, always correct the press yourself. In my 24th Maxim, a most erudite and important one, the word *nachash* is printed *nechadadi.* After this, let no conjectural emendation be deemed too wild. When we see sh [ש] converted by a printer into dhdhj [דדי], what blunders must not have been made in the days of MSS.! And yet you hear fools prating about the impropriety of meddling with the text.

Maxim Eighty-second.

MAXIMS are hard reading, demanding a constant stretch of the intellectual faculties. Every word must be diligently pondered, every assertion examined in all its bearings, pursued with a keen eye to its remotest consequences, rejected with a philosophic calmness, or treasured up with the same feeling as a "κτημα ες αει" — a "possession to eternity."

Maxims of O'Doherty.

PART THE THIRD.

Introduction.

GENTLE READER,

I HAVE already said that I do not fear the danger of cloying you with this my Series of Maxims. *Toujours perdrix*, &c., is a true saying, no doubt, for you do get tired of partridges, [which, *ut obiter dicam*, that is, in plain English, *en passant*, are very so-so in France,] but there is no danger of your getting tired of a varied dinner. Thus, in this affair of mine, if it were, like the *New Monthly Magazine*, a series of humdrum papers eternally upon the same subjects, you would certes feel no little lassitude. But I humbly submit to your superior judgment, that I am not by any means in the predicament of that old-womanly journal, edited by my friend Tom Campbell of Glasgow, a man for whom I have a particular esteem, and concerning whom I shall probably tell a good story next month.

I honestly have stuck by my original bargain with you, gentle reader, and give you downright and actual observations on human life. There is not a Maxim which I have not tried, as Dr. William Kitchener did his cookery recipes. In all other books of Maxims which I have read, the greater proportion by far is mere moonshine, of no practical utility whatever. I have a vague recollection of having read a book by Dr. Hunter, of York, I believe, from which all I gleaned—certainly all that has stuck to my memory—is an advice to have your stairs painted stone colour to save soap—to send your cards to your bookbinder to shave off their edges, which will permit you to play with them three times as long as you otherwise would—and if your wife wears a wig, never to look at her bare skull, for it is a hideous spectacle. Of which the two first are piperly, and the third I know nothing about, not being enrolled in the ranks of matrimony.

So also in "Lacon, or Few Things in Many Words," I defy you to point out a solid practical Maxim; at least I cannot recollect one.* And if not practical, they are naught. The contrary of the law of theology holds in this case. In Scotland I have heard people say, "It is no sound doctrine, it is the law o' warks." Now, unless apophthegms are exclusively confined *to works*, their doctrine is not sound. While writing this, I have happened perchance to take up a morning paper, wherein I find excerpts from the Maxims of one Balthasar Gracian; and what are they? "Learn to obtain and preserve reputation," a pretty copy-line for a school-boy, I own. "Learn to command your passions. The passions are the breeches of the mind;" he might as well have said the petticoats of the Celtic. Who learns any thing by such twaddle?

In a word, gentle reader, these things pass away. If they glitter or dazzle, they are but a kind of *Fata Morgana,* which is baseless and transient, and altogether different from the *Effata Morgana,* by which name you may, if you like, call the dicta of,

Unalterably thine,
Gentle Reader,
MORGAN ODOHERTY.

AMBROSE'S, ATHENS,
August 27, 1824.

---

* Lord Byron, who had been satirized in a heavy poem by the Rev. C. C. Colton, author of "Lacon, or Many Things in Few Words," was the first to say that the book should have been entitled "Few Things in Many Words."—M.

Maxim Eighty-third.

We moderns are perhaps inferior to our ancestors in nothing more than in our epitaphs. The rules, nevertheless, for making a good epitaph, are exceedingly simple. You should study a concise, brief, and piquant diction; you should state distinctly the most remarkable points in the character and history of the defunct, avoiding, of course, the error into which Pope so often fell, of omitting the name of the individual in your verses, and leaving it to be tagged to the tail or beginning of the piece, with a separate and prosaic "*hic jacet.*" Thirdly, there should be, if possible, some improvement of the subject,—some moral or religious or patriotic maxim,—which the passenger carries with him, and forgets not. I venture to present, as a happy specimen, the following, which is taken from a tombstone in Winchester churchyard, and which tradition ascribes to a late venerable prelate of that see, Dr. Hoadly:*—

"Private John Thoms lies buried here,
Who died of drinking cold small beer:—
Good Christian! drink no beer at all,
Or, if you will drink beer, don't drink it small."

Nothing can exceed the nervous pith and fine tone of this, both in the narrative and the didactic parts. It is really a gem, and confers honor on the Bishop—on whom, by the way, a clever enough little epitaph was written shortly after his death, by a brother Whig and D. D. Bishop Hoadly was, in this doctor's opinion, a heretical scribe, and his monument encroached too much on one of the great pillars of the Cathedral.

"Here lying Hoadly lies, whose book
Was feebler than his bier.—
Alive, the Church he fain had shook,
But undermines it here.

---

* Dr. Benjamin Hoadly (born in 1676), a famous Whig, in the reign of Queen Anne, was created Bishop of Bangor in 1715; and successively translated to the sees of Hereford, Salisbury, and Winchester; and died in 1761. He differed so essentially from the doctrines of the church of England, that he was described as "the greatest dissenter that ever wore a mitre."—M.

Maxim Eighty-fourth.

There is not a truer saying in this world, than that truth lies on the surface of things. The adage about its lying in a well was invented by some solemn old ass, some "passymeasures pagan," as Sir Toby Belch calls him, who was ambitious of being thought deep, while, in point of fact, he was only muddy. Nothing that is worth having or knowing is recondite or difficult to be discovered. Go into a ball-room, and your eye will in three seconds light (and fix) on *the* beauty. Ask the stupidest host in the world to bring you the best thing he has in his house, and he will, without doubt, set a bottle of claret forthwith on your table. Ask the most perfect goose of a bookseller who is the first poet in the world, and he will name Shakspere. Ask Macvey* which is the best Magazine, and he will utter in response the name of Blackwood. I have never been able to understand the advantages of hard study, deep researches, learned investigations, &c. &c. &c. Is there any really good author lying concealed among the litter of lumber ransacked only the fingers of the Bibliomaniacs? Is there any thing equal to punch, with which the drinking public in general remains unacquainted? I think not. I therefore take things easy.

Maxim Eighty-fifth.

Few idiots are entitled to claver on the same form with the Bibliomaniacs; but, indeed, to be a *collector* of any thing, and to be an *ass*, are pretty nearly equivalent phrases in the language of all rational men. No man *collects* any thing of which he really makes use. Who ever suspected Lord Spencer or his factotum, little Dibdin,† of *reading?* The old Quaker at York,

* Macvey Napier. — M.

† Earl Spencer (born in 1758, died in 1834), though in office, under Fox as well as under Pitt, is more worthy of notice as a book-collector than as a statesman. He encouraged literature and the fine arts; was a conspicuous member of the Roxburgh Club, in its zenith; and formed a rare and costly library (including the Valdarfar edition of Boccaccio, purchased at a vast price), of which the Rev. T. F. Dibdin, his librarian, published an account in three volumes. Dib-

who has a museum of the ropes at which eminent criminals have dangled, has no intention to make an airy and tassel-like termination of his own terrestrial career—for that would be quite out of character with a man of his brims. In like manner, it is now well known that the three thousand three hundred and thirty-three young ladies who figure on the books of the Seraglio, have a very idle life of it, and that, in point of fact, the Grand Seignior is a highly respectable man. The people that collect pictures, also, are, generally speaking, such folk as Sir John Leicester, the late Angerstein, and the like of that.* The only two things that I have any pleasure in collecting, are bottles of excellent wine, and boxes of excellent cigars—articles, of the first of which I flatter myself I know rather more than even Lord Eldin does of pictures;† and of the latter whereof I make rather more use than old Mustapho can be supposed to do of his 3333 knick-knacks in petticoats—or rather, I beg their ladyships' pardon, in trowsers.

Maxim Eighty-sixth.

SOMETHING I was saying recalls to my mind the intense scorn I have for what they call *seeing sights!* When you go out to visit a friend in the country, "I am so glad to see you, my dear fellow," says he—"come away, and you shall feast your eyes on our grand cascade—abbey—lake—castle—plain—forest," or whatever the sight of that vicinity may happen to be. If he took you out to his field, and said, "Look at these sheep—are you a judge?—which of them shall I order to be killed?"

din, nephew of the song-writer, was born in 1775, and died in 1847. His bibliographical publications, which were numerous and valuable, are long since out of print, and sell for five times their original price. Despite Odoherty's sneer, Dibdin and his noble patron were book-readers as well as book-collectors.—M.

* Sir John Leicester (created Lord Farnborough by George IV.) was a liberal patron of the fine arts in England at the time these Maxims were originally published.—John Julius Angerstein (born at St. Petersburgh in 1735, died in London in 1822) was a wealthy merchant, whose noble collection of paintings, purchased by the English Government for £60,000, formed the nucleus of the present National Gallery of England.—M.

† John Clerk, Lord Eldin, a Scottish judge—for whom is claimed the origi-

or asked one to give him an opinion about the state of his hot-house, to inspect the drawing of his fish-pond, or any thing of this kind, the man might be borne with. But, in general, in-door prospects are the best. What purling brook matches the music of my gurgling bottle? What is an old roofless cathedral compared to a well-built pie?

Maxim Eighty-seventh.

Of late they have got into a trick of serving up the roasted pig without his usual concomitants. I hate the innovating spirit of this age; it is my aversion, and will undo the country. Always let him appear erect on his four legs, with a lemon in his mouth, a sprig of parsley in his ear, his trotters bedded on a lair of sage.* One likes to see a pig appear just as he used to do upon the board of a Swift, a Pope, an Arbuthnot. Take away the customs of a people, and their identity is destroyed.

Maxim Eighty-eighth.

Claret should always be decanted. I find it necessary to observe this, because the vile Frenchified fashion of shoving the black bottles about is fast coming into vogue in certain quarters. These outlandish fellows drink their wine out of the black bottle for two reasons—first, that they can't afford crystal; and, secondly, because, sending all their best wine over to us, they, of course, are in the habit of consuming weak secondary trash among themselves, which will not keep, and has therefore no time for depositing grounds. But why should we imitate such creatures as these? The next thing, I suppose, will be to have ruffles without a shirt, and to masticate frog's blubber. No good can come of lowering our good old national pride, antipathies, and principles in general.

nal proposal of breaking the line in naval warfare—had one of the finest picture galleries in Scotland, in 1824.—M.

* What Washington Irving has said, in his Sketch Book, as to the serving-up of the boar's head, at Oxford (with a lemon in his mouth) may be taken as referring also to roast pig—immortalized by gentle "Elia."—M.

Maxim Eighty-ninth.

LIBERALITY, Conciliation, &c. &c., are roundabout words for humbug in its lowest shape. One night lately I had a very fine dream. I dreamt I was in heaven. Some of the young angels were abusing the devil bitterly. Hold, hold! said an ancient-looking seraph, in a very long pair of wings, but rather weak in the feather,—you must not speak in this way. Do not carry party-feelings into private life. The devil is a person of infinite talent—a very extraordinary person indeed. Such a speaker! &c, &c. &c. In regard to dreams, I have now adopted the theory of the late Dr. Beattie, author of the Minstrel, a poem; for I had been supping that night among the Pluckless.

Maxim Ninetieth.

THERE are *two* kinds of drinking which I disapprove of—I mean dram-drinking and port-drinking. I talk of the drinking of these things in great quantities, and habitually; for as to taking a few drams and a few glasses of port every day, that is no more than I have been in the custom of doing for many years back. I have many reasons that I could render for the disgust that is in me, but I shall be contented with one. These potables, taken in this way, fatally injure a man's personal appearance. The drinker of drams becomes either a pale, shivering, blue-and-yellow-looking, lank-chopped, miserable, skinny animal, or his eyes and cheeks are stained with a dry, fiery, dusky red, than which few things can be more disgusting to any woman of real sensibility and true feminine delicacy of character. The port-drinkers, on the other hand, get blowsy about the chops, have trumpets of noses, covered with carbuncles, and acquire a muddy look about the eyes. Vide the Book of the Church,* *passim*. For these reasons, do not, on any account, drink port or drams, and, *per conversum*, drink as much good claret, good punch, or good beer, as you can get hold of, for these liquors make a man an Adonis. Of the three, claret conveys

* "The Book of the Church," by Southey, the poet-laureate.—M.

perhaps the most delicate tinge to the countenance; nothing gives the air of a gentleman so completely as that elegant lassitude about the muscles of the face, which accompanied with a gentle rubicundity, marks the man whose blood is in a great proportion *vin-de-Bordeaux*. There is a peculiar delicacy of expression about the mouth also, which nothing but the habit of tasting exquisite claret, and contemplating works of the most refined genius, can ever bestow. Punch, however, is not without its own peculiar merits. If you want to see a fine, commanding, heroic-looking race of men, go into the Tontine Coffee-room of Glasgow, and behold the effects of my friend Mr. Thomas Hamilton's rum, and the delicious water of the *Arns* fountain, so celebrated in song; or just stop for a minute at the foot of Millar Street, and see what you shall see. Beer, though last, is not least in its beautifying powers. A beer-drinker's cheek is like some of the finest species of apples,

——" the side that's next the sun."

Such a cheek carries one back into the golden age, reminding us of Eve, Helen, Atalanta, and I know not what more. Upon the whole, I should, if called upon to give a decided opinion as to these matters in the present state of my information and feelings, say as follows: Give me the cheek of a beer-bibber—the calf of a punch-bibber—and the mouth of a claret-bibber—which last, indeed, I already have.

N. B.—Butlers should be allowed a good deal of port, for it makes them swell out immensely, and gives them noses *à-la-*Bardolph; and the symptoms of good eating and drinking should be set forth a little *in caricaturâ* upon the outward man of such folk, just as we wish inferior servants to wear crimson breeches, pea-green coats, and other extravaganzas upon finery. As for dram-drinking, I think nobody ought to indulge in it except a man under sentence of death, who wishes to make the very most of his time, and who knows that, let him live never so quietly, his complexion will inevitably be quite spoilt in the course of the week. A gallon of good stout brandy is a treasure to a man in this situation; though, if I were in his place, I rather think I should still stick to my three bottles of claret and dozen cigars *per diem;* for I should be afraid of the other system's effects upon my nervous system.

Maxim Ninety-first.

In one of my previous Maxims I have laid it down, that "the intensely amorous temperament, in a female, stamps melancholy on her eyelid." This, I find, has given rise to much remark, and a considerable controversy is still going on in one of the inferior periodicals. Shakspere, however, is entirely on my side. When he was a young man, and wrote his Troilus and Cressida,* he appears indeed to have thought otherwise. It was then that he made his Ulysses say,—

> ——"Fie, fie upon her!
> There's language in her eye, her cheek, her lip!
> Nay, her foot speaks: her wanton spirits look out
> At every joint and motion of her body.
> Oh, these encounterers! so glibe of tongue,
> That give accosting welcome ere it comes,
> And wide unclasp the tablet of their thoughts
> To every ticklish reader. Set them down
> For sluttish spoils of opportunity,
> And daughters of the game——"

Animated and beautifully said, but the theory of the sage Greek quite false! The same poet, after looking at human nature for a number of years, arrived at truer views. It was then that he represented Juliet—

> "See! how *she leans her cheek upon her hand!*"

It was then that he conceived the rich and meditative voluptuousness of the all-accomplished Cleopatra, and described the pious resolves of "the curled Antony," as feeble and ineffectual when opposed to the influence of that

> ——————"Grave charm,
> Whose eye beck'd forth his wars, and call'd them home;—
> Whose bosom was his crownet, his chief end."

Helen, in Homer, is also uniformly represented as a melancholy creature; and the most pathetic thing that has ever been written, is her lamentation over her virtue in the 24th Iliad. To

* "Troilus and Cressida" was *not* written when Shakspere was a young man. It came out as late as 1609, when Shakspere was 45 years old.—M.

conclude, the late Rev. Lawrence Sterne (a prime connoisseur) has recorded, in distinct terms, his opinion as to which is "the most serious of all passions." We four, then, are of the same way of thinking as to this matter.

Maxim Ninety-second.

IN helping a lady to wine, *always* fill the glass to the very brim, for custom prevents them from taking many glasses at a time; and I have seen cross looks when the rule has been neglected by young and inexperienced dandies.

Maxim Ninety-third.

THE King, if Sir Thomas Lawrence's last and best picture of him may be believed, wears, when dressed for dinner, a very short blue surtout, trimmed with a little fur, and embroidered in black silk upon the breast, all about the button-holes, &c.—black breeches and stockings, and a black stock.* I wish to call general attention to this, in the hopes of seeing his Majesty's example speedily and extensively adopted. The modern *coat* is the part of our usual dress which has always given most disgust in the eye of people of taste; and I am, therefore, exceedingly happy to think that there is now a probability of its being entirely exploded. The white neckcloth is another abomination, and it also must be dismissed. A blue surtout, and blue trowsers richly embroidered down the seams, form the handsomest dress which any man can wear within the limits of European costume.†

Maxim Ninety-fourth.

MEDIOCRITY is always disgusting, except, perhaps, mediocrity of stature in a woman. Give me the Paradise Lost, the Faerie Queen, the Vanity of Human Wishes, that I may feel

* This is the celebrated portrait, engraved by Finden (who was three years at work on the plate) on which the late Mr. Turveydrop, in *Bleak House*, took his last lessons on "deportment."—M.

† Maginn's almost invariable attire was a blue frock coat.—M.

myself elevated and ennobled; give me Endymion, or the Flood of Thessaly, or Pye's Alfred, that I may be tickled and amused.* But on no account give me an eminently respectable poem of the Beattie or Campbell class, for that merely sets one to sleep. In like fashion, give me, if you wish to make me feel in the heaven of heavens, a *hookah.* There is no question that this is the Paradise Gained of the smoker. But, if you cannot give me that, give me a cigar; with which whoso is not contented deserves to inhale sixteen pipes of assafœtida *per diem in secula seculorum.* What I set my face against is the vile mediocrity of *a pipe,* properly so called. No pipe is *cleanly* but the common Dutch clay, and that is a great recommendation, I admit; but there is something so hideously absurd in the appearance of a man with a clay pipe in his mouth, that I rather wonder any body can have courage to present himself in such a position. The whole tribe of *meerschaums,* &c., are filthiness itself. These get saturated with the odious oil of the plant, and are, in fact, poisonous. The only way in which you can have a pipe at once gay-looking and cleanly, is to have a glass tube within it, which can be washed with water immediately after use; but then the glass gets infernally hot. On the whole, unless you be a grandee, and can afford to have a servant expressly devoted to the management of your smoking concerns, in which case a *hookah* is due to yourself, the best way is to have nothing but cigars.

Maxim Ninety-fifth.

THE Havana cigar is unquestionably at the head. You know it by the peculiar beauty of the firm, brown, smooth, delicately-textured, and *soft* leaf; and if you have any thing of a nose, you can never be deceived as to its odour, for it is a perfect *bouquet.* The *Chinese* cheroots are the next in order; but the devil of it is, that one can seldom get them, and then they are always dry beyond redemption. The best Chinese cheroots

* Endymion, by John Keats; the Flood of Thessaly by Barry Cornwall: Alfred, an epic poem, by Henry James Pye, poet-laureate from 1790 to his death in 1813.—M.

have a delicate grayish tinge; and, if they are not complete sticks, put them into an air-tight vessel, with a few slices of a good juicy melon, and, in the course of a few hours, they will extract some humidity from their neighbours. Some people use a sliced *apple*, others a *carrot*, either of which may do when a melon is not to be had, but that is the real article, when attainable. As to all the plans of moistening cigars by means of tea-leaves, rum-grog, &c., they are utterly absurd, and no true smoker ever thinks of them. Manilla cigars occupy the third station in my esteem, but their enormous size renders them inconvenient. One hates being seen sucking away at a thing like a walking-cane. I generally find that Gliddon, of London, has the best cigars in the market. George Cotton, of Edinburgh, is also very *recherché* in these articles. But, as I believe I once remarked before, a man must smuggle, in the present state of the code.

N. B. It will be observed that I have changed my views as to some very serious parts of this subject, since the year of grace 1818, when I composed my verses to my pipe—

"Divine invention of the age of Bess," &c.

which John Schetky is so fond of reciting, and which Byron plagiarised so audaciously in his mutineering production.* As my friend Mr. Jeffrey lately said, when toasting Radical Reform, "Time makes us all wiser."

Maxim Ninety-sixth.

Cold whisky-punch is almost unheard of out of Ireland, and yet, without instituting any invidious comparisons, it is a liquor of most respectable character, and is frequently attainable where cold *rum*-punch is not. The reason why it has got a bad name in Great Britain is, that they make it with cold water, whereas it ought always to be made with boiling water, and allowed to concoct and cool for a day or two before it is put on the table. In this way, the materials get more intensely amalgamated than *cold* water and *cold* whisky ever do get. As to the beautiful mutual adaptation of cold rum and cold water, that is beyond all

* See page 44 in this volume. Schetky was an artist in Edinburgh.—M.

praise, and indeed forms a theme of never-ceasing admiration, being one of Nature's most exquisite achievements.* Sturm has omitted it, but I mean to make a supplement to his Reflections when I get a little leisure.

Maxim Ninety-seventh.

No real smoker uses any of these little knick-knackeries they sell under the name of cigar-tubes, and the like of that. The chief merit of the thing is the extreme gentleness and delicacy with which the smoke is drawn out of the leaf by the loving and animated contact, and eternally varying play and pressure of that most wonderful piece of refined mechanism, the lip of man; whereas, if you are to go to work upon a piece of silver, ivory, horn, wood, or whatever these concerns are made of, you lose the whole of this, and, indeed, you may as well take a pipe at once.

Maxim Ninety-eighth.

The reason why many important matters remain in obscurity and doubt is, that nobody has adopted the proper means for having them cleared up. For example, one often hears of a man making a bargain with *one* friend of his, that whichsoever of the pair happens to die first will, if possible, revisit the glimpses of the moon, and thereby satisfy the survivor of the existence of ghosts. This, however, is ridiculous, because it is easy to see that there may be special circumstances to prevent this particular spirit from doing what is wanted. Now, to put an end to this at once, I hereby invite one and all of my friends who peruse this maxim to pay me a visit of the kind alluded to. Surely you cannot all be incapable of doing the thing, if it is to be done at all.

* Odoherty refers, no doubt, to the far-famed Glasgow Punch, in which cold rum and cold water certainly do bear part, but not exclusively. The receipt for making a quart jug of it is as follows: — Melt lump sugar in cold water, with the juice of a couple of lemons, passed through a fine hair-strainer. This is Sherbet, and must be well mingled. Then add old Jamaica rum — one part of rum to five of the sherbet. Cut a couple of limes in two, and run each section rapidly round the edge of the jug or bowl, gently squeezing in some of the delicate acid. This done, the punch is made. Imbibe. — M.

Maxim Ninety-ninth.

IN order to know what cod really is, you must eat it at Newfoundland. Herring is not worthy of the name, except on the banks of Lochfine in Argyleshire; and the best salmon in the whole world is that of the Boyne.* Dr. Kitchener, in all probability, never tasted any one of these things, and yet the man writes a book upon cookery! It is really too much for a man to write about salmon, who never eat it until it had been kept for ten days in a tub of snow, which is the case with all that comes to London, excepting the very few salmon caught in the Thames,† and these are as inferior in firmness and gusto to those of a mountain stream, as the mutton of a Lincolnshire squire is to that of Sir Watkin of Wales‡ or Jamie Hogg of Ettrick. This fish ought to be eat as soon as possible after he is caught. Nothing can then exceed the beautiful curdiness of his texture, whereas your kept fish gets a flaccidity that I cannot away with.

N. B. Simple boiling is the only way with a salmon just caught; but a gentleman of standing is much the better for being cut into thickish slices—cut across, I mean—and grilled with cayenne. I have already spoken as to the sauce.||

Maxim One Hundredth.

THE best of all pies is a grouse-pie; the second a blackcock-pie; the third a woodcock-pie (with plenty of spices); the fourth a chicken-pie (ditto.) As for a pigeon-pie, it is not worthy of a

* Dublin Bay herrings are the best. It is impossible to say whence the *best* salmon comes. There is fine salmon in the Wye and the Severn. From the north of Ireland a great quantity is now railed off, in ice, to the London market. In the Dee, between Aberdeen and Ballater, many salmon are caught on the leap, instantly cleaned out, crimped, and boiled within a few yards of the river. The fish thus caught and thus treated, is very fine indeed.—M.

† It may safely be averred that not "within the memory of the oldest inhabitant" has salmon been caught in the Thames.—M.

‡ The late Sir William Watkins Wynn, of Winnstay, from his vast property and great influence in the Principality, was called "King of Wales."—M.

|| The Odoherty salmon-sauce (as described in Maxim XXXII.) is made of vinegar, mustard, Cayenne pepper, and parsley.—M.

place upon any table, so long as there are chickens in the world. A rook-pie is a bad imitation of that bad article; and a beefsteak-pie is really abominable. A good pie is excellent when hot; but the *test* of a good pie is, "How does it eat cold?" —Apply this to the examples above cited, and you will find I am correct.

Maxim One Hundred and First.

NEVER taste any thing but whisky on the moors. Porter or ale blows you up, and destroys your wind. Wine gets acid immediately on an empty stomach. And put no water to your whisky, for if you once begin swilling water, you will never stop till you make a bag of yourself. A thimbleful of neat spirits once an hour is the thing; but one bumper at starting, and another exactly at noon, is found very wholesome.

Maxim One Hundred and Second.

NO man need be afraid of drinking a very considerable quantity of neat whisky, when in the wilds of Ireland or Scotland. The mountain air requires to be balanced by another stimulus;* and if you wish to be really well, you must always take a bumper before you get out of bed, and another after getting into it, according to the fashion of the country you are in.

Maxim One Hundred and Third.

THE Scotch writers of our day seem to consider it as an established thing, that their country furnishes the best breakfast in Europe; but this I cannot swallow—I mean the assertion, not the breakfast, which I admit to be excellent, but deny to be peerless. The fact is, that breakfast is among the things that have never yet received any thing like the attention merited. The best breakfast is unquestionably that of France; their cof-

* The mountain air really has the effect here attributed to it. A man who, in ordinary cases, would pause before he committed the enormity of drinking a glass of neat spirits, will take two or three glasses, after he is braced by the mountain air, and fatigued by the steep mountain ascent. But there is no occasion for taking any neat spirits whatever.—M.

fee, indeed, is not *quite* equal to that of Germany, but the eatables are unrivalled; and I may be wrong, but somehow or other I can never help thinking that French wines are better in the morning than any others. It is here that we are behind every other nation in Europe—the whole of us, English, Scotch, and Irish; we take no wine at breakfast.

A philosophic mind devoted to this subject, would, I think, adopt a theory not widely different from the following, which, however, I venture to lay down with much diffidence. I say, then, that a man's breakfast should be adapted to his pursuits—it should come home to his business as well as to his bosom. The man who intends to study all the morning, should take a cup or two of coffee, a little well-executed toast, and the wing of a partridge or grouse, when in season; at other times of the year, a small slice of cold chicken, with plenty of pepper and mustard; this light diet prepares him for the elastic exercise of his intellectual powers. On the other hand, if you are going to the fox-chase, or to the moors, or to any sphere of violent bodily exertion whatever, in this case your breakfast will be good and praiseworthy, exactly in proportion as it approaches to the character of a good and praiseworthy dinner. Hot potatoes, chops, beefsteaks, a pint of Burgundy, a quart of good old beer—these are the sort of materials a sportsman's dejeune should consist of. Fried fish is an excellent thing also—particularly the herring. If you have been tipsy over night, and feel squeamish, settle your heart with half a glass of old cogniac, ere you assume the knife and fork; but on no account indulge the whimsies of your stomach, so as to go without a real breakfast,—"*L'appetit vient en mangeant*," quoth the most veracious of adages—therefore begin boldly upon something very highly peppered, and as hot as Gomorrah, and then no fear of the result. You will feel yourself another man, when you have laid in a pound of something.

Of tea, I have on various occasions hinted my total scorn. It is a weak, nervous affair, adapted for the digestion of boarding-school misses, whose occupation is painting roses from the life, practising quadrilles, strumming on the instrument, and so forth. Old people of sedentary habits may take chocolate if they like it; I, for my part, stick to coffee when I am studious.

Maxim One Hundred and Fourth.

By eating a hearty breakfast, you escape the temptation of luncheon — a snare into which he who has a sufficient respect for his dinner will rarely fall.

Maxim One Hundred and Fifth.

I agree with Falstaff, in his contempt for the prevalent absurdity of eating eggs, eggs, eggs at breakfast. "No pullet-sperm in my brewage," say I. I prefer the chicken to the egg, and the hen, when she is really a fine bird, and well roasted or grilled, to the chicken.

Maxim One Hundred and Sixth.

Cold pig's face is one of the best things in the world for breakfast, but it should not be taken unless you are to be active shortly after, for it is so good that one can scarcely help taking a great deal when one begins to it. Eat it with shallot, vinegar and French mustard. Fruit at breakfast is what I cannot recommend;* but if you will take it, be sure not to omit another dram after it, for if you do, you will certainly feel heavyish all the morning.

N. B. — The best breakfast-dram is whisky, when it is really very old and fine, but brandy is more commonly to be had in perfection among the majority of my readers. Cherry brandy is not the thing at breakfast; it is too sweet, and not strong enough. In the Highlands of Scotland, people of extraordinary research give you whisky strongly impregnated with a variety of mountain herbs. And this, I am bound to admit, is attended with the most admirable consequences; — but they will not part with their receipts, therefore it is not worth while for me to do more than merely allude to the fact. Be sure you take it when on the spot.

* Yet the old proverb says, "Fruit is gold in the morning; silver at noon; and lead at night." — M.

Maxim One Hundred and Seventh.

SOME people wear Cossacks* with silk stockings—nothing can be in worse taste. These gentlemen seem to think that their Cossacks smack of the *Don*, whereas nothing can be so decidedly *oriental*.

Maxim One Hundred and Eighth.

NEVER wear a coat with a velvet collar—not even a surtout.† This maxim is, however, almost unnecessary; for no tailor, whose coat it is possible to wear, would ever think of putting a velvet collar on any vesture intended to be worn on the west side of Temple-bar.

Maxim One Hundred and Ninth.

NEVER eat turtle at the West End of the Town, except at the houses of the West Indians. The turtle at the occidental coffee-houses is always lean and poor, and wants the oriental richness and flavour of Bleaden's.‡

Maxim One Hundred and Tenth.

THERE is nothing so difficult as the invention of a new tie. You might almost as easily find out a sixth order of architecture. I once made a drawing of a *nodus* from a Lachrymatory found at Herculaneum, and found it had a good effect when reduced to practice. Its great beauty was, that you did not know where the knot began, nor where it ended. Even of the origi-

* The present trowsers were introduced into England in 1814, when the emperor Alexander of Russia brought some of his loose-trowsered Cossacks over to England. Before that time, tight pantaloons or breeches (these last with or without boots) were the fashion.—M.

† In the year 1855, the tailor will justly dissent from this Maxim. A third of all the coats now in use are made with velvet collars.—M.

‡ Bleaden kept a well-known hostelrie, called The King's Head, in a court off Cheapside, London, and was famous for his soups—particularly his turtle, with an accompaniment of cold iced punch.—M.

nality of this tie, I was for some time doubtful, till one evening at the Opera I heard Hughes Ball* exclaim, in an ecstasy of surprise and admiration,—"By G—d, there's a new tie!"

Maxim One Hundred and Eleventh.

MAN and wife generally resemble each other in features, never in disposition. A goodnatured man marries a shrew—a choleric man, an insensible lump of matter—a witty man, an insipid woman—and *a very great fool*, a blue-stocking.

The reason of the resemblance in face I take to be this: every man thinks himself the handsomest person in existence; and therefore, in looking out for a wife, he always chooses the woman that most nearly resembles himself.

The reason for dissimilarity in disposition, is even more plain. Every one respects another for the quality, good or bad, which he himself wants. Besides, this sort of opposition prevents the holy and happy state from getting flat, as it otherwise would, and produces upon it the same effects as acids upon an alkali The worthy Bishop of Durham was lamenting to Dr. Paley the death of his wife—"We lived nineteen years together," said his lordship, "and never had two opinions about any thing in all that time. What think you of that, Doctor?"—"Indeed, my Lord," rejoined Paley, in his broad Carlisle accent, "I think it must ha' been vera flat." I am orthodox, and quite agree with Dr. Paley.

Maxim One Hundred and Twelfth.

SOME people talk of devils; all our common devils are damnable. The best devil is a slice of roast ham which has been basted with Madeira, and then spiced with Cayenne.

* Mr. Hughes Ball, a man of great wealth, fell in love with a *danseuse* at the Italian Opera in London, who was called Signora Mercandotti, and married her. For a short time (anterior to his marriage) he was looked up to by the small dandies as a veritable "arbiter elegantiarum." The story went that this Golden Ball, as he was familiarly called, had disbursed £1000 for a dressing-case, the fillings-up of which were of solid gold! He subsided into a respectable married man, and is yet alive.—M.

Maxim One Hundred and Thirteenth.

In Paris there is no restaurateur whose house unites all the requisites for dining well.* I have had long experience of them, and can speak with authority. Beauvilliers' is a good quiet house, where you get all the regular French dishes admirably dressed. His *fricassées de poulet* are not to be surpassed; they have a delicate flavour of the almond, which is quite inimitable — and his *patés* and *vol-au-vents* are superb. But he has neither his vegetables nor his venison so early as Véry. I don't by any means agree with those people who extol the cookery at Véry's; it is excellent, certainly — but not better than that of the other firstrate houses. The thing in which Véry really surpasses all the rest, is in his *desserts;* his fruits are magnificent, and look as if they came from the gardens of Brobdignag. I used to like the cookery and the chambertin of the *Trois frères Provençaux,* but I think this house has fallen off latterly in everything but those delicious salads — "Spots of greenery," as Mr. Coleridge calls them. The cookery at Grignon's I think decidedly bad; but his white wines, and particularly the Haut Barsac, have what my friend Goethe call a paradise clearness and odour. The only place where one can dine well, from soup down to Curaçoa, is at the *Rocher de Cancale,* though it stands in a villanous dirty street. If anybody wants to know how far the force of French cookery can go, let him dine at the *Rocher* — especially if he is a piscivorous person, like myself. The soups are beyond all praise — and the *potage prentanière* (spring soup) absolutely astounds you by the prematurity of vegetation which it proves. I ate asparagus soup at the *Rocher de Cancale,* on the 18th of January. *Rupes Cancaliensis, esto perpetua!*

Maxim One Hundred and Fourteenth.

At a restaurateur's, when you ask for any wine above the pitch of *vin ordinaire,* always examine the cork before you

* This represents a state of things, in Paris, fully 30 years ago, and is not applicable to its present status as regards the means and appliances of dining well. — M.

allow the *sommelier* to draw it. This is a maxim worth any money. The French have an odious custom of allowing people to have half bottles of the higher wines. The waiters, of course, fill up the bottle with an inferior sort, and seal it again; so that you frequently get your Sauterne christened with Chablis. I am sorry to be obliged to say, that at the *Rocher de Cancale,* this trick is very commonly played off. It certainly injures the respectability of the house, and even endangers the throne of the Bourbons. I ought here in gratitude to mention, that at *Prévot's,* one of the best of the second-rate restaurateurs, I have drunk delicious *Chateau grillê*—a wine very rarely found in the *cartes.*

Maxim One Hundred and Fifteenth.

In Paris, when you have two invitations for the same evening, (one from an English, and one from an Irish lady,) always accept the latter. You may be quite sure of having supper at the Irish house, which will not be the case at the English one; and you may depend upon having the best punch.

Maxim One Hundred and Sixteenth.

As a general rule, never accept an invitation to a French Soirée, unless you are fond of *Eau sucrée Ecarté* at night, and disorder of the colon next morning.

Maxim One Hundred and Seventeenth.

When you have an invitation to one or more parties in the same evening, always accept that of an *old maid* (if you receive one) in preference to the others. You are sure of being better received, and—I don't know for what reason, but the fact is so—old maids are generally fond of that last of the day, commonly called supper. Your attention, besides, to the lots of iced punch, dispenses you from paying much to the ladies *à la glace,* who muster in great force on such occasions.

Maxim One Hundred and Eighteenth.

NEVER wear a bright purple coat*—it does not harmonise well with any colour of trousers.

Maxim One Hundred and Nineteenth.

ALL the poets whom I have ever seen, except Sir Walter Scott, look lean and hungry. I do not except Coleridge, because he never writes.

Maxim One Hundred and Twentieth.

THE best coffee in Paris is made at the *Café des Colonnes;* —or, as Mr. Jeffrey rejoiceth more to spell it, the CAFFEE *des* MILLES *Colonnes;* and the liqueurs are superb. The Belle Limonadière, alas! hath passed away—but the rooms are more splendid than ever.† There is a paradise opened lately on the Boulevard, called the *Café Turc;* but then it is on the Boulevard du Temple—and who ever went there since the Revolution? The gardens are but half lighted—so as to throw a delicious and dreamy twilight about you—and this contrasts admirably with the blaze of glory which flashes on you as you enter the saloon itself, all glittering with mirrors, and glowing with gold, and fretted with what seem diamonds, rubies, and amethysts. The *Café* is built in the form of a superb Turkish hall, and is gorgeous as the Opium-Eater's Oriental Dreams, or a Chapter in Vathek! Mr. Wordsworth describes this *Café:*

> "Fabric it seems of diamond and of gold,
> With golden column upon column high
> Uplifted—towers, that on their restless fronts
> Bear stars—illumination of all gems—
> Far sinking into splendour, without end!"

---

* This is supposing an almost impossible case. No persons, except the livery servants of Archbishops and Bishops, wear purple coats.—M.

† When I last saw it [Nov. 1852] nothing could look more dingy and shabby genteel than *The Thousand-pillar Café*, with its gilding changed to black by time, gas, and neglect.—M.

Maxim One Hundred and Twenty-first.

NOTHING is so humiliating to a man of reflection, on awaking in the morning, as the conviction which forces itself upon him that he has been drunk the night before. I do not mean, gentle reader, that he repents him of having been drunk — this he will, of course, consider meritorious — but he cannot help the intruding persuasion, that all the things he uttered after he entered into a state of civilation* (if he recollects any thing about them) were utter stupidities, which he mistook at the time for either wit, wisdom, or eloquence.

Maxim One Hundred and Twenty-second.

PEOPLE often say of a man that he is a cunning fellow. This can never be true — for if he were, nobody could find out that he was.

Maxim One Hundred and Twenty-third.

CAYENNE pepper in crystal is a most meritorious invention of those worthy lads, the Waughs in Regent Street.† Before their time the flavour of Cayenne could never be equally distributed through soups and sauces.

Maxim One Hundred and Twenty-fourth.

NO artist or musician, that was ever good for any thing *as such*, was ever good for any thing else. Even Michel Angelo was a very indifferent poet — though Mr. Wordsworth has taken the trouble to translate some of his sonnets.

Maxim One Hundred and Twenty-fifth.

IT is singular that scarcely any tailor who can make a coat well, can make pantaloons. Such tailors are like those histori-

* When a man, very drunk, utters the word *civilation*, as a substitute for *civilization* (which then is too difficult to be uttered correctly in full) it may safely be anticipated that he has exceeded the bounds of sobriety. — M.

† The Waughs were brothers, of the Quaker sect, who failed about 1834, and had, in their time, the handsomest drug-shop in London. — M.

cal painters who could paint figures, but not landscapes. Stulze is the Raphael of tailors, but he is falling fast into a hard and dry style of cutting: Nugee is the Correggio:—but there is no Michel Angelo—no master of the *gran Contorno.* Place is the Radical tailor—but since he became a Westminster reviewer, he is more engaged in cutting up than cutting out.* I wonder if he sends in his bills quarterly as well as his reviews! Cameron & Co., the army tailors of Henrietta Street, make the best pantaloons in London: and nobody can achieve like them a pair of tight pantaloons—a thing, as Dr. Johnson pathetically observes, always expected, and never found!

Maxim One Hundred and Twenty-sixth.

THERE is one sort of tie which it is very difficult to make, and which I cannot explain to my readers without a diagram. It contains in itself, however, the elements of all other ties: and when a man can make this one well, he has the secret of all the rest.

Maxim One Hundred and Twenty-seventh.

MUCH is said about the French politeness. I do not think them a polite people, and for this reason: In France, if you ever do get drunk, it must be while the ladies are at table—for they quit it along with you. Now, I hold it to be a proof of utter want of politeness to get drunk before women—and not to get drunk at all, proves a man to be equally unfit for a state of civilation.

Maxim One Hundred and Twenty-eighth.

DESPISE humbug—I once dined with Wilberforce, in company with a black who had been manumitted. Mr. Wilber-

* Francis Place, who kept a tailor's shop at Charing Cross, was a strong liberal, with great influence over the Electors of Westminster. He wrote ably on Political Economy, and contributed largely to the *Westminster Review,* when conducted on the Benthamite principle of "the greatest happiness for the greatest number of persons."—M.

force's reasons for placing him at table with gentlemen was, that "he was a man and a brother." I think Mr. Wilberforce's white servants must have thought their case very hard as compared with that of the ex-slave.

Maxim One Hundred and Twenty-ninth.

Of Whisky there are more numerous varieties than of any other spirit. Perhaps, however, in this I may be deceived, for my greater intimacy with that fluid may make me more sensitive as to the minute distinctions of taste. It is probable that in France the palate of the connoisseur is equally cognoscent of the varieties of brandy. I repent that, during my late tour in that country, I did not make inquiries on this most important point; but I shall decidedly ask my friend, the Vicomte d'Arlincourt* — a man for whom I have a particular esteem — concerning it, when I next shall have the pleasure of seeing him at Ambrose's.

Maxim One Hundred and Thirtieth.

With respect to the last maxim, it is to be remarked, in corroboration of the hypothesis there hinted at, (*hinted at*, I say, for I by no means pledge myself to the dead certainty of the fact,) that a most particular diversity of taste exists in the several rums. Antigua has a peculiar smack and relish, by which it is to be known from Jamaica at first gulp. Yet it is very possible, *experto crede*, to bam even a connoisseur by giving him good whisky — free from the empyreumatic taste which is *frequently* observable on several even of licensed whiskies, and *always* on *potheen* — mixed subdolously with burnt brown sugar. It is a great imitation.

* The Vicomte d'Arlincourt, a French novelist, who flourished some thirty years ago. One of his productions, in which he had pedantically paraded his knowledge of geology, got a terrible peppering from Odoherty, in No. VII. of the Noctes Ambrosianæ. — M.

Maxim One Hundred and Thirty-first.

To return to whisky. Inishowen is generally accounted the best potheen; but, as far as regards my own private drinking, I prefer that manufactured at Roscrea, in the county of Tipperary, where I have frequently drunk it with the Rev. John Hamilton, who, by-the-bye, is most untruly and unfairly abused by the little Whig libeller, Tom Moore, in his Fudge Family, (p. 61,) in company, to be sure, with much higher people, which, of course, is a consolation.* Potheen improves much by age. I must say, that one principal reason of its being preferred to Parliament whisky, arises from the natural propensity to do what is forbidden; and I add, as my candid opinion, that if it were taxed, it would not be in such estimation as that procured by scientific distillation from large stills—that is, if the great distillers could be depended upon for honesty, and were not to be suspected shrewdly of making use of other ingredients than malt.†

N. B.—I here intended to have gone in at some length to the divers qualities of all the whisky fluids of the empire, and, with a minute and critical, and, on mine honor, an impartial survey of the whole, to have given my opinion on their various merits or demerits: but I fear that the consideration would be too

* The Rev. John Hamilton, rector of Roscrea, deserved to be abused. Wishing that the district in which he resided should be considered as disturbed by Whiteboy movements, he put a stuffed figure in one of his windows, to represent himself, went out on the lawn and shot at it, and strongly asseverated that the Whiteboys had attempted to assassinate him! Moore's allusion is as follows:—

"I doubt not you could find us, too,
Some Orange Parsons that might do;
Among the rest, we've heard of one,
The Reverend—something—Hamilton.
Who made a figure of himself
(Delicious thought!) and had it shot at,
To bring some Papist to the shelf,
That couldn't otherwise be got at—
If *he*'ll but join the Association,
We'll vote him in by acclamation."—M.

† A great portion of the whisky in Scotland and Ireland is manufactured from raw grain.—M.

lengthy for a list of mere maxims. Brevity is the very soul (not of wit, to be sure, in this case, for that vain and frivolous ingredient ought to be far from our thoughts when discussing subjects of interest to the human race, but—) of apophthegms; but when these my Maxims are gathered, as, God willing, they shall be, into a separate volume, I shall, about this part of them, insert a long and deeply-meditated paper, in which I shall chemically, scientifically, compotically, and empirically — a word which I here use, Mr. Coleridge, in its true and original sense — discuss the whole subject, in such a way, that, like Dr. Barrow preaching before King Charles the Second, it will be universally conceded to me that I have exhausted it. Mr. William Thomas Brande and Sir Humphry Davy* have kindly consented to draw up the chemical tables, with the same precision as they have already done those for wines. I have also in hand a paper written by a couple of ingenious philosophers, "On the Uses and Abuses of Porter," seriously summed up by them with that skill and talent which so truly marks these eminent and erudite men; and that, too, I shall insert in some conspicuous part of my volume. It will be found to be a very instructive and interesting paper.

Maxim One Hundred and Thirty-second.

In parts out of Ireland, you can not convince people of the right method of pronouncing and spelling POTHEEN. They will have it that it is Potch-cheen, or some such thing. It is simply the diminutive of *pot,* and would, indeed, be more correct without the medial *h,* which, however, has gained insertion in consequence of the thick utterance of the people. So *squire* makes *squireen,* a poor little squire, as

> "We 'll take it kind if you provide
> A few *squireens.*" THOMAS MOORE.

Devotee, contracted (by aphœresis) to *'votee,* becomes *'voteen,* to signify a little, mean, superstitious worshipper. *Buckeen* is a

* Davy was the leading, because the most philosophical, chemist of his day. Brande, who has published the "Elements of Chemistry," was long attached to the London Institution, in Albemarle street, in which Faraday now fills Davy's place. — M.

poor attempt at being a *buck*, such as you see in Prince's Street, Edinburgh, for instance, &c., &c. So Potteen corrupted to Potheen, is a little pot; and thence, by a natural metonomy, signifies the production of that utensil.

A curious book might be written on mispronunciations. Is there a man in ten who calls Bolivar correctly? Every one almost is ready to rhyme him as

Bold Simon Bolivar,
Match for old Oliver, &c., &c.

Whereas it should be

Few can deceive, or
Baffle Bolivar.*

Maxim One Hundred and Thirty-third.

In playing domino, you can not be said to have a good hand unless you have five of one number, and one of these a double. This well played, with first move, ought in general to win the game.

Maxim One Hundred and Thirty-fourth.

In vino veritas is an old saying, but scarcely a true one.† Men's minds, when elevated by wine, or anything else, become apt to exaggeration of feeling of every kind. I have often found *In vino asperitas* to be a much truer *dictum*.

Maxim One Hundred and Thirty-fifth

Some people tell you that you should not drink claret after

* Odoherty is wrong in this pronunciation—if Byron be right, as I believe he is, in putting the accent on the last syllable. Thus (in the Age of Bronze), we have—

" While Franklin's quiet memory climbs to heaven,
Calming the lightning which he thence had riven,
Or drawing from the no less kindled earth
Freedom or peace to that which boasts his birth;
While Washington 's a watchword, such as ne'er
Shall sink while there's an echo left to air:
While even the Spaniard's thirst of gold and war
Forgets Pizarro to spout Bolivar."—M.

† But in Maxim XLII. we find Odoherty saying " that no man ever says or does that brutal thing when drunk, which he would not also say and do when sober, *if he durst*."—M.

strawberries. They are wrong, if the claret be good. The milky taste of good claret coheses admirably with the strawberry—somewhat like cream. If the claret be bad, it is quite a different affair; and suspect it, if you find the master of the house anxious not to make the test. George Faulkner of Dublin—I was going to say, my friend Faulkner, until I recollected that he was dead some thirty odd years before I was born—Swift's printer, Foote's Peter Paragraph*—who does not know George?—used to sit a whole night with a solitary strawberry at the bottom of his glass, over which he used to pour generally four bottles of claret. I do so, George would say, because a doctor recommended it to him for its cooling qualities. The idea that cold wine should not be drunk er cool fruit is nonsense. If you feel the claret chill you, you will find the remedy in the seventy-fifth maxim of this series.†

Maxim One Hundred and Thirty-sixth.

If you be an author, never disturb yourself about little squibs, &c., against you. If you do, you will never be at rest. If you want to annoy the squibber, pretend never to have heard of them. It is only five days ago since I was in company with Rogers and Tom Moore, and no pair could harmonize better.—Yet who does not know Tom's epigram on Sam? Rogers had made him a present of a copy of Paradise Lost, in which there was the very common frontispiece of the devil, in the shape of a serpent, twining round down the tree of knowledge, with the fatal apple in his mouth, which he was in the act of presenting to Eve; and under it Tom, instigated no doubt by the evil spirit whose picture he was inspecting, wrote—

* Alderman George Faulkner, of Dublin, caricatured in one of Foote's farces as "Peter Paragraph," was printer and editor of the *Dublin Journal.* Foote hit off his personal peculiarities so well that all of Faulkner's compositors and apprentices having been sent to the theatre to hiss the play and the player, vehemently applauded both. Faulkner, who was present, upbraided them, but was met with the retort, "Ah, Master, sure you wouldn't have us hiss your own sweet self, that was on the stage."—M.

† The remedy is, that "when cold claret begins to chill the stomach, a glass of brandy after every four glasses of claret corrects the frigidity."—M.

"WITH EQUAL GOOD NATURE, GOOD GRACE, AND GOOD LOOKS,
AS THE DEVIL GAVE APPLES, SAM ROGERS GIVES BOOKS."

An unkind return, certainly, for civility, The cut at the looks was particularly unfair, as Mr. Rogers is a bachelor; but he only laughed, as he always does, and the thing passed off like water from a duck's back.

Maxim One Hundred and Thirty-seventh.

NEVER repine on account of that mediocrity of station in which it has pleased Providence to place you. Why should you do so? Would you wish to be the King? I, for one, should unquestionably consider that situation as a decided bore. What! submit to have all your motions placarded in the papers? low scribes spouting away, pro and con, every time you alter your dress, your house, your ministers, your tipple—any thing, in short? What! to be surrounded by an eternal retinue of lords and grooms, and God knows all what? A shocking state of suffering, indeed, and demanding more than Christian endurance. I would not be king, in any thing like a free country, at least, upon any possible terms. If one were a real despot, the case might be better, I admit; for then one could appoint some under-scrub of a viceroy, or lord-lieutenant, or captain-general, or so, to hold the courts, give the grand dinner, sign the death-warrants, ride in state, and all the rest of it, in place of one; while you enjoyed yourself, as it pleased your fancy, in some central retreat, such as Capreæ, or the Happy Valley in Rasselas. But even that is not what I envy. I have no wish to exercise despotic power, and therefore I have no wish to possess it. Any crown would be to me so much *du trop*. What is the object of human life? to be happy—admitted. In what does happiness consist? In deciding who shall, and who shall not, be hung? In having a flag on the top of the house? In talking politics with Canning, Eldon, Liverpool, Metternich, Hardenberg, Pozzo di Borgo?*—I despise all such doings.

* In 1824, George Canning was Foreign Secretary, Lord Eldon was Lord Chancellor, and Lord Liverpool was Premier of England, Prince Metternich and Prince Hardenberg were respectively Prime Ministers of Austria and

Does a man enjoy his beefsteak, his bottle of excellent port or claret, his cigar, his flirtation, his any thing you please to think of, a bit the more for being called King, or Duke, or Emperor, or so? Not one bit. I utterly deny the thing. Were I not Morgan ODoherty, I should like to be Mustapha Abn Selim.

Maxim One Hundred and Thirty-eighth.

I SCARCELY look upon it as much better to be a duke than to be a king. On the contrary, I have often thought it is almost as bad. You are annoyed with the same eternal troop of hangers-on, only they are, if possible, of a still more inferior description. Your house is not your own, nor your time either; for the one is always full of humdrum bores, crack-wits, assenting idiots, lions, lionesses, and I know not what trash; and the other is taken up all the after-part of every day with doing the civil to these creatures; and all the morning you have cursed letters to write about country gentlemen's sons wanting to be promoted, learned lads wanting livings, dandies that aspire to sit in the Foreign Office, political tracasseries, farms to let, money to raise, bonds, mortgages, promises to and from Mr. Peel—in short, as I said before, you are never your own man. The late Duke of Norfolk, to be sure, used to dine every day by himself, in one of the boxes of a common coffee-house in Covent-Garden, drink two bottles of port, and then rumble home to St. James's Square in a jarvie.* He did so.—Well, and can't I do the same thing quite as well, without being called "Your Grace" at the end of every pint of wine? I can, and I know it. Nay, I am of opinion that I can do the same thing more comfortably than the Duke, for I can do it without any human creature taking the slightest notice of what I do. He was not merely the stout gentleman in the gray coat, and I am the tall one in the blue—

Prussia. Count Pozzo di Borgo was high in the diplomatic service of Russia.—M.

* This was the man who, from his distaste for water (save when mingled with brandy), was emphatically called "The *dirty* Duke." He became a Protestant, that he might take his seat in the House of Lords, and was chiefly distinguished for his enormous capacity for eating and drinking, and his excellent judgment on wine.—M.

no, there was always some suspicion of his rank floating about, or at least suspected of doing so — no real sense of the delights of perfect obscurity. In point of fact, such adventitious affairs have no influence whatever on the real sum of human felicity. I remember one day I was walking with my friend Dr. Mullion, and we came in front of Burlington House.* "Mull," says I, "What a noble mansion this is? Look at it attentively, my hearty." He fixed his fine gray eye upon the stately pile, and after perusing it with the utmost diligence of admiration for some space, made answer, "It *is* a grand house indeed, man. Hech me, man! what a dinner I could eat in a house like that!" Chewing the cud of this philosophical reflection, we jogged along for a minute or two, till the well-known azure pillars of Cork Street† happened to attract my friend's notice. My mind was still brimfull of the beautiful architecture, stately air, grand outline, &c. &c. &c. of the patrician mansion which we had just left to leeward, when, lo and behold! the Doctor gives me a little touch on the elbow, just as much as to hint whereabouts we were. "Pooh, pooh!" said I, starting round upon him — "Confound your blood, Dr. Mullion, what makes you attract my attention to this low, shabby, dirty, abominable, piece of plebeian brick-work, ornamented in front with two vile, shapeless wooden posts with, with foreheads villanous low, and daubed over with a little sky-blue paint! — pooh, pooh!" — "Weel, aweel," quoth Mull, "say what you like — but, hech me, man! what a dinner I could eat in a house like that!" This did me.

Maxim One Hundred and Thirty-ninth.

IT was a long while ere I discovered the most convenient method of supporting my drawers. It is a bore to have a separate pair of braces, and the usual schemes of looping are, all of

* Burlington House, Piccadilly — the London residence of the Duke of Devonshire. — M.

† The Blue Posts, in Cork street, off Bond street, is a respectable hotel, not to be confounded with its namesake in the Haymarket, nearly opposite the theatre, which is the resort of loose fish, of both sexes, at all hours of the day and night. — M.

them, liable to objections. The true way is, have two small pieces of tape placed *horizontally* along the waistband of the nether integuments, at those parts of them which correspond to the parts of the upper touched by the extremities of the braces; have these horizontal tapes, say three inches to each, attached firmly to the substance of the waistband; and then pass the brace under the open part of the tape, before you bring it in contact with the button on the breeches. This is one of those inventions which will stand the test so long as the present general system of breeches-making is retained; but that, I freely admit, appears to me to be by no means free from radical defects. The pressure comes too exclusively on particular parts of the shoulders. By a row of buttons all round, this evil might be remedied. That again would involve inconveniences of quite another, though perhaps an even more distressing order. On the whole, this is a matter which modern artists have too much neg lected; and I hereby promise, by means of a separate and distinct MAXIM, to make not only the fame, but the fortune, of the man who, within six months from this date, satisfies me that he has paid proper attention to the hint now conveyed.

Maxim One Hundred and Fortieth.

NO young lady should ever go to a masquerade in any dress associated in the minds of mankind with the habits of an inferior order of society. Put you on the dress of a pretty Abigail, and the devil is in it, if there be no gay lad ready enough to treat you as he would treat a pretty Abigail. The same objection applies to the whole race of milk-maids, hay-makers, nuns, &c. &c. Every one thinks it fair to be a little particular in his attentions to beings of these orders. So, if you go after the publication of this Maxim, we shall all know what you are expecting.

Maxim One Hundred and Forty-first.

INSTEAD of a Maxim there ought to be a volume, ay, a quarto, upon the order to be observed in the wines handed round during dinner I have long ago mentioned, that I disapprove, on general and philosophical principles, of a great mixture of wines during the repast; but this was said with an eye to those, on the one side, who, unlike myself, are of a delicate stomachic organization, and to those, on the other, who, like myself intend to take a proper dose after dinner is down. The man who has the stomach, or the man who intends to exemplify the sobriety, of a horse, may mix wines to a very considerable extent, nay, in fact, ought to do so. The rule is this: Begin with the wines of the most delicate aroma and flavour, and terminate with those of a more decided character. Let the burgundies come immediately after the soup, then the champagnes, the hocks last. Burgundy, after any thing sweet has touched the mouth, is not worth drinking. After champagne, and still more after hock, it is quite insipid. Attend to this carefully, for I often see things grievously misplaced.

Maxim One Hundred and Forty-second.

THE preceding Maxim will probably give rise to much and anxious discussion. To narrow the field, therefore, I take this opportunity of declaring, that there are two liquids which may be eternally varied in their application during dinner, with which you may begin and end, and which you may intersperse, *ad libitum*, whenever you like, and whatever you have been eating and drinking. These two gifts are sherry and cold rum-punch. With regard to them you never can go wrong. They can no more be out of place in a dinner, than a fine tree in a landscape, or a fine woman in a boudoir.*

* It was Maginn's intention to have continued these Maxims, the republication of which, in book form, he was fond of anticipating. But he never got beyond these three Parts. His "Maxims to Marry by," (pp. 363—374) in this volume, may be taken as a continuation.—M.

Don Juan Unread.

YARROW UNVISITED.

WORDSWORTH.

FROM Stirling Castle we had seen
The mazy Forth unravell'd;
Had trod the banks of Clyde and Tay,
And with the Tweed had travelled;
And, when we came to Clovenford,
Then said my "*winsome Marrow*,"
"What'er betide, we'll turn aside
And see the Braes of Yarrow."

"Let Yarrow Folk, *frae* Selkirk Town,
Who have been buying, selling,
Go back to Yarrow, 'tis their own,
Each Maiden to her Dwelling!
On Yarrow's banks let herons feed,
Hares couch, and rabbits burrow!
But we will downwards with the Tweed,
Nor turn aside to Yarrow.

DON JUAN UNREAD.*

BYRON.

OF Corinth Castle we had read
The amazing Siege unravelled,
Had swallowed Lara and the Giaour,
And with Childe Harold travelled;
And so we followed cloven-foot†
As faithfully as any,
Until he cried, "Come, turn aside
And read of Don ‡Giovanni."

"Let Whiggish folk, *frae* Holland House,
Who have been lying, prating,
Read Don Giovanni, 'tis their own,
A child of their creating!
On jests profane they love to feed,
And there they are — and many;
But we, who link not with the crew,
Regard not Don Giovanni.

---

* This, one of the earliest of Maginn's contributions to *Blackwood*, appeared in November, 1819, together with the translation, into English verse, of the first fitte of Chevy Chase — the ballad which, Sir Philip Sydney said, "stirs the heart like a trumpet." It was thus prefaced: — "Mr. Editor, I composed the following poem on Tuesday night last, between the hours of eleven and twelve o'clock, during a sound sleep, into which I had fallen while in the act of attempting to peruse *Constable's Magazine*. While I slept I was busily employed in versifying, and should, I am sure, have composed much more, but that I unfortunately threw the Magazine off the table upon my foot, which instantly awaked me. A half-hundred could not have descended with more weight, a circumstance which proves how very heavy the articles contained in that work must be; and I feel the effects of it yet. I send my lines merely as a psychological curiosity like Kubla Khan. It is a remarkable fact, that a poem of Mr. Wordsworth's, '*Yarrow Unvisited*,' bears a resemblance to this of mine; how to account for this coincidence I know not." — In the first collective edition of Byron's Works, (17 vols., published by Murray, of London,) "Don Juan Unread" was quoted, as Maginn's, among the "Testimonies of Authors." The first Cantos of "Don Juan" were published in July, 1819. — M.

† A recollection of the usual accoutrements of the prince of the air, to whose service the poem of Don Juan is devoted, will account for this epithet being applied to its author. — W. MAGINN.

‡ Italice for Juan, which is Hispanice for John. — W. M.

"There's Gala Water, Leader Haughs,
Both lying right before us;
And Dryborough, where with chiming
Tweed
The Lintwhites sing in chorus;
There's pleasant Tiviot Dale, a land
Made blithe with plough and harrow;
Why throw away a needful day
To go in search of Yarrow?

"What's Yarrow but a River bare
That glides the dark hills under?
There are a thousand such elsewhere
As worthy of your wonder."
—Strange words they seem'd of slight
and scorn;
My true-love sigh'd for sorrow;
And look'd me in the face, to think
I thus could speak of Yarrow!

"Oh! green," said I, "are Yarrow's
Holms,
And sweet is Yarrow flowing!
Fair hangs the apple frae the rock,
But we will leave it growing.
O'er hilly path, and open Strath,

"There's Godwin's daughter, Shelley's
wife,*
A writing fearful stories;
There's Hazlitt, who, with Hunt and
Keats
Brays forth in Cockney chorus;
There's pleasant Thomas Moore, a lad
Who sings of Rose and Fanny;†
Why throw away these wits so gay
To take up Don Giovanni.

"What's Juan but a shameless tale,
That bursts all rules asunder?
There are a thousand such elsewhere
As worthy of your wonder."
Strange words they seem'd of slight
and scorn;
His lordship look'd not *canny*;‡
And took a pinch of snuff, to think
I flouted Don Giovanni.

"O! rich," said I, "are Juan's rhymes,
And warm its verse is flowing!
Fair crops of Blasphemy it bears,
But we will leave them growing.
In Pindar's|| strain, in prose of Paine,

---

* Mrs. Shelley, wife of the poet, was daughter of William Godwin, (author of "Political Justice," and several novels, of which "Caleb Williams" and "St. Leon" are best remembered,) and the no less celebrated Mary Wolstoncroft, his wife, who wrote a "Vindication of the Rights of Woman." Mrs. Shelley was born in 1797, and died in 1851. The "fearful story" above alluded to was "Frankenstein," published in 1817. Among other works of hers is her "Lives of Eminent Literary Frenchmen," in *Lardner's Cyclopædia*. She edited, with notes, her husband's poems.—M.

† "Come, tell me, says Rosa, as kissing and kissed," &c. and "Sweet Fanny of Timmol," with many other equally edifying little *pieces*.—W. M. [These lyrics, which are certainly not the most modest *chansons*, in the world, have been omitted in the collection of Moore's works edited by himself.—M.]

‡ Scottice for—I do not exactly know what—but it signifies something pleasant, comfortable, knowing, snug, or the like.—W. M.

|| Peter, to wit.—W. M. [Dr. John Wolcott, who satirized George III. and others, under the *nom de plume* of "Peter Pindar," was born in 1738 and died in 1819. The temporary and personal nature of his subjects has deprived his

We'll wander Scotland thorough;
But, though so near, we will not turn
Into the Dale of Yarrow.

"Let Beeves and home-bred Kine partake
The sweets of Burn-mill meadow;
The Swan on still St. Mary's Lake
Float double, Swan and Shadow!
We will not see them; will not go,
To-day, nor yet to-morrow:
Enough if in our hearts we know,
There's such a place as Yarrow.

"Be Yarrow Stream unseen, unknown!
It must, or we shall rue it:
We have a vision of our own;
Ah! why should we undo it?
The treasured dreams of times long past
We'll keep them, winsome Marrow!
For when we're there, although 'tis fair
'Twill be another Yarrow!

"If Care with freezing years should come,
And wandering seem but folly,

And many another Zanny,
As gross, we read, so where's the need,
To wade through Don Giovanni.

"Let Colburn's town-bred cattle snuff
The filths of Lady Morgan,*
Let Maturin to amorous thémes
Attune his barrel organ!†
We will not read them, will not hear
The parson or the granny;‡
And, I dare say, as bad as they,
Or worse, is Don Giovanni.

"Be Juan then unseen, unknown!
It must, or we may rue it;
We may have virtue of our own;
Ah! why should we undo it?
The treasured faith of days long past,
We still shall prize o'er any;
And we shall grieve to hear the gibes
Of scoffing Don Giovanni.

"When Whigs with freezing rule shall come,‖
And piety seem folly;

---

writings of much of their interest, but their peculiar humour and racy freshnees have scarcely ever been equalled. — M.

* In the day when these stanzas were written, it was the Tory policy personally to assail all writers of Whig politics. Lady Morgan, who avowed very liberal opinions, was the frequent object of attack in *Blackwood* and the *Quarterly Review:* — as a woman, and therefore comparatively defenceless, the Tory wits and libellers safely assailed her. — M.

† The Rev. R. C. Maturin, who was compelled to publish plays, sermons, poetry, and novels, to assist the very narrow income he derived from the Church, in which he had a Dublin curacy — had rendered himself somewhat liable to the reproach above-written, by the somewhat too vivid colouring of some scenes in his romance of "Melmoth the Wanderer." — M.

‡ Vulgariter for grandmother, not that I mean to assert that Lady M. *is* a grandmother, but to insinuate, that as she is old enough to be one, she has a fair claim to the title. — M. [A mistake. Lady Morgan was not 45 years old in 1819. — M.]

‖ The Whigs *did* come in, and Tories *went out*, in 1830, and have continued in office twenty years out of the twenty-five since that date. — M.

Should we be loth to stir from home,
And yet be melancholy;
Should life be dull, and spirits low,
'Twill soothe us in our sorrow
That earth has something yet to show,
The bonny Holms of Yarrow!"

When Cam and Isis* curbed by Brougham,
Shall wander melancholy;
When Cobbet, Wooler, Watson, Hunt,†
And all the swinish many,
Shall rough-shod ride‡ o'er church and state,
Then hey! for Don Giovanni."

---

* Rivers, on the banks of which certain Universities much indebted to the learned jurisconsult mentioned in the text for his kind attention to their interests, are seated. — W. M. [Brougham, contrary to the poet's anticipation, did "curb" Cambridge and Oxford, from 1830 to 1834 — his position, as Lord Chancellor of England, giving him *ex officio* authority over these Universities. — M.]

† Of the four worthies named here, notable liberals at this period, Cobbett and Hunt eventually became members of Parliament. Dr. Watson, accused of sedition, and suspected of treason, found safety in retreat to the United States; Wooler, a very able man, editor of "The Yellow Dwarf," a Radical Journal, outlived Maginn many years, but died obscurely. — M.

‡ "We shall ride roughshod over Carlton House." — Speech of all the talents through the mouth-piece of Lord ———, on hearing of the assassination of Mr Percival. — W. M. [The Whigs, who came into office in 1806, headed by Fox, were on such good terms with themselves that "All the Talents" was their own self-assumed *sobriquet*. In May, 1812, on Percival's death, the Marquis Wellesley was empowered to ask the Whig leaders (Lords Grey and Grenville) to form a Government. The Prince Regent, who desired to retain his household, (the heads of which were his personal friends,) was disgusted with Lord Grey's haughty intimation that, as a preliminary, all its members must resign, and his Lordship's boast in private that "he would ride roughshod through Carlton House." This caused the Prince to place Lord Liverpool and the Tories in office, which the Whigs did not obtain until November, 1830. — M.]

The Irishman and the Lady.

(*To be sung with boisterous expression.*)

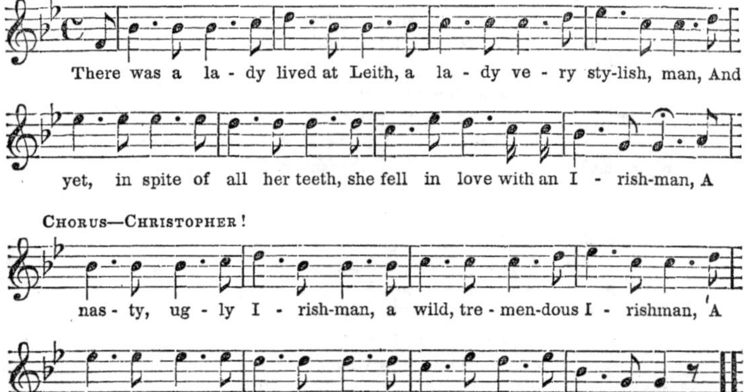

I.

THERE was a lady lived at Leith,
  A lady very stylish, man;
And yet, in spite of all her teeth,
  She fell in love with an Irishman.
    A nasty, ugly Irishman,
    A wild, tremendous Irishman—
A tearing, swearing, thumping, bumping, ramping, roaring Irishman.

II.

His face was no ways beautiful,
  For with small-pox 'twas scarr'd across;
And the shoulders of the ugly dog
  Were almost doubled a yard across.
    O, the lump of an Irishman,
    The whisky-devouring Irishman—
The great he-rogue, with his wonderful brogue, the fighting, rioting, Irishman.

III.

One of his eyes was bottle-green,
  And the other eye was out, my dear;
And the calves of his wicked-looking legs
  Were more than two feet about, my dear,

O, the great big Irishman,
The rattling, battling Irishman —
The stamping, ramping, swaggering, staggering, leathering swash of an Irishman.

IV.

He took so much of Lundy-Foot,
That he used to snort and snuffle — O;
And in shape and size, the fellow's neck,
Was as bad as the neck of a buffalo.
O, the horrible Irishman,
The thundering, blundering Irishman —
The slashing, dashing, smashing, lashing, thrashing, hashing Irishman.

V.

His name was a terrible name, indeed,
Being Timothy Thady Mulligan;
And whenever he emptied his tumbler of punch,
He'd not rest till he filled it full again.
The boozing, bruising Irishman,
The 'toxicated Irishman —
The whisky, frisky, rummy, gummy, brandy, no dandy Irishman.

VI.

This was the lad the lady loved,
Like all the girls of quality;
And he broke the skulls of the men of Leith,
Just by the way of jollity.
O, the leathering Irishman,
The barbarous, savage Irishman —
The hearts of the maids, and the gentlemen's heads, were bother'd, I'm sure, by this Irishman.*

---

* This song was introduced by Odoherty, (to be sung with boisterous expression,) in the first of the NOCTES AMBROSIANÆ, (March, 1822,) and is to be found, set to music, in Vol. I, page 153, of the collective edition of that work, published by Redfield, and annotated by myself.— M.

Here Let me Dine.

'Tis not when on turtle and venison dining,
And sipping Tokay at the cost of his Grace;
Like the plate on his sideboard, I'm set to be shining—
(So nearly a mug may resemble a face.)
This is not the dinner for me—a poor sinner;
Where I'm bound to show off, and throw pearls before swine.
Give me turnips and mutton,—(I ne'er was a glutton)—
Good friends and good liquor—and *here* let me dine.

Your critic shows off, with his snatches and tastes
Of odd trash from Reviews, and odd sorts of odd wine;
Half a glass—half a joke—from the Publisher's stock
Of Balaam and Hock, are but trash, I opine.
Convérsazioni—are not for my money,
Where Blue Stockings prate about Wylie and Pen;*
I'd rather get tipsy with *ipsissimi ipsi*—
Plain women must yield to plain sense and plain men.

Your dowager gives you good dinners, 'tis true;
She shines in liqueurs, and her Sherry's antique;
But then you must swear by her eye's lovely blue,
And adore the bright bloom that is *laid* on her cheek.
Blue eyes in young faces are quite in their places;
One praises and gazes with boundless delight
And juvenile roses ne'er trespass on noses,
As the custom of those is, I've cut for to-night.

Your colonels talk but of a siege or a battle—
Your merchants of naught but the course of exchange—
Your squires, of their hounds, of the corn-bill or cattle—
Your doctors their cases and cures will arrange—
Your lawyer's confounding, on multiple poinding—
Your artists are great on expression and tone—
Parsons sport *Moderators* and *Church-procurators*,
Each set is the devil when feeding alone.

But *here*, where all sets and all topics are mingled—
The hero—the dentist—the parson—the squire—
No *one* branch of blarney's selected or singled,—
But our wine and our wit each discussion inspire;

---

* Popular novels of that period—viz, "Sir Andrew Wylie" by Galt, and "Pen Owen" by Hook, cousin of Theodore's.—M.

Where the pun and the glass simultaneously pass;
  Where each song seems quite heavenly, each bumper divine;
Where there's drinking and smoking, and quizzing and joking,
  But nothing provoking — HERE! HERE! let me dine.*

Ana.†

I. EVERY one knows that in Burns' song which begins,

"Is there for honest poverty?"

the bard indulged in a *levelling* strain of sentiments, which some of his readers have blamed; yet one of the most forcible stanzas might have been borrowed (if Burns had ever borrowed) from a person who was not likely to have encouraged *levelling* principles, or to have underrated the authority of the *princes* of the earth. I mean King Lewis the XIV. of haughty and magnificent memory.

Burns says,

"A king may mak a belted knight,
  A marquis, duke, and a' that;
But an honest man's aboo his might,
  Gude faith he maunna fa' that."

Freron tells us, that Lewis walking one day in the garden of Versailles, with all his nobles around him uncovered, directed Mansard, an able architect and amiable man, who was, it seems, unwell, to put on his hat — the courtiers looked astonished at so great a condescension, but the monarch rebuked them by saying, "Gentlemen, I can make as many dukes as I please, but I never could make a man like Mansard." Freron, vol. ix p. 36.‡

II. The Jesuits of Dole had two fine convents and estates, the one called L'Arc (the bow) in Lorrain, and La Fléche (the

* This song appeared in "THE NOCTES," for May, 1822. — M.

† These Ana appeared in *Blackwood* in 1819, and are presented here not so much for their intrinsic merit (though they are curious, and show how discursive Maginn's reading had been) but because they are among the very first of the Doctor's contributions. — M.

‡ Henry VIII. of England, had previously applied the same words to Hans Holbein, the painter. — M.

arrow) in Anjou; when the latter was given them by Henry the IV. the following distich appeared,

> *Arcum* dola dedit, dedit illis alma *Sagittam*
> Francia, quis chordum, quem meruere, dabit?
>
> *Howell's Fam. Epist.*
>
> Dole gave these monks the bow—a shaft, the king;
> But who will give, what they deserve, a string!

The anagram is pleasant; but, it seems, the Jesuits know how to have *two strings to their bow.*

III. Pope exposes, in admirable poetry, the idle vanity of those whose

> ———ancient, but ignoble blood,
> Has crept through scoundrels ever since the flood.

But I never have met this folly more strikingly exemplified than in an account of the family of Rosencrantz, in Hofman's Historical Portraits of the Worthies of Denmark. "This family, through a long train of descents of persons filling the highest offices, offers few events worthy of attention, except that one nobleman of this name was executed for forging, and another banished for a libel."

IV. *A Curious Trial by Jury.*—Christiern the II. had a mistress named Dyvele, with whom he suspected one of his nobles, named Forben Oxe, to have been too familiar. She, however, died, and after her death the king asked Oxe to tell him sincerely if his suspicions were well founded. I own, said Oxe, I tried, but never could succeed with her. The furious king ordered Oxe to be tried for this intended crime before the senate—he was, of course, acquitted; if, said the enraged and disappointed tyrant, his neck were as thick as an ox's, I would have his head. He called, therefore, together *twelve* peasants, and forming a square with four spears, into which they entered, (an odd jury box,) he forbade them to separate till they should have agreed to their verdict upon Oxe. The peasants, perplexed what to do, returned a special verdict which would have done no discredit to a jury of Jesuits—"We can not try him," said they, "when his own confessions have already condemned him." This was enough for Christiern, and poor Oxe did lose his head accordingly.—Frer. ix. 54.

V. That madman Rousseau wrote to a farce called *Narcissus* a preface as full of the most absurd self-love, as the story of Narcissus itself—But Ovid painted his maniac with a soft and harmonious pencil; Rousseau's portrait of himself is in the style of Spagnoletto—Amongst other fine sentiments which he means for philosophy, he says, "In laboring to acquire *my own* esteem (it does not seem to have required much labor) I have learned to do very well without the esteem of others." Thus the clear and Christian duty of satisfying, in the first place, one's own conscience is parodied by Rousseau into an expression of that morbid vanity which can extract internal satisfaction from the disapprobation of all mankind.

VI. The character of Louis XVIII. has been so long obscured, formerly by his exile, and latterly by the eclipsing glory of the Sieur Caze,* his favorite, that one must look thirty years back to find any traces of his real disposition, which is the more material, under present circumstances, inasmuch as it has given rise to the reproach so commonly thrown out against the Ultras of France, that they are "*more Royalist than the King.*" A little examination into the early history of the revolution will show that it was hardly possible to be *less Royalist* than Louis XVIII. was in those days of trial. We can not suspect that he was paralyzed by the same vile and odious motives which excited the activity of Philip Egalité; but undoubtedly the circumstance in which he stood,—of being the *second* in succession to the *crown*, and the *first* in succession to the *regency*, ought, as a matter of mere good taste, to have made his affection towards his unhappy and persecuted brother a little more prominent. It was surely a singular and unlucky coincidence, that he should be, of all his family after the Dauphin, the nearest to the throne and after Egalité, the dearest to the Jacobins. It is true that this disgraceful popularity was softened down by the very qualities which perhaps contributed to create it. His manners were low; his tastes were rather worse than his manners, and what-

* M. Decazes, who succeeded Fouché (in September, 1815), as Minister of Police, is the person indicated here. He was personally a great favorite with Louis XVIII., not only because of his strong Royalist predilections, but on account of his elegant manners. Eventually he became Premier.—M.

ever abilities he may have possessed, were so buried under the sensuality and selfishness of his mode of life, that they gave neither hopes nor fears to the discontented nor to the loyal. Observe, we speak of thirty years ago. It is to be hoped, and indeed there is reason to believe, that these thirty years of adversity (if the king considered that to be adversity during which he never wanted two courses) may have in some degree improved the personal character of this prince. But it is surely not too much to say, that somewhat of his original and natural indolence and selfishness is likely still to adhere to him, and to render him as indifferent to what may be the state of France uuder his younger brother, as he was to what was the state of France under his elder brother. In 1789, a patriotic wit attributes to each of the royal family a song, the first line of which is supposed to be characteristic. The Count D'Artois* sings,

"I am a soldier and a gentleman;"

but the Comte de Provence (Louis XVIII.) only mutters,

"I am no king; and what is worse, no prince."

Again—in another *jeu d'esprit*, also from a *patriot* pen, where characteristic residences in the different streets of Paris are assigned to the royal family, Egalité is lodged in the Rue de Louis le Grand; the Count D'Artois (whose devotion to his brother was so honorable that even his enemies respected it) is placed in the Place Royale, while Monsieur (Louis XVIII.) is trundled into the Rue *des Francs Bourgeois*—a street, says St. Foix, which has its name from being inhabited by the lowest and the meanest of the people. These not unimportant trifles are to be found in the *Memoires pour servir a l'Histoire de* 1789, pp. 30 and 116. But this, you will perhaps say, is the malice of the Jacobins. Not altogether, for the Jacobins detested M. D'Artois; yet, as we see, did him some kind of justice; and why should we take it for granted that they did not also do justice to M. de Provence? But let us see what the Royalists thought of him. In the 15th volume of the *Actes des Apotres*, p. 128, there is one of those satirical songs called by the French *Noels:* the verse in which Louis XVIII. is described, may be quoted

* Afterward the unfortunate Charles the Tenth.—M.

as an additional proof of what the public opinion even of the Royalists of 1790, was with regard to him:—

Grand ami du silence,
Du bon vin, du repos.
Le Comte de Provence
Balbutia ces mots;
"Souffrez que promptement chez moi je me retire,
"Je crains trop de l'embarras;
"*Mon frère est dans un vilain pas,*
"Mais, helas! *qu'il s'en tire.*"

which may be thus imitated:—

Very active at clearing his plate,
Very clever at holding his tongue;
In size he is Louis the great,
And thus he half hiccupp'd half sung:
"Permit me to make my escape,
"I'm a poor, inoffensive good man;
"My brother, who's in a d——d scrape,
"Must get out o't as well as he can."

We think one may now safely say, that it is no very great crime in the French Royalists to be *more Royalist* than Louis XVIIIth, who seeing his brother, his king, "*in a d——d scrape,*" is represented as leaving him "*to get out of it as well as he could.*"

Chevy Chase; A Poem—Idem Latine Redditum.*

BEING of Sir Philip Sidney's opinion, that the ballad of Chevy Chase stirs the heart like the sound of a trumpet, and being moreover willing that other nations should have at least some idea of that magnificent poem, I have translated it into the universal language of Europe — Latin; and I send you my translation of the first fytte; — you will perceive that I have retained the measure and structure of the verse most religiously — I wish I could say that I have preserved also the fire and spirit of the original. Bold, at the desire of Bishop Compton, translated into Latin the more modern ballad of Chevy Chase — as also did Anketeil, a Presbyterian Clergyman (I believe) in the north of Ireland. Lord Woodhouselee, in his excellent Essay on Translation, has quoted the first verse of Anketeil's translation apparently without knowing the author. But to say nothing of the inferiority of the poem they translated, I flatter myself that I out-top them by the head and broad shoulders, in the superior richness and melody of my double rhymes. Print this, then, by all means — so no more from your servant at command. — O. P.

First Fytte.	*Pars Prima.*
1.	1.
THE Percy out of Northumberland,†	PERSÆUS ex Northumbria
And a vow to God made he,	Vovebat, Diis iratis,
That he would hunt in the mountains	Venare inter dies tres
Of Cheviot within days three,	In montibus Cheviatis,
In the mauger of doughty Douglas,	Contemtis forti Douglaso
And all that with him be.	Et omnibus cognatis.

* This first fytte of "Chevy Chase," the earliest contribution of any moment by Maginn to *Blackwood*, appeared in the number for November, 1819. It was signed O. P. — which Mr. Blackwood subsequently extended into "Dr. Olinthus Petre, Trinity College, Dublin." It was under this signature that Maginn severely attacked the late Sir John Leslie, (Professor of Natural Philosophy in Edinburgh University,) accusing him, among other things, of abusing the Hebrew language without even knowing its alphabet! Leslie brought a libel-suit against Blackwood for this, and obtained — a farthing damages, which was, in fact, a defeat. — M.

† I have modernized the spelling of the old ballad. — W. M.

2.

The fattest harts in Cheviot
He said he'd kill and carry away:
"By my faith," said doughty Douglas,
"I'll let* that hunting if I may."

3.

The Percy out of Bamborough came,
With him a mighty meany;
With fifteen hundred archers bold;
They were chosen out of shires three.

4.

This began on Monday at morn,
In Cheviot the hills so high;
The child may rue that is unborn;
It is the more pity!

5.

The drivers through the woods went,
For to raise up the deer;
Bowmen bickered upon the bent,
With their broad arrows clear.

6.

Then the wild through the woods went,
On every side sheer;
Grayhounds through the groves glent,
For to kill their deer.

7.

This began in Cheviot the hills above,
Early on a Monday;
By that it drew to the hour of noon,
A hundred fat harts dead there lay.

8.

They blew a mort upon the bent;
They 'sembled on sides sheer:
To the quarry then the Percy went,
To see the brittling of the deer.

9.

He said—"It was the Douglas' promise,
This day to meet me here,

2.

"Optimos cervos ibi," ait,
"Occisos reportabo;"
"Per Jovem," inquit Douglasus,
Venatum hunc vetabo."

3.

Ex Bamboro Persæus it,
Cum agmine potenti;
Nam tribus agris lecti sunt
Sagittarii ter quingenti.

4.

Ad Cheviatos graditur,
In Lunæ die mane;
Puer nondum natus fleret hoc;
Quod est dolendum sane!

5.

Viri, qui cervos agerent,
Per nemora pergebant;
Dum sagittarii spiculas
Ex arcubus fundebant.

6.

Tum diffugerunt† penitus
Per omnem sylvam feræ;
Et eas canes Gallici
Sequentes percurrêre.

7.

Hunc matutino tempore
Venatum sic cæperunt;
Et centum sub meridiem
Pingues cervi ceciderunt.

8.

Tum tubæ taratantara‡
Convocat dissipatos;
Comes Persæus visum it
Cervos dilaniatos.

9.

Dicens, "Promisit Douglasus
Mî hic occursum ire,

---

* *Let:* —to hinder.—M.

† Percy's translation of *sheer.*—W M.

‡ So Ennius. At tuba terribili sonitu *taratantara* dixit.—W. M.

But I wist he would fail verament,"
A great oath the Percy sware.

Sed* scivi quod non faceret."
His dictis jurat mirè.

10.

At last a squire of Northumberland
Looked at his hand full nigh —
He was ware of the Douglas coming,
With him a mighty meany;

10.

Tandem armiger Northumbriæ
Aspexit venientem
Prope ad manum Douglasum,
Et agmina ducentem.

11.

Both with spear, bill, and brand,
It was a mighty sight to see;
Hardier men of heart and hand
Were not in Christianity.

11.

Cum hastis, pilis, ensibus,
Magnifici iverunt;
Fortiores in fidelibus
Domini non fuerunt.

12.

They were twenty hundred spearmen good.
Withouten any fail;
They were born along by the water of
Tweed,
In the bounds of Tividale.

12.

Bis mille procul dubio
Hastati bonæ notæ,
Ad aquas Tuedæ nati sunt,
In finibus Tiviotæ.

13.

"Leave off the brittling of the deer,"
he said,
"And to your bows take heed;
For never since you were on your moth-
ers born
Had ye such meikle need."

13.

"Mittite cervos, sumite,
Sagittas nullâ morâ;
Nunquam tam opus fuit, ex
Nostrâ natali horâ."

14.

The doughty Douglas on a steed
He rode his men beforne;
His armour glittered as did a glede —
A bolder bairn was never born.

14.

In primo fortis Douglasus
Equitans veniebat;
Lorica prunæ similis
Ardenti resplendebat.

15.

"Tell me what men ye are," he says,
"Or whose men that ye be;
Who gave ye leave to hunt in this
Cheviot Chase in the spite of me?"

15.

Et, "Quinam estis, cedo," ait,
"Aut cujus viri sitis?
Quis misit vos venatum hic,
Nobis admodum invitis?"

16.

The first man that an answer made,
It was the Lord Percy —

16.

Persæus autem Douglaso
Respondit longe primus,

* Consult the Edinburgh Reviewer of Falconer's Strabo for this construction of *scio quod* — the "paltry" dog will remember something about it, as sure as my name is not Copplestone.— W. M.

"We will not tell what men we are,
Nor whose men that we be;
But we will hunt here in this chase.
In the spite of thine and thee.

"Qui sumus haud narrabimus,
Aut cujus viri simus;
Sed hic, invitis omnibus,
Venatum statim imus.

17.

"The fattest harts in Cheviot
We have killed, and cast to carry away."
"By my troth," said the doughty Douglas,
Therefore the one of us shall die this day."

17.

"Cervorum hic pinguissimos
Occisos auferemus."
"Idcirco," dixit Douglasus
"Necèsse est ut pugnemus."

18.

Then said the doughty Douglas
Unto the Lord Percy,
"To kill all these guiltless men,
Alas! it were great pity;

18.

Et dixit fortis Douglasus
Hæc verba nunc Persæo,
"Necare hos innoxios
Non esset gratum deo;

19.

"But, Percy, thou art a lord of land,
I am an earl in my own country;
Let all our men upon a party stand,
And do the battle of thee and me."

19.

"Sed tu, Persæë, princeps es,
Sum ego comes quoque,
Cernamus soli, agmine
Manente hic utroque."

20.

"Now Christ's curse on his crown," said the Lord Percy,
"Whosoever thereto says nay!
Bv my troth, doughty Douglas," he says,
"Thou shalt never see that day,

20.

Persæus inquit, "Pereat is
Qui huic vult obviam ire
Nam, hercle, dies aderit
Nunquam, Douglàse dire,

21.

"Neither in England, Scotland, nor France,
Nor for no man of woman born;
But an fortune be my chance,
I dare meet him one for one."

21.

"Quum Angliâ, Scotiâ, Galliâ,
Negaverim tentare
Sortem cum ullo homine
In pugnâ singulari."

22.

Then bespake a squire of Northumberland,
Rog. Witherington was his name—
"It shall never be told in South England
To King Harry the fourth for shame

22.

Tunc armiger Northumbriæ
R. Withringtonus fatur,
"Nunquam Henrico principi
In Anglia hoc dicatur;

23.

"I wot ye be great lords two,
I am a poor squire of land,
I will never see my captain fight in a field
And look on myself and stand;*
But while I may my weapon wield,
I will not fail both heart and hand."

23.

"Vos estis magni comites
Et pauper miles ego,
Sed pugnaturum dominum,
Me otioso, nego:
Sed corde, manu, enseque,
Pugnabo quamdiu dego."

24.

That day, that day, that dreadful day—
The first fytte here I find;
An' ye will hear more of the hunting of Cheviot,
Yet there is more behind.

24.

O dies! dies, dies trux!
Sic finit cantus primus;
Si de venatu plura vis,
Plura narrare scimus.

FINIS PARTIS PRIMÆ.

P. S.—I am aware that "Douglassius" is consecrated; but I am not without authority for Douglasus.—I have also translated this into Greek, and I send you the first verse as a specimen.

Περσαῖος ἐκ Νορθύμβριας
Εὔχετο τοῖς θεοῖσι,
Θηρᾷν ἐν τρισὶν ἡμέραις
'Εν οὔρεσί Χεβιατοίσι,
Κἄν ἀντέχῃσι Δούγλασος
Σὺν πᾶσιν ἑτάροισι.

Don't say a word of this, however, to Hallam—"classic Hallam, much renowned for Greek," as Lord Byron justly styles him—lest he should mistake my verses for Pindar's, and consequently declare them not Greek. Apropos, is it not a good joke to see Hallam putting a Greek motto to his book on the Middle Ages after all? I was thinking of translating old Chevy into Hebrew—for I am a Masorite; but as Professor Leslie has declared Hebrew to be a "rude and poor dialect," in his book on Arithmetic, I was afraid to come under the censure of that learned gentleman. To be sure he does not know (*as I can prove from his writings*) even the alphabet of the language he abuses, but still I am afraid he would freeze me if I had any thing to do with it.

---

* In Bishop Percy—"And stand myself and look on." But correct it, meo periculo.—W. M.

Chevy Chase.

*Second Fytte.**

1.

†The English men had their bows bent,
Their hearts were good enow,
The first‡ of arrows that they shot off,
Seven score spearmen they slew.

2.

Yet bides Earl Douglas on the bent,
A captain good enough;
And that was seen verament,
For he wrought them wo and wouch.

3.

The Douglas parted his host in three,
Like a chief chieftain of pride;
With sure spears of mighty tree,
They came in on every side.

4.

Through our English archery
Gave many a wound full wide;
Many a doughty they made to die,
Which gained them no pride.

5.

The English men let their bows be,
And pulled out brands that were bright;
It was a heavy sight to see
Bright swords on helmets light.

Pars Secunda.

1.

Angli perstrenui animis
Tunc arcus intenderunt,
Et vicies septem homines
Primo jactu necaverunt.

2.

Attamen mansit Douglasus
In boni ducis morem;
Quod patuit cum perniciem
Effudit et dolorem.

3.

Trifariam struxit aciem,
Periti ducis arte;
Cum hastis ligni validi
Ruunt ex omni parte.

4.

Ediderunt stragem plurimam
Per ordines Anglorum:
Heroum vitas dempserunt§
Non amplius superborum.‖

5.

Stringunt, omissis arcubus,
Angli gladios fulgentes:
Quos miserum fuit cernere
In cassibus descendentes.

---

* This second fytte of "Chevy Chase" did not appear in *Blackwood* until June, 1820.—M.

† I have, as before, modernized the spelling of the old ballad, and in a few places the language.—W. M.

‡ *i. e.* First Flight. Percy.—W. M.

§ Dr. Carey (Prosody, p. 199, &c.) condemns this license. I therefore give him leave to alter my systolated præterites into preterpluperfects, as he has done in all the passages which stand in the way of his rule. I have no doubt that he will discover some new picturesque mood and tense beauty in the change, quite unknown to the author.—W. M.

‖ I hope I have hit the sense of my original.—W. M.

6.

Through rich mail and myne-ye-ple*
Many stern they struck down straight;
Many a ficke that was full free
There under foot did light.

6.

Armorum plicas splendidas
Mucro strictus penetravit:
Et multos quondam nobiles
Pes vilis conculcavit.

7.

At last the Douglas and the Percy met,
Like two captains of might and main;
They swept together, till they both sweat,
With swords of fine Milain.†

7.

Persæus mox et Douglasus
(Dux contra vires ducis)
Pugna concurrunt ensibus
Mediolani cusis.

8.

These worthy fickes for to fight,
Thereto they were full fain,
Till the blood out of their helmets sprung,
As ever did hail or rain.

8.

Hi comites fortissimi
Perstiterunt pugnando,
Donec cruor saliit cassibus,
Ut imber vel ut grando.

9.

"Hold thee, Percy," said the Douglas,
"And i' faith I will thee bring,
Where thou shalt have an earl's wages
Of James, our Scottish king:

9.

"Si cedas," inquit Douglasus,
"Perducam te, Persæe,
Ubi ut comes viveres
Sub rege Scotiæ meæ:

10.

"Thou shalt have thy ransom free—
I bid thee hear this thing;
For the manfullest man art thou,
That ever I conquered in field-fighting."

10.

"Et ‡lytrum nullum peterem,
Nam vere potest dici,
Te virum esse optimum,
Quem prælio unquam vici."

11.

"Nay, then," said the Lord Percy
"I told it thee beforne,
That I would never yielded be
To no man of woman born."

11.

Dixit Persæus, "Iterum,
Quod antea dixi, edam;
Id est, quod nunquam homini,
Ex fæmina nato cedam."

12.

With that there came an arrow hastily
Forth of a mighty one;

12.

Ex forti arcu calamus
Tum rapide volavit

---

* "Perhaps many plies or folds. Monyple is still used in this sense in the north, according to Mr. Lambe," Bp. Percy. I have followed him.—W. M.

† Swords made of Milan Steel. Percy.—W. M.

‡ Græce, λύτρον. Ennius uses it, or rather its plural, lytra, as the name of a play concerning the ransom of Hector's body. If this be not thought sufficient authority, the reader may substitute *prœtium* in the text with all my heart.—W. M.

It hath stricken the Earl Douglas
  In at the breast-bone.

Et inter verba Douglasum
  In pectore vulneravit.

13.

Through liver and lungs both
  The sharp arrow is gone;
That never after in his life days
  He spake more words than *one.
"Fight ye my merry men while you may,
  For my life days are gone."

In jecore et pulmonibus
  Hæsit sagita cita;
Et postea verbum unicum
  Hoc tantum dixit ita,
"Pugnate strenue, socii,
  Nam ego cedo vita."

14.

The Percy leant upon his brand,
  And saw the Douglas die;
He took the dead man by the hand,
  And said, "Wo is me for thee.

Persæus nitens gladio
  Douglassi vidit mortem,
Et manu capta mortui
  Ploravit ejus sortem.

15.

"To have saved thy life I'd have parted with
  My lands for years three;
For a better man of heart nor hand
  Was not in all the north country."

"Tribus annis agros dederem
  Servare virum talem;
Nam fortior nemo fuit per
  Regionem borealem."

16.

Of all that saw a Scottish knight,
  Was named Sir Hugh Montgomery;
He saw the Douglas to death was dight;
  He spanned a spear a trusty tree.

Hugo Montgomoræus hunc
  Cœsum vulnere indigno
Vidit, et hastam arripit
  Ex strenuo factam ligno.

17.

He rode upon a courser
  Through an hundred archery;
He never stinted nor never stopped
  Till he came to the good Lord Percy.

Et equitavit fortiter
  Per sagittarios centum;
Donec ad Anglum comitem
  Ab eo erat ventum.

18.

He set upon Lord Percy
  A dint that was full sore,

Persæum gravi vulnere
  Dicto citius sauciavit,

---

* From this it appears that Jerry-Benthamism is of an older date than the superficial commonly imagine. Fight-you-my-merry-men-while-you-may-for-my-life-days-are-gone; or, as the original has it, Fyghte-ye-my-merry-men-whylles-ye-may-for-my-lyff-days-ben-gan, is as pretty a *single* word as any we can find in the lucid pages of this most Euphuistical radical, and most radical Euphuist, who commonly passes in our days for the inventor of the many-words-clubbing-to-make-one style. We have here a much older authority; so that Jerry must be set down as one of the *servum pecus* in that instance.—W. M.

With a sure spear of a trusty tree,
Clean through the body he the Percy bore.

Nam corpus hasta rigidâ
Penitus perforavit.

19.

At the other side that a man might see
A large cloth yard and mare.
Two better Captains were not in Christianty
Than that day slain was there.

19.

Hasta ex læso corpore
Exivit ulnæ spatio;
Meliores cæsis ducibus
Non tenuit ulla natio.

20.

An archer of Northumberland,
Saw slain was the Lord Percy;
He bare a bent bow in his hand,
Was made of trusty tree.

20.

Sagittarius ex Northumbria
Vidit dominum necatum;
In manu arcum tenuit
Ex arbore fabricâtum.

21.

An arrow that a cloth-yard long,
To the hard steel haled he;
A dint that was both sad and sore
He set on Sir Hugh Montgomery.

21.

Tres pedes longum calamum
Perduxit ad mucronem,
Et vulnere mortifero
Interimit Hugonem.

22.

The dint it was both sad and sore,
That he on Montgomery set;
The swan-feathers that his arrow bore
With his heart's-blood were wet.

22.

Pertriste fuit vulnus, quod
Hugo accipiebat:
Sagittæ alas cygneas
Cor sanguine tingebat.

23.

There was never a ficke one foot woul fly,
But still in storm did stand,
Hewing on each other while they might drie
With many a baleful band.

23.

Nulli volebant fugere;
Sed strenue simul stantes*
Dimicabant quamdiu licuit,
Se mutuo laniantes.

24.

This battle began on Cheviot,
An hour before the noon,
And when even song-bell was rung,
The battle was not half done.

24.

Cœperunt hora cernere
Antemeridiana;
Et prælium sæviit vesperis
Cum sonuit campana.

25.

They took on, on either hand,
By the light of the moon;

25.

Etiam sub Lunæ radiis
Perstabant sic pugnare;

* An attempt at imitating the alliteration of the original.—W. M.

Many had no strength to stand,
In Cheviot the hills aboun.

Donce sauciati plurimi
Non potuerunt stare.

26.

Of fifteen hundred archers of England
Went away but fifty and three:
Of twenty hundred spearmen of Scotland
But even five and fifty.

26.

Quinquaginta tres rediere ex
Anglorum ter quingentis;
Quinquaginta quinque tantum ex
Bis millibus Scotæ gentis.

27.

But all were slain, Cheviot within,
They had no strength to stand on high;
The child may rue that is unborn;
It was the more pity.

27.

Ceciderunt sane cæteri
In montibus Cheviatis;
Puer nondum natus fleret hoc
Quod est dolendum satis.

28.

There was slain with the Lord Percy
Sir John of Agerstone;
Sir Roger, the kind Hartley,
Sir William the bold Heron.

28.

Occisi cum Persæo sunt*
Johannes Agerstonus,
Rogerus mitis Hartlius,
Gulielmus et Heronus;

29.

Sir George the worthy Lovel,
A knight of great renown,
Sir Ralph, the rich Rokeby,
With dints were beaten down.

29.

Et Georgius dignus Lovelus,
Bellator famæ veræ,
Rodolphus dives Rokebius
Confossi cecidere.

30.

For Withrington my heart is wo,
That ever he slain should be:
For when his legs were hewn in two,
He knelt, and fought upon his knee.

30.

Pro Withringtono doleo
Quem fatum triste stravit;
Nam binis fractis cruribus
In genibus pugnavit.

31.

There was slain with the doughty Douglas
Sir Hugh Montgomery,

31.

Montgomoræus cecidit
Cum Douglaso die eo;

---

* How beautifully Homeric! How like the catalogues of the slain in the lines of the Prince of poets! Particularly, how like the following:

Καὶ σὺν Περσαῖῳ ἐδάμεν 'Αγαττώνος ἀμύμων,
'Αρτλεῖος τ' ἀγαθὸς, 'Ηρώνος θ' ἱππότα δῖος;
Καὶ Λοβέλος κρατερὸς αἰχμητῆς, ἠδὲ 'Ροβαῖος
'Αφνειος βιότοιο πέσον χαλκοῖο τυπῇ.

The names in the Greek are not expressed so roughly as in the English, but there is a manifest resemblance between the passages.—W. M.

Sir David Liddel, that worthy was.
  His sister's son was he.

Atque Liddelus, dignus vir
  Nepos Montgomeræo.*

32.

Sir Charles Murray in that place,
  That never a foot would fly,
Sir Hugh Maxwell, a lord that was,
  With the Douglas did he die.

32.

Moræus, virtus bellica
  Quem fugere non sivit;
Hugo Maxwellus dominus
  Cum Douglaso obivit.

33.

So on the morrow they made them biers
  Of birch and hazel gray;
Many widows, with weeping tears,
  Came to fetch their mates away.

33.

Feretra luce postera
  Ex betula fecerunt;
Et lachrymantes viduæ
  Maritos avexerunt.

34.

Tividale may carp of care!
  Northumberland may make great moan!
For two such captains, as slain were there,
  Of the march party shall never be none.

34.

Tiviotæ vallis lugeat!
  Northumbris sint dolores!
Nam nunquam erunt finibus
  Principes meliores.

35.

Word is come to Edinburgh,
  To James the Scottish king,
That doughty Douglas, lieutenant of the march,
  He lay slain Cheviot within.

35.

Edinam regi Scotico
  Mox nuncium est relatum,
Marchiarum prasidem Douglasum
  Esse collibus necatum.

36.

His hands did he weal and wring,
  He said, "Alas! and wo is me!
Such another captain Scotland within,"
  He said, "I'faith shall never be."

36.

Fædavit pugnis pectora,
  Exclamans voce tristi,
Væ mihi! quis in Scotia
  Est comparandus isti?

37.

Word is come to lovely London,
  To the fourth Harry our king,
That Lord Percy, lieutenant of the marches,
  He lay slain Cheviot within.

37.

Londinumque amabilem†
  Henrico est relatum,
Persæum finium præsidem
  Esse collibus necatum.

* I confess that I am not sure whether the author means that Sir David Liddel was nephew to Earl Douglas or Sir H. M., but as the latter is more syntactical, I have preferred it. — W. M.

† Another Homerism, Αὐγειὰς ἐρατεινὰς. *Iliad*, B. 532, 583. 'Αρήνην ἐρατεινὴν. 591. Μαντινέην ἐρατεινὴν. 607, and a thousand other places. The author had manifestly made Homer his study. — W. M.

38.

"God have mercy on his soul," says king Harry,
"Good Lord if thou will it be!
I have a hundred captains in England,
As good as ever was he.
But, Percy, an I brook my life,
Thy death well quit shall be."

38.

Salus sit animæ, inquit Rex,
Si ita placeat deo!
Sunt pares fortitudine
Centum duces regno meo;
Sed tamen Scotos puniam
Pro nobili Persæo.

39.

As our noble king made his avow,
Like a noble prince of renown,
For the death of the Lord Percy,
He did the battle of Humbledown.

39.

Et Homilduni fortis rex
Patravit id quod dixit;
Ubi propter cæsum comitem
Cum hostibus conflixit.

40.

Where six-and-thirty Scottish knights
On a day were beaten down;
Glendale glittered with their armour bright,
O'er castle, tower, and town.

40.

Ubi quater novem equites
Scoti simul periere;
Glendalæ turres castraque
Sparsis armis micuere.

41.

(This* was the hunting of the Cheviot;
That tear began this spurn;
Old men, that knew the ground well enough,
Call it the battle of Otterburn.

41.

Et causam dedit prælii
Venatio Cheviata;
Pugna, loci gnaris senibus,
Otterburni esl vocata.

42.

At Otterburn began this spurn
Upon a Monday;
There was the doughty Douglas slain,
The Percy never went away.)

42.

Otterburni die Lunæ sic
Incepi hic venatus;
Ibi Persæus cecidit,
Et Douglasus est stratus.

---

* Bp. Percy suspects these two verses, 41, 42, to be spurious. So do I, as they stand at present; but I think we might make a good verse out of the two; thus:

This was the hunting of the Cheviot,
Upon a Monday;
There was the doughty Douglas slain,
The Percy never went away.

This will get off the confusion with regard to the battle of Otterburn, and the strange language of these verses. Percy's interpretation of "That tear began this spurn," is, "That tearing or pulling occasioned this spurn or kick." I have followed him, though I confess I am not satisfied with it. — W. M.

43.

There never was a time on the march parties,
  Since the Douglas and the Percy met,
But it was marvel an the red blood ran no
  As the rain does on the street.

43.

Cum se in marchiis Douglasus
  Persæo obviam daret,
Fuit mirum, si effusius
  Cruor imbre non manaret.

44.

Jesus Christ our *bales bete,
  And to the bless us bring!
This was the hunting of the Cheviot;
  God send us all good ending!

44.

Miserere nostrum domine!
  Et nos salute dona.
Venatio ista finiit sic;
  Sit nobis finis bona!

Explyceth Richard Sheale† temp. Henr. VI.

Explicit O. P. temp. Geo. IV.

PERORATIO.

1.

Vale! I, carmen meum, i,
  Pulcherrimam Edinam,
Et ibi pete illico
  Blackwodi Magazinam.

2.

Invenias tum Christophorum
  A Borea nominatum.
Cui tuum spero numerum
  Rhythmicum fore gratum.

3.

Quid agam, si interroget,
  Respendeas, "Nihil sane;
Est, bibit, garrit, dormitat,
  Meridie, vespere, mane."

4.

Et addas, "Te, Christophore
  (Ut liquido juravit)
In tribus, cum me mitteret,
  Cantharis propinavit."

5.

Finiamus nunc. Lectoribus
  (Si ulli sint lectores)
Arrideant, precor, veneres,
  Et gratiæ, et amores.

---

* *i. e.* Better our bales, remedy our evils. Bp. Percy. — W. M.

† The author of this ballad, as the reader may see by the expliceth, is RICHARD SHEALE, a gentleman not to be confounded, as honest old Tom Hearne has done, with a Richard Sheale who was living in 1588. Nor is he to be confounded with a Richard Sheil who is alive in 1820, writing tragedies and other jocose performances. I waive the objection arising from Chronology, as that is a science I despise, therein imitating Lady Morgan, the Edinburgh Reviewers, Major Cartwright, and various other eminent persons. For (to take one instance from the works of the first-cited authority) might not Mr. Richard Sheil of 1820, be as capable of writing a ballad in the days of Henry VI. as the wife of the Grand Condè of intriguing with a king who was dead before she was born? (See, if extant, Lady Morgan's France.) My objections to their identity are of a graver and more critical nature. 1*st*, Richard Sheil of Chevy Chase is an original writer, which nobody accuses Richard Sheil of Evadne of being. 2*ndly*, Although in verse 33, Second Fytte, the ballad-monger had an opportunity of bringing up the children with their mothers, to serve as a clap-trap, he has not done so; an omission of which the tragedy-monger

I have done with Chevy Chase; but as I am in a garrulous disposition, I wish to add a few words. Every true lover of English literature, must acknowledge the great benefit conferred on it by Bishop Perry, in publishing his Relics. That work has breathed a spirit of renovated youth over our poetry; and we may trace its influence in the strains of higher mood, uttered by the great poets of our own days. The Bishop was qualified for this task by exquisite poetical feeling, a large share of varied antiquarian knowledge, and general literary acquirements—united accomplishments which he possessed in a greater degree perhaps than any of his contemporaries. But since his time, and in a great measure in consequence of his work, and those which it called forth, so much more is known with respect to early English literature—I might say with respect to early English history—and the taste of the public is so much more inclined to such studies, that I think a general collection of our old English ballads, comprising of course those of Percy, Ritson, and others, which may merit preservation, is a great desideratum. Little skilled as I am in such subjects, I could point out deficiencies in the plan or the details of every work of the kind I have ever seen—deficiencies, however, which I have not time to notice, nor perhaps would this be the proper place to do it, or I the proper person, after travestying the first of old ballads into Monkish Latin. I should require in the editor high poetic taste, a deep and minute knowledge of the history and antiquities of the country, a profound acquaintance with the customs, the language, the heraldry, the genealogy of our ancestors, a critical judgment with respect to ancient poetry, and a perfect familiarity with all our poetic stores, ancient and modern—besides, what are not so common as may be imagined, undeviating honesty and fidelity. Yours, &c. &c. O. P.

DUBLIN, *May* 31, 1820.

of Ballemira would never have been guilty. 3*dly*, The people in the poem of the rhymester are decent men, who talk plain language; whereas, the people in The Apostate are stalking-talking rogues, who discourse in the most sarsenet phraseology. 4*thly*, and *lastly*, The ballad of the Percy and Douglas (teste Sir P. Sidney) moves the heart like the sound of a trumpet, whereas, the tragedy of Adelaide puts one to sleep more effectually than a double dose of diacodium. Wherefore, I am of opinion, that Mr. R. Sheil now extant, is *not* the author of Chevy Chase. Q. E. D.—W. M.

The Man in the Bell.*

In my younger days, bell-ringing was much more in fashion among the young men of ———, than it is now. Nobody, I believe, practises it there at present except the servants of the church, and the melody has been much injured in consequence. Some fifty years ago, about twenty of us who dwelt in the vicinity of the Cathedral, formed a club, which used to ring every peal that was called for; and, from continual practice and a rivalry which arose between us and a club attached to another steeple, and which tended considerably to sharpen our zeal, we became very Mozarts on our favorite instruments. But my bell-ringing practice was shortened by a singular accident, which not only stopped my performance, but made even the sound of a bell terrible to my ears.

One Sunday, I went with another into the belfry to ring for noon prayers, but the second stroke we had pulled shewed us that the clapper of the bell we were at was muffled. Some one had been buried that morning, and it had been prepared, of course, to ring a mournful note. We did not know of this, but the remedy was easy. "Jack," said my companion, "step up to the loft, and cut off the hat;" for the way we had of muffling was by tying a piece of an old hat, or of cloth (the former was preferred) to one side of the clapper, which deadened every second toll. I complied, and mounting into the belfry, crept as usual into the bell, where I began to cut away. The hat had been tied on in some more complicated manner than usual; and I was perhaps three or four minutes in getting it off; during which time my companion below was hastily called away, by a message from his sweetheart I believe, but that is not material

* This story first appeared in *Blackwood* for November, 1821. It is briefly characterized by Mr. Kenealy as "a paper worthy of Victor Hugo." In an Epistle General, which closed the number, and professed to be addressed to Correspondents, it was quizzically said "Mr. Brougham will see that we have lost no time in inserting 'The Man in the Bell.' He can best explain the true meaning of this most mysterious and appalling narrative." But, in its earlier days, *Blackwood* was fond of such mystifications. — M.

to my story. The person who called him was a brother of the club, who, knowing that the time had come for ringing for service, and not thinking that any one was above, began to pull. At this moment I was just getting out, when I felt the bell moving; I guessed the reason at once—it was a moment of terror; but by a hasty, and almost convulsive effort, I succeeded in jumping down, and throwing myself on the flat of my back under the bell.

The room in which it was, was little more than sufficient to contain it, the bottom of the bell coming within a couple of feet of the floor of lath. At that time I certainly was not so bulky as I am now, but as I lay it was within an inch of my face. I had not laid myself down a second, when the ringing began.—It was a dreadful situation. Over me swung an immense mass of metal, one touch of which would have crushed me to pieces; the floor under me was principally composed of crazy laths, and if they gave way, I was precipitated to the distance of about fifty feet upon a loft, which would, in all probability, have sunk under the impulse of my fall, and sent me to be dashed to atoms upon the marble floor of the chancel, an hundred feet below. I remembered—for fear is quick in recollection—how a common clock-wright, about a month before, had fallen, and bursting through the floors of the steeple, driven in the ceilings of the porch, and even broken into the marble tombstone of a bishop who slept beneath. This was my first terror, but the ringing had not continued a minute, before a more awful and immediate dread came on me. The deafening sound of the bell smote into my ears with a thunder which made me fear their drums would crack.—There was not a fibre of my body it did not thrill through: it entered my very soul; thought and reflection were almost utterly banished; I only retained the sensation of agonizing terror. Every moment I saw the bell sweep within an inch of my face; and my eyes—I could not close them, though to look at the object was bitter as death—followed it instinctively in its oscillating progress until it came back again. It was in vain I said to myself that it could come no nearer at any future swing than it did at first; every time it descended, I endeavored to shrink into the very floor to avoid being buried under the down sweeping mass; and then reflecting on the danger of pressing too weightily on my frail support, would cower up again as far as I dared.

At first my fears were mere matter of fact. I was afraid the pullies above would give way, and let the bell plunge on me. At another time, the possibility of the clapper being shot out in some sweep, and dashing through my body, as I had seen a ramrod glide through a door, flitted across my mind. The dread also, as I have already mentioned, of the crazy floor, tormented me, but these soon gave way to fears not more unfounded, but more visionary, and of course more tremendous. The roaring of the bell confused my intellect, and my fancy soon began to teem with all sort of strange and terrifying ideas. The bell pealing above, and opening its jaws with a hideous clamor, seemed to me at one time a ravening monster, raging to devour me; at another, a whirlpool ready to suck me into its bellowing abyss. As I gazed on it, it assumed all shapes; it was a flying eagle, or rather a roc of the Arabian story-tellers, clapping its wings and screaming over me. As I looked upward into it, it would appear sometimes to lengthen into indefinite extent, or to be twisted at the end into the spiral folds of the tail of a flying-dragon. Nor was the flaming breath, or fiery glance of that fable animal, wanting to complete the picture. My eyes inflamed, bloodshot, and glaring, invested the supposed monster with a full proportion of unholy light.

It would be endless were I to merely hint at all the fancies that possessed my mind. Every object that was hideous and roaring presented itself to my imagination. I often thought that I was in a hurricane at sea, and that the vessel in which I was embarked tossed under me with the most furious vehemence. The air, set in motion by the swinging of the bell, blew over me, nearly with the violence, and more than the thunder of a tempest: and the floor seemed to reel under me, as under a drunken man. But the most awful of all the ideas that seized on me were drawn from the supernatural. In the vast cavern of the bell hideous faces appeared, and glared down on me with terrifying frowns, or with grinning mockery, still more appalling. At last, the devil himself, accoutred, as in the common description of the evil spirit, with hoof, horn, and tail, and eyes of infernal lustre, made his appearance, and called on me to curse God and worship him, who was powerful to save me. This dread suggestion he uttered with the full-toned clangor of the bell. I had him within an inch of me, and I thought on the fate of the Santon Barsisa. Strenuously and desperately I defied him, and bade him be gone. Reason, then, for a moment, resumed her sway, but it was only to fill me with fresh terror, just as the lightning dispels the gloom that surrounds the benighted mariner, but to shew him that his vessel is driving on a rock, where she must inevitably be dashed to pieees. I found I was becoming delirious, and trembled lest reason should utterly desert me. This is at all times an agonizing thought, but it smote me then with tenfold agony. I feared lest, when utterly deprived of my senses, I should rise, to do which I was every moment tempted by that strange feeling which calls on a man, whose head is dizzy from standing on the battlement of a lofty castle, to precipitate himself from it, and then death would be instant and tremendous. When I thought of this, I became desperate. I caught the floor with a grasp which drove the blood from my nails; and I yelled with the cry of despair. I called for help, I prayed, I shouted, but all the efforts of my voice were, of course, drowned in the bell. As it passed over my mouth, it occasionally echoed my cries, which mixed not with its own sound, but preserved their distinct character. Perhaps this was but fancy. To me, I know, they then sounded as if they were the shouting, howling or laughing of the fiends with which my imagination had peopled the gloomy cave which swung over me.

You may accuse me of exaggerating my feelings; but I am not. Many a scene of dread have I since passed through, but they are nothing to the self-inflicted terrors of this half hour. The ancients have doomed one of the damned, in their Tartarus, to lie under a rock, which every moment seems to be descending to annihilate him—and an awful punishment it would be. But if to this you add a clamor as loud as if ten thousand furies were howling about you—a deafening uproar banishing reason, and driving you to madness, you must allow that the bitterness of the pang was rendered more terrible. There is no man, firm as his nerves may be, who could retain his courage in this situation.

In twenty minutes the ringing was done. Half of that time passed over me without power of computation—the other half appeared an age. When it ceased, I became gradually more quiet, but a new fear retained me. I knew that five minutes would elapse without ringing, but, at the end of that short time the bell would be rung a second time, for five minutes more. I could not calculate time. A minute and an hour were of equal duration. I feared to rise lest the five minutes should have elapsed, and the ringing be again commenced, in which case I should be crushed, before I could escape, against the walls or frame-work of the bell. I therefore still continued to lie down, cautiously shifting myself, however, with a careful gliding, so that my eye no longer looked into the hollow. This was of itself a considerable relief. The cessation of the noise had, in a great measure, the effect of stupifying me, for my attention, being no longer occupied by the chimeras I had conjured up, began to flag. All that now distressed me was the constant expectation of the second ringing, for which, however, I settled myself with a kind of stupid resolution. I closed my eyes, and clenched my teeth as firmly as if they were screwed in a vice. At last the dreaded moment came, and the first swing of the bell extorted a groan from me, as they say the most resolute victim screams at the sight of the rack, to which he is for a second time destined. After this, however, I lay silent and lethargic, without a thought. Wrapt in the defensive armor of stupidity, I defied the bell and its intonations. When it ceased, I was roused a little by the hope of escape. I did not, however, decide on this step hastily, but, putting up my hand with the utmost caution, I touched the rim. Though the ringing had ceased, it still was tremulous from the sound, and shook under my hand, which instantly recoiled as from an electric jar. A quarter of an hour probably elapsed before I again dared to make the experiment, and then found it at rest. I determined to lose no time, fearing that I might have lain then already too long, and that the bell for evening service would catch me. This dread stimulated me, and I slipped out with the utmost rapidity, and arose. I stood, I suppose, for a minute, looking with silly wonder on the place of my imprisonment, penetrated with joy at escaping, but then rushed down the stony and irregular stair with the velocity of lightning, and arrived in the bell-ringer's room. This was the last act I had power to accomplish. I leant against the wall, motionless and deprived of thought, in which posture my companions found me, when, in the course of a couple of hours, they returned to their occupation.

They were shocked, as well they might, at the figure before them. The wind of the bell had excoriated my face, and my dim and stupified eyes were fixed with a lack-lustre gaze in my raw eye-lids. My hands were torn and bleeding: my hair dishevelled; and my clothes tattered. They spoke to me, but I gave no answer. They shook me, but I remained insensible. They then became alarmed, and hastened to remove me. He who had first gone up with me in the forenoon, met them as they carried me through the church-yard, and through him, who was shocked at having, in some measure, occasioned the accident, the cause of my misfortune was discovered. I was put to bed at home, and remained for three days delirious, but gradually recovered my senses. You may be sure the bell formed a prominent topic of my ravings, and if I heard a peal, they were instantly increased to the utmost violence. Even when the delirium abated, my sleep was continually disturbed by imagined ringings, and my dreams were haunted by the fancies which almost maddened me while in the steeple. My friends removed me to a house in the country, which was sufficiently distant from any place of worship, to save me from the apprehensions of hearing the church-going bell; for what Alexander Selkirk, in Cowper's poem, complained of as a misfortune, was then to me as a blessing. Here I recovered; but even long after recovery, if a gale wafted the notes of a peal toward me, I started with nervous apprehension. I felt a Mahometan hatred to all the bell tribe, and envied the subjects of the Commander of the Faithful the sonorous voice of their Muezzin. Time cured this, as it does most of our follies; but, even at the present day, if, by chance, my nerves be unstrung, some particular tones of the cathedral bell have power to surprise me into a momentary start.

The Lost (and Found) Memorandum Book.*

Preliminary letter—Extracts—Strictures on Political Economy, wherein a Remedy for the Poor Laws is Divulged—Diary—Cockney Letter and Love Song—The Somnambulatory Butcher, an Episode—Ailie Mushat's Cairn—Japanese Poetry; Ode on the Death of Yahmahsseero—Stanzas on Despair, and Thoughts on a New Conjugation.

To CHRISTOPHER NORTH, *Esq.*

SIR,—While lately travelling through part of England, a thing which is customary with me twice a year, for the transaction of business, I happened, in the stage between Bath and ———, to meet with a circumstance, which is the occasion of my now addressing you.

As I do not happen to be of the melancholic temperament, and am rather fond, than otherwise, of society, it is not unusual for me, as I am a bachelor, and have the happiness or misery of travelling alone, when I fall in with a landlord of genteelish manners, and good nature, to ask him to a participation of my supper. By good luck, it fell out that I here found a man to my mind. After supper was discussed, and our rummers charged for the second time, the spirit of my host began to expand; and, in the midst of his hilarity, he let me into numerous anecdotes of his own; some of which might have been spared, and many of which were entertaining enough. I shall confine myself to that which is the subject of my present epistle.

About two years ago, a military gentleman, of what rank he could not learn, except that his companions sometimes called him General, took up abode with him for eight days; and lived, during the whole of that time, to use a proverbial expression, "at rack and manger." Every stranger that arrived within that time, at the inn, seemed to be of his acquaintance; or, if they were unknown to him, a friendship was soon begun and cemented; and ere they were a couple of hours together, one could have sworn that they had been born in the same village—edu-

* These "Extracts from a lost (and found) Memorandum Book," appeared in *Blackwood* for March, 1821.—M.

cated at the same school — or, to bring forward a still stronger link of association, which the author of Rob Roy has mentioned, "had read from the same Bible at church." Whoever was with him, whether the social or the serious, he regularly obliged them to sit till three in the morning, when he sent them, or, more properly speaking, led them, to their bed rooms.

At length, having ordered breakfast one morning, he disappeared, and the landlord could never afterwards find one token or trace of him. He left behind him a green net purse, (containing more than the amount of his bill,) and the chambermaid drowned in tears. He was remarkably tall, of rather a spare habit of body, wore neatly curled brown whiskers, a gray surtout, Wellington boots, with spurs, and a South-Sea cap, with a gold band. He had no baggage with him; and the only relique of his visit was a little book, which he had inadvertently left in his bed room.

I begged a sight of this relique from my host, and was not a little struck with its contents. It is a small volume, in red binding, fastened with tape — on the back, in gilt letters, is marked "Memorandum Book." After looking over a few pages, I was highly amused with its contents, and expressed myself so to my host, who obligingly told me it was of no use to him, and that I was most welcome to it. Its contents are of a most miscellaneous nature, and written, in some parts, in a rather illegible hand. I have made one of my young men transcribe a piece from it, here and there, which you will receive along with this, and which you may make public if you please. Should I observe this to be the case, I may transmit you a few farther extracts from time to time. I remain yours, &c.

J—— T——N.

February 10, 1821.

EXTRACTS.

No. I.

STRICTURES ON POLITICAL ECONOMY, WHEREIN A REMEDY FOR THE POOR LAWS IS DIVULGED.

Insula, sole occidente, viridi, seculis plurimis elapsis, præclarus vir militaris apparebitque florebit. Ille non modo omni sapientiæ re, sed omni philosophiæ discet et docebit; poeta etiamque celebris. — *Frag. M. S. Vet. apud. Vatican.**

It is only of late years that political economy has raised itself to the dignity of a science. Doctrines, that men believed to be as true as Father Paul's history of the Council of Trent, were nevertheless neglected; and other theories, as unsubstantial as the morning mist, though known and acknowledged to be false, substituted in their stead, and acted on. As Jeffrey said of Wordsworth's Excursion, "this would never do." The chaff has been sifted from the wheat — the truth has been purified from the error — and the facts that before were scattered, like the twelve tribes of Israel, over the face of society, have been brought together, and cemented into a regular and almost complete fabric, under the auspices of Malthus, Godwin, Weyland Say, James Graham, M'Culloch, Jeremy Bentham, and the writer of the present article.

But what is the rising of the stocks to him who has no capital ? — What is the question about the balance of trade to him who has no merchandise ? And what is the worth of our knowing the right principles, if we find it impossible to act on them ? — It is of no use to know the nature of the disease, if we have not a plaster to apply, or a remedy to prescribe.

We cannot make as good silks in England as we can get from India; nor can we afford to sell them as cheap, we want *materiel*. But then it would overpower the feelings of our humanity to ruin the 40,000 families, that are employed in that branch of manufacture. The silk spun in this country is by no means so good; whether it be the case that the silk-worm does not keep its health in our northern latitudes, or not, I have too little confidence in my own opinion to say: but this I can tell from experience, that we are more apt to be mistaken as to the animal

* This quotation is imaginary, of course. — M.

itself, thereby rendering all our labour fruitless, and our efforts abortive. The writer of this article bought several papers full of the embryos of the silk-worm, but after waiting in eager expectation for a twelvemonth, to his utter consternation and astonishment, they turned out to be nought else but common maggots.

The poor-rates are a great bore in this country, but it is all owing to the excess of population, and for this I would here suggest a remedy. If the overplus of the population were to be called together, and some able speaker, say one of the advocates of the Scottish bar, selected to address them, and lay down to them in a placid and precise manner, the hardships they entail on society, and the impropriety of their ever having been born, unquestionably then the overplus of population, provided they consisted of well-educated, decent, and sensible people, could have no objection either to be transported beyond seas, or despatched in as gentle a manner as could be devised. Until a great national meeting is called for the purpose, we must be content to put up with many evils. Mendicity is not the least of these, and to the public in general we recommend the following plan, which is as yet in private circulation, and does not seem to have reached the ear of the Society for the Suppression of Begging. It originated from the ingenuity of one of that useful class of the community, a French cook; but as he had been for several years domesticated in this country, no other realm can presume to come in for a share of the honour, which is purely national. It is said that M. Say, Benjamin Constant, and Carnot, claim it for France; but this is only a report.

The house in which this ingenious French cook served, was infested from morning to night, and the court-yard literally swarming with beggars, as "thick as the motes that people the sun-beams." The proprietor was dunned with petitions, and the watch-dog, which was chained at the outer gate, had actually worn down his teeth to the stumps in biting the intruders. No further service could thus be expected from him. Long did the French cook ponder, during his evening reveries over his tumbler by the kitchen fire, what could be done in the present unfortunate dilemma. For a long series of evenings he beat his brains to no purpose; at length, after a long hour's silence, he one night started up, and almost severed, with his heel, the butler's gouty toe from his body, exclaiming—"Eureka! I have found it!!"

He set about preparing a most hellish decoction, which he seasoned with Cayenne pepper, (the Capsicum Annuum of Linnæus,) until it was enough, without a metaphor, to set the stomach on fire, and cause an "interna conflagratio."

Next morning he set about putting his project in practice, and the first beggar that approached he beckoned him to come in, shut the kitchen door, and having filled out a bumper, bade him whip it off, and be gone, lest his master should appear. The mendicant, glad of the treat, turned up his little finger in a twinkling, and retreated as fast as his legs could carry him, but not far; for his eyes threatened to start from his head, and the saliva ran from the corners of his mouth, after the fashion of a waterspout. Thus was one despatched; he came no more. Again—again—a hundred times was the project tried, and uniformly with the same success; till, in less than three weeks, not one beggar was to be seen in that country side. The French cook is, we understand, at present putting in for a patent, which we have no doubt will be granted.

By this the public may observe, that the way to get quit of beggars is by the immediate use of the hellish decoction; and not by following the vain, void, visionary, childish, and nugatory schemes, at present inculcated by the writers on political economy.* M. O.

July 10th.—Settled with Bullock and Badcock for the "Poems by a Military Amateur." Balance in my favour of £3 : 15 : 11 1-2. Very bad concern. Cost me three months'

* This ironical remedy, suggested with so much mock gravity, "is almost worthy, (Kennealy says,) of standing beside Swift's *Project for eating children.*" Who would have thought that, in 1843, the Duke of Norfolk should seriously have proposed that hot water, highly seasoned with Cayenne, should be taken by the poor, to assuage the pangs of hunger?—M.

severe composition.* Cannot fathom what the reading public of this age would swallow: What I write most carelessly they relish best. Hope I shall succeed better with my "Treatise on the education of young ladies."

July 12*th.*—Went to Newmarket. Bet three to one, at starting, on the blue body and buff sleeves; fairly taken in, as he came last; or rather never came in, being distanced. Gulled out of a guinea and half, and got very angry. Run, after the race, a foot match with Lieutenant Finch; shammed lameness at first, and then beat him hollow; running the last fifty yards backwards. Out of pocket by this excursion 10s. 6d.

13*th.*—Played three hours at billiards with a knowing one, who took me in. Proposed whist, at which I am a dead hand, and fairly came paddy over him. Rose in a passion, and broke off farther connexion with me, swearing there was foul play. Gained by my acquaintance with him £2 : 10 : 3. Got drunk.

14*th.*—Headach in the morning. Wrote sonnet to Despondency—ditto to Despair. Got up and shaved, felt better—went out at twelve to a match at cricket—returned successful—a dinner and drink at stake—dressed at five—excellent claret—got drunk. Returned home, and read Roger's Human Life—did not much like it—too wirewove. Took up Story of Rimini—thought more highly of it—last book admirable.

15*th.*—Dreamt all night of Cockaigne—terrible jargon these fellows speak. Felt squeamish; but after despatching a bottle of soda water, sate down and composed the following letter and love song.

LOVE SONG,

By a Junior Member of the Cockney School.

TO THE EDITOR OF LA BELLE ASSEMBLEE.

(This letter is private, so you must not print it.)

SIR,—As I am not at all pleased with the strain of sentiment and affectation, that disfigures and runs through the love poems of

* "The Feast of Bellona, and other Poems, by a Military Amateur," (an imaginary volume, published by Bullock & Badcock, imaginary booksellers in London,) was reviewed with extracts in *Blackwood* for May, 1819, and professed to have been written by Odoherty. It would seem that Maginn, to carry on the joke, adopted it; but the antique extracts were by another hand, and want the true attic flavour of Odoherty.—M.

Burns and Byron, I have endeavoured to hit on a key somewhat nearer to the well-head of the human heart, and somewhat truer to the feelings of domestic nature, mutual endearment and connubial felicity. Descriptions of simple life, and rural nature, are very well to those who have had an opportunity of seeing them; but to me, and the multitudes like me, who live in the great city, it is but just that the writers of the present age should adopt something that would come home to our feelings and businesses. A friend of mine, that came off a far journey last week, very jauntily told me, that cabbages grew on fir trees, that cows can eat potatoes, and that they feed sheep on cider in Kent; but I was not such a spoonie as to believe him. If the accompanying poem be adapted to your miscellany, please insert it, and believe me,

Your most obliged Friend,

WM. TIMS GOODENOUGH.

Oh! lovely Polly Savage,
O! charming Polly Savage,
Your eye beats Day and Martin,
Your cheek is like red cabbage.

As I was going down the Strand
It smote my heart with wonder,
To see the lovely damsel,
A-sitting at a vinder.
Oh! lovely Polly Savage, &c.

Oh! once I loved another girl,
Her name it was Maria;
But, Polly dear, my love for you
Is forty-five times high*er*.
O! lovely Polly Savage, &c.

We'll take a shop in Chicken Lane,
And I will stand prepared,
To sell fat bacon by the pound,
And butter by the yard.
O! lovely Polly Savage, &c.

And when at five o'clock, my love,
We sit us down to dine,
How I will toast your darling health,
In draughts of currant *v*ine.
Oh! lovely Polly Savage, &c.

Oh then our little son shall be
As wanton as a spaniel,
Him that we mean to christen'd be,
Jacques Timothy Nathaniel.
Oh! lovely Polly Savage, &c.

And if we have a little girl,
I'm sure you wont be sorry
To hear me call the pretty elf
Euphemiar Helen Laura*r*.
Oh! lovely Polly Savage, &c.

Then fare-thee-well a little space,
My heart can never falter,
And next time when I see your face,
'Twill be at Hymen's *h*altar.
Oh! lovely Polly Savage &c.

18*th.*—Wet morning,—could not venture to stir abroad,—just shows us how much men alter. A few years ago, when my country demanded my services, I braved the dangers of every clime, the torrid heats of a Spanish summer, and the damp atmosphere of the United States. Dare say, however, that I could do so again, if occasion required. Took a chair by the fire, and read over again Crabbe's Borough. Think the Reverend Gentleman shows pluck; but do not remember in all his pictures of human life, ever observing the portrait of one butcher introduced. Pondered whether I might venture to remedy this defect, and send him my delineation* to be hung up in the Gallery of Portraits, in the next edition of his admirable work.

Wrote what follows in twenty minutes, and copied it verbatim, as under.

THE SOMNAMBULATORY BUTCHER.—*An Episode.*

Reflections —birth, — parentage, — boyish tricks, — education, — change of dress, — apprenticeship, — bladders and Dr. Lavement, — bad habits, — ditto cured by his mother, — caution, — and moral.

Men's legs, if man may trust the common talk,
Are engines put in motion when men walk;
But when we cross our knees, and take a chair
Beside the fire, they're not in motion there:
So this we learn by wisdom, art, and skill,
That legs are made to stir, or to sit still.
Yet sometimes I have heard, that when the head
In woollen cap lay snoring on the bed,
The legs, without the sanction of the brain,
Were fond to wander on the midnight plain,
Pursue, mid darkness, tasks of common day,
Yet come, as will'd Caprice, unharm'd away;
Which to illustrate, let the reader bend
A willing ear, and list his warning friend.

James Neckum Theodore Emmanuel Reid,
Was meanly born, and was ignobly bred,
Lived upon pottage, slept within a shed;
His mother, — But it were in vain to look —
Her's was no marriage by the session book;
His mother, fool, had never taken pains
To gird her neck with matrimonial chains,

* This is rather a parody on the imitation, in the Smith's "Rejected Addresses," than on the actual poetry of Crabbe. — M.

And he, her leman, seeing what would be,
Turn'd a blue-neck'd marine, and cross'd the sea;
So, in neglect and wrath the child was born,
While neighbours chuckled with their looks of scorn;
But fast he throve, and fat he grew, and that
Was felt most keenly by the tortured cat,
Whose ears he pinch'd, whose tail he drew, until
'Twas forced, when fairly vanquish'd, to lie still;
The chickens too, no sinecure of life
Had with the boy, who pull'd their necks in strife,
Till from their sockets started their black eyes,
And died their vanish'd voice in feeble cries.

At length a cap upon his head was braced,
Shoes shod his feet, and breeches girt his waist;
Tall as a leek he grew, his hair was long,
And through its folds the wild winds sang a song;
From mother's clutches oft would he elope,
And little knew his morning face of soap;
Till, having spent the morn in game and play
With comrades dirty, frolicsome, and gay,
As duly as the village clock struck two,
As duly parted he from ragged crew,
And homewards wended, fast and nothing loth,
To dip his whispers in his mother's broth.

The boy grew strong; the master of the school
Took him in charge, and with a birch did rule;
Full long and oft he blubber'd; but, at length,
Within a week he learned to letter tenth;
And ere six moons had waxed, and waned, and set,
He had reached z, and knew his alphabet.

His education finish'd, choice he made
Of a most lucrative and wholesome trade;
The leathern cap was now dismiss'd; and red,
Yea fiery, glow'd the cowl upon his head:
And, like a cherry dangling from the crown,
A neat wool tassel in the midst hung down;
Around his waist, with black tape girded tight,
Was tied a worsted apron, blue and white;
His Shetland stockings, mocking winter's cold,
Despising garters, up his thighs were roll'd,
And, by his side, horn-handled steels, and knives,
Gleam'd from his pouch, and thirsted for sheep's lives.
For, dexterous, he could split dead cows in halves,
And, though a calf himself, he slaughter'd calves.

But brisker look'd the youth, and nothing sadder,
For of each mother's son he got the bladder,
And straight to Galen's-head in joy he bore it,
Where Dr. Lavement gave a penny for it.

But he had failings as I said before,
So, duly as his nose began to snore,
His legs ran with his body to the door:
And forth he used to roam, with sidelong neck,
To—as the Scot's folks term it—lift the sneck.
All in his shirt and woollen cap he strayed,
Silent, though dreaming; cold, but undismay'd.
The moon was shining 'mid the depth of Heaven,
And from the chill north, fleecy clouds were driven
Athwart its silver aspect, till they grew
Dimmer, and dimmer, in the distant blue;
The trees were rustling loud; nor moon, nor trees,
Nor cloud, could on his dreaming frenzy seize,
But, walking with closed eyes across the street,
He lifted handsomely his unshod feet,
Till nought, at length, his wandering ankles propt,
And head and heels into the pond he dropt.

Then rose the loud lament; the earth and skies
Rung with his shouts, and echoed with his cries;
The neighbours, in their night-caps, throng'd around,
Call'd forth in marching order at the sound;
They hauled young Neckum out, a blanket roll'd
Around his limbs with comfortable fold,
Hurried him home, and told him, cursing deep,
"That if again with cries he broke their sleep,
Him they would change into a wandering ghost,
Draw from the pond, but hang him on a post."

Oh! reader, learn this truth most firm and sure,
That vicious practices are hard to cure;
That error girds up with a serpent fold,
Hangs on the youth, but clings about the old.—
Night after night, if rainy, cold, or fair,
Forth went our hero, just to take the air;
Ladies were terrified, and, fainting, cried,
A ghost in white had wander'd by their side!
The soldier home his quaking path pursued,
With hair on end, gun cock'd, and bayonet screw'd
And frightful children run to bed in fear,
When mothers said the ghost in white was near!

'Twas a hard case, but Theodore's mother quick
Fell on a scheme to cure him of the trick;
Hard by his bed a washing-tub she placed,
So, when he rose, it washed him to the waist;
And loud he roar'd, — while startled at the sound,
Old women bolted from their beds around —
"Save, save a wandering sinner, or he's drown'd!!!"

He rose no more, as I'm informed in sleep,
But duly fell'd down cows, and slaughter'd sheep,
Took to himself a wife, a pretty wench,
Sold beef by pounds, and cow-heel on a bénch;
In ten years had seven boys, and five fair girls,
With cheeks like roses, and with teeth like pearls
Lay still in bed like any decent man,
Pursued through life a staid and honest plan,
And lived beloved, while honours thicken'd o'er him,
Justice of Peace, and Custos Rotulorum.

So all my readers from this tale may learn,
The right way from the wrong way to discern;
Never by dreams and nonsense to be led,
Walk when they wake, and slumber when in bed!

——Read last night a volume of the Heart of Mid-Lothian. The author's name as well known to me as if he had put it on the title-page. "None but himself can be his parallel." Well may we say, as my friend Ovid said of Telamon Ajax,

"None but himself, himself could overthrow."

This book knits my heart more firmly than ever to the "land of the mountain and the flood." When sitting in my chamber, I am transported there in a twinkling; the scenes rise before me in all their native majesty — the Castle, the High-street, and the Porteous mob. Am most pleased with the scenes at Davie Dean's cottage, Leonard's Hill, and Arthur's Seat. Many a time have I, reclining among the ruins of St. Anthony's Chapel, surveyed, in extatic admiration, the magnificent prospect around; — the blue and castellated majesty of Dunedin, "throwing its white arms to the sea;" — the variegated succession of woodlands, and pasture, and green fields; — the broad expanse of the Forth, with its multitude of gliding sails; — and, far in the north, the pale green, or the remoter hazy blue mountains of Fife and

Stirlingshire. At my feet, the Palace of Holy-rood, the habitation of kings, the mansion of the Stuarts, with the Gothic ruins of its chapel, its gray towers, and its desolate garden, spotted with dark-green shrubs, and melancholy flowers; — and, stretching around me in emerald smoothness, the far extending park, with its well-trodden pathway. Often have I, returning half cut, from dining at the mess of my fellow soldiers at Piershill, felt an inward trepidation in entering that park, and instinctively grasped my sword, when I thought on the ghost of Ailie Mushat, who is said, yet to

> "Visit the glimpses of the moon,
> Making night hideous."

N. B. — A good subject for poetry; to remember it the first idle hour.

(After a few pages, — commemorative of a battle between two of the Fancy, written in the cant style, — the review of a corps of sharpshooters, with whose manœuvres the writer finds great fault, — and an elaborate criticism on a charity sermon, which had been recently preached, — we find this promise fulfilled to the letter, as follows,) —

AILIE MUSHAT'S CAIRN.

A Vision-like remembrance of a Vision.

The night was dark; not a star was view'd
Mid the dim, and cloudy solitude;
I listen'd to the watchman's cry,
  And to the midnight breeze, that sung
Round the ruins of St. Anthony,
  With dismal, and unearthly tongue:
I scarcely felt the path I trode;
  And I durst not linger to look behind,
For I knew that spirits were abroad,
  And heard their shrieks on the passing wind;
When lo! a spectacle of dread and awe
With trembling knees, and stiffening hair I saw!

A grave-light spread its flames of blue,
  Its flames of blue and lurid red,
And, in the midst, a hellish crew
  Were seated round the stony bed

Of one, whom Murder robb'd of life!—
I saw the hand that held the knife,
It was her husband's hand, and yet
With the life-gore the blade was wet,
Dripping like a fiery sheath,
On the mossy cairn beneath!
The vision changed; and, on the stones,
    With visage savage, fierce, and wild,
Above the grave that held her bones,
    The ghost of Ailie Mushat smiled;
It was a sight of dread and fear—
    A chequered napkin bound her head,
Her throat was cut from ear to ear,
    Her hands and breast were spotted red;
She strove to speak, but from the wound
Her breath came out with a broken sound!

  I started! for she strove to rise,
And pierced me with her bloodshot eyes;
She strove to rise, but fast I drew
    Upon the grass a circle round;
I said a prayer, and she withdrew
    Slowly within the stony mound—
And trembling, and alone I stood,
In the depth of the midnight solitude.

Aug. 4.—Am glad to observe from the philosophical journals, the newspapers, and other authentic sources, that several of the barbarous tribes are paying attention to literature and the fine arts.—The Japanese poem I have seen pleases me extremely, though the subject can scarcely be said to be well adapted for poetry. My translation is not so bad. M. Titsingh's Latin paraphrase is also very good. The English is literal.

ODE ON THE DEATH OF YAHMASSEERO, COUNCILLOR OF STATE.

Japanese.

Kee rah ray tah vah
Bah kah to see yo ree to
Kee koo tah fah yah
Yah mah mo o see ro mo
Sah vah goo sin bahn.

Latin.

Præcidisse
Consiliarium minorem
Nuper audivi,
In montis castello
Turbas excitantem, novum custodem.

English.

I have just learned that one of the new guards has excited a tumult in the

Free Translation.

Pray, have you heard the news?
  One of the footguards drew

castle, by assassinating a councillor in his folly.

His cutlas; in a rage
His anger to assuage,
  A councillor he slew!

II.

Yah mah see ro no
Ser ro no o ko so day
Tshay mee so mee tay
Ah kah do see yo ree to
Fee to vah yoo nahr.

The white robe of Yahmahsseero is stained with blood, and all call him the red councillor.

II.

Yahmahsseero
Candidam togam
Cruore tinctam
Rubentemque consiliarium
Omnes viderunt.

Yahmahsseero's robe
  Is stained with fiery gore,
And each that doth him meet,
Calls him upon the street,
  The crimson councillor.

III.

Ah soo mah see no
Sahn no no vah tahree nee
Mee soo mah see tay
Tah no mah mo kee ray tay
O tsoo too yah mah see ro.

The current which, on the eastern road, crosses the village Sahnno, has swelled, and penetrated the dike round the fen, and the high castle of the mountain has fallen.

III.

In via orientali
Per vicum *Sahnno* irruentes,
Aquae profluentes,
Terram lacunae perfosserunt
Rutique *montis* castellum.

The current to the east
  By Sahnno, little town,
Hath overflown, and burst the dike
With fury, and the castle, like
  A fool, hath fallen down.

IV.

Fah tsee oo yay tay
Oo may gah sah koo rah ta
Sah koo fahn mah vo
Tah ray tah kee tsoo kay tah
Sahn no mee kee ray say tah.

Who has cast into the fire the plum and cheery trees? — Valuable trees, which are planted in boxes, for the sake of their agreeable flowers? *Sahnno* has cut them down.

IV.

Pretiosas in vasis arbores,
Prunos et cerasos
Floribus amœnas
Quis in ignem projecit?
Sahnno quidem eas præcidit.

Who has felled the cherry trees?
  And who has felled the plum?
Trees planted in neat boxes,
And anything but hoaxes
  For odoriferous gum.

V.

Kee rah ray tah vah
Bah kah do see yo ree to
Yoo oobay kay mee
Sahn no sin sah yay mee moo
Ho ray gah ten mei.

V.

Præcidit (consiliarium)
Vesanus consiliarius
Dicere possumus
Si prius talia unquam audiverimus
Hoc puisse *Cæli Mandatum.*

A councillor in his madness hath been overthrown; if ever such an event was heard of, it may be said to be a judgment from heaven.

A councillor hath been knocked
From off his legs,—most true;
If ever such a thing was heard,
It may most safely be averr'd
That it hath been—adieu!

Aug. 8.—Blue stockings are not to my taste, unless their attention be only paid to polite literature—the play that is just to come out, or the last new poem.

Last night's party, however, the most agreeable of the kind that I have met; if the young lady with the blue eyes could have been contented with only smiling and showing us her fine teeth, and not disturbed herself about the alteration in the criminal laws, and the effects which the corn-bill might have had. Rather too theatrical in the other young lady, Miss ———, to recite Coleridge's ode to the Departing Year, with such emphatic pith, and such vehemence of gesticulation. The MS. poems handed round insufferably bad. Elegies in the measure of "Oh, Miss Bailey, unfortunate Miss Bailey," and Odes, in which sound gave sense no opportunity of coming forward in self defence. Must learn the particulars of that sweet, modest, and melancholy young creature, who sate on the end of the sopha, nearest the door. Am certain that I caught her sighing several times. Must be at the bottom; having been teazing myself whether the unfortunate passion, the theme of the stanzas which she handed about, as her picnic share of the literary banquet, can be only an effusion of sentiment, or whether they have originated in dread reality. At all events, she may wait long enough, till her verses come round to her again; as, in the heat of conversation, I stowed them along with my snuff-box into my waistcoat pocket. They are not amiss.

STANZAS.

Oh mine be the shade, &c.

Oh! mine be the shade where no eye may discover,
Where in silence and sorrow alone I may dwell;
Give scorn to the maid, who is false to her lover;
A tear unto her, who has loved but too well!

Alas for the heart, when affection forsaking
  The vows, it has pledged, and has cherish'd through years;
For no refuge remains to that lone heart but breaking,
  The silence of grief, and the solace of tears!

Farewell the bright prospects that once could allure me
  To think this poor earth was a promise of Heaven;
Since he, who once doated, no more can endure me,
  Too much with the darkness of fate I have striven;
The flowers with their odours — the birds with their singing —
  The beauties of earth, and the glories of sky,
Dear — sad recollections are constantly bringing —
  And all that remains upon earth is — to die!!

To die — or to be married. It is a lottery indeed, but still "I have stout notions on the marrying score," to use the words of an eminent poet.* Truly I am not a little taken with this sweet young creature; and perhaps, after all, this

Was *not* taught her by the dove,
To die, and know no second love.

If I thought so, — I do not know, but that I might make proposals; if she has any rhino, so much the better; let her put it in her pocket, and it will prevent the wind from blowing her away. But the deuce is, I am afraid of that evil genius of mine, Mrs. M'Whirter. What misery a rash step entails upon us. I wish a hurricane would blow her and the lecturer to the river of the Amazons for ever and a day.

* * * * * * * *

* Leigh Hunt, in "Rimini."—M.

Familiar Letter from the Adjutant.*

DEAR KIT,

I write this in the earnest hope of its finding you less molested by your inveterate enemy in the great toe, and brimful of the delight, which your modesty and diffidence can not prevent you feeling, in hearing it acknowledged from all quarters, that yours is the most excellent work of its kind, which has appeared in any country, since the invention of printing. Do let me know what the *Edinburgh Review* people are saying about it, or, if they are at last fairly beat to a stand still, and seriously thinking of giving up the concern. I heard, indeed, that a meeting of their contributors has been lately convened, either for that purpose or perhaps for petitioning you to make your journal a general receptacle for speculations of all kinds; and that, thus, such of them as were capable, might be transferred to the legion of Blackwood, and not utterly cast destitute. But this is a matter, friend North, on which I would advise you to proceed with cautious circumspection—it might prove like marriage—alas! the day—a step not easy to be remedied. Many of your supporters would find a delicacy in making common cause with the generality of these folks, as they have uttered such a quantity of unsound and unsatisfactory stuff, in every branch and department of human knowledge, and ridiculed every thing worthy of respect and veneration. *Exempli gratia*, but that's a trifle, there is your humble servant, who could not, with any degree of honor, act in concert with men, who depreciated the late glorious war, and every battle in it, mid whose bloodshed, and under whose "sulphrous canopy" he plucked a leaf of laurel for his brow. But we shall drop the subject, as not worth speaking about—conscious that where the glory of his country, and the reputation of his work is concerned, no man will direct the helm with a more intrepid spirit, or maul the invaders with a more unerring hand, than yourself, the redoubted Christopher North, Esquire.

* This Familiar Letter ("containing projects, promises, and imitations") appeared in *Blackwood* for May, 1821.—M.

You asked me in your last, if I ever now-a-days read any? and if so, what books occupy my attention and time? A question with a vengeance. Do you think that my knowledge comes to me by intuition? After having written above half a hundred articles to you, in every department of human knowledge, you ask me if ever I read any. That reminds me of the tower of Babel—you might as well ask if it reared itself. But, in writing so, I doubt not you have only made a *lapsus linguæ*, or at any rate a joke on my multitudinous researches. All kinds of books come welcome enough to me. I have a capacity of digestion rather ostrich-like, and capable of managing a great farrago; and assimilating the same into solid nourishment. I like the drama very much; and Alexander Macpherson being now in the middle of the fifth act, will soon show whether or not the genius of the drama loves me. Novels are "an appetite and a feeling" which I can not resist—Political economy I like better than I do some of its professors—Metaphysics are excellent food for me; and, over a ten-hours' mathematical proposition, I am as cool as a cucumber; but *entre nous*, theological controversy is my favorite study; but don't mention this, as the Roman Catholic clergy like nothing better than to have a bull-baiting with me; and, in spite of all my asseverations and protestations to the contrary, they will insist that I am a little loose both in my moral and religious principles; but I am thoroughly convinced that they are wrong.

When you see Wastle, tell him I have found it quite out of my power to be over, according to promise, at the walking of the Commissioner; but hope yet to have that honor along with him. At all events, I am determined to be over at the Edinburgh races, as I have got possession of as fine a bit of horse-flesh as ever put hoof to turf; and I would like to know what success Salamanca would have, in taking a few rounds for the hunter's plate. If he be successful, it will be a good speculation; if not, I will sell him the next day at Wordsworth's* out of pure vexation, although I had him as a present from a military friend of mine, who rode him at the battle of Waterloo. He has not yet lost tooth-mark, and gallops like a fury. The

* A horse-dealer in Edinburgh.—M.

best of it is, that the longer he runs he continues to improve; and, if there be above three four mile heats, I never saw the horse, mare, or gelding, that I would not back him against, at considerable odds. He is a little stiff for the first mile or so after starting but when he begins to warm, you never beheld a finer personification of the fine idea, which Lord Byron has applied to denote the beauty and swiftness of Mazeppa's charger,

> Who looked as though the speed of thought
> Were in his limbs.

I have him in training already, and hope to show him off in style to you in July. If I was not so lengthened in the nether extremities, I would not care much to jockey him myself; but that, to be sure, is an after consideration.

Do give us a paper from your editorial pen on the Pope and Bowles controversy. I cannot fathom what Campbell and Byron would be at. Lord Byron compares the poetry of Pope to a Grecian temple, and the poetry written by Campbell, Scott, Wastle, Southey, Wordsworth, Hogg, Coleridge, himself, myself, &c. to the tower of Babel. A pretty comparison of a surety; but it is all in my eye, Betty Martin, that men, like Campbell and Byron, should imagine that the essence of poetry consisted in the manners and morals of society; in drawing pictures of merchants with spectacles, and goose quills stuck behind their ears pondering over their legers; of awfully ancient spinsters, leering from behind their fans, and looking unutterable things; of grocers' apprentices, sanding the sugar, watering the tobacco, and then walking aloft to prayers; of the lack-a-daisical exclamations of boarding school misses, and the pettifogging dandyism of lawyers' clerks — and yet, that these poets, in hostility to their own doctrines, should write of such natural personages as a Corsair, with "one virtue, and a thousand crimes;" of a Lord Lara, who, seeing a ghost, broke out into a perspiration, and spoke Gaelic or some other outlandish tongue; of Count Manfred, alias Dr. Faustus, jun. who

> —— saw more devils than vast hell can hold,
> The madman.

Of the Giaour, who turned an infidel monk, because he ran away with another man's wife, who was sewed up in a sack, and thrown into the sea;—or of such a true and natural person as Andes, "Giant of the western star," sitting with his cheek reclined on his dexter hand, and a flambeau in his left fist, looking over in the dark from America to Europe;—or of a gentleman of the second-sight, begging his master not to go to battle, as he had a presentiment that he would be much safer at home;—and a thousand other things, well enough adapted to poetry in my humble opinion, but having as slight an application to the practice of life as can well be imagined. Sir Walter Scott must immediately send Lord Cranstoun's goblin page an errand to the Red Sea, and let him be for ever "lost! lost! lost!" And as for his redoubted namesake, Michael, the flag-stone must be no more lifted from his grave;—Coleridge must tie the Auncient Marinere to a stake, and have a shot at *him* with the cross-bow, as he so treated the "harmless Albatross;"—and as for the Lady Christabel, he must, without delay, scribble four dozen of letters, inviting his friends to her funeral—let him employ a patent coffin, as she is rather a restless and unruly subject.—Wordsworth must despatch the Danish Boy to the land of shadow;—and Hogg should purchase a pennyworth of saddle-tacks, and, with a trusty hammer, nail the ears of the Gude Grey Catte to his stable door, to frighten away the rats, as she will no longer be able to act as governess to the Seven Daughters of the Laird of Blair. As for Miss Kilmeny, when she comes back at the end of the next seven years, let him give her a furlough, specifying perpetual leave of absence.—Dr. Southey ought to send a specimen of a Petrified Glendoveer to the College Museum, ere the species becomes utterly extinct, that future antiquarians may not be completely puzzled, if their bones be found, like those of the mammoth, in a fossil state; and he ought to give the witch Maimuna in Thalaba, that was perpetually singing, a half-crown's worth of the most choice ballads, to set her up in a decent line of trade, and have done with her. Thomas Moore's Veiled Prophet, without the nose, should get a proper certificate, and be sent to the Chelsea Hospital; and, on proper representation being made, the Peri, who had neither house nor hold, may be received into the Charity-Workhouse.—Do, North, convince both Mr. Campbell and his lordship, that the world is tolerably well contented with the poetry they have foolishly thought proper to give it; that though Mr. Campbell's criticism is sometimes a little vapid, yet that his verses are generally excellent; and that, if Lord Byron's system of moral and ethical poetry be after his old way — that is, if Beppo and Don Juan, like the brick of the pedant in Hierocles, are specimens of the materials of which it is to be composed, we should think, that the world will be contented with the specimens it has already enjoyed. Enough is as good as a feast; "where ignorance is bliss, 'tis folly to be wise;" and, as I am tired of it, I will drop the subject.

Friend North, I have a crow to pluck with you,—You are as strange a fellow as ever fell within the circle of my acquaintance, always excepting Mrs. M'Whirter, for she beats cockfighting. You will pretend, now, that you did not know to whom the memorandum-book belonged, out of which you treated your readers, or rather the world, for all the world are your readers, a month or two ago. Really this is provoking, and I do not take it altogether well at your hands. Would it not have been more creditable to you, instead of creating a few smiles at my expense, to have written to the wandering sinner of a Bagman, into whose hands my book fell, that you knew the proprietor; and that you would thank him to transmit it to you, that you might transmit it to the proper owner? It would not surprise me much, though you were yet to write me a letter, professing your entire ignorance of the whole transaction; and that you are free to give your oath, that you had not so much as the smallest suspicion that the memorandum-book could possibly belong to me. Do you think me innocent enough to believe any stuff of this sort? Though I am not a Highlander, I have enough of the second-sight to see clearly through trifles of this kind. But I will waste no more words on the subject; and, though we are hundreds of miles apart, our hearts are always together. I can take a joke, and can give one; so we will shake hands and forget the whole matter: Indeed I am almost sorry that I mentioned it; but don't give any more extracts without my consent.

Tell our divan, the first time you all meet in Ambrose's, to remember me in their prayers; as I am sure that I never empty a tumbler or two, *solus*, without toasting them all alternately; and, as I allow each a bumper, it sometimes obliges me to have a third brewing. Let them know, that I will see them all in July, and that I have a budget of famous anecdotes and rencontres to entertain them with; some of them out-hector Hector, and they are all personal, *ipsò teste*, as Maturin says. But I shall drop the subject, as I do not wish to promise. "There's a braw time coming," as the deacon's son observes.

What would you think of it, I have been amusing myself with some imitations of the living authors; — it was during the time I was confined to my room, from having sprained my left ankle, in leaping over a five-bar gate for a wager, and I intend to make a complete cabinet of them. I have already allowed Hazlitt a complete ration of epigram, antithesis, and paradox. Goodwin sails in a parachute of theory, suspended to a balloon inflated with sulphureted hydrogen; Cobbet writes an official document, *currente calamo*, with all the courtier-like dignity becoming a secretary to her majesty; and Charley Phillips, with his fists tied into large bladders, knocks arguments from off their feet by repeated douces on either side of the chops, with his unceasing one, twos. I have, likewise, a complete set of the poets, good, bad, and indifferent. The Cockneys I found it desperately hard to imitate, as I could not make my genius to descend so low. I do not know, but that I have caricatured some of them a little; but this was unintentional, as they have fairly baffled me in many particulars.

As you seem interested in my literary doings, I will treat you with two or three short specimens, as I see you are already in for a double postage. To begin with the mightiest man of our age, do you think that in the following, I have caught the chivalrous flow, the tone of the olden time, the grace, and the harmony, and the strength, that characterize the poetry of the Ariosto of the North? The Lay of the Last Minstrel, and Marmion, form eras in the mind of every true living admirer of poetical excellence.

The hounds in the kennel are yelling loud,
The hawks are boune for flight;

For the sun hath burst from his eastern shroud,
And the sky is clear, without a cloud,
  And the steed for the chase is dight:
The merry huntsmen, up in the morn,
Crack the long whip, and wind the horn.

Lord Timothy rubbed his eyes, and rose
  When he heard the merry crew;
He scarce took space to don his clothes,
  And his night-cap quick he threw
Back on the pillow, and down the stair,
Disdaining brush or comb for hair,
  With lightning speed he flew;
And in the twinkling of a fan,
With frock and cap, the gallant man,
Caparison'd all spick and span,
  Was with the waiting crew.
Sir Abraham rode his bonny gray;
    Sir Anthony his black;
Lord Hector hath mounted his sprightly bay;
Lord Tom, Lord Jack, and all are away;
Curvet, and demivolte, and neigh,
Mark out their bold and brisk array,
With buckskins bright, and bonnets gay,
    And bugles at each back.

They had hardly ridden a mile, a mile,
  A mile but barely ten,
As each after each they leaped a stile,
When their heart play'd pit-a-pat the while,
  To see a troop of armed men,
A troop of gallant men at drill,
With well soap'd locks, and stiffen'd frill;
Each in his grasp held spear or sword,
Ready to murder at a word,
And ghastly was each warrior's smile,
Beneath his barred aventayle;
Buff belts were girt around each waist;
Steel cuisses round each thigh were braced;
Around each knee were brazen buckles;
And iron greaves to save their knuckles;
High o'er each tin-bright helmet shone
The casque, and dancing morion,
Which reach'd to where the tailor sets,
On shoulder, woollen epaulets;
Their blades were of Toledo steel,
Ferarra, or Damascus real;

Yea! human eye did never see,
Through all the days of chivalry,
Men more bedight from head to heel, &c.

Lady Alice she sits in the turret tower,
A-combing her raven hair;
The clock hath tolled the vesper hour,
Already the shadows of evening lower
To veil the landscape fair.
To the jetty fringe of her piercing eye
She raised her opera glass,
For she was anxious to espy
If her worthy knight should pass.—
"Lo! yonder he comes,"—she sigh'd and said,
Then with a rueful shake of head—
"Shall I my husband ne'er discover—
'Tis but the white cow eating clover!"
She looked again,—"Sure yon is he,
That gallops so fast along the lea!
Alas! 'tis only a chestnut tree!!
Standing as still as still can be!!!"
—"Come hither, come hither, my little foot page,
And dance, my anguish to assuage;
And be it jig, or waltz, or reel,
I care not, so it doth conceal
The ghosts, that of a thousand dies,
Float evermore before mine eyes;
And I, to make thee foot it gay,
With nimble finger, by my fay,
Upon the tambourine will play!" &c.

But I must not give you too much of it, as it will spoil the interest of the work, which will shortly appear in three octavo volumes, printed uniformly, and with portraits; something like Peter's Letters. The imitation extends to three cantos, together with an introductory epistle to my friend Dr. Scott.—Under the head of Coleridge, you will find the continuation of Christabel,* and the Auncient Waggonere; both of which were ushered into public notice by your delightful and discriminating work, together with the following

* The continuation of Christabel, published in *Blackwood*, was written, not by Maginn, but by the late D. M. Moir, the "Delta" of Maga.—M.

FRAGMENT OF A VISION.

A dandy, on a velocipede,*
  I saw in a vision sweet,
Along the highway making speed,
  With his alternate feet.
Of a bright and celestial hue
Gleam'd beauteously his blue surtout;
While ivory buttons, in a row,
Show'd like the winter's cavern'd snow,
Which the breezy North
Drives sweeping forth,
To lodge in the cave below:
Ontario's beaver, without demur,
To form his hat did lend its fur:
His frill was of the cambric fine,
And his neckcloth starch'd, and aquiline;
And oh, the eye with pleasure dwells
On his white jean indescribables;
And he throws the locks from his forehead fair,
And he pants, and pants, and pants for air;
What is the reason I cannot tell,—
There is a cause — I know it well;
Too firmly bound — too tightly braced,
The corsets grasp his spider waist,
Till his coat tails are made to fly
Even from the back they glorify.
Look again, he is not there —
Vanish'd into the misty air!
Look again! — do ye see him yet?
Ah no! the bailiff hath seized him for debt;
And, to and fro, like a restless ghost,
When peace within the grave is lost,
He paces as far, as far he should,
Within the bounds of Holyrood!

His Lordship of Byron, I have not handled roughly enough; I cannot yet forget the tower of Babel; what a speech! — as if we were a parcel of jackasses! I shall yet have at him for it. What do you think of The Galiongee, — A fragment of a Turkish Tale?

* The velocipede was a slight carriage on which a man sat astride, and had his pedestrian motions rapidly accelerated by its large wheels.— M.

THE GALIONGEE.

A Fragment of a Turkish Tale.

Advertisement.—The Author of this tale begs to inform the public, that the scattered fragments which it presents were collected from an improvisatore, who recited during the time that the author drank his fifth cup of Mocha with that civilest of all gentlemen, Ali Pacha.

THE Pacha sat in his divan,
With silver-sheathed ataghan;
And call'd to him a Galiongee,
Come lately from the Euxine Sea
To Stamboul; chains were on his feet,
  And fetters on his hands were seen,
  Because he was a Nazarene:
When, duly making reverence meet,
With haughty glance on that divan,
And curling lip, he thus began:

  "By broad Phingari's silver light,
When sailing at the noon of night,
Bismillah! whom did we descry
  But dark corsairs, who, bent on spoil,
  Athwart the deep sea ever toil!—
We know their blood-red flags on high:
The Capitan he call'd, belike,
With gesture proud, to bid us strike,
And told his Sonbachis to spare
Of not one scalp a single hair,
Though garbs of green showed Emirs there!
It boots not, Pacha, to relate
  What souls were sent to Eblis throne,
How Azrael's arrows scatter'd fate,
  How wild, wet, wearied, and alone,
When all my crew were drench'd in blood,
Or floated lifeless on the flood,
I fought, unawed, nor e'er thought I
To shout 'Amaun,' the craven's cry.—
  I took my handkerchief to wipe
  My burning brow, and then I took,
With placid hand, my long chibouque,
That is to say, my Turkish pipe,
And having clapp'd it in my cheek,
Disdaining ere a word to speak,
I shouted to the pirate, 'Now,
You've fairly beat me, I allow,'" &c.

Perhaps, — as I know that Childe Harold's Pilgrimage is one of your first favorites, — you will find an account of his step-brother, Childe Paddy's* banishment to New Holland, more to your taste. This is the commencement:

Oh! mortal man, how varied is thy lot,
  Thy ecstasies of joy and sorrow, how
Chill'd, sunk, and servile art thou, or how hot
  Flashes indignant beauty from thy brow!
  Times change, and empires fall; the gods allow
Brief space for human contemplation, and
  Above all partial dictates disavow
Unequal love; how can we, at their hand,
For individual fate a gentler boon demand!

Childe Paddy parted from his father's cot;
  It was not castle proud, nor palace high,
Extraneous symmetry here glitter'd not,
  But turf-built walls and filth did meet the eye;
  Loud was the grumph and grumble from hog-stye;
Swans gleam'd not here, as on the Leman lake,
  But goose and ducklings, famed for gabbling cry,
With quack, quack, quack, did make the roofs to shake,
Till in their utmost holes the wondering rats did quake!

He thought of father, whom he loved, and left;
  He thought of mother, at her booming wheel;
He thought of sister, of his care bereft;
  He thought of brethren dear; and, to conceal
  The endless pangs that o'er his brain did reel,
As through the vale his pensive way he took,
  For fear his onward purpose would congeal
He sung, while pacing with right-forward look,
"Sweet Kitty of Coleraine," and "Fair of Donabrooke!"

I rejoice that your prophecy, as to the popularity of Hogg's Tales, has been abundantly verified. Natural power and genius will fight their way, in spite of opposition, and "disdainful of help or hindrance." I doubt not that his better half has had a hand in the purgation of the new edition. Give my compliments to him; tell him I shall never forget the kindness I experienced at Altrive Lake; and, above all, ask him how he likes the following stanzas, the opening of a ballad, as long as "Kirkma-

* It was first written "Childe Raddy," but I was afraid of angering the Scotsman.— M. O.

breck," that celebrated modern Timon, or rather she-Timon, or woman hater.

Theyre wals ane Brounie offe mucle faime
  Thatte ussit too cumme too ane aulde fairme housse
Ande evir the maydes fro theyre beddes came,
  Alle theyre werke wals dune, soo cannye and douce.

The cauppis wure cleanit; the yerne wals spunne,
  Ande the parritche aye maide forre the oulde guidman,
The kye wure milkit, the yill wals runne,
  Ande shininge lyke goude wals the ould brasse pan.

Ande mickle theye wonderit, and mair theye thocht,
  But neivir ane wurde too theyre minny spake theye,
Theye lukit aye too the braas theye hadde cofft,
  Too buske theyre hayre, and to maike theme gaye.

Thenne outte spake Jennye, the youngeste ane,
  "I'm shure to mye Jocke itte wull gie delyghte,
Ande maike the laddye a' fidginge faine,
  Too see the luffes offe mye handes soe whyte."

Thenne outte spake Kirstene, as doune she satte
  Before the glasse toe kaim herre hayre,
"Oh! luke," quoth she, "I amme gettinge soe fatte,
  Thatte I offe idlesse muste beware.

"The neiburs theye wille kenne noe mee,
  Forre I'm scrimply aible to gaung aboutte,
Iffe I gette on soe, ye wulle brieflye see
  A hurlye cofft toe carrye mee outte," &c.

Speaking of Wordsworth, what he is dreaming about? The published part of the Excursion does not extend to a week, and we have had no more of it for the last seven years; if the poet's life and peregrinations are to occupy an equally proportionate space, published at the same distance of time, the world may expect to see the conclusion of the work at much about the same time when Blackwood's Magazine intends retiring from public notice, that is to say, somewhere about the year 3000. The following is a small portion of a fifty-page episode. It is entitled

THE KAIL POT.

If e'er, in pensive guise, thy steps have stray'd
At eve or morn, along that lofty street,
Yclept the Canongate, exalt thine eyes,

And lo! between thee and the azure sky,
Dangling in negro blackness beautiful,
A kail pot hangs, upon an iron bar
Suspended, and by iron chains hung down.
Beneath it yawns a threshold, like the den
Of Cacus, giant old, or like the caves
Of sylvan satyrs in the forests green;—
There enter, and, amid his porter butts,
In conscious wisdom bold, sits Nathan Goose,
Worshipping the muses and a mug of ale!

Sweet are the songs of Nathan Goose, and strong
Yea! potent is the liquor that he sells;
On many a cold and icy winter night,
When stars were sparkling in the deep blue sky,
Have, circling round his board, a jovial throng,
Tippled until the drowsy chime of twelve.
Strange has it seem'd to me, that we, who breathe
Vapours, as watery as the cooling drops
Of Rydal Mere, should drink combustibles,
And perish not; yet, thereby, of the soul
The cogitations are disturb'd; its dreams
Are hollows by reality and time
Fulfill'd not, and the waking spirit mourns,
When shines the sun above the eastern sea,—
The ocean seen from Black Comb's summit high,
And throws his yellow light against the pane
Of chamber window,—window deep embower'd
With honey-suckle blossoms;—o'er the wrecks
Of such fantastical, and inane stuff,
Shadows, and dreams, and visions of the night.—
Then follow headaches dreadful, vomitings
Of undigested biscuit, mingled with
The sour and miserable commixture of
Hot aqua vitæ, with the mountain lymph,—
If city water haply be so call'd,—
The lymph of Fountain-well, hard by the shop
Where seeds and roots are sold, above whose door
The black-eyed eagle spreads his golden wings.

Hard is the lot of him, whom evil fates
Have destined to a way of life unmeet;
Whose genius and internal strength are clogg'd
By drudgery, and the rubs of common men.
But I have gazed upon thee, Nathan Goose,
Gazed on the workings of thy inward soul—
Hail'd with delight thy planet in the sky,
And mid the constellations planted thee! &c.

As you are one of the prime admirers of the Lyrical Ballads, as who, with the smallest pretensions to poetical taste, does not acknowledge most of them to be extremely fine, and studded over with the very pearls of poetry,—I have copied over for you a lyrical ballad of the true breed. I do not know but that you will like it almost as well as the Wagoner, or Peter Bell.

BILLY BLINN.

I knew a man that died for love,
His name, I ween, was Billy Blinn;
His back was hump'd, his hair was gray,
And, on a sultry summer day,
We found him floating in the linn.

Once as he stood before his door,
Smoking, and wondering who should pass,
Then trundling past him in a cart
Came Susan Foy, she won his heart,
She was a gallant lass.

And Billy Blinn conceal'd the flame
That burn'd, and scorch'd his very blood;
But often was he heard to sigh,
And with his sleeve he wiped his eye,
In a dejected mood.

A party of recruiters came
To wile our cottars, man and boy;
Their coats were red, their cuffs were blue,
And boldly, without more ado,
Off with the troop went Susan Foy!

When poor old Billy heard the news,
He tore his hairs so thin and gray;
He beat the hump upon his back,
And ever did he cry, "Alack,
Ohon, oh me!—alas a-day!"

His nights were spent in sleeplessness,
His days in sorrow and despair;
It could not last—this inward strife;
The lover he grew tired of life,
And saunter'd here and there.

At length, 'twas on a moonlight eve,
The skies were blue, the winds were still;
He wander'd from his wretched hut

And, though he left the door unshut,
He sought the lonely hill.

He look'd upon the lovely moon,
He look'd upon the twinkling stars;
"How peaceful all is there," he said,
"No noisy tumult there is bred,
And no intestine wars."

But misery overcame his heart,
For all was waste and war within;
And rushing forward with a leap,
O'er crags a hundred fathoms steep,
He plunged into the linn.

We found him when the morning sun
Shone brightly from the eastern sky;
Upon his back he was afloat—
His hat was sailing like a boat—
His staff was found on high.

Oh, reckless woman, Susan Foy,
To leave the poor, old, loving man,
And with a soldier, young and gay,
Thus harlot-like to run away
To India or Japan.

Poor Billy Blinn, with hair so white,
Poor Billy Blinn was stiff and cold;
Will Adze he made a coffin neat,
We placed him in it head and feet,
And laid him in the mould!

I dare say you will suppose that there is no end to my prosing. But hold, my pen!—For the present I am determined to have done. As to Southey, Lamb, Milman, Croly, Shelley, Wastle, Wilson, Campbell, Hunt, Montgomery, Bowles, Dr. Scott, Frere, Rogers, Bloomfield, Herbert, Thurlow, Willison Glass, &c., you shall have more of them in my next; and meantime believe me, more than ever has been yet professed by

Yours, &c.

MORGAN ODOHERTY.

COLERAINE, *Red Cow Inn*, *April* 30.

And, though he left the door unshut,
He sought the lonely hill.

He look'd upon the lovely moon,
He look'd upon the twinkling stars;
"How peaceful all is there," he said,
"No noisy tumult there is bred,
And no intestine wars."

But misery overcame his heart,
For all was waste and war within;
And rushing forward with a leap,
O'er crags a hundred fathoms steep,
He plunged into the linn.

We found him when the morning sun
Shone brightly from the eastern sky;
Upon his back he was afloat—
His hat was sailing like a boat—
His staff was found on high.

Oh, reckless woman, Susan Foy,
To leave the poor, old, loving man,
And with a soldier, young and gay,
Thus harlot-like to run away
To India or Japan.

Poor Billy Blinn, with hair so white,
Poor Billy Blinn was stiff and cold;
Will Adze he made a coffin neat,
We placed him in it head and feet,
And laid him in the mould!

I dare say you will suppose that there is no end to my prosing. But hold, my pen!—For the present I am determined to have done. As to Southey, Lamb, Milman, Croly, Shelley, Wastle, Wilson, Campbell, Hunt, Montgomery, Bowles, Dr. Scott, Frere, Rogers, Bloomfield, Herbert, Thurlow, Willison Glass, &c., you shall have more of them in my next; and meantime believe me, more than ever has been yet professed by

Yours, &c.

MORGAN ODOHERTY.

COLERAINE, *Red Cow Inn, April* 30.

There's not a Joy that Life can give,* &c.

1.

There's not a joy that WINE *can give like that it takes away,*
When slight intoxication yields to drunkenness the sway,
'Tis not that *youth's smooth cheek* its *blush* surrenders to the nose,
But the stomach turns, the forehead burns, and all our pleasure goes.

2.

Then the few, who still can keep their chairs amid the smash'd decanters,
Who wanton still in witless jokes, and laugh at pointless banters—
The magnet of their course is gone—for, let them try to walk,
Their legs, they speedily will find as jointless as their talk.

3.

Then the mortal hotness of the brain, like hell itself, is burning,
It cannot feel, nor dream, nor think—'tis whizzing, blazing, turning—
The heavy wet, or port, or rum, has mingled with *our tears,*
And if by chance we're weeping drunk, each drop our cheek-bone sears.

4.

Though fun still flow from fluent lips,† and jokes confuse our noddles
Through midnight hours, while punch our powers insidiously enfuddles,
'Tis but as ivy leaves were worn by Bacchanals of yore,
To make them still look fresh and gay while rolling on the floor.

5.

Oh! could I walk *as I have* walk'd, *or* see *as I have* seen;
Or even roll as I have done on many a carpet green—
As port at Highland inn seems sound, all corkish though it be,
So would I the Borachio kiss, and get blind drunk with thee.‡

---

* The actual title of these "Stanzas for Music" (as they are called in Byron's Poems,) is not correctly given here. The first stanza runs thus:

"There's not a joy the world can give like that it takes away,
When the glow of early thought declines in feeling's dull decay;
'Tis not on youth's smooth cheek the blush alone, which fades so fast,
But the tender bloom of heart is gone, ere youth itself be past."

These lines bear date March, 1815.—M.

† The *ipsisima verba* are "Though wit may flash from fluent lips."—M.

‡ This parody was put into Byron's mouth, as chanted by him at the symposium with Odoherty, at Pisa, in July, 1822.—M.

'Tis in vain to complain.

1.

'Tis in vain
To complain,
In a melancholy strain,
Of the days that are gone, and will never come again.
Be we gay,
While we may,
At whatever time of day,
Be our locks berry brown, or mottled o'er with gray,
Be our locks berry brown, or mottled o'er with gray.

2.

We have laughed,
We have quaffed,
We have raked it fore and aft,
But out of pleasure's bowl have not emptied all the draught.
Never mind
Days behind,
But still before the wind,
Float after jolly souls, full flasks, and lasses kind,
Float after jolly souls, full flasks, and lasses kind.*

Chanson a Boire.

1.

Time and we should swiftly pass;
He the hour-glass, we the glass.—
Drink! yon beam which shines so bright
Soon will sink in starless night:
    Ere it sink, boys, ere it sink—
    Drink it dim, boys! drink, drink, drink!

2.

Drink before it be too late—
Snatch the hour you may from fate;
Here alone true wisdom lies,
To be merry 's to be wise.—
    Ere ye sink, boys—ere ye sink—
    Drink ye blind, boys! drink, drink, drink!†

---

* This appeared in THE NOCTES, for August, 1823.—M.
† From THE NOCTES, March, 1823.—M.

Song of a Fallen Angel over a Bowl of Rum-Punch.

BY T. M., ESQ.

HEAP on more coal there,
And keep the glass moving,
The frost nips my nose,
Though my heart glows with loving.
Here's the dear creature,
No skylights — a bumper;
He who leaves heeltaps
I vote him a mumper.
With hey cow rumble O
Whack! populorum,
Merrily, merry men,
Push round the jorum.

What are Heaven's pleasures
That so very sweet are?
Singing from psalters,
In long or short metre.
Planked on a wet cloud
Without any breeches,
Just like the Celtic,*
Met to make speeches.
With hey cow rumble, &c.

Wide is the difference,
My own boozing bullies,
Here the round punch-bowl
Heap'd to the full is.
Then if some wise one
Thinks that up "yonder"
Is pleasant as we are,
Why — he's in a blunder.
With hey cow rumble, &c.†

---

* The Celtic Society, at their annual dinner, always wore the kilt. — M.

† First published in THE NOCTES for July, 1823. It is a parody on Moore — and not a very good one. — M.

Pococurante.*

I DO not care a farthing about any man, woman, or child, in the world. You think that I am joking, Jemmy; but you are mistaken. What! you look at me again with those honest eyes of yours staring with wonder, and making a demi-pathetic, demi-angry appeal for an exception in your favour. Well, Jemmy, I *do* not care about you, my honest fellow, so uncork the other bottle.

Did you ever see me out of humour in your life for the tenth part of a second?—Never, so help me, God!—Did you ever hear me speak ill of another? I might, perhaps, have cracked a joke—indeed, I have cracked a good many such in my time—at a man's expense behind his back; but never have I said anything which I would not say to his face, or what I would not take from him with treble hardness of recoil, if it so pleased him to return it; but real *bona fide* evil-speaking was never uttered by me. I never quarrelled with any one. You are going to put me in mind of my duel with Captain Maxwell. I acknowledge I fought it, and fired three shots. What then? Could I avoid it? I was no more angry with him, when I sent the message, than I was at the moment of my birth. Duelling is an absurd custom of the country, which I must comply with when occasion requires. The occasion had turned up, and I fought of course. Never was I happier than when I felt the blood trickling over my shoulders—for the wise laws of honour were satisfied, and I was rid of the cursed trouble. I was sick of the puppyism of punctilio, and the booby legislation of the seconds, and was glad to escape from it by a scratch. I made it up with Maxwell, who was an honest, though a hot-headed and obstinate man—and you know I was executor to his will. Indeed, he dined with me the very day-week after the duel.

* This very peculiar composition, in which deep feeling is mingled with an affectation of contempt for men, gods, and columns, ("Homines, Dii, et columnæ,") was published in *Blackwood* for August, 1823, and was referred to, more than once, by Maginn, in proof of his ability to be intense, as well as amusing.—M.

Yet, spite of this equanimity, I repeat it, that I do not care for any human being on earth, (the present company always excepted,) more than I care for one of those filberts which you are cracking with such laudible assiduity.

Yes—it is true—I have borne myself towards my family unexceptionably, as the world has it. I married off my sisters, sent my brothers to the colleges, and did what was fair for my mother. But I shall not be hypocrite enough to pretend to high motives for so doing. My father's death left them entirely to me, and what could I do with them? Turn them out? That would be absurd, and just as absurd to retain them at home without treating them properly. They were *my* family. My own comforts would have been materially invaded by any other line of conduct. I therefore executed the filial and fraternal affections in a manner which will be a fine topic of panegyric for my obituary. God help the idiots who write such things! *They* to talk of motives, and feelings, and the impulses that sway the human heart! They, whose highest ambition it is to furnish provender, at so much a line, for magazine or newspaper. Yet from them shall I receive the tribute of a tear. The world shall be informed in due time, and I care not how soon, that "DIED at his house, &c. &c. a gentleman, exemplary in every relation of life, whether we consider him as a son, a brother, a friend, or a citizen. His heart," and so on to the end of the fiddle faddle. The winding up of my family affairs, you know, is, that I have got rid of them all; that I pay the good people a visit once a-month, and ask them to a humdrum dinner on my birth-day, which you are perhaps aware occurs but once a-year. I am alone. I feel that I am alone.

My politics—what then? I am, externally at least, a Tory, *à toute outrance*, because my father and my grandfather (and I cannot trace my genealogy any higher) were so before me. Besides, I think every gentleman should be a Tory; there is an easiness, a suavity of mind, engendered by Toryism, which it is vain for you to expect from fretful Whiggery, or bawling Radicalism, and such should be a strong distinctive feature in every gentleman's character. And I admit, that, in my youth, I did many queer things, and said many violent and nonsensical matters. But that fervour is gone. I am still outside the same; but inside how different! I laugh to scorn the nonsense I hear vented about me in the clubs which I frequent. The zeal about nothings, the bustle about stuff, the fears and the precautions against fancied dangers, the indignation against writings which no decent man thinks of reading, or against speeches which are but the essence of stupidity; in short, the whole tempest in a tea-pot appears to me to be ineffably ludicrous. I join now and then, nay very often, in these discussions; why should not I? Am I not possessed of the undoubted liberties of a Briton, invested with the full privilege of talking nonsense? And, if any of my associates laugh inside at me, why, I think them quite right.

But I have dirtied my fingers with ink, you say, and daubed other people's faces with them. I admit it. My pen has been guilty of various political jeux d'esprit, but let me whisper it, Jemmy, on *both* sides. Don't start, it is not worth while. My Tory quizzes I am suspected of; *suspected* I say, for I am not such a goose as to let them be any more than mere matters of suspicion; but of quizzes against Tories I am no more thought guilty than I am of petty larceny. Yet such is the case. I write with no ill feeling; public men or people who thrust themselves before the public in any way, I just look on as phantoms of the imagination, as things to throw off common-places about. You know how I assassinated Jack ****, in the song which you transcribed for me; how it spread in thousands, to his great annoyance. Well, on Wednesday last, he and I supped tete-a-tete, and a jocular fellow he is. It was an accidental rencounter—he was sulky at first, but I laughed and sung him into good humour. When the second bottle had loosened his tongue, he looked at me most sympathetically, and said, May I ask you a question?—A thousand, I replied, provided you do not expect me to answer them.—Ah, he cried, it was a shame for you to abuse me the way you did, and all for nothing; but, hang it, let bygones be bygones.—You are too pleasant a fellow to quarrel with. I told him he appeared to be under a mistake.—He shook his head—emptied his bottle, and we staggered home in great concord. In point of fact, men of sense think not of such things, and mingle freely in society as if they never occurred.

Why then should I be supposed to have any feeling whatever, whether of anger or pleasure about them?

My friends? Where are they? Ay, Jemmy, I do understand what that pressure of my hand means. But where is the other? Nowhere! Acquaintances I have in hundreds—boon companions in dozens—fellows to whom I make myself as agreeable as I can, and whose society gives me pleasure. There's Jack Meggot—the best joker in the world—Will Thomson—an unexceptionable ten-bottle man—John Mortimer, a singer of most renowned social qualities—there's—but what need I enlarge the catalogue? You know the men I mean. I live with them, and that right gaily, but would one of them crack a joke the less, drink a glass the less, sing a song the less, if I died before morning. Not one—nor do I blame them, for, if they were engulfed in Tartarus, I should just go through my usual daily round—keep moving in the same monotonous tread-mill of life, with other companions to help me through, as steadily as I do now. The friends of my boyhood are gone—ay—all—all gone!—I have lost the old familiar faces, and shall not try for others to replace them. I am now happy with a mail-coach companion, whom I never saw before, and never will see again. My cronies come like shadows, so depart. Do you remember the story of Abon Hassen, in some of the Oriental tales? He was squandering a fine property on some hollow friends, when he was advised to try their friendship by pretending poverty, and asking their assistance. It was refused, and he determined never to see them more—never to make a friend—nay, not even an acquaintance; but to sit, according to the custom of the East, by the way-side, and invite to his board the three first passers-by, with whom he spent the night in festive debauchery, making it a rule never to ask the same persons a second time. My life is almost the same—true it is that I know the exterior conformation, and the peculiar habits of those with whom I associate, but our hearts are ignorant of one another. They vibrate not together; they are ready to enter into the same communication, with any passer-by. Nay, perhaps, Hassen's plan was more social. He was relieved from inquiries as to the character of his table-mates. Be they fair, be they foul, they were nothing to him. I am tormented out of my life by such punctilios as I daily must submit to. I wonder you keep company, says a friend—*friend!* well, no matter—with R. He is a scoundrel—he is suspected of having cheated fifteen years ago at play, he drinks ale, he fought shy in a duel business, he is a Whig—a Radical, a Muggletonian, a jumper, a moderate man, a Jacobin; he asked twice for soup, he wrote a libel, his father was a low attorney, nobody knows him in good society, &c. &c. &c. Why, what is it to me? I care not whether he broke every commandment in the decalogue, provided he be a pleasant fellow, and that I am not mixed up with his offences. But the world will so mix me up in spite of myself. Burns used to say, the best company he was ever in was the company of professed blackguards. Perhaps he was right. I dare not try.

My early companions I *did* care for, and where are they? Poor Tom Benson, he was my class-fellow at school; we occupied the same rooms in college, we shared our studies, our amusements, our flirtations, our follies, our dissipations together. A more honourable or upright creature never existed. Well, sir, he had an uncle, lieutenant-colonel of a cavalry regiment, and at his request Tom bought a cornetcy in the corps. I remember the grand-looking fellow strutting about in the full splendour of his yet unspotted regimentals, the cynosure of the bright eyes of the country town in which he resided. He came to London, and then joined his regiment. All was well for a while; but he had always an unfortunate itch for play. In our little circle it did him no great harm; but his new companions played high, and far too skilfully for Tom—perhaps there was roguery, or perhaps there was not—I never inquired. At all events, he lost all his ready money. He then drew liberally on his family; he lost that too; in short, poor Tom at last staked his commission, and lost it with the rest. This, of course, could not be concealed from the uncle, who gave him a severe lecture, but procured him a commission in an infantry regiment destined for Spain. He was to join it without delay; but the infatuated fellow again risked himself, and lost the infantry commission also. He now was ashamed or afraid to face his uncle, and enlisted (for he was a splendid looking young man, who was instantly accepted,) as a private soldier in the twenty-sixth foot. I suppose that he found his habits were too refined and too firmly fixed to allow him to be satisfied with the scanty pay, and coarse food, and low company, of an infantry soldier. It is certain, that he deserted in a fortnight after enlistment. The measure of poor Tom's degradation was not yet filled up. He had not a farthing when he left the twenty-sixth. He went to his uncle's at an hour when he knew that he would not be at home, and was with difficulty admitted by the servant, who recognized him. He persuaded him at last that he meant to throw himself on the mercy of his uncle, and the man, who loved him,—everybody of all degrees who knew him loved him,—consented to his admission. I am almost ashamed to go on. He broke open his uncle's escritoire, and took from it whatever money it contained—a hundred pounds or thereabouts—and slunk out of the house. Heavens! what were my feelings when I heard this—when I saw him proclaimed in the newspapers as a deserter, and a thief! A thief!—Tom Benson a thief! I could not credit the intelligence of my eyes or my ears. He whom I knew only five months before—for so brief had his career been—would have turned with scorn and disgust from any action deviating a hair's-breadth from the highest honour. How he spent the next six months of his life, I know not; but about the end of that period a letter was left at my door by a messenger, who immediately disappeared. It was from him. It was couched in terms of the most abject self-condemnation, and the bitterest remorse. He declared he was a ruined man in character, in fortune, in happiness, in everything, and conjured me, for the sake of former friendship, to let him have five guineas, which he said would take him to a place of safety. From the description of the messenger, who, Tom told me in his note, would return in an hour, I guessed it was himself. When the time came, which he had put off to a moment of almost complete darkness, I opened the door to his fearful rap. It was he—I knew him at a glance, as the lamp flashed over his face—and, uncertain as was the light, it was bright enough to let me see that he was squalid, and in rags; that a fearful and ferocious suspicion, which spoke volumes, as to the life he had lately led, lurked in his side-looking eyes; those eyes that a year before spoke nothing but joy and courage, and that a premature grayness had covered with pie-bald patches the once glossy black locks which straggled over his unwashed face, or through his tattered hat.

I had that he asked,—perhaps more—in a paper in my hand. I put it into his. I had barely time to say "O Tom!" when he caught my hand, kissed it with burning lips, exclaimed "Don't speak to me—I am a wretch!" and, bursting from the grasp with which I wished to detain him, fled with the speed of an arrow down the street, and vanished into a lane. Pursuit was hopeless. Many years elapsed, and I heard not of him—no one heard of him. But about two years ago I was at a coffee-house in the Strand, when an officer of what they called the Patriots of South America, staggered into the room. He was very drunk. His tawdry and tarnished uniform proclaimed the service to which he belonged, and all doubt on the subject was removed by his conversation. It was nothing but a tissue of curses on Bolivar and his associates, who, he asserted, had seduced him from his country, ruined his prospects, robbed him, cheated him, and insulted him. How true these reproaches might have been I knew not, nor do I care, but a thought struck me that Tom might have been of this army, and I inquired, as, indeed, I did of everybody coming from a foreign country, if he knew anything of a man of the name of Benson. "Do you?"—stammered out the drunken patriot—"I do," was my reply.—"Do you care about him?" again asked the officer. "I did—I do," again I returned. "Why then," said he, "take a short stick in your hand, and step across to Valparaiso, there you will find him two feet under ground, snugly wrap up in a blanket. I was his sexton myself, and had not time to dig him a deeper grave, and no way of getting a stouter coffin. It will just do all as well. Poor fellow, it was all the clothes he had for many a day before." I was shocked at the recital, but Holmes was too much intoxicated to pursue the subject any farther. I called on him in the morning, and learned that Benson had joined as a private soldier in this desperate service, under the name of Maberly—that he speedily rose to a command—was distinguished for doing desperate actions, in which he seemed quite reckless of life—had, however, been treated with considerable ingratitude—never was paid a dollar—had lost his baggage—was compelled to part with almost all his wearing apparel for subsistence, and had just made his way to the sea-side, purposing to escape to Jamaica, when he sunk, overcome by hunger and fatigue. He kept the secret of his name till the last moment, when he confided it, and a part of his unhappy history, to Holmes. Such was the end of Benson, a man born to high expectations, of cultivated mind, considerable genius, generous heart, and honourable purposes.

Jack Dallas I became acquainted with at Brazen Nose. There was a time that I thought I would have died for him—and, I believe, that his feelings towards me were equally warm. Ten years ago we were the Damon and Pythias—the Pylades and Orestes of our day. Yet I lost him by a jest. He was wooing most desperately a very pretty girl, equal to him in rank, but rather meagre in the purse. He kept it, however, a profound secret from his friends. By accident I found it out, and when I next saw him, I began to quiz him. He was surprised at the discovery, and very sore at the quizzing. He answered so testily, that I proceeded to annoy him. He became more and more sour, I more and more vexatious in my jokes. It was quite wrong on my part; but God knows I meant nothing by it. I did not know that he had just parted with his father, who had refused all consent to the match, adding injurious insinuations about the mercenary motives of the young lady. Dallas had been defending her, but in vain; and then, while in this mood, did I choose him as the butt of my silly witticisms. At last something I said—some mere piece of nonsense—nettled him so much, that he made a blow at me. I arrested his arm, and cried, "Jack, you would have been very sorry had you put your intentions into effect." He coloured as if ashamed of his violence, but remained sullen and silent for a moment, and then left the room. We never have spoke since. He shortly after went abroad, and we were thus kept from meeting and explaining. On his return, we joined different coteries, and were of different sides in politics. In fact, I did not see him for nearly seven years until last Monday, when he passed me, with his wife—a different person from his early passion, the girl on account of whom we quarrelled—leaning on his arm. I looked at him, but he bent down his eyes, pretending to speak to Mrs. Dallas. So be it.

Then there was my brother—my own poor brother, one year younger than myself. The verdict—commonly a matter of course—must have been true in his case. What an inward revolution that must have been, which could have bent that gay and free spirit, that joyous and buoyant soul, to think of self-destruction. But I cannot speak of poor Arthur. These were my chief friends, and I lost the last of them about ten years ago; and since that time I know no one, the present company excepted, for whom I care a farthing. Perhaps, if they had lived with me as long as my other companions, I would have been as careless about them, as I am about Will Thomson, Jack Megget, or my younger brothers. I am often inclined to think, that my feelings towards them are but warmed by the remembered fervour of boyhood, and made romantic by distance of time. I am pretty sure, indeed, that it is so. And, if we could call up Benson innocent from the mould of South America—Could restore poor, dear Arthur—make Dallas forget his folly—and let them live together again in my society, I should be speedily indifferent about them too. My mind is as if slumbering, quite wrapped up in itself, and never wakes but to act a part. I rise in the morning, to eat, drink, talk—to say what I do not think, to advocate questions which I care not for—to join companions whom I value not, to indulge in sensual pleasures which I despise—to waste my hours in trifling amusements, or more trifling business, and to retire to my bed perfectly indifferent as to whether I am ever again to see the shining of the sun. Yet, is my outside gay, and my conversation sprightly. Within I generally stagnate, but sometimes there comes a twinge, short indeed, but bitter. Then it is that I am, to all appearance, most volatile, most eager in dissipation; but could you lift the covering which shrouds the secrets of my bosom, you would see that, like the inmates of the hall of Eblis, my very heart was fire.

Ha—ha—ha!—say it again, Jemmy—say it again, man—do not be afraid. Ha—ha—ha!—too good—too good, upon honour, I was crossed in love! *I* in love. You make me laugh—excuse my rudeness—ha—ha—ha! No, no, thank God, though I committed follies of various kinds, I escaped *that* foolery. I see my prosing has infected you, has made you dull. Quick, unwire the champagne—let us drive spirits into us by its generous tide. We are growing muddy over the claret. *I* in love! Banish all gloomy thoughts,

"A light heart and a thin pair of breeches
Goes thorough the world, my brave boys."

What say you to that? We should drown all care in the bowl—fie on the plebeian word,—we should dispel it by the sparkling bubbles of wine, fit to be drank by the gods; that is your only true philosophy.

"Let us drink and be merry,
Dance, laugh, and rejoice,
With claret and sherry,
Theorbo and voice.

"This changeable world
To our joys is unjust;
All pleasure's uncertain,
So down with your dust.

"In pleasure dispose
Your pounds, shillings, and pence,
For we all shall be nothing
A hundred years hence."

What, not another bottle?—Only one more!—Do not be so obstinate. Well, if you must, why, all I can say is, good night.

* * * * * * *

He is gone. A kind animal, but a fool, exactly what is called the best creature in the world. I have that affection for him that I have for Towler, and I believe his feelings towards me are like Towler's, an animal love of one whom he looks up to. An eating, drinking, good-humoured, good-natured varlet, who laughs at my jokes, when I tell him they are to be laughed at, sees things exactly in the light that I see them in, backs me in my assertions, and bets on me at whist. I had rather than ten thousand pounds be in singleness of soul, in thoughtlessness of brain, in honesty of intention, in solid contented ignorance, such as Jemmy Musgrove. That I cannot be. *N'importe.*

Booby as he is, he did hit a string which I thought had lost its vibration—had become indurated like all my other feelings. Pish! It is well that I am alone. Surely the claret has made me maudlin, and the wine is oozing out at my eyes. Pish!—What nonsense. Ay, Margaret, it is exactly ten years ago. I was then twenty, and a fool. No, not a fool for loving you. By Heavens, I have lost my wits to talk this stuff! the wine has done its office, and I am maundering. Why did I love you? It was all my own perverse stupidity. I was, am, and ever will be, a blockhead, an idiot of the first water. And such a match for her to be driven into. She certainly should have let me know more of her intentions than she did. Indeed—Why should she? Was she to caper after my whims, to sacrifice her happiness to my caprices, to my devotions of to-day, and my sulkinesses, or, still worse, my levities of to-morrow? No, no, Margaret: never—never—never, even in thought, let me accuse you, model of gentleness, of kindness, of goodness, as well as of beauty. I am to blame myself, and myself alone.

I can see her now, can talk to her without passion, can put up with her husband, and fondle her children. I have repressed that emotion, and, in doing so, all others. With that throb lost, went all the rest. I am now a mere card in the pack, shuffled about eternally with the set, but passive and senseless. I care no more for my neighbour, than the King of Diamonds cares for him of Clubs. Dear, dear Margaret, there is a lock of your hair enclosed unknown to you in a little case which lies over my heart. I seldom dare to look at it. Let me kiss its auburn folds once more, and remember the evening I took it. But I am growing more and more absurd. I drink your health then, and retire.

> Here's a health to thee, Margaret,
> Here's a health to thee;
> The drinkers are gone,
> And I am alone,
> So here's a health to thee.

Dear, dear Margaret.

An Hundred Years Hence.

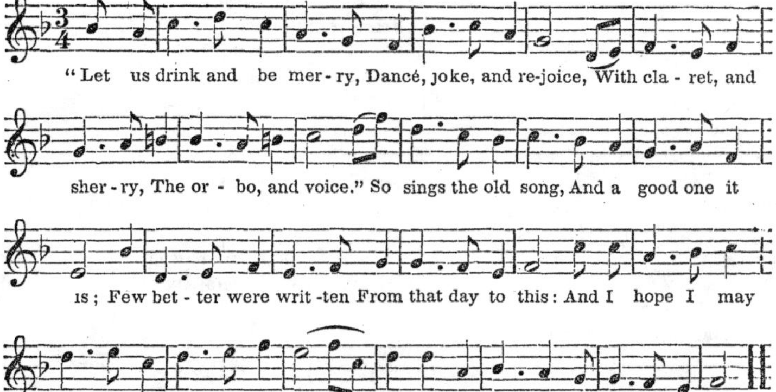

I.

"Let us drink and be merry,
  Dance, joke, and rejoice,
With claret and sherry,
  Theorbo and voice."
So sings the old song,
  And a good one it is;
Few better were written,
  From that day to this:
And I hope I may say it,
  And give no offence,
Few more will be better,
  An hundred years hence.*

II.

In this year eighteen hundred
  And twenty and two,
There are plenty of false ones
  And plenty of true.
There are brave men and cowards;
  And bright men and asses;
There are lemon-faced prudes;
  There are kind-hearted lasses.
He who quarrels with this
  Is a man of no sense,
For so 'twill continue
  An hundred years hence.

III.

There are people who rave
  Of the national debt,
Let them pay off their own
  And the nation's forget;
Others bawl for reform,
  Which were easily done,
If each would resolve
  To reform Number One;

* The old chant of "An Hundred Years Hence" was a great favorite of Maginn's. He has quoted from it in the preceding article, ("Pococurante,") and he made another version of it many years' later. The present version was given in *Blackwood* for December, 1822, as sung at No. VI. of THE NOCTES.—M.

For *my* part to wisdom
  I make no pretence,
I'll be as wise as my neighbors
  An hundred years hence.

IV.

I only rejoice, that
  My life has been cast
On the gallant and glorious
  Bright days which we've past;
When the flag of Old England
  Waved lordly in pride,
Wherever green Ocean
  Spreads his murmuring tide:
And I pray that unbroken
  Her watery fence
May still keep off invaders,
  An hundred years hence.

V.

I rejoice that I saw her
  Triumphant in war,
At sublime Waterloo,
  At dear-bought Trafalgar;
On sea and on land,
  Wheresoever she fought,
Trampling Jacobin tyrants
  And slaves as she ought:
Of CHURCH and of KING
  Still the firmest defence:—
So may she continue
  An hundred years hence.

VI.

Whey then need I grieve, if
  Some people there be,
Who, foes to their country,
  Rejoice not with me;
Sure I know in my heart,
  That Whigs ever have been
Tyrannic, or turnspit,
  Malignant, or mean:
THEY WERE AND ARE SCOUNDRELS
  IN EVERY SENSE,
AND SCOUNDRELS THEY WILL BE
  AN HUNDRED YEARS HENCE.

VII.

So let us be jolly,
  Why need we repine?
If grief is a folly,
  Let's drown it in wine!
As they scared away fiends
  By the ring of a bell,
So the ring of the glass
  Shall blue devils expel:
With a bumper before us
  The night we'll commence
By toasting true Tories
  An hundred years hence.

A Dozen Years Hence.

I.

"LET's drink and be merry,
Dance, sing, and rejoice,"—
So runs the old carol,
"With music and voice."
Had the Bard but survived
Till the year thirty-three,
Methinks he'd have met with
Less matter for glee;
To think what we were
In our days of good sense,
And think what we shall be
A dozen years hence.

II.

O! once the wide Continent
Rang with our fame,
And nations grew still
At the sound of our name;
The pride of Old Ocean,
The home of the free,
The scourge of the despot,
By shore and by sea,
Of the fallen and the feeble
The stay and defence—
But where shall our fame be
A dozen years hence?

III.

The peace and the plenty
That spread, over all
Blithe hearts and bright faces
In hamlet or hall;
Our yeomen so loyal
In greenwood or plain,
Our true-hearted burghers
We seek them in vain;
For Loyalty's now
In the pluperfect tense,
And *freedom's* the word
For a dozen years hence.

IV.

The Nobles of Britain,
Once foremost to wield
Her wisdom in council,
Her thunder in field,
Her Judges, where learning
With purity vied,
Her sound-headed Churchmen,
Time-honour'd, and tried;
To the gift of the prophet
I make no pretence,
But where shall they all be
A dozen years hence?

V.

Alas! for old Reverence,
Faded and flown;
Alas! for the Nobles,
The Church, and the Throne,
When to Radical creeds,
Peer and Prince must conform,
And Catholics dictate
Our new Church Reform;
While the schoolmaster swears
'Tis a useless expense,
Which his class won't put up with
A dozen years hence.

VI.

Perhaps twere too much
To rejoice at the thought,
That its authors will share
In the ruin they wrought;

---

* In *Blackwood*, for February, 1833, appeared this second imitation, or rather paraphrase, of Maginn's favourite old ballad. At that date, (just after the defeat of the Tories, by the accession of the Whigs to office, and the passing of the Reform Bill, after a two years' struggle between the Liberals and the Boroughmongers, in which the Irish party, headed by O'Connell, supported Reform,) Maginn, a violent partisan, was extremely indignant, as these stanzas evince.—M.

That the tempest which sweeps
All their betters away,
Will hardly spare Durham,
Or Russell, or Grey:*
For my part I bear them
No malice prepense,
But I'll scarce break my heart for't,
A dozen years hence.

VII.

When Cobbett shall rule
Our finances alone,
And settle all debts
As he settled his own;
When Hume shall take charge
Of the National Church,
And leave his old tools,
Like the Greeks,† in the lurch!
They may yet live to see
The new era commence,
With their *own* "Final Measure,"
A dozen years hence.‡

VIII.

Already those excellent
Friends of the mob,
May taste the first fruits
Of their Jacobin Job;
Since each braying jackass
That handles a quill,
Now flings up his heels
At the poor dying Bill;
And comparing already
The kicks with the pence,
Let them think of the balance
A dozen years hence.

IX.

When prisons give place
To the swift guillotine,
And scaffolds are streaming
Where churches have been;
We too, or our children,
Believe me, will shake
Our heads—if we have them—
To find our mistake;
To find the great measure
Was all a pretence,
And be sadder and wiser
A dozen years hence.

* The late Earl of Durham, son-in-law of Lord Grey, was in the Reform Ministry as Lord Privy Seal. Born in 1792, he sat in Parliament for many years as Mr. Lambton. In 1828, he was created Baron Durham, and was made Earl in 1833. He was, *personally*, the most thorough aristocrat of his time: *politically*, few public men held such ultra-liberal principles. After having been two years in Russia, as Ambassador, (during which time he became persuaded that the Emperor Nicholas was an extremely mild and liberal man,) he became Governor-General of Canada with powers almost equal to those of a dictator—but was blamed, by the British Government, for exercising some of them, and threw up his appointment in anger, and returned to England. He died in 1840. Lord John Russell, who owes his station as a public man, to that accident of an accident—the having a Duke for his father, introduced the Reform Bill into the House of Commons, on March 1, 1831.—M.

† Cobbett, who had borrowed a thousand pounds from Sir Francis Burdett, contrived *not* to repay it. Mr. Hume, while the Greeks were struggling for independence, had speculated on the stock issued as acknowledgment of their Loan, and—had not *lost* by thus putting his pounds and patriotism into the same venture.—M.

‡ Lord John Russell's declaration that the Reform Bill was "a final measure" obtained him the *sobriquet* of Lord John Finality, and disgusted the movement party, whose support had carried the Bill.—M.

The Pewter Quart.

A NEW SONG TO AN OLD TUNE — WRITTEN AND COMPOSED FOR THE JOLLIFICATION OF BIBBERS OF BEER, PORTER, ALE, STOUT, NAPPY, AND ALL OTHER CONFIGURATIONS OF MALT AND HOP.*

Preface to the Reader, which serves also for Invocatiou.

Gentle Reader!
Poets there were, in ages back,
Who sung the fame of the bonny Black Jack;
Others tuned harmonious lays
In the Leathern Bottle's praise;
Shall not I then lift my quill,
To hymn a measure brighter still?
Maidens, who Helicon's hill resort,
Aid me to chaunt of the Pewter Quart.

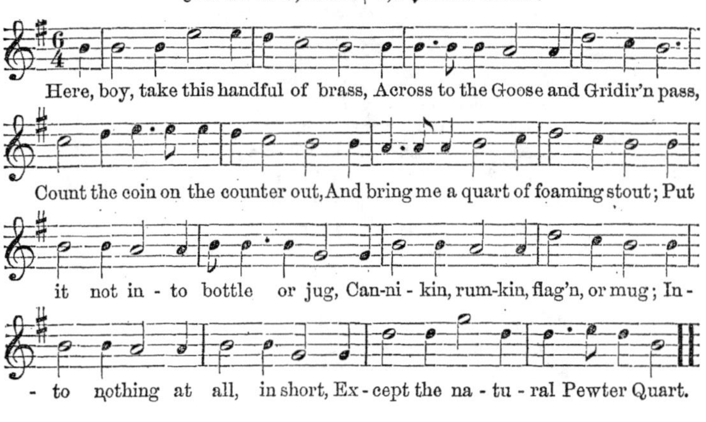

2.

As for the glass, though I love it well,
Yet the quart I take to be prefera—ble;
For it is solid and stout, like what
Bubbles and froths inside the pot:
Why should anything, brittle or frail,
Fence ENGLAND'S liquor, VALOROUS ALE!
He was a man of taste and art,
Who stowed it away in a Pewter Quart.

* *Blackwood* for November, 1823, contained the "Pewter Quart." — M.

3.

In the bowels of ENGLAND's ground,
Its materials all are found,
From its sides should flow again,
What cheers the bowels of ENGLAND's men:
Can the same be said, I ask,
In favour of foreign flagon or flask?
None can of them the good report,
We can of our national Pewter Quart.

4.

Pleasant it is their shine to see,
Like stars in the waves of deep Galilee;
Pleasant it is their chink to hear,
When they rattle on table full charged with beer;
Pleasant it is, when a row's on foot,
That you may, when you wish to demolish a brute,
Politely the man to good manners exhort,
By softening his skull with a Pewter Quart.

5.

As for the mallet-pate, pig-eye Chinese,
They may make crockery if they please;
Fit, perhaps, may such vehicle be,
For marrowless washes of curst Bohea;
That is a liquor I leave to be drunk
By Cockney poet and Cockney punk;
Folks with whom I never consort,
Preferring to chat with my Pewter Quart.

6.

Silver and gold no doubt are fine,
But on my table shall never shine;
Being a man of plain common sense,
I hate all silly and vain expense,
And spend the cash these gew-gaws cost,
In washing down gobbets of boiled and roast,
With stingo stiff of the stiffest sort,
Curiously pulled from a Pewter Quart.

7.

Bakers and bowls, I am told, of wood,
For quaffing water are counted good;
They give a smack, say the wat'ry folks,
Like drinking after artichokes,

Devil may care! I never use
Water in either my belly or shoes;
And shall never be counted art or part
In putting the same in a Pewter Quart.

8.

Galvani one day, skinning a frog,
To pamper his paunch with that pinch-gut prog,
Found out a science of wonderful wit,
Which can make a stuck pig kick out in a fit.
Make a dead thief dance a Highland reel,
And butcher a beast without cleaver or steel:
And he proves by this science with erudite art,
That malt must be drunk from a Pewter Quart.

9.

If Hock then loves the glass of green,
And champagne in its swan-necked flask is seen;
If Glasgow punch in a bowel we lay,
And twist off our dram in a wooden quaigh;
If, as botanical men admit,
Everything has its *habitat* fit,
Let Sir John Barleycorn keep his court,
Turban'd with froth in his Pewter Quart.

10.

So, boy, take this handful of brass,
Across to the Goose and Gridiron pass,
Count the coin on the counter out,
And bring me a quart of foaming stout;
Put it not into bottle or jug,
Cannikin, rumkin, flagon, or mug—
Into nothing at all, in short,
Except the natural Pewter Quart.

HERE FOLLOWS

A DISSERTATION ON THE LEATHER BOTTLE AND THE BLACK JACK.

In the works of the ingenious D'Urfey, which he who studies not with nocturnal and diurnal attention, is worthy of infinite reprobation, not to say worse, will be discovered two poems, which have not, as yet, excited the notice of the learned in the manner which they deserve.* I shall therefore, as briefly as

* Thomas D'Urfey, author of thirty-one comedies which have sunk into deserved forgetfulness, by reason of their licentiousness, and of six volumes of

the importance of the matter will admit of, dissertate somewhat upon them; inviting the attention of the sage and erudite to my remarks; perfectly regardless of the approbation or disapprobation of those whom my friend, the Reverend Edward Irving, calls "the flush and flashy spirits of the age;" thereby making an agreeable and euphuistical alliteration at head and tail.*

In the third volume of "Pills to Purge Melancholy," the two hundred and forty-seventh page, and first verse, will be found these words: —

The Leather Bottle.

Now God above, that made all things,
Heaven and earth, and all therein;
The ships upon the seas to swim,
To keep foes out, they come not in.
Now every one doth what he can
All for the use and praise of man.
 I wish in Heaven that soul may dwell
 That first devised the leathern bottle.

A more splendid exordium is not in the whole compass of our poetry. The bard, about to sing of a noble invention, takes high ground. His eyes, with a fine frenzy rolling, glances at the origin of the world, the glories of Heaven, and the utilities of earth; at old ocean murmuring with its innumerable waves, and the stately vessels walking the waters in all their magnificence; and then, by a gradual and easy descent, like Socrates bringing philosophy from the abodes of the gods to the dwellings of men, chaunts the merits of him who, for the use and praise of man, devised the Leathern Bottle. Compare Pindar's celebrated opening with this, and you will see how short is the flight of the Bœotian muse, contrasted with that of our own swan. Observe, moreover, the solid British feeling of the illustrious

songs and party lyrics, called "Laugh and be Fat; or, Pills to Purge Melancholy," was a boon companion of Charles II., and in high request among the wits and profligates of that monarch's court. He died, 1723. — M.

* In his Orations, published in 1823, Irving had denounced "unhallowed poets, and undevout dealers in science, and intemperate advocates of policy, and all other pleaders before the public mind," as "the flush and flashy spirits of the age." — M.

poet. No sooner does he mention ships, than the national spirit breaks forth.

> The ships upon the seas to swim,
> To keep foes out, they come not in.

Had the man who wrote this, one idea inconsistent with the honour and glory of Britain?—I lay a thousand pounds he had not. Had he lived in our days, he would have consigned the economists to the devil and the Scotsman. Conceive, for a moment, this great man, big with beer, and thoroughly impressed with veneration for our walls of wood, reading that article in the Edinburgh on the Navigation Laws. What an upcurled lip of indignation would he not display! How hearty would be his guffaw of contempt! How frequent his pulls at the vessel inserted in his dexter paw, in order to wash down the cobweb theories he was endeavouring to swallow! How impatiently would the pigtail turn under the nether-gum, until at last, losing patience, he would fling the Balaam over the bannisters, and exclaim, "Here, John, take it away from me, and put it in the only place where it can be at all for the use and praise of man." What place that is, it is not necessary for me to mention.

> Now, what do you say to the canns of wood?
> Faith, they are nought, they cannot be good;
> When a man for beer he doth therein send,
> To have them filled, as he doth intend:
> The bearer stumbleth by the way,
> And on the ground his liquor doth lay;
> Then straight the man begins to ban,
> And swears it, 'twas long of the wooden can;
> But had it been in a leathern bottle,
> Although he stumbled, all had been well;
> So safe therein it would remain,
> Until the man got up again.
> And I wish in heaven, &c.

The ambling pace of the verse cannot be sufficiently commended. Here we go on jog trot, as Sancho Panza on Dapple. Nothing stops the full gush of poetry poured out in a ceaseless, murmuring flow, like a brook rolling at the feet of two lovers by moonlight. Remark, too, the insight this verse gives us of the manners of the poet. His habits are completely anti-domestic;

that have what King Leigh* calls "all the freshness of out-of-doors life." He has no store at home. When he wants to drink, he sends for the quantity required. All the bother of butlers is done away with. The whole tribe of tapsters are his footmen, and the wide world his cellar. You perceive, too, the habits of his household: it is in a state of perpetually blissful intoxication. Nothing can be more a matter of course than that any messenger of his should stumble by the way; it is a regular affair of ordinary speculation. And then see his magnanimity. Grieved as he is at the loss of his liquor, he has no indignation against the drunken bearer, but transfers his wrath to the vessel, resolving henceforward to alter his measures. In all this, there is something Christian-like and philanthropic.

Now for the pots with handles three,
Faith, they shall have no praise of me,
When a man and his wife do fall at strife,
(As many, I fear, have done in their life,)
They lay their hands upon the pot both,
And break the same, though they were loth;
Which they shall answer another day,
For casting their liquor so vainly away:
But had it been in a bottle filled,
The one might have tugged, the other have held;
They both might have tugged till their hearts did ake,
And yet no harm the bottle would take.
And I wish in heaven, &c.

The philosophy of this verse is worthy of Lord Bacon or his commentator. The philosopher, knowing the pugnacity of human nature, feels no surprise at a matrimonial scuffle, but instantly his great object occurs to his mind. "Fight it out," quoth he; "fight it out by all means; but don't spill the drink." The whole forms a pleasant domestic picture; the husband on one side of the table, warming his bunnions at the fire; the wife, mending a pair of breeches at the other; and a three-handled pot, lying in quiet serenity between them, upon a deal table.

* Leigh Hunt, spoken of, in those days, as the King of Cockaigne or Cockney-land. — M.

† The commentator here alluded to was Professor Macvey Napier, whose article "On the scope and tendency of Bacon" was constantly ridiculed in the earlier volumes of *Blackwood*. — M.

Suddenly arises a storm, occasioned by what we are not informed by the poet, but most probably by an unequal division of the contents of the aforesaid pot—and a combat ensues. Both seize the pot, and the liquor is spilt. How touchingly, and yet with a just indignation, does our friend reflect on this!

For which they shall answer another day,
For casting their liquor so vainly away.

The solemnity of this threat is awfully impressive. It sounds like a voice from Delphi, or like a deep-toned imprecation, uttered from the mystic groves of Eleusis. There is nothing like it in all Paradise Lost.

Now what of the flagons of silver fine?
Faith, they shall have no praise of mine.
When a nobleman he doth them send
To have them filled, as he doth intend,
The man with his flagon runs quite away,
And never is seen again after that day.
Oh, then his lord begins to ban,
And swears he hath lost both flagon and man:
But it ne'er was known that page or groom,
But with a leathern bottle again would come.
And I wish in heaven, &c.

You see here the touches of a fine archaic simplicity. The silver flagon indicating that its possessor is a nobleman—the provision for life which it affords the flying footman, *who never again is seen after that day*—the baronial swearing of his lordship—and his regret at the loss of his property, first in the flagon, and then in the man; all take us back to the feudal times, and make us think of beetle-browed castles frowning over foaming cataracts; of knights clad in the panoply of plate and mail pricking forth upon the plain; of ladye love, and chivalrye;

Of tilting furniture, emblazoned shields,
Impresses quaint, caparisons and steeds,
Bases and tinsel trappings, gorgeous knights,
At tilt and tournament; then marshall'd feast,
Served up in hall with sewers and seneschals.

It is agreeable to yield the mind occasionally to these soft delusions of fancy, and to let our souls revel in the beauties and splendours of times past by. But, alas! as Burke says, "the day of chivalry is gone, and the glory of Europe is departed."

I agree with that great orator, but shall nevertheless proceed with the Leathern Bottle.

Now, what do you say to these glasses fine?
Faith, they shall have no praise of mine,
When friends are at a table set,
And by them several sorts of meat,
The one loves flesh, the other fish;
Among them all remove a dish;
Touch but a glass upon the brim,
The glass is broke; no wine left in:
Then be your table-cloth ne'er so fine.
There lies your beer, your ale, your wine;
And, doubtless, for so small abuse,
A young man may his service lose.
And I wish, &c.

I am sorry the poet wrote this verse. There is something flunkeyish and valleydeshammical in the whole passage. Something, in fact, Moorish — I mean Peter-Moorish ;* and, I suspect, an interpolation. What need we care for the discarded skip, or the stained diaper? Get it washed. Warrant it will not add a shilling to your washerwoman's bill in the twelvemonths. But perhaps you are afraid of the stains remaining to offend your optic nerve. Make your mind easy on the subject. You will find your remedy in the two hundred and ninety-ninth page of the Book of Rundell.† "Rub your part," says that she-Kitchener, "on each side with yellow soap; then lay on a mixture of starch in cold water, very thick; rub it well in, and expose the linen to the sun and air, till the stain comes out. If not removed in three or four days, rub that off, and renew the process. When dry, it may be sprinkled with a little water." Observe, it *may* be sprinkled; for she does not insist on *that*

* Peter Moore, Whig M. P. for Coventry, deserves to be remembered for his kindness to Sheridan when dying, and for having placed a tombstone over the wit's remains, at his own proper cost, in Westminster Abbey. — M.

† Mrs. Rundell's "Domestic Cookery," published by John Murray, of London. It was (and is) extremely popular and Murray realized a large fortune out of this book and Byron's poetry. The wife of the senior partner in the great form of Rundell and Bridges, jewellers, London, was the author, and presented the manuscript to Mr. Murray. When she found that it was successful and profitable, she claimed some share in the pecuniary results, and received £1,000. Nearly half a million copies have been sold, in the last forty-five years. — M.

with dogged pertinacity. Nothing can be more simple than the process; and I am sorry the matter was mentioned. If it really be a *bona-fide* part of the composition, I must only class it among the follies of the wise; and mourn over the frail condition of human nature.

Now when this bottle is grown old
And that it will no longer hold,
Out of the side you may cut a clout,
To mend your shoe when worn out;
Or hang the other side on a pin,
'Twill serve to put many odd trifles in,
As nails, awls, and candles' ends;
For young beginners need such things.
  I wish in Heaven his soul may dwell
  That first invented the Leathern Bottle.

This is a brilliant verse, and displays a genius for mechanical invention, which would do honour to a Perkins. The thrifty management, too, is highly commendable; and the care he manifests for young beginners, marks a parental and humane disposition, which converts our admiration of the poet into love for the man. He appears to be of the opinion of that eminent statesman—the Mr. Maberley* of his day—who declared that there is nothing like leather. Much may be, and indeed has been, said, on both sides of the question; but though the controversy is far from being set at rest, I shall not agitate it on the present occasion.

Let me now turn to the second head of my discourse; namely, the Black Jack.

'Tis a pitiful thing, that now-a-days, sirs,
Our poets turn Leathern Bottle praisers;
But if a leathern theam they did lack,
They might better have chosen the bonny Black Jack;
For when they are both now well worn and decayed,
For the Jack, than the bottle, much more can be said.
  And I wish his soul much good may partake,
  That first devised the bonny Black Jack.

I, for one, am free to admit, that I do not like this commencement. There is something, as Leigh Hunt says, base and

* Maberley, long M. P. for the borough of Abington, became a bankrupt in his later years.—M.

reviewatory in it. Why need he disparage the valuable labours of his predecessor bard? The world was large enough for them both. But the poetic tribe is irritable. This very moment, there is barbarous civil war going on among them. Southey calls Byron Satan; and Byron compliments the Laureate with the soothing title of Rogue. Bernard Barton has been heard to declare, that he did not think ODoherty's poetry had any thing Miltonian about it — to be sure it was in private; and he qualified the assertion by adding, that he gave it merely as matter of opinion; but after all, it was shabby on the part of Broadbrim.* I say nothing; and mention the business just in illustration.

And now I will begin to declare
What the conveniences of the Jack are.
First, when a gang of good fellows do meet,
As oft at a fair, or a wake, you shall see't;
They resolve to have some merry carouses,
And yet to get home in good time to their houses;
Then the bottle it runs as slow as my rhime,
With Jack, they might have all been drunk in good time.
  And I wish his soul in peace may dwell,
  That first devised that speedy vessel.

The writer of this is evidently an intensely moral and domestic man. It being an object of necessity to get drunk, the question arises how this is to be done with the most decorous propriety. Arguing then, with Macbeth, that when a thing is to be done, 'twere well that it were done quickly; and, anxious to delight the family at home with an early visit, he naturally prefers the jack, or, as he most poetically calls it, the Speedy Vessel. He manifestly hates loitering and lingering in any work in which he is engaged, and is quite shocked at the idea of intruding on domestic arrangements by any absence of his. He feels the duties of the head of a household too keenly; he is too much interested in the proper ordering of affairs at home. Certain I am that family prayers were the regular order of the day in his establishment.

* Bernard Barton, a quaker, (born in 1784, died in 1849,) wrote a great many very tolerable verses, which made him popular — chiefly as contributor to Magazines and Annuals. — M.

And therefore leave your twittle twattle,
Praise the Jack, praise no more the Leathern Bottle;
For the man at the bottle may drink till he burst,
And yet not handsomely quench his thirst:
The master hereat maketh great moan,
And doubts his bottle has a spice of the stone;
But if it had been a generous Jack,
He might have had currently what he did lack:
  And I wish his soul in Paradise,
  That first found out that happy device.

The lament of the unsated beer-bibber is given here with a pathos which must draw tears from the eyes even of the most hard-hearted. No words are thrown away. We see him endeavouring to effect his purpose at the bottle's mouth, and finding his efforts vain, he "*thereat maketh great moan.*" How simple, yet how tender! Had Sheil, or any other poetaster of that stamp, such a passage in his hands, into what a bladder of wordy amplification would he not have blown it! We should infallibly have had the wife and children drawn in to participate in the father's sorrow; but here we have a strain of higher mood.

Be your liquor small, or thick as mud,
The cheating bottle that cries good, good;
Then the master again begins to storm,
Because it said more than it could perform:
But if it had been in an honest Black Jack,
It would have proved better to sight, smell, and smack;
  And I wish his soul in Heaven may rest,
  That added a Jack to Bacchus's feast.

On this verse I make no remark, as I am sure that by this time the reader of moderate abilities, or proper application, will be able to discover its scope and tendency.

No flagon, tankard, bottle, or jug,
Is half so fit, or so well can hold tug;
For when a man and his wife play at thwacks,
There is nothing so good as a pair of Black Jacks:
Thus to it they go, they swear, and they curse,
It makes them both better, the Jack's ne'er the worse;
For they might have banged both, till their hearts did ake,
And yet no hurt the Jacks could take:
  And I wish his heirs may have a pension,
  That first produced that lucky invention.

I am afraid my friend Joe Hume would hardly agree with this last prayer, but it is evident that Joseph has no taste for the fine arts. The philological student will discover in this verse the origin of the phrase, "leathering a man's wife." On the moral propriety of conjugal fisticuffery I had prepared some copious remarks, when I received information from a sure hand, that my Lord Holland has a folio on the subject nearly ready for the press, and I bow to his Lordship's superior talents and experience.

Socrates and Aristotle
Sucked no wit from a Leather Bottle;
For surely I think a man as soon may
Find a needle in a bottle of hay:
But if the Black Jack a man often toss over,
'Twill make him as drunk as any philosopher;
When he that makes Jacks from a peck to a quart,
Conjures not, though he lives by the black art.
And I wish, &c.

I care not a fig for the black art, and defy the foul fiend, Prince Hohenlohe, and Ingleby the Emperor of the Conjurers* —so shall make no remark on the last two lines. It would lead us into too deep a historico-metaphysical disquisition, were I to enter into a history of the fortunes of the Aristotelian philosophy. During the life of Aristotle, he was looked on as the prince of philosophers; and such did his estimation continue, as long as there were minds in the world manly enough to understand him. While Europe was sunk in darkness, he was taken up by the acute Arabians, then at the head of the intellect of the earth. From them the schoolmen caught him, badly translated and imperfectly understood; and when their day was over, the puny whipsters who had got possession of the ear of the metaphysical world, thought nothing could be finer than to disparage, because he had been caricatured, him whom they could not read; and we see, in our own day, Stewart† mumping and mumbling

* Prince Hohenlohe, about 1823, was stated to have restored diseased and afflicted persons to health, by praying for them. — Ingleby, who called himself "Emperor of the Conjurers," was an adroit practitioner of legerdemain. — M.

† Dugald Stewart, Professor of Moral Philosophy in the University of Edinburgh: born in 1753, died in 1828. — M.

pretty little nothings, with full assurance that the Peripatetic whom he cannot construe, or who, if construed for him, is far above any reach of thought he could bring to the consideration, is unworthy to unloose the latchet of his shoe. But to his fortune in our poetry I may briefly advert: it is a fine illustration of the elder Mr. Shandy's theory of the influence of a name. That he was a hard drinker I hope, for he was a great man; but whether he was or not, no name of the ancients occurs so often in juxta-position with the bottle. See the verse above. So also the eminent Harry Carey,*

Zeno, Plato, Aristotle,
All were lovers of the bottle.

So in MS. penes me,

To moisten our throttle,
We'll call the third bottle,
For that was the practice of wise Aristotle.

All owing to the two last syllables of his name. With respect to the remark in the text, that

If the Black Jack a man often toss over,
'Twill make him as drunk as any philosopher.

I can vouch, from my own experience, that the illustration is correct; for I have had the honour of being intimately acquainted with fifteen of the first philosophers of the age, fourteen of whom went to bed drunk as widgeons every night of their lives, and the fifteenth retired when he found himself tipsy.

Besides, my good friend, let me tell you, that fellow
That framed the bottle, his brains were but shallow;
The case is so clear, I nothing need mention,
The Jack is a nearer and deeper invention;
When the bottle is cleaned, the dregs fly about,
As if the guts and the brains flew out;
But if in a cannon-bore Jack it had been,
From the top to the bottom all might have been clean.
And I wish his soul no comfort may lack,
That first devised the bouncing Black Jack.

I am not antiquarian enough to decide on the correctness of the above objurgation against the uncleanliness of the bottles of

* Henry Carey was not only a musician, but also author of many ballads, among which "Sally in our Alley" was praised by Addison for its words, and by Geminiani for its music. He committed suicide in 1743. — M.

the olden time, and willingly leave the consideration of the matter to Mr. John Nichols, who presides, and long may he preside, over the archæologists who wield the pen for the Gentleman's Magazine,* in which, perhaps, he will favour us with an engraved likeness of a leathern bottle, as, I think, churches are running rather low. But, be that as it may, he must have little gusto for the sublime who can fail to admire the splendid epithet of the CANNON-BORE Jack. What vast ideas of stupendous bibosity does not it excite? Conceive a nine-pounder-like machine charged with ale, levelled on your table, in full range against your brains! Nay, the very word is good. It makes us think of battle and blood—of square column and platoon mowed down in unrelenting sweep—of Sir William Congreve,† the Duke of Wellington, and the field of Waterloo—of Buonaparte, St. Helena, and Sir Hudson Lowe—and thence, by the association of ideas, of Barry O'Meara,‡ and the horse-whipping of old Walter of the Times. I shall lump my dissertation on the four following verses:—

Your leather bottle is used by no man
That is a hair's-breadth above a plowman;
Then let us gang to the Hercules pillars,
And there let us visit those gallant Jack swillers;
In these small, strong, sour, mild, and stale,
They drink orange, lemon, and Lambeth ale:
The chief of heralds there allows,
The Jack to be of an ancienter house.
  And may his successors never want sack,
  That first devised the long Leather Jack.

Then for the bottle, you cannot well fill it,
Without a tunnel, but that you must spill it;

* John Nichols, (born in 1744, died in 1828,) conducted *The Gentleman's Magazine* for nearly half a century.—M.

† Inventor of the rockets which bear his name. They have fallen into disrepute. He was born in 1772, and died in 1828.—M.

‡ Barry Edward O'Meara, born 1778, died in 1836. Napoleon's surgeon at St. Helena, in July 1818, (when he was recalled and deprived of his rank,) and author of "A Voice from St. Helena." Byron, in "The Age of Bronze," speaking of Napoleon, says that

"The stiff surgeon, who maintained his cause,
Hath lost his place, and gained the world's applause."—M.

'Tis as hard to get in, as it is to get out,
'Tis not so with a Jack, for it runs like a spout
Then burn your bottle, what good is in it,
One cannot well fill it, nor drink nor clean it;
But if it had been in a jolly Black Jack,
'Twould come a great pace, and hold you good tack.
And I wish his soul, &c.

He that 's drunk in a Jack, looks as fierce as a spark,
That were just ready cockt to shoot at a mark;
When the other thing up to the mouth it goes,
Makes a man look with a great bottle nose;
All wise men conclude, that a Jack, new or old,
Tho' beginning to leak, is however worth gold;
For when the poor man on the way does trudge it,
His worn-out Jack serves him for a budget.
And I wish his heirs may never lack sack,
That first contrived the leather Black Jack.

When bottle and Jack stand together, fie on't,
The bottle looks just like a dwarf to a giant;
Then have we not reason the Jack for to choose,
For they can make boots, when the bottle mends shoes;
For add but to every Jack a foot,
And every Jack becomes a boot:
Then give me my Jack, there's a reason why,
They have kept us wet, they will keep us dry.
I now shall cease, but as I am an honest man,
The Jack deserves to be called Sir John.
And may they ne'er want, for belly nor back,
That keep up the trade of the bonny Black Jack.

Amen! and virtue be its own reward!

On the above, four things are to particularly noticed.

I. That the Hercules Pillars is the *ne-plus-ultra* of signs.

II. That the progress of time has extinguished various sorts of ales—for who, now-a-days, drinks Orange, Lemon, or Lambeth—they sleep with the Chians and Falernians of the days of Greece and Rome.

III. That a partiality for a man's favourite pursuit may lead him to bestow on it unjust and undeserved praise; for, after various and repeated experiments in drinking out of every vessel under the sun, I can give it as my unbiassed opinion, that the shape of the instrument imparts no additional value to the liquor drunk, and that therefore the idea that he, who imbibes from a black jack, acquires a superior fierceness or martiality of aspect, must be classed among such innocent delusions as induced the barber to recommend whitehandled razors as the best fitted for abrading of beards.

Lastly and finally, we cannot help being pleased by the vein of genuine and unaffected piety which runs through both these dignified compositions. The prayers which in both conclude each verse, though more varied and poetical in the latter, are not more solemn and impressive than the solitary ejaculations of blessing bestowed upon the earlier production. There is something striking, which sinks in to the soul, in the constant choral-like repetition of the one formulary which amply compensates for the picturesque diversity, which excites our admiration, but fills us not with awe. The one goes to the head—the other to the heart. To conclude, if the brows of the inventors of the Bottle and Jack deserve to be bound with snow-white fillets, as being men who civilized life by new productions of art and genius, the bards who hymned their exploits may justly claim the same honour, as being pious poets, who spoke things worthy of Apollo.

M. OD.

An Idyl on the Battle.*

FISTS AND THE MAN I sing, who, in the valleys of Hampshire,
Close to the borough of Andover, one fine day of the spring-time,
Being the twentieth of May, (the day, moreover, was Tuesday,)
Eighteen hundred and twenty-three, in a fistical combat,
Beat, in a handful of rounds, Bill Neat, the butcher of Bristol.
What is the hero's name? Indeed, 'tis bootless to mention.
Every one knows 'tis Spring — Tom Spring, now Champion of England.†
Full of honours and gout, Tom Cribb surrendered his kingdom,
And in the Champion's cup no more he quaffs as the Champion.
Who is to fill his place? the anxious nation, inquiring,
Looks round the ring with a glance of hope and eagerness blended.
Everywhere would you see deep-drawn and puckered-up faces,
Worn by the people in thought on this high and ponderous matter.
Spain and Greece are forgot — they may box it about at their pleasure;
Newport‡ may brandish his brogue unheard at the Sheriff of Dublin;

---

* This imitation (so far as the metre goes,) of Southey's "Vision of Judgment," appeared in *Blackwood* for July, 1823.— M.

† Tom Spring's real name was Thomas Winter. He was a native of Herefordshire. In stature he was tall, in strength great, in science superb, in pluck unrivalled, in honesty above all doubt, in aspect pleasing, in manners mild. For many years after he left the Ring he kept the well-known public-house yclept "The Castle," in Holborn, London, not far from the principal entrance to Gray's Inn. He was particularly placid in temper and unassuming in demeanor. Always attired in black, with an irreproachable white cravat, he gently moved among the pewter-pots, in his bar, reminding one more of a clergyman than of the Champion of England. At night he presided in a free-and-easy, celebrated for its vocalization, in his own hostelrie, and many went thither to see him in the chair. But his proper place was in the little parlor behind the bar, every inch of its walls covered with portraits of pugilists — save one little corner, which contained a few shelves on which were ranged sundry volumes of the Racing Calendar, (for Tom Spring latterly affected to patronize the Turf,) and the whole of Pierce Egan's "Boxiana." In that little snuggery, where a substantial joint ever ornamented the table, punctually at half-past one, I have met with members of parliament, authors, barristers, doctors, and country gentlemen who were on friendliest terms with Tom. Perhaps, also, they might come to see the bright eyes of Tom's niece — the rosiest and plumpest of feminines! Tom Spring was a fair fighter and an honest man. He realized a considerable sum by his business of innkeeper.— M.

‡ The late Sir John Newport, a patriot in the Irish and a placeman in the English Parliament. He was Comptroller of the Exchequer, with £2000 a year salary, for many years, but lent himself to a scandalous job, connected

Canning may give the lie to Brougham,* and Brougham be a Christian;
Hume may be puffing Carlile,† or waging a war upon Cocker;
Byron may write a poem, and Hazlitt a Liber Amoris;‡
Nobody cares a fig for the Balaam of Baron or Cockney.
All were absorbed at once in the one profound speculation,
Who was the man to be the new pugilistical Dymoke.§
Neat and the Gasman put up, and the light of Gas was extinguished.
Woe is my heart for Gas! accursed be the wheel of the waggon
Which made a pancake‖ of blood of the head of that elegant fellow.
He had no chance with Neat; the fist of that brawny Bristolian
Laid him in full defeat on the downs of Hungerford prostrate.
Great was the fame of Bill; the ancient city of Bristol
[Bristol, the birth-place dear of the Laureate LL.D. Southey—
Bristol, the birth-place too of Thomas Cribb the ex-Champion]

---

with it, in 1839. At that date, the Melbourne Ministry was so nearly "done up" that some of its members, whose private fortune was small, looked out for the loss of place and pay. Among these was Mr. Spring Rice, Chancellor of the Exchequer, with £5000 a year salary. He prevailed on Old Newport to resign his £2000 per annum as Comptroller of the Exchequer, obtained a retiring pension of £1000 out of the public revenue, made up another £1000 a year out of his own pocket, and had himself appointed to the then vacated Comptrollership, which he has held ever since. Newport lived for a few years—at a cost to the country of £1000 a year and of as much more to Mr. Spring Rice, who was created Lord Monteagle on quitting the Ministry.—M.

* Alluding to Canning's celebrated response "I rise to say that that is false" to Brougham, who charged him, in Parliament, with being guilty of "most monstrous political tergiversation."—M.

† Richard Carlile who, for many years, kept a shop in Fleet street, London, for the sale of irreligious publications, was repeatedly convicted and imprisoned, and finally became an itinerant preacher of the Gospel.—M.

‡ "Liber Amoris, or the Modern Pygmalion," was an unfortunate book, by William Hazlitt, in which is detailed how he loved a tailor's daughter and was jilted by her.—M.

§ Dymoke of Scrivelsbaye is hereditary Champion of England, and one of the family appeared, as such, at the gorgeous Coronation of George IV.—M.

‖ "My troth, gin yon chield had shaved twa inches nearer you, your head, my man, would have lookit very like a bluidy pancake."—*Reginald Dalton.*

You see I agree with Southey, a man for whom I have a particular esteem, that people ought to indicate the most minute sources of information. Yet the Doctor is not always so fair—the most splendid passage in his Roderick is merely a transcript of a conversation I had with him on the top of one of the Bristol coaches in the year 1814; and yet I do not recollect that he anywhere alludes to the circumstance. Indeed, he seldom mentions my name in any of his writings. Yet I respect him highly, and frequently mention him in *my* works.—M. OD.

Hailed him with greetings loud; and, boldly declaring him matchless,
Challenged the boxing world to try his valour in contest.
  London replied to the call — the land of the Cockneys, indignant
At this *yokel attempt to set up a Champion provincial,
Looked with its great big eyes at Spring, and Spring understood it,
Everything soon was arranged; the time was fixed for the battle;
Cash on each side was posted, a cool two hundred of sovereigns;
And the affair was put beneath the guidance of Jackson.†
I sha'n't delay my song to say, how some Justices tasteless
Twice by the felon hand of power prevented the combat.‡
Vain the attempt as base — as well the clashing of comets
Would be prevented by them, as the onslaught of pugilist rivals.
  When the great day arrived, big with the glory of Britain,
Bustle be sure there was, and riding, and running, and racing;
Nay, for three days before, the roads were wofully crowded;
All the inns were beset, each bed had a previous engagement;
So, if you came in late, you were left in a bit of a hobble —
Either to camp in the street, or sleep on three chairs in the bar-room.
Chaises, coaches, barouches, taxed carts, tilburies, whiskeys,
Curricles, shandry-dans, gigs, tall phaetons, jaunting cars, waggons,
Cabriolets, landaus, all sorts of vehicles rolling,
Four-wheeled, or two-wheeled, drawn by one, two, three, or four horses;
Steeds of various degrees, high-mettled racer, or hunter,
Bit of blood, skin-and-boner, pad, hack, mule, jackass, or donkey;§
Sniffers on foot in droves, by choice or economy prompted;
Grumbling Radical, pickpocket Whig, and gentleman Tory,
Down from ducal rank to the rascally fisher of fogles,‖
Poured from London town to see the wonderful action.
Thirty thousand at least were there; and ladies in numbers
Rained from their beautiful eyes sweet influence over the buffers.
  Well the ground was chosen, and quite with the eye of a poet;
Close to the field of fight, the land all rises around it,
Amphitheatrical wise, in a most judgmatical fashion.
There had the Johnny-raws of Hants ta'en places at leisure,

---

* *Yokel.* — Provincial, I opine; but am not sure. If wrong, shall correct in second edition; or, at all events, in time for the third. — M. OD.

† Jackson, once a prize-fighter; afterward a teacher of pugilism. Lord Byron, who was one of his pupils, has repeatedly mentioned him — always with praise. In his more advanced years, when I saw him, the gravity of his aspect and gentleness of his manners were particularly observable. — M.

‡ A magistrate in England always possesses, and sometimes has exercised, the power of preventing prize-fights — as leading to breaches of the peace. — M.

§ *Jackass, or donkey.* — I mean the four-footed animals. No allusion whatever to any he or she Whig — they being biped. — M. OD.

‖ *Fisher of fogles,* i. e. pickpocket. A fogle is a handkerchief. — M. OD.

Many an hour before the combatants came to the turn-up.
 We were not idle, be sure, although we waited in patience;
Drink of all sorts and shapes was kindly provided to cheer us;
Ales from the famous towns of Burton, Marlboro', Taunton;
Porter from lordly Thames, and beer of various descriptions;
Brandy of Gallic growth, and rum from the isle of Jamaica;
Deady, and heavy wet, blue ruin, max, and Geneva;
Hollands that ne'er saw Holland, mum, brown stout, perry, and cyder;
Spirits in all ways prepared, stark-naked, hot or cold watered;
Negus, or godlike grog, flip, lambswool, syllabub, rumbo;
Toddy, or punch, or shrub, or the much sung stingo of gin-twist;
Wines, in proportions less, their radiance intermingling.*
Flowed like a stream round the ring, refreshing the dry population.
Glad was I in my soul, though I missed my national liquor,
And with a tear in my eye my heart fled back into Ireland.
†Whiskey, my jewel dear, what though I have chosen a dwelling
Far away, and my throat is now-a-days moistened by Hodges,—
Drink of my early days, I swear I shall never forget thee!
Round the ring we sat, the stiff stuff tipsily quaffing.‡
[Thanks be to thee, Jack Keats; our thanks for the dactyl and spondee
Pestleman Jack, whom, according to Shelley, the Quarterly murdered§
With a critique as fell as one of his own patent medicines.]
 Gibbons appeared at last; and, with adjutants versed in the business,
Drove in the stakes and roped them. The hawbuck|| Hottentot Hantsmen
Felt an objection to be whipped out of the ring by the Gibbons.
Fight was accordingly shewn, and Bill, afraid of the numbers,
Kept his whip in peace, awaiting the coming of Jackson.
Soon did his eloquent tongue tip off the blarney among them;

---

* *Their ra-di-ance inter-mingling.*—There is a fine spondaic fall. What do you think of that, Doctor Carey? Read the line over three times before you answer. It must put you in mind of

———"Ag-mi-na circum-spexit."—*Virg.*—M. OD.

† *Whiskey, my jewel dear*, &c.—These fine lines are imitated from the Vision of Judgment. See the passage beginning, "Bristol, my birth-place dear, what though I have chosen a dwelling," &c. &c.—M. OD.

‡ *Tipsily quaffing.*—From a poem about Bacchus, written by poor Jack Keats, a man for whom I had a particular esteem. I never can read the Quarterly of late, on account of the barbarous murder it committed on that promising young man. Murray can never come to luck. Indeed, since Keat's death, he has been publishing Sardanapalus, and Cain, and Fleury's Memoirs, &c. &c. which must give some satisfaction to the injured shade of the deceased.—M. OD.

§ "Strange that the soul, that very fiery particle,
Should let itself be muffled out by an article."—M.

|| *Hawbuck.*—Johnny Raw to the last degree.—M. OD.

And what force could not do, soft talk performed in a jiffy.
Arm-in-arm with his backer and Belcher, followed by Harmer,
Neat in a moment appeared, and instantly flung down his castor.
In about ten minutes more, came Spring, attended by Painter;
Cribb, the illustrious Cribb, however, acted as second.*
Compliments, then, were exchanged, hands shaken, after the fashion
Of merry England for ever, the beef-eating land of the John Bulls.
Blue as the arch of Heaven, or the much-loved eyes of my darling,
Was the colour of Spring — to the stakes Cribb tied it in person.
Yellow, like Severn streams, when the might of rain has descended,
Shone forth the kerchief of Neat. Tom Belcher tied it above Spring's —
But with a delicate twist, Tom Cribb reversed the arrangement,
Putting the blue above. The men then peeled for the onset.
Twenty minutes past One P.M. — So far for a preface.

Round the First.

Spring was a model of manhood. Chantrey, Canova, or Scoular,†
Graved not a finer form; his muscles firmly were filled up,
And with elastic vigour played all over his corpus;
Fine did his deltoid show; his neck rose towering gently
Curved from the shoulder broad; his back was lightsomely dropt in.
Over his cuticle spread a slightly ruddy suffusion,
Shewing his excellent state, and the famous care of his trainers;
Confidence beamed from his face; his eye shone steady in valour.
Valiantly, too, looked Neat, a truly respectable butcher,
But o'er his skin the flush was but in irregular patches:
Even on his cheeks, the bloom was scarce the breadth of a dollar.
Gin, thou wert plainly there! I would he had left thee to Hazlitt,‡
Ay, or to any one else, all during the process of training!
Bootless 'tis now to complain — Bill Neat, you were bothered by Daffy!§
Long did they pause ere they hit — much cautious dodging and guarding
Shewed their respect for each other; four tedious minutes, ere either
Struck, had elapsed; at last Tom Spring hit out with the left hand,
So did Bill Neat with the right, but neither blow did the business,
Neat then made up for offence, and flung out a jolly right-hander,
Full for the stomach of Spring; but Spring judiciously stopped it,

---

* Thomas Cribb, ex-Champion of England. Like most of his calling, he devoted his later years to keeping a public house, and (also like most ex-pugilists) was gentle as a lamb in private life.— M.

† *Scoular.* His head of D. Bridges ranks with Chantrey's of Sir W. Scott.

‡ Hazlitt, thus labelled as a gin-drinker, invariably made "potations pottle deep" of—*tea.* He took it very strong, and in such large quantities that it assisted to shatter his nervous system.— M.

§ Gin.— M.

Else it had flattened the lad as flat as the flattest of flounders:
Even as it was, it contused the fleshy part of his fore-arm.
Neat tried the business again—'twas now more happily parried.
Spring, with a smile at the thought of the smash he had given to Bill's fist,
Put down his hands for a while, but soon gathered up to the onset;
Hit and re-hit now passed, but Neat threw off a right-hander
Meant for certain effect. The true scientifical manner
Shewn by William in this was loftily cheered by the audience,
Thunders of clapping ensued, and the whole ring roared like a bullock,
Neat grew offensive now, but the stop and parry of Winter
[Winter is Spring's real name, though they call him, for brevity, Tom Spring.]
Punished him step by step, as Bill drove him into the corner.
"Now is the time," cried Belcher, and Bristol waited the triumph,
But the position of Spring prevented all awkward invasion.
In-fighting then was tried, that came to a close and a struggle:
Under came Billy Neat, as Ajax under Ulysses.
Spring came over him hard—and 3 to 2 was the betting.

Round the Second.

Spring shewed the same strong guard, but ever ready for action.
Neat began to breathe short, when, WAP! came a flushy right-hander,
Plump on his fore-head, and, lo! the stream of the claret was flowing,
*Sanguine as butchers will bleed, not at all like the ichor of angels.
Out did he hit to the right—Spring sprung back—Neat again tried it,
But, on the side of the head, he got such a lump of a twister,
That he was turned quite round, and nearly saluted his mother.†
Stupid and senseless he looked like a young whig lawyer of Embro'—
(Some little mealy-faced pup, amazed with a recent suffusion
From the uplifted leg of some big boardly bull-dog of Blackwood)—
Then did the hooting arise, from various people indignant;
And, in the hubbub loud, "Cross, Cross!" was frequently mentioned.
This brought Neat to his senses, and straight he took to in-fighting.
Bloody hard hits came from both—'twas head-work chiefly between them:
Down in the end went Neat, and blue looked the betters of Bristol!

Round the Third.

Neat tried his hand at hard hitting—and then were the heavy exchanges.
But in one counter-hit, his blow was heavier than Tommy's,
For it sent him away. Bill Neat then burst out a-laughing,

---

* *Sanguine as butcher's will bleed, not at all like the ichor of angels.*—
——"From the gash
A stream of nectareous humour issuing, flowed
Sanguine, such as celestial spirits may bleed."—MILTON.—M. OD.

† *His mother*, i e. the Earth. This I explain for the groundlings.—M. OD.

Like the Olympian Gods at Vulcan handing the stingo.
He followed up his success; and after ringing the changes,
Planted a terrible lunge on the short-rib department of Thomas.
Then he gave all his weight to a blow, and floored his opponent,
Coming down with him himself. On this, a terrible uproar
Rose from the Men of the West—a shout of jubilant cheering.
Short is the vision of man! that very round had undone him,
For, in the counter-hit, he broke a bone in his fore-arm.
What is the name of the bone?—Well, since you ask me the question,
Radius, 'tis called by Cline, a most anatomical surgeon.*

Round the Fourth.

Firm was the guard of Spring; Neat worked most anxious to get in—
Vainly—for Spring baffled all his attempts, just as if he was sparring.
Soon he took the offensive, and the woful yokels of Avon
Heard his fists, right and left, rap! rap! on the body of Billy.†
One—two nobbers, besides, did he administer freely;
All the while poor Bill felt out for the ribs with the left hand;
Every hit being short, and the right hand quite ineffective:
Backward and forward jumped Spring, and grasping his burly opponent,
Caught him up from the ground, and fell down fairly upon him.
Glorious! sublime was the feat, and there was no saying against it.
Bristol looked very blank, as blank as the Island of Byron.‡
Loud did the Westerns cry, "Bill, what has become of your right hand?
Gemini, man! My eyes! Hey! Go it! What are you *arter?*"§
Betting was 5 to 1.—In fact, Bill Neat was defeated.

Rounds Fifth and Sixth.

Lump we a couple of rounds, for I'm in a devilish hurry,
Being invited to dine at the Dog and Duck with Pierce Egan‖

* Henry Cline, who was "a most anatomical surgeon," was also held in high repute by his pupils and the profession, as a lecturer and demonstrator. He died in 1827.—M.

† *Heard his fists, right and left, rap! rap! on the body of Billy.*—Imitated from

"Heard the bell from the tower toll! toll! in the silence of evening."
SOUTHEY.—M. OD.

‡ "The Island; or Christian and his Comrades," the last written of Byron's tales, bears date "Genoa, October, 1823."—M.

§ *Arter.*—Bristolian for *after.*—M. OD.

‖ Pierce Egan, author of "Boxiana" and "Life in London," was a great sporting authority thirty years ago, and, as such, often referred to by the contributors to *Blackwood.*—M.

Neat was quite stupified now,* a mere Phrenological fellow,
Who, as we happen to know, can not tell a man's head from a turnip.
All his hits were at random; on getting a bodier slanting,
Down he'd have gone for time, but Spring, with the kindest intentions,
Lent him a merry-go-down, to freshen his way in the tumble.
Murmurs then were of foul play, as if he had fallen out of fancy
Without the aid of a hit; but Jackson, unerring as Delphi,
Stated the fact as it was, and decision dwelt on his dictate.
As for round the sixth, 'tis hardly worth the relating.
Neat was pelted about, and knocked down like a cow in the shambles.

Round the Seventh.

Still there was pluck in Bill; Spring feared a customer rummish.
Cautiously, therefore, he fought and parried the sinister lunges.
One, however, took place on the right lower ribs of the hero,
Whereon he sparred for a hit, which he planted with ease and affection,
Right on the brain-box of Neat, who, though not given to praying,
Sunk on his marrow-bones straight, in a fashion godly and pious.
Instantly rose a shout, a riff-raff-ruffianly roaring,
Hallabulloo immense, a most voluminous volley;
Cockneyland crowed like a cock, and the hills gave an echo politely.

Round Eighth and Last.

Neat came up once more, but the fight was over; again he
Hit with the dexter arm, and *felt* that he now was defeated.
Spring in a moment put in a ramstam belly-go fister—
Down to the ground went Neat, and with him down went the battle.
"It is no use," said Bill; "my arm, do you see me, is injured—
Therefore I must give in." He spoke—and, mournfully placing
On the sore part his hand, he shewed the fracture to Tom Spring.
Seven-and-thirty minutes it lasted—ten of them wasted
In the first round alone. The glorious news came to London
Somewhere about eight o'clock; but still incredulous people
Held the report as false; and, even approaching to midnight,
Bets were laid on Neat—so much was Spring undervalued.
  Woe was in Bristol town—woe, woe on the Severn and Avon;
Clifton, the seat of the gay, looked dull and awfully gloomy;
Grief was in Bath the polite; a mournful air of dejection
Reigned o'er the tables of whist; and mugs, as fair as the morning,

---

* *A mere Phrenological fellow, who, as we happen to know, cannot tell a man's head from a turnip.*—See the organization of that celebrated Swede, Professor Tornhippson, as developed in those two scientific works, the Transactions of the Phrenological Society, and the Noctes Ambrosianæ, No. VIII.—M. OD.

Looked like the ten of spades, or the face of my Lord Grim-Grizzle.*
Round the old Redcliff church† was held an aggregate meeting,
‡Stormy and sad by fits — where some, with sceptical speeches,
Doubted the fact of the case — or, cunningly crooking the fingers,
Made a ✕ in the open air, affronting the moon-beams;
Others but shook the head, and jingled the coin in their pockets,
Cheering themselves with the much-loved sound of the gold for the last time.
But in the shambles of Bristol, among the butcherly people,
There was the blackness of sorrow; loud oaths, or sorrowful moaning,
Rung in the seat of slaughter — but slaughter now was suspended;
Mute was the marrow-bone now, the ancient music of Britain;
Cleaver, and bloody axe, steel, hand-saw, chopping-block, hatchet,
Lay in a grim repose; and the hungry people of Bristol
Could not the following day get a single joint for their dinner.
But when the cross was suggested, §the whole black body of butchers
Raged, like a troubled sea, with a wild and mutinous uproar.
Such was the state of the West. Meanwhile Spring travelled to London,
There to be hailed as the Champion bold of merry Old England.
Neat he saw in bed — his arm was fastened with splinters —
And in the heel of his fist Tom nobly inserted some shiners.
Bill was sulky, however; and still he lustily vaunted,
That, if his arm had not broke, he must have been hailed as the Champion—
That can be known, however, to the Fates and Jupiter only.
Where are the chaffers now, who swore that Spring was no hitter?
That he could scarce make a dint in a pound or a half-pound of butter? —
Melted all fast away, like the butter of which they were speaking.
Long live the Champion Spring! and may his glorious annals
Shine in the pages of Egan‖ as bright as the record of Tom Cribb!
One man more must be fought, however; — Arise to the combat,

---

* *Face of my Lord Grim-Grizzle.*— An acquaintance of Mr. Lambton's, who calls him the Erl-King. Mark the spondaic again, Dr. Carey.— M. OD. [Earl Grey, father-in-law of Mr. Lambton, afterward Earl of Durham.— M.]

† Redcliff Church, in Bristol, the scene of Chatterton's early studies.— M.

‡ *Stormy and sad by fits.*— See Homer, Il. 7. "A meeting of Trojans was held," says the old fellow,

Δεινη και τετρηχυια. κ. τ. λ.

Is not mine something like? — M. OD.— [Of course.— C. N.]

§ *The whole black body of butchers raged like a troubled sea, with a wild and mutinous uproar.*— Imitated from

——" The whole dense body of darkness
Raged like a troubled sea, with a wild and mutinous uproar."— SOUTHEY.

I quote from memory. — M. OD.

‖ Pierce Egan was not only author of "Boxiana," but Editor of the sporting paper, *Bell's Life in London.*— M.

Rise for the Champion's crown, arise, I say, Joshua Hudson!*
That will be the fight—meanwhile Spring lords the ascendant;
Therefore huzza for Spring—and I make my bow to the public.
["To-morrow for fresh fights and pastures new."]—MILTON.

M. OD.

*** It is an undoubted historical fact, that Neat's brotherhood, the butchers of Bristol, betted particularly thick upon him. He must be a rigid moralist, indeed, who would condemn this. "*Butcherus* sum, *butcheriani* nihil a me álienum puto," will hold as truly, ay, and more truly, than the original passage of the dramatist, which asserted, that all human cares were participated in by all human beings. The butchers, consequently, were severe sufferers; one poor flesher bled to the tune of six hundred pounds—an amiable man, with an interesting wife and six small children. The green visage of the Sheriff was seen in the market; and a vast quantity of the implements by which the most powerful of cattle fell, fell themselves in turn under the fatal hammer of the auctioneer. It is not wonderful, under such circumstances, that the butchers should shew much sore flesh. Among them it is a general belief that Neat did cross it; and accordingly he is not so popular a preacher as the Reverend Neddy Irving, by several degrees. Besides, national pride is against the belief, that a Herefordshire man, bred in London, should subdue the flower of Bristol, the wonder of the western land. Neat, however, is indignant at the idea, and lays the whole circumference of the blame upon his broken radius. We happened to be by in Bristol, when a young gentleman, six feet two high, of a mild countenance, slightly pitted with the small-pox, and considerably blown up with brandy, was coming off a Southampton coach, in company with his father, a very decent-looking seventeen-stone old body. The father and son were conversing affably about the late event, which has brought more ruin on the western empire than any disaster since the days of Honorius; and the son, just as he stepped down, remarked gently, "By ——, Neat sold the fight." A man of a certain appearance, with his right arm in a sling, was standing by, and asked, with more energy than politesse, "Who the blazes dost thee speak of?"—"Why," said the youth, "Neat,

* Josh Hudson did *not* fight Spring.—M.

who sold the fight." On which the man of the arm, putting forth his sinister bunch of fives, saluted the youngster under the ear with a blow that projected him about seven feet six inches across the street, deposited him in a place of safety in the sink, and sent the blood gushing forth, with the most fluent liberality, from mouth, nose, and ears. "Now," said the striker, "I'm Neat; what dost thee say to that?"—"Nothing at all," replied the strikee, "only that I am satisfied."

But forty thousand knock-down blows would not satisfy the body-politic of the butchers. We were ourself in company with a very interesting and ingenious person of that tribe, with whom we had much conversation. He is a truly fine and amiable butcher, who had lost a quantity of cash on the fight. He vented his indignation sadly against Bill Neat, and his wrath would not be appeased. He ventured to suggest, that Bill's arm being broken, quite did up all his chance; and hinted, that, in fact, he had no chance even without the smash of his bone. In truth, we may as well at once tell the reader, that we look upon Spring as the better man—tardy to be sure, something like a British reviewer, but still of guard inpenetrable, great coolness, great courage, and great science. Neat is a man more of genius than cultivation—in ruffianing superb, in skill defective. Now, as we know that they are men of equal weight, or that the difference, if any, is for Spring, he being 3 pounds heavier, and that he has the advantage of being a nicer height, viz. 5 feet 11½ inches, while Neat is 6 feet ¼ inch, we say that no ruffianosity can ever beat science under such circumstances. This we stated with our utmost eloquence to our friend the butcher, but in vain. He had a preconceived theory that Neat *could* beat, and *would* not, which no facts could conquer. Undoubtedly, however, our friend, the feller of oxen, is a man of genius; for he wrote a song in the height of his indignation, of which he kindly gave us a copy, on condition that we should keep it a secret. We therefore commit it in confidence to our readers:—

LAMENT OF A BIG BRISTOL BUTCHER.

1.

I was as raw as butcher's meat,
  I was as green as cabbage,

When I sported blunt on Billy Neat,
 The ugly-looking savage.

2.

I was as dull as Bristol stone,
 And as the Severn muddy,
Or I should have had the humbug known,
 Of that big bruiser bloody.

3.

I was as dull as a chopping-block,
 As stupid as a jack-ass,
Or I'd not have laid on such a cock
 One whiff of my tobaccoes.

4.

For budding flower, or leafing tree,
 I now don't care a splinter;
For Spring is a colder thought to me
 Than the bitterest day of Winter.

5.

Woe, woe unto the market-place!
 Woe, woe among the cleavers!
For sad is every greasy face
 Among Bill Neat's believers.

6.

I'm rooked of notes both small and great,
 I'm rooked of every sovereign;
So bloody curses on Bill Neat,
 Whatever king may govern!

We do not hesitate to say, that the author of these verses is a poet, and are not without a hope, that the same age, which saw raised from humble degree to the heights, or at least declivities, of Parnassus, such souls as those of our own, our dear friend Hogg the Shepherd of Ettrick, or, to leave him out of the question, of Clare the hedger, Cunningham the mason, Bloomfield the herd, Keats the apothecary, and Mrs. Yearsley the milkwoman, will also have the happiness of witnessing the rise and progress of the author of this Lament, Humphry Huggins, the butcher.

Quod Testor,

M. OD.

A Twist-imony in Favour of Gin-Twist.*

An humble imitation of that admirable Poem, the Ex-ale-tation of Ale, attributed by grave authors to Bishop Andrews, on which point is to be consulted, Francis, Lord Verulam, a celebrated Philosopher, who has been lately bescoped-and tendencied by Macvey Napier, Esq.

Running Index of Matters.

1.

Proœm.

At one in the morn, as I went staggering home,
With nothing at all in my hand, but my fist,
At the end of the street, a good youth I did meet
Who ask'd me to join in a jug of gin-twist.

2.

Gin-twist.

"Though 'tis late," I replied, "and I'm muggy beside,
Yet, an offer like this I could never resist;
So let's waddle away, sans a moment's delay,
And in style we'll demolish your jug of gin-twist."

3.

Wines.

The friends of the grape, may boast of rich Cape,
Hock, Claret, Madeira, or Lachryma Christ,
But this muzzle of mine was never so fine,
As to value them more than a jug of gin-twist.

4.

Brandy.

The people of Nantz, in the Kingdom of France,
Bright brandy they brew, liquor not to be hiss'd;
It may do as a dram, but, 'tis not worth a damn,
When water'd, compared with a jug of gin-twist.

5.

Rum.

Antigua, Jamaica,—they certainly make a
Grand species of rum, which should ne'er be dismiss'd;
It is splendid as grog, but never, you dog,
Esteem it as punch, like a jug of gin-twist.

---

* This curious poem, in which such a variety of words are pressed into the service, as rhymes to *gin-twist*, appeared in *Blackwood* for November, 1822. The fluid thus immortalized is nothing more nor less than punch—made of gin instead of whiskey, and rather freely flavoured with a greater quantity of the essential oil of lemon, obtainable by rubbing a lump of sugar on the rind of a lemon, or by infusing thin parings of said lemon-rind into the sugared and spirited hot fluid.—M.

6.

Cold Punch.

Ye Bailies of Glasgow! Wise men of the West!
  Without your rum bowls, you'd look certainly ***tristes;***
Yet I laugh when I'm told, that liquor so cold
  Is as good as a foaming hot jug of gin-twist.

7.

Potsheen.*

The bog-trotting Teagues, in clear whiskey delight,
  Preferring potsheen to all drinks that exist;
I grieve, ne'ertheless, that it does not possess
  The juniper smack of a jug of gin-twist.

8.

Farintosh.

Farintosh and Glenlivit, I hear, are the boast
  Of those breechesless heroes, the Sons of the Mist;
But, may I go choke, if that villainous smoke
  I'd name in a day with a jug of gin-twist.

9.

The Celtic.

Yet the Celtic I love, and should join them, by Jove!
  Though Glengarry should vow I'd no right to enlist;
For that Chief, do you see, I'd not care a bawbee,
  If strongly entrench'd o'er a jug of gin-twist.

10.

Kilts.

One rule they lay down is the reason, I own,
  Why from joining their plaided array I desist;
Because they declare, that no one shall wear
  Of breeches a pair, o'er their jugs of gin-twist.

11.

Breeches.

This is plainly absurd, I give you my word,
  Of this bare-rump'd reg'lation I ne'er saw the gist;
In my gay corduroys, can't these philabeg boys
  Suffer me to get drunk o'er my jug of gin-twist?

12.

Rack.

In India they smack a liquor call'd rack,
  Which I never quaff'd, (at least that I wist;)
I'm told 'tis like tow in its taste, and so,
  Very different stuff from a jug of gin-twist.

13.

Porter and Ale.

As for porter and ale—'fore Gad, I turn pale,
  When people on such things as these can insist;
They may do for dull clods, but, by all of the gods!
  They are hog-wash when match'd with a jug of gin-twist,

---

* *Potsheen* is not the word, (as may be found by reference to Maxim 132,) but *potheen*—as made in a little pot.—M.

14.

Why tea we import, I could never conceive; Tea.
To the mandarin folk, to be sure, it brings grist;
But in our western soils, the spirits it spoils,
While to heaven they are raised by a jug of gin-twist.

15.

Look at Hazlitt and Hunt, most unfortunate pair! Hazlit, Hunt, Bohea.
Black and blue from the kicks of a stern satirist; Z*
But would Mynheer IZZARD once trouble their gizzard,
If bohea they exchanged for a jug of gin-twist?

16.

Leibnitz held that this earth was the first of all worlds, Leibnitz.†
And no wonder the buck was a firm optimist;
For 'twas always his use, as a proof to adduce,
Of the truth of his doctrine, a jug of gin-twist.

17.

It cures all the vapours and mulligrub capers; Howard.
It makes you like Howard, the philanthro-pist;
Woe, trouble, and pain, that bother your brain,
Are banish'd out clean, by a jug of gin-twist.

18.

You turn up your nose at all your foes, Law of libel.
Abuse you, traduce you, they may if they list:
The lawyers, I'm sure, would look very poor,
If their clients would stick to their jugs of gin-twist.

19.

There's Leslie, my friend, who went ramstam to law, Mr. Leslie and Dr. Olinthus Petre.‡
Because PETRE had styled him a poor Hebraist;
And you see how the Jury, in spite of his fury,
Gave him comfort far less than one jug of gin-twist.

20.

And therefore, I guess, Sir, the *celebre* Professor, Leslie and Kit North.
Even though culpably quizz'd as a mere sciolist,

---

* Sundry articles, in each number of *Blackwood*, on the Cockney School of Poetry, signed "Z.," and most personal on Hunt and Hazlitt, were generally attributed to Lockhart. — M.

† The actual optimist theory of Leibnitz was that an infinite number of worlds are possible in the divine understanding; but, of all possible ones, God has chosen and formed the best. Also, that each being is intended to attain the highest degree of happiness of which it is capable, and is to contribute, as a part, to the perfection of the whole. — M.

‡ Dr. Olinthus Petre, — one of Maginn's *noms de plume*, and that under which he attacked Sir John Leslie. — M.

Would have found it much meeter, to have laugh'd at old
PETRE,
And got drunk with Kit North o'er a jug of gin-twist.

21.

Stranguary.

Its medical virtues * * * * * *
* * * * * * * * * *
* * * * * * * * * *
* * * * * * * a jug of gin-twist.

22.

Brockden Brown.

By its magical aid, a toper is made,
Like Brockden Brown's hero, a ventriloquist;
For my belly cries out, with an audible shout,
"Fill up every chink with a jug of gin-twist."

23.

Cosmogony.

Geologers all, great, middling, and small,
Whether fiery Plutonian or wet Neptunist,
Most gladly, it seems, seek proofs for their schemes,
In the water, or spirit, of a jug of gin-twist.

24.

Geology.

These grubbers of ground, (whom God may confound!)
Forgetting *transition*, trap, hornblende, or schist,
And all other sorts, think only of quartz—
I mean, of the quarts in a jug of gin-twist.

25.

Parnassus.

Though two dozen of verse I've contriv'd to rehearse,
Yet still I can sing like a true melodist;
For they are but asses, who think that Parnassus
In spirit surpasses a jug of gin-twist.

26.

The Massora.

It makes you to speak Dutch, Latin, or Greek;
Even learning Chinese very much 'twould assist:
I'll discourse you in Hebrew, provided that ye brew
A most Massorethical jug of gin-twist.

27.

The Picturesque.

When its amiable stream, all enveloped in steam,
Is dash'd to and fro by a vigorous wrist,
How sweet a cascade every moment is made
By the artist who fashions a jug of gin-twist!

28.

Whiggery.

Sweet stream! there is none but delights *in* thy flow,
Save that vagabond villain, the Whig atheist;

For done was the job for his patron, Sir Bob,*
When he dared to wage war 'gainst a jug of gin-twist.

29.

Don't think, by its name, from Geneva it came, John Calvin.
The sour little source of the Kirk Calvinist —
A fig for Jack Calvin, my processes alvine
Are much more rejoiced by a jug of gin-twist.

30.

Let the Scotsman delight in malice and spite, Michael Angelo Taylor, Esq., M. P., &c.†
The black-legs at Brookes's, in hazard or whist;
Tom Dibdin in books — Micky Taylor in cooks,
My pleasure is fixed in a jug of gin-twist.

31.

Though the point of my nose grow as red as a rose, Precious stones.
Or rival in hue a superb amethyst,
Yet no matter for that, I tell you 'tis flat,
I shall still take a pull at a jug of gin-twist.

32.

There was old Cleobulus,‡ who meaning to fool us, Wise Men of Greece.
Gave out for his saying, ΤΟ ΜΕΤΡΟΝ ΑΡΙΣΤ';
But he'd never keep measure, if he had but the pleasure
Of washing his throat with a jug of gin-twist.

---

* Sir R. Walpole; justly turned out for taxing gin. He was the last decent man who committed Whiggery, nevertheless. — M. OD. [The statement there is incorrect. When Walpole returned to office in 1721, (on the retirement of Lord Sunderland, who was implicated in the South Sea scheme,) he shewed himself a practical free-trader by abolishing the greater part of the petty duties and impoverishing taxes which distracted the exportation of British manufactures, and lessened the importation of the most necessary commodities. Twelve years later, he introduced his plan for subjecting the duties on wine and tobacco to the laws of excise — a measure so unpopular that he could not carry it. This was in 1733, but certainly did not turn Walpole out of office, for he continued prime minister until February, 1742, when he resigned, and was created Earl of Oxford, with a pension of £4,000 a year. — M.]

† Michael Angelo Taylor, M. P., who resided near the House of Commons, and was very popular with the Whig party, during the Regency and earlier years of the reign of George IV., on account of his keeping a sort of free table for his legislative friends and colleagues. — M.

‡ Cleobulus, one of the Seven Wise Men of Greece, born at Rhodes, in the 6th century before Christ. — M.

33.

Kisses.

There are dandies and blockheads, who vapour and boast
Of the favours of girls they never have kiss'd;
That is not the thing, and therefore by jing!
I kiss while I'm praising my jug of gin-twist.

34.

Plato

While over the glass, I should be an ass,
To make moping love like a dull Platonist;
That ne'er was my fashion, I swear that my passion
In as hot as itself for a jug of gin-twist.

35.

Θαλαττα θαλαττα.

Although it is time to finish my rhyme,
Yet the subject's so sweet, I can scarcely desist;
While its grateful perfume is delighting the room,
How can I be mute o'er a jug of gin-twist?

36.

GOD SAVE THE KING.

Yet since I've made out, without any doubt,
Of its merits and glories a flourishing list,
Let us end with a toast, which we cherish the most,
Here's "GOD SAVE THE KING!" in a glass of gin-twist.

37.

Moral.

Then I bade him good night in a most jolly plight,
But I'm sorry to say that my footing I missed;
All the stairs I fell down, so I batter'd my crown,
And got two black eyes from a jug of gin-twist.

Irish Songs.*

THERE is, I perceive, a disinclination becoming very visible on the part of the English, to believe us Irish people, when we tell them that they know nothing about us. They look upon it as a sort of affront, and yet nothing is more true. And as example is much better than any theory, I shall just beg leave to prove my assertion, by that they put into our mouths when they think fit to write as Irish.

The first book I lay my hand on will do. It is a collection of Irish songs, published in London, without date, printed by Oliver and Boyd. It contains all the popular Irish songs which you hear sung at the theatres, public-houses, Vauxhall, and other such fashionable places of resort. There are ninety of them in all, and I shall patiently examine these specimens of Irish wit—these would-be flowers of the Hibernian Parnassus.

The first song is a great favourite. The Sprig of Shillelah, and it is not much amiss. It contains an immensity of blarney to us, which, of course, is palatable. I suspect the author of never having been in Ireland, nevertheless, from these lines:—

> "Who has e'er had the luck to see Donnybrook fair,
> An Irishman all in his glory is there;"

for I have had the "luck" to see that fair, and I never could see any glory in it. It is a paltry thing, if compared with Bartholomew fair, or any of the great fairs in London; and like them is a nuisance which gathers the blackguard men and women of a metropolis, to indulge in all kinds of filth. I should call it the worst specimen of Ireland. Would a Scotchman think his national character would be favourably exhibited by a collection of the cadies and baker-boys, and gutterbloods of Edinburgh, with their trulls? And as Dublin is three times the size of Edinburgh, the sweepings of its streets must be three times as disgusting. The squalid misery, too, which is mixed up with the drunken riot of the fairs of Donnybrook, has always been quite revolting to my eyes, and I should rather see the magis-

* This article appeared in *Blackwood*, for March, 1825.—M.

tracy of Dublin employed in suppressing it, than hear silly song-writers using their rhymes in its panegyric.

The next is Paddy MacShane's Seven Ages; a stupid parody on Shakespeare. A great knowledge of Ireland is shewn here. Mr. MacShane, it appears, was a native of Ballyporeen, and fell in love with a lady there—but

> "She asked me just once that to see her I'd come,
> When I found her ten children and husband at home,
> A great big whacking chairman of Ballyporeen!"

Now Ballyporeen, Heaven bless it, is a dirty village, of about fifty houses, at the foot of the Kilworth mountains, as you enter Tipperary, on the mail-coach road from Cork to Dublin. When I passed through it last, the only decent-looking house I saw there was the inn; and a poor one enough even that was. I leave it to yourself to judge what a profitable trade that of a chairman would be in such a place as that; or how probable it is that a woman with a husband and ten children could pass off, incog., as unmarried, upon a native. You would walk from one end to the other of it in three minutes.

Again he tells us that

> "I turned servant, and lived with the great justice Pat,
> A big dealer in p'ratoes at Ballyporeen,
> With turtle and venison he lined his inside,
> Ate so many fat capons," &c.

Potatoes are somewhere about the price of three half-pence a-stone in Ballyporeen, and they are cultivated by almost every one in it; so that this excellent justice had a fine merchandize of it. As for turtle, I imagine that the name of it was never heard of in the village; indeed, as Tipperary is quite an inland county, it must be a rarity to every part of it—and capons! I am quite sure the dish is unknown altogether. The bard shews great knowledge of the Irish magistracy, even by the way he mentions his justice—Justice Pat!

We have then,

> "There was an Irish lad—Who loved a cloistered nun.'

A good song, and perhaps Irish. One verse is like the idiom. When the hero could not get at his mistress,

> "He stamped and raved, and sighed and prayed,
> And many times he swore,
> The devil burn the iron bolts!
> The devil burn the door!"

Then follows,

> "Mulrooney's my name, I'm a comical boy,
> A tight little lad at Shillelah,
> St. Patrick wid whiskey he suckled me, *joy*,
> Among the sweet bogs of Killalah."

I must protest that I never heard the word "joy" so used in Ireland by anybody, and yet it is a standing expression put into our mouths by every writer of Irish characters. Of the existence of Killalah, I am ignorant. We have Killalah in Connaught, but it rhymes to tallow. But appropos of rhymes, listen to those put into Mr. Mulrooney's mouth,

> "But thinks I, spite of what fame and glory *bequeath*,
> How conceited I'd look in a fine laurel *wreath*,
> Wid my hand in my mouth, to stand picking my *teeth*."

I flatter myself that the "comical boy" would say *bequaith* and *wraith*, rhyming to *faith*, and never think of screwing up his mouth to squeezing these into *bequeeth* and *wreeth*.

Of Dermot and Sheelah, I shall only quote the chorus,

> "Beam, bum, *boodle*, loodle, loodle,
> Beam, bum, *boodle*, loodle, loo."

Pretty writing that—and very much on a par, in point of sense and interest, with Barry Cornwall's humbugs to Appollor—rather more musical I own. But is it Irish? *Negatur*. I deny it poz! Boodles! why, Boodles is a club of good hum-drum gentlemen, kept by Cuddington and Fuller, at 31, St. James Street; but not particularly Hibernian. A chorus in the same taste concerning them, would run thus,

> "Bow, wow, boodle, noodle, doodle,
> Bow, wow, boodle, noodle, pooh!"

Close following comes Paddy O'Blarney, a misnomer on the face of it. Blarney is a village and a baronial castle. You might as well say, Sawney M'Linlighgow, or Archy O'Goosedubs. The song is a brutal attempt at wit, and mock-Irish, *ex. gr.*

13*

"I found one who larnt grown-up *Jolmen* to write,
Just to finish gay Paddy O'Blarney."

Jolmen! what's that? Put for *jontlemen*, I suppose. This fellow had a fresh idea of the tongue. Such a word never was heard among us. By the way, our plebeians generally say, jintlemen, though the folks who write for us think otherwise.

Hear the next bard,

"I'm a comical fellow"

En passant, I may remark that I never heard any one say he was a comical fellow, that he did not prove an ass, and the rule holds here,

"I'm a comical fellow, I tell you no fib,
And I come from the bogs of Killaley."

a various reading, I suppose, of the celebrated unknown district, commemorated in another song, by the name of Killalah.

"You see I'm the thing by the cut of my jib,
And they christen'd me Teddy O'Reilly."

Observe the name O'Reilly rhymes plainly to "highly." Ask for O'Raly anywhere, and you will not be understood. But the Christian name is equally destructive to its Irish pretensions. Teddy, a Cockney vulgarism for Edward, and that too confined to the raff of Cockaigne. Thady is a common Irish name, which, as you know, is the abbreviation of Thaddeus, the name of one of the apostles, according to Saints Matthew and Mark, but Teddy is unheard of. Yet it occurs in half a dozen songs of this volume.

What part of the world the next song comes from, needs no ghost to tell us. One rhyme will denote it.

"As the board they put out was too narrow to *quarter*,
The first step I took I was in such a *totter*."

It is, you see, marked with the indelible damned Cockney blot, and, in all probability, proceeds from the pen of Leigh Hunt. An Irishman who sounds the R as fiercely as ever that canine letter rung from human organ, could never have been guilty of it.

Cushlamachree, which succeeds, is, 'tis said, from the pen of Curran, and the first verse is, I think, a good and warm one.

"Dear Erin, how sweetly thy green bosom rises,
An emerald set in the ring of the sea:
Each blade of thy meadows my faithful heart prizes,
Thou queen of the West—the world's Cushlamacree."

We soon come to a strain of another mood in Sheelah's Wedding, which, for magnificent ignorance of the country in which the scene is laid, is just as good as can be conceived. I extract the whole second verse as a sample of various beauties.

"Well, the time being settled, to *church* they were carried,
With some more lads and lasses, to see the pair married,
Who vowed that too long from the *parson* they tarried;
For who should such sweet things be scorning?
Then at *church*, arrah, yes, you may fancy them there;
Sure the *priest* tied them fast, you may very well swear;
And when it was done,
Och, what laughing and fun
Took place about something, and throwing the stocking,
While the blythe boys and GIRLS
Talked of ringing the BELLS
On St. Patrick's day in the *morning*."

The rhyme here marks this brute to be a bestial Cockney. The mixture of the words "parson" and "priest" convicts him of not knowing Irish phraseology, which restricts the latter word to the Roman Catholic clergy, who are not parsons. By the name, Sheelah, the lady is decidedly Catholic—and then how consistently we have the talk about the "church" and the "bells!" Roman Catholic places of worship all through Ireland are called *chapels*, and they have no bells, very few having even one. And the morning marriage! there the ape, if he knew any thing of Ireland, must have known that Catholic marriages there are celebrated in the *evening*. I have been at some hundreds of them.

In the next song, and several others, we have "taef" for "thief," which is enough. The vulgarism inter Hibernos, is "teef." In the next we have the adventures of a certain Mr. *Teddy*, of whom I have already disposed. I may pass Mr. Grimgruffenhoff, and Bumper Squire Jones, for different reasons. The latter is a capital song indeed, and written by an Irish

Baron of Exchequer. The breed of such judges is not extinct, while we have Lord Norbury, whom God preserve.*

Mr. O'Gallogher falls in love in the next song with a lady named Cicely,—what part of Ireland he found her in is not mentioned. It never was my lot to meet with one of her name—and the same remark I must extend to the heroine of the following chaunt—the celebrated Looney Mactwolter's mistress, Miss Judy *O'Flannikin,*—who is evidently transmuted from O'Flannegan, to rhyme the opening line,

"Oh! whack, Cupid's a *Mannikin.*"

Looney itself is a dubious *Christian* name. I have known plebeians of that *surname,* and when they rise in society, if they ever do, they change it always to Loane.

"Murphy O'Casey,"—heads the next—Psha! the name will not pass muster. You might as well say Blackwood O'Jeffrey. Nor can I panegyrize in another song Father O'Rook, for an Irishman would certainly call him O'Rourke.

I skip a parcel of mere vulgarity to give you

"I'm Larry O'Lashem, was born in Killarney,"

one of whose adventures is described in the following dialect:

"I amused myself laughing, to see how the HINDER
Wheels after the fore ones most furiously paid, [Qu?]
Till a wheel broke its leg, spilt the coach out of the WINDER,
While my head and the pavement at nutcracking played."

Winder! Poet of Cockneyland! the compliments of the season to you. I disclaim you as a countryman. Nor shall I claim the bard, who, singing of the Siege of Troy, tells you that

"—— the cunning Ulysses, the Trojans to *cross,*
Clapt forty fine fellows on one wooden *horse.*"

From the theme of the poem—those old down-looking Greeks—and this rhyme, it is evident that it was written by the late Mr. Keats. May I be shot if *he* was an Irishman!

Molly Astore is a beautiful tune to namby-pamby New-Monthly-looking words, and the parody on it is quite a poor thing. I flatter myself I have made better.

* Lord Norbury, Chief-Justice of the Common Pleas, in Ireland, from 1800 until 1827, was born in 1745, and died in July 1831.—He was the subject of one of the most graphic "Sketches of the Irish Bar," by Sheil.—M.

A poet farther on, treats us to the following description of a Kerryman:

> "His hair was so red, and his eyes were so bright."

No doubt there are red-haired Kerryman, but they are not one in fifty. The complexion is dark olive, and the hair black, they being in all probability descended from the Spaniards. The poet was thinking of a Highlander. Now the knights of Kerry wear breeches, and are in a small degree civilized.

Another Irishman from Cockneyshire, sings of

> "——Cormac O'Con,
> Of the great Con grandsire,
> With the son of Combal the Greek sire,
> Whose name sounded afar,
> As great Ossian's *papa*."

If I met this fellow, who has our Irish names so glib at his fingers' ends, at the top of the highest house of the city, I should kick him down stairs. A Ludgate-Hill pawnbroker could not be more impertinent, if he wrote of the fine arts.

In the same *de haut en bas* fashion should I kick him who informs us that

> "I were astonish'd as much as e'er *man was*,
> To see a sea-fight on an ocean of *canvass*."

You hear the barbarian saying canvass—I long to pull his nose.

I apprehend the author of the Irish Wedding (see Jon Bee) is a Scot.

> "First book in hand, came Father Quipes."

What part of the world does that name belong to?—

> "——came Father Quipes,
> With the bride's dada, *the Bailie, O.*"

Bailies we have none in Ireland, and if we had, they should be all Protestants, and thereby out of the pale of Father Quipes.

A piece of politics, in another ditty, is quite diverting to us, who know a thing or two.

> "Though all taxes I paid, yet no vote I could pass O——"

and was in consequence, though

> "With principles pure, patriotic, and *firm*,
> Attach'd to my country, a friend to *reform*,"

obliged to fly. His case was certainly hard in not having a vote, when every farmer or labourer in Ireland may have one if he likes, or rather if his landlord likes. In the county of Cork there are 25,000 voters, in Down about 20,000, and so on; so that his grievance about the want of suffrage is rather singular.

There is no use in bothering the public with any more remarks on such a subject. I hope nobody will think I have any spleen against this collection of songs, which is just as good as any other similar one, but I wished to shew that I had some ground for saying, that we are not quite wrong in accusing our English friends of ignorance of our concerns. Some time or other, perhaps, I may in the same way get through the usual stage characters, in which we figure and prove them equally remote from truth.

It would, perhaps, be a good thing to go over some of the political speculations on Ireland in the same manner, but I never liked Irish politics, and now I particularly detest them. I frequently admire the intrepidity of the heads which John Black* spins out for the edification of the Whigamores, whenever he takes us in his hand. Evidently wishing to patronize us, he nevertheless treats us as mere barbarians. I remember reading one morning in the Chronicle, that, except Dublin and Cork, there were no large towns in Ireland, which accounts for its want of civilization, while Scotland was indebted for her superiority over us, to her possessing such eminent cities as Edinburgh, Glasgow, Paisley, Aberdeen, Dundee, Inverness, and some others which I forget. Now Limerick is larger and more populous than any except the first two; Waterford, Galway, Kilkenny, and Belfast, fall little short of them; and, taking out the first half dozen of Scotch towns, you would seek in vain through Scotland for towns to compare with Drogheda, Sligo, Carlow, Clonmell, Derry, Youghall, and several others. This is but a small sample of his accuracy.

He of the Courier knows, *in his writings*, something more, but *personally*, Mudford is quite horror-struck at the notion of us.† The Roman Catholic Association, professedly friends of

* John Black, who conducted the *Morning Chronicle*, in London, for many years.—M.

† William Mudford, Editor of the *Courier*, a ministerial newspaper, in London, during the whole period of the war with Napoleon, and for nearly twenty

the liberty of the press, have brought an information against him for inserting some remarks of a correspondent on Maynooth College, and availed themselves of an obscure law, to lay the venue against him in Cork. The very wind of the word has frightened my friend Mudford out of his seven senses. Some Cockney blackguard, with that spirit of personality so disgustingly the distinction of the Cockney school, once called him "a pile of fleecy hosiery,"—but that name is every day becoming less and less applicable. He looks on the Corkagians as no better than Ashantees, and, no doubt, anticipates, from the jaws of long John Brixon, mayor of that beef-abounding city, the fate of poor Sir Charles M'Carthy.* Let him be comforted. Cork, I can assure him, is well munitioned with victual and drink, and he has but a small chance of being eaten alive there, particularly as he remains but a fortnight. Nor let him dread the hostile countenances of a grand jury, empannelled by Jack Bagnell and Ned Colburn, best of little men—sheriffs of the aforesaid bailiwick. And even if that is improbable, the thing comes to a petit jury, even before them—let him pluck up courage. Men there are to be found on all sides of the banks of

> The spreading lee, that like an island fayre,
> Encloseth Corke with its divided flood,

who would devour the boot from the silk twist that hems its upper-leather, to the iron horse-shoe which guards its heel, sooner than give a verdict against the right. Counselled by these reflections, let him devour turbot, hot (as the old cookery books have it) from the bank in the harbour—let him swallow salmon, creaming in overlasting curd from the Lee—let Kinsale feed him with hake, fish of delicious flavour, unheard of in Augusta Trinobantum—from Cove let him gulp down oysters capacious as his well-fleshed hand. Kerry will supply him mutton to masticate, small, but lively. Cork itself will offer its beef and

years later. He wrote several works, of which his romance "The Five Nights of St. Alban" is best known.—M.

* Sir Charles M'Carthy, an Irish officer, commanded in Cape Coast in 1821–3. In the latter year he marched against the Ashantees—but his black troops ran away, his white soldiers were defeated, his body was eaten by the victors, and his head (carefully pickled) was placed as an ornament on the great war drum of the enemy, in January, 1824. In a subsequent battle it was recaptured.—M.

butter, peerless throughout the land. Pork is, I own, inferior to the flesh of Anglia pigs;—but Wicklow can send her turf-dried hams, easily procurable, that will scarce vail bonnet to those of Wiltshire. He may, no doubt, regret the crammed poultry of London,—but a turkey in native flavour, will smoke upon his board for two tenpennies. Does he long for dainties more rich and rare? In a harbour, yawning for the West Indies, he need not desiderate turtle—in a city within easy march of sporting hills and dales, he need not be afraid of wanting game or venison. As for drink, is he fond of port? Vessels from Oporto will justle the boat that brings him to the quay—if of claret, he must be unskilled in bibulous lore, if he knows not the value set upon the claret of Ireland. But as his stay is short, I recommend whiskey-punch. *That* he cannot get for love nor money in London. Let him there ingurgitate that balmy fluid. There's Walker—there's Wise—there's Calaghan—there's Hewitt—excellent artists all*—they will sell it to him for from 6s. 6d. to 7s. 6d. a gallon—and a gallon will make sixty-four tumblers—I have often calculated it—and that is three times as much as he should drink in an evening. So doing, he will be happy, and fearless of the act of Judge Johnson.

But what is this I am about? digressing from a disquisition on songs, pseudo-Irish, to the way in which a stranger, who knows how, could live in Cork. It can't be helped—I have lost the thread of my argument. So I think I had better conclude.

M. OD.

* Distillers of whiskey, in Cork.—M.

Cork is the Aiden for you, love, and me.*

Air—"*They may rail at this life.*"

I.

THEY may rail at the city where I was first born,
But it's there they've the whiskey, and butter, and pork,
An' a *nate* little spot for to walk in each morn,
They calls it Daunt's Square, and the city is Cork!
The Square has two sides, why, one east, and one west;
And convanient's the ragion of frolic and spree,
Where salmon, drisheens, and beef-steaks are cook'd best,
Och! *Fishamble's* the *Aiden* for you, love, and me.

II.

If you want to behold the sublime and the beauteous,
Put your toes in your brogues, and see sweet Blarney Lane,
Where the parents and *childer* is comely and duteous,
And "dry lodgin" both rider and beast entertain;
In the cellars below dines the slashin' young fellows,
What comes with the butter from distant Tralee;
While the landlady, chalking the score on the bellows,
Sings, Cork is an *Aiden* for you, love, and me.

III.

Blackpool is another sweet place of that city,
Where pigs, twigs, and wavers, they all grow together,
With its small little tanyards—och, more is the pity—
To trip the poor beasts to convert them to leather!
Farther up to the east, is a place great and famous,
It is called Mellow Lane—antiquaries agree
That it holds the *Shibbeen* which once held King *Shamus*:—
O! Cork is an *Aiden* for you, love, and me.

IV.

Then go back to Daunt's Bridge, though you'll think it is *quare*
That you can't see the bridge—faix! you ne'er saw the like
Of that bridge, nor of one-sided Buckingham Square,
Nor the narrow Broad lane, that leads up to the Dyke!
Where turning his wheel sits that Saint "Holy Joe,"
And *numbrellas* are made of the best quality,
And young *varginls* sing "*Colleen das croothin a mo*"†
And Cork is an *Aiden* for you, love, and me.

---

* Sang by Odoherty at THE NOCTES, May, 1828.—M.

† *Colleen das croothin a. mo,*—An Irish phrase, signifying "The pretty girl milking her cow." There is a delightful Irish Melody bearing this name.—M.

V.

When you gets to the Dyke, there's a beautiful prospect
  Of a long gravel walk between two rows of trees;
On one side, with a beautiful southern aspect,
  Is Blair's Castle, that trembles above in the breeze!
Far off to the west lies the lakes of Killarney,
  Which some hills intervening prevents you to see;
But you smell the sweet wind from the wild groves of Blarney—
  Och! Cork is the *Aiden* for you, love, and me!

VI.

Take the road to Glanmire, the road to Blackrock, or
  The sweet Boreemannah, to charm your eyes,
If you doubt what is *Wise*, take a dram of Tom Walker,
  And if you're a *Walker*, toss off Tommy Wise!*
I give you my word that they're both lads of *spirit;*
  But if a "*raw-chaw*," with your gums don't agree,
Beamish, Crawford, and Lane, brew some porter of merit,
  Tho' *Potheen* is the nectar for you, love, and me.

VII.

Oh, long life to you, Cork, with your pepper-box steeple,
  Your girls, your whiskey, your curds, and sweet whey!
Your hill of Glanmire, and shops where the people
  Gets decent new clothes down *beyont* the Coal Quay.
Long life to sweet Fair Lane, its pipers and jigs,
  And to sweet Sunday's well, and the banks of the Lee,
Likewise to your *coort*-house, where judges in wigs
  Sing, Cork is an *Aiden* for you, love, and me!

---

* Walker and Wise were rival distillers of whiskey, in Cork. Beamish & Crawford and Lane are eminent brewers.—M.

English Songs.*

I HAVE been tumbling over Ritson's songs† listlessly this morning, for want of something better to do, and cannot help thinking, that a much better selection and arrangement might be made. He assigns 304 pages to love-songs, and but 228 to all others. The collection of ancient ballads, which concludes the volume, is not very much in place in a book of *songs;* and, besides, is far inferior to what we now know such a collection ought to be. Now, I submit, without at all disparaging that "sublime and noble — that sometimes calm and delightful — but more frequently violent, unfortunate, and dreadful passion" of love, as Ritson calls it, — in does not fill such a space, in the *good* song-writing of any country, as a proportion of fifteen to eleven, against all other species. I say of *good* song-writing, for I know of namby-pamby, it fills nine parts out of ten.

And precisely of namby-pamby are composed nine parts out of ten of Ritson's most pedantic divisions into classes — classes sillily planned at first, and not clearly distinguished in execution afterwards. The second song of the first class, by Miss ‡Aiken, concludes with this verse —

"Thus to the rising god of day
Their early vows the Persians pay,
And bless the spreading fire:
Whose glowing chariot mounting soon,
Pours on their heads the burning noon,
They sicken and expire."

This is not song-writing — it is only a bombastic repetition of a middling thought, which had been already expressed ten thou

* From *Blackwood* for April, 1825. — M.

† Joseph Ritson, an antiquarian, who exhibited more industry than taste in his researches into and criticism on early English poetry, died in 1803. His "Collection of English Songs," in 3 vols., is here referred to by Odoherty.— M.

‡ Afterwards Mrs. Barbauld. She died a very short time ago. — M. OD. [Anna Letitia Barbauld, authoress of Hymns, and Early Lessons for Children, was born in 1743, and died in 1825. — M.]

sand times. It is, in short, a verse out of a poor *ode,* in the modern sense of the word.

In Otway's song, p. 4.

> "To sigh and wish is all my ease,
> Sighs which do heat impart
> Enough to melt the coldest ice,
> Yet cannot warm your heart."

Is this verse worth printing?—this frigid, trivial conceit, which has been tossed about by the verse-writers of all the nations in the world?

In the same page sings Viscount Molesworth,

> "Almeria's face, her shape, her hair,
> With charms resistless wound the *heart,*"

which, it is needless to say, is rhymed by "*dart.*"

In short, of the eighty-four songs of the first class, with the exception of "Take, O take those lips away!"—"To all ye ladies now at land,"—"My time, O ye muses, was happily spent,"—which, though far too long for a song, contains many ideas and lines perfectly adapted for that style of composition—and perhaps half-a-dozen others, all are of the same cast; and, what makes it more provoking, we see affixed to some of them the names of Dryden, Prior, &c., as if the editor had a perverse pleasure in showing us that these men could write as tritely and trivially as their neighbours on some occasions. Colin and Lucy, and Jemmy Dawson, which this class contains, are no more songs than Chevy Chace, or the Children of the Wood.

The second class, in which "love is treated as a passion," is better; for even attempts at writing in the language of passion are generally at least readable, if they are often absurd. What we cannot tolerate is inanity. There is a kind of noisy gallantry about

> "Ask me not how calmly I
> All the cares of life defy;
> How I baffle human woes,
> Woman, woman, woman knows,"

which is pleasant. Song XII. is excellent; compare the very sound of

> "Over the mountains,
> And over the waves,

> Under the fountains,
> And under the graves,
> Under floods that are deepest
> Which Neptune obey,
> Over rocks which are steepest,
> Love will find out his way," &c.

with the trim nothingness of the very next—

> "Oft on the troubled ocean's face,
> Loud stormy winds arise,
> The murmuring surges swell apace,
> And clouds obscure the skies:"
> But when the tempests' rage is o'er—

what follows? Why,

> "Soft breezes smooth the main,
> The billows cease to lash the shore,
> And all is calm again!!"

Compare, again, song XXII.

> "Would you choose a wife for a happy life,
> Leave the court, and the country take,
> Where Susan and Doll, and Hanny and Moll,
> Follow Harry and John, whilst harvest goes on,
> And merrily merrily rake," &c.

with song XXIV.,

> "Happy the world in that blest age
> When beauty was not bought and sold,
> When the fair mind was uninflamed
> With the mean thirst of baneful gold."

What jejune trash! and how absurd and abominable an attempt it is to put into this creeping dialect what we have read in Greek all but divine, and in Italian almost as delicious as Greek! I say, compare such passages as these together, and if you be not thoroughly sensible of the vast inferiority of the songs by persons of quality, and the propriety of utterly ejecting them from collections of songs, you will be fit to comment on them in the style of Gilbert Wakefield, and to receive panegyrics accordingly from Tom Dibdin.*

* What is written above of English Songs, will, of course, apply to the songs of all nations. I shall give a specimen in French. I shall first quote a song by Antoine Ferrand, [a Parisian, a Counsellor on the Court of Aids, who died in 1719.—*Anth. Fran.* vol. I. p. 117.] It runs thus:—

The third class opens beautifully, indeed, with "He that loves a rosy cheek." Few poems in our language resemble so much as the first two verses of this song (the third is provokingly inferior) the admirable and indefinable beauty of the

Iris est plus charmante
Que l'Aurore naissante;
La Jeunesse brillante
N'eut jamais tant d'appas.
Tout le monde l'adore;
Flore
Est moins fraiche et moins belle,
Qu' elle:
Venus même n'a pas
Tant d' amours qui marchent sur ses pas, &c.

Here we have Venus, Flora, and Aurora, in full fig; and, in the name of the three goddesses, is the song worth a farthing? Now take a song which you may vote low if you have a mind, but it is a good song nevertheless, and worth a cart-load of the above rubbish. I shall copy it all:—

1.

Malgré la bataille
Qu' on donne demain,
Ca, faisons ripaille,
Charmante Catein:
Attendant la gloire,
Prenons le plaisir,
Sans lire au grimoire
Du sombre avenir.

2.

Si la Hallebarde
Je peux mériter,
Pres du corps du garde
Je te fais planter;
Ayant la dentelle,
Le soulier brodé,
La blouque à l'oreille
Le chignon cardé.

3.

Narguant tes compagnes,
Méprisant leurs vœux,
J'ai fait deux campagnes
Roti de tes feux.
Digni de la pomme,
Tu reçus ma foi,
Et jamais rogome
Ne fut bu sans toi.

4.

Tien, serre ma Pipe,
Garde mon briquet;
Et si la Tulipe
Fait le noir trajet,
Que tu sois la seule
Dans le régiment,
Qu' ait le brule-gueule
De son cher amant.

5.

Ah! retien tes larmes,
Calme ton chagrin;
Au nom, de tes charmes
Achéve ton vin.
Mais, quoi! de nos bandes
J' entends les Tambours?
Gloire! tu commandes,
Adieu mes amours.

The author of this song is Christopher Mangenot, brother of the Abbe Mangenot of the Temple. It was written during our war with France in 1744. It was generally attributed to the pen of Voltaire, but I doubt if he could have written in this vein. I wish somebody would translate it into English.—M. OD—(Do it yourself.—C. N.)

Greek epigrams. I, however, do not remember one exactly in point. Those following (except the jocular ones, as, "Why so pale, fond lover?"—"Tom loves Mary passing well,"—"My name is honest Harry."—"My passion is as mustard strong," &c.) are not particularly worthy of applause. It contains, to be sure, "Mary, I believed thee true,"—"Still to be neat, still to be drest," and some others; but the staple commodity is,

"But passion's wild impetuous sea
Hurries me far from peace and thee—
'Twere vain to struggle more.
Thus the poor sailor slumbering lies,
While swelling tides around him rise,
And push his bark from shore:
In vain he spreads his helpless arms;
His pitying friends, with fond alarms,
In vain deplore his state.
Still far and farther from the coast,
On the high surge his bark is tost,
And, foundering, yields to fate."

Is not this the quintessence of absurdity now-a-days? Fine, pretty, good-for-nothing verses, I admit them to be, never intended or fitted to be sung; and besides, have I not read somewhere,

"Heu! quoties fidem
Mutatosque Deos flebit, et aspera
Nigris æquora ventis
Emirabitur insolens,
Qui nunc te fruitur credulus aurea!"

I own I have no patience when I see things, which have been once beautifully expressed, re-said in a manner blundering and diluted.

Class Fourth is devoted solely to expressions of love for the fair sex*—not a hopeful subject. Love to them is too serious a thing to be jested with, [See Lord Byron's Don Juan, and also see Ovid, from whom Lord Byron has *conveyed* the idea,] and they are too proud to complain, if slighted. They would be

* In this class, Ben Jonson's "Drink to me only" is inserted, I think, wrongly, for it appears to be an address from a man, not a woman. By Ritson's remark, p. lxxix, it would appear that he did not know it was from the Greek. —M. OD.

wrong if they did; it is *our* part to sue, it is *theirs* to slight or to accept. They should take the advice of Shakespeare—

"Sigh no more, ladies, sigh no more,
Men were deceivers ever,
One foot at sea, and one on shore,
To one thing constant never.
Then sigh not so,
But let them go,
And be you blithe and bonny."

If the ladies *will* not write their feelings, I am afraid we *can* not. At all events, this fourth class is completely *fadé*. There are some middling songs in it, but the majority are like those from Mr. Mosy Mendez.

"Vain is every fond endeavour,
To resist the tender dart;
For examples move us never;
We must feel to know the smart."

Which is just as much poetry as,

Vain, quite vain, the toil you spend is,
When your time in verse you pass;
For, good Mr. Moses Mendez,
You are nothing but an ass.

The ideas in Soame Jenyn's song, No. X., are very pretty. The appeal to a lover acknowledged triumphant,

"Say, would you use that very power
You from her fondness claim,
To ruin, in one fatal hour,
A life of spotless fame?
Ah! cease, my dear, to do an ill,
Because, perhaps, you may;
But rather try your utmost skill
To save me, than betray,"

is elegantly thought and expressed. There is something like the idea in the life of Gilbert Earle,* when the lady urges her lover not to take advantage of her tenderness to betray her honour.

In the Fifth Class are some very good songs. It contains, among others, three most especial favourites of mine, "Sally in

* "Passages in the Life of Gilbert Earle," sometimes incorrectly attributed to Lockhart, was written by the late Barry St. Leger, an Irishman.—M.

our Alley," by poor Harry Carey, (Goldsmith's own song, by the way,) "Black-eyed Susan," and Bishop Percy's "O Nanny, wilt thou gang with me?" But I rather think I am not peculiar in this taste. It contains also a good deal of very good nonsense. In general, of the 287 songs of the volume, I think we might fairly, for one reason or another, dispense with at least 200.

Our second division is drinking. Ritson was a water-drinker, and therefore says, "he candidly owns that he was not sorry to find every endeavour used to enlarge this part of the collection with credit (and he may, probably, as it is, have been too indulgent) prove altogether fruitless; a circumstance, perhaps, which will some time or other be considered as not a little to the honour of the English muse." This is stuff. I shall not eulogize drinking, but I am not to be humbugged with the idea, that *any* production of the English muse ever soared within five hundred yards of him who sings of

Ηδυν θεσπεσιον θειον ποτον;

or that any *songs* we have can beat those of Anacreon. If future generations differ with this dictum of mine, they may with all my heart, but I shall retain to myself the privilege of thinking such generations asinine to a great degree. Ritson's selections, however, are tolerable. Drinking-songs may be divided pretty fairly into two classes:—the meditative, which, in the Egyptian manner, brings the skeleton into the banquet-room, and bids you think of the fleetingness of life as the chief stimulus to make the most of its enjoyments while it lasts.

"Heu, heu, nos miseros, quam totus homuncio nil est,
Quam fragilis tenero stamine vita cadit!
Sic erimus cuncti, postquam nos auferet Orcus,
Ergo vivamus, dum licet esse bene—"

as Trimalchio sings. The second class is the joyous, which bids us use the goods the gods provide us, because we like them—because they exhilarate us; when the song bursts forth from mere animal spirits, or, to talk Pindarically, when—

"Θαρσυλέυ δὲ παρὰ
Κρητῆρα βωνὰ γίνεται."

and we cry—

"Ἐγκιρνάτω τίς μιν, γλυκὺν
Κώμου προράτευ."

Of the former kind, "An hundred years hence," has always appeared to me particularly good:—

"Let us drink, and be merry,
Dance, joke, and rejoice,
With claret and sherry,
Theorbo and voice.
The changeable world
To our joy is unjust,
All treasures uncertain;
Then down with your dust!
In frolics dispose
Your pounds, shillings, and pence,
For we shall be nothing
An hundred years hence."

Of the more roaring jovial songs, I do not see any worth extracting in Ritson. I think your own pages, Mr. Editor, contain some far superior to any which he sports.

What stories a commentator thoroughly versant with this subject could tell in every part of this department! I see here some of the ditties of Tom D'Urfey, whose whole life, properly written, would be a history of the joviality of England for half a century. I see here some of the songs of Tom Brown, a fellow of deeper thought than generally is to be found among the bards of the bottle. Then we have "Ye Goodfellows all," by Baron Dawson, the friend of Carolan, last of the Irish bards, and the companion of Dr. King, poet of Cookery. We see the names of Gay, Lord Rochester, Harry Carey, old Sheridan the purple-snouted, Ben Jonson the rare, Milton, and the Duke of Wharton. Let any one who knows the literary history of the country just pause for a moment at the last names I have quoted, and run over at a mental glance the events of their lives, and how various a blending of thoughts will he not experience! I confess, that reading convivial songs is to me a melancholy amusement. Every page I turn presents me with verses which I heard in merry hours from voices now mute in death, or removed to distant lands, or estranged in affection. But—

"'Tis in vain
To complain,
In a melancholy strain,
Of the days that are gone, and will never come again."

Is the story true that Wolfe either wrote or sung "How stands the glass around," the night before the battle,

"When that hero met his fate on the heights of Abram?"

I heard he did—but I forget my authority.

"The Ex-ale-tation of Ale," page 63, is not properly a song, but it is a pleasant extravaganza. There is one phenomenon mentioned in it, which I submit to Sir Humphrey Davy or some other great chemist, for I cannot resolve it.

"Nor yet the delight that comes to the sight,
To see how it flowers and mantles in graile,*
As green as a leek with a smile on the cheek,
The *true orient colour* of a pot of good ale."

How was it green? I know not, neither can I conjecture. The third part of Miscellaneous Songs has our usual favourites joined to others quite unworthy. Strange to say, it contains neither "God save the King," nor "Rule Britannia." Could this have arisen from the cankered Jacobinism of citizen Ritson? If so, it was shabby even for a Jacobin. I cannot pass over this list, without thanking Tom Campbell for "Ye mariners of England." I never read it without forgiving him all his Whiggery, and lamenting the Ritter Bann and Reullura.

As for the fourth part—the old ballads, I say nothing, except that it is poor enough, and I think uncalled for here. The last ballad is by Sir W. Scott—a translation from the Norman French, the original of which, the editor says, cannot now be retraced. Had it ever any existence? It is a splendid thing, and I do not recollect seeing it in his works. Therefore here it goes—

BALLAD

ON THE DEATH OF SIMON DE MONTFORT,

EARL OF LEICESTER,

AT THE BATTLE OF EVERSHAM, 1226.

(*Literally versified from the Norman French.*)

BY WALTER SCOTT, ESQ.

"IN woeful wise my song shall rise,
My heart impels the strain;

* *i. e.* Small particles. Spenser uses the word for gravel.—M. OD.

Tears fit the song, which tells the wrong,
  Of gentle Barons slayn.
Fayr peace to gaine they fought in vayn;
  Their house to ruin gave,
And limb and life, to butcheryng knyfe,
  Our native land to save.

CHORUS.

"Now lowly lies the flower of pries,*
  That could so much of weir:†
Erle Montfort's scathe, and heavy death,
  Shall cost the world a tear.

"As I here say, upon Tuesdaye,
  The battle bold was done;
Each mounted knight, there fell in fight,
  For ayd of foot was none:
There wounds were felt, and blows were dealt,
  With brands that burnish'd be,
Sir Edward stoute, his numerous route,
  Have won the maisterie.
    Now lowly lies, &c.

"But, though he died, on Montfort's side
  The victorie remain'd;
Like Becket's fayth, the Erle's in deathe,
  The martyr's palm obtain'd;
That holy Saint would never graunt,
  The church should fall or slyde;
Like him, the Erle met deadly peril,
  And like him dauntless dyed.
    Now lowly lies, &c.

"The bold Sir Hugh Despencer true,
  The kingdom's Justice he,
Was dom'd to die unrighteouslye,
  By passynge crueltie;
And Sir Henry, the son was he
  To Leister's nobile lord,
With many moe, as ye shall know,
  Fell by Erle Gloster's sword.
    Now lowly lies, &c.

"He that dares dye, in standing by
  The country's peace and lawe,
To him the Saint the meed shall graunt
  Of conscience free from flawe.

---

* Price. † War.

Who suffers scathe, and faces death,
  To save the poor from wrong,
God speed his end, the poor man's friend,
  For suche we pray, and long!
          Now lowly lies, &c.

"His bosom here, a treasure dere.
  A sackclothe shirt, they founde;
The felons there full ruthless were
  Who stretched hym on the grounde.
More wrongs than be in butcherye,
  They did the knight who fell,
To wield his sword, and keep his worde,
  Who knew the way so well.
          Now lowly lies, &c.

"Pray as is meet, my brethern sweet,
  The maiden Mary's son,
The infant fair, our noble heir,
  In grace to guide him on.
I will not name the habit's* claym,
  Of that I will not saye;
But for Jesus' love, that sits above,
  For churchmen ever pray.
          Now lowly lies, &c.

"Seek not to see, of chivalrye,
  Or count, or baron bold;
Each gallant knight, and squire of might
  They all are bought and sold;
For loyaltie and veritie,
  They now are done awaye—
The losel vile may reign by guile,
  The fool by his foleye.
          Now lowly lies, &c.

"Sir Simon wight, that gallant knight,
  And his companye eche one,
To heaven above, and joye and love.
  And endless life, are gone.
May He on rood who bought our good,
  And God, their paine relieve,
Who, captive ta'en, are kept in chaine,
  And depe in dungeon grieve!

---

* The clerical habit is obviously alluded to; and it seems to be cautiously and obscurely hinted, that the church was endangered by the defence of De Montfort.—M. OD.

"Now lowly lies the flower of pries,
That could so much of weir;
Erle Montfort's scathe, and heavy death,
Shall cost the world a tear."*

On the whole, the really good songs of Ritson might be gathered into a single volume. His preliminary dissertation is pleasant enough, and might be retained with improvements. Another volume of additional songs might be collected, and then it would be tolerably complete. I should agree with Ritson as to the propriety of rejecting all political songs, for I think they should make a separate work, which is a desideratum in our literature. Songs of free-masonry also I should exclude, though I do not think with him (p. x.) that they would disgrace the collection, some of them being pretty good, but because they are not intelligible to the uninitiated. The only one in favour of which I should break my rule, that I recollect just now, is Burns's "Adieu, a heartwarm fond adieu, dear brethren of the mystic tie."

Some time or other, what I propose will be effected. Blackwood should publish it.—M. OD.

* It was the object of the translator to imitate, as literally as possible, the style of the original, even in its rudeness, abrupt transitions, and obscurity. Such being the particular request of Mr. Ritson, who supplied the old French of this ballad minstrelsy.—*Note by Sir Walter Scott.*

Lament for Lord Byron.*

Air — The Last Rose of Summer.

LAMENT for Lord Byron,
  In full flow of grief,
As a sept of Milesians
  Would mourn o'er their chief!
With the loud voice of weeping,
  With sorrow's deep tone,
We shall keen o'er our poet,
  "All faded and gone."

Though in far Missolunghi
  His body is laid;
Though the hands of the stranger
  His lone grave have made;
Though no foot from Old England
  Its surface will tread,
Nor the sun of Old England
  Shine over its head;

Yet, bard of the Corsair,
  High-spirited Childe;
Thou who sang'st of Lord Manfred
  The destiny wild!
Thou star, whose bright radiance
  Illumined our verse,
Our souls cross the blue seas,
  To mourn o'er thy hearse.

Thy faults and thy follies,
  Whatever they were,
Be their memory dispersed
  As the winds of the air;
No reproaches from me
  On thy course shall be thrown, —
Let the man who is sinless
  Uplift the first stone.

In thy vigor of manhood
  Small praise from my tongue

---

* Written immediately after Byron's death; sung by Odoherty at THE NOCTES; published in *Blackwood* for June, 1824.— M

Had thy fame or thy talents,
  Or merriment wrung;
For that Church, and that State, and
  That monarch I loved,
Which too oft thy hot censure
  Or rash laughter moved.

But I hoped in my bosom
  That moment would come,
When thy feelings would wander
  Again to their home.
For that soul, O lost Byron!
  In brillianter hours,
Must have turn'd to its country—
  Must still have been ours.

Now slumber, bright spirit!
  Thy body, in peace,
Sleeps with heroes and sages,
  And poets of Greece;
While thy soul in the tongue of
  Even greater than they,
Is embalm'd till the mountains
  And seas pass away.

Odoherty's Dirge.*

Oh! when I am departed and passed away,
Let's have no lamentations or sounds of dismay—
Meet together, kind lads, o'er a three-gallon bowl,
And so toast the repose of Odoherty's soul.
                Down, derry down.

If my darling girl pass, gently bid her come in,
To join the libation she'll think it no sin;
Though she choose a new sweetheart, and doff the black gown,
She'll remember me kindly when down—down—down—
                Down, derry down.

---

* Chanted by Odoherty, at THE NOCTES, and published in *Blackwood* for June, 1824.—M.

A Story without a Tail.*

CHAP. I.—HOW WE WENT TO DINE AT JACK GINGER'S.

So it was finally agreed upon that we should dine at Jack Ginger's chambers in the Temple, seated in a lofty story in Essex Court. There was, besides our host, Tom Meggot, Joe Macgillicuddy, Humpy Harlow, Bob Burke, Antony Harrison, and myself. As Jack Ginger had little coin and no credit, we contributed each our share to the dinner. He himself provided room, fire, candles, tables, chairs, tablecloth, napkins—no, not napkins; on second thoughts we did not bother ourselves with napkins—plates, dishes, knives, forks, spoons, (which he borrowed from the wig-maker,) tumblers, lemons, sugars, water, glasses, decanters—by the by, I am not sure that there were decanters—salt, pepper, vinegar, mustard, bread, butter, (plain and melted,) cheese, radishes, potatoes, and cookery. Tom Meggot was a cod's head and shoulders, and oysters to match—Joe Macgillicuddy, a boiled leg of pork, with peas-pudding—Humpy Harlow, a sirloin of beef roast, with horseradish—Bob Burke, a gallon of half-and-half, and four bottles of whiskey, of prime quality ("Potteen," wrote the whiskeyman, "I say, by Jupiter, but of which *many*-facture *He* alone knows")—Antony Harrison, half-a-dozen of Port, he having tick to that extent at some unfortunate wine-merchant's—and I supplied cigars *à discretion*, and a bottle of rum, which I borrowed from a West Indian friend of mine as I passed by. So that, on the whole, we were in no danger of suffering from any of the extremes of hunger and thirst for the course of that evening.

We met at five o'clock—*sharp*—and very sharp. Not a man was missing when the clock of the Inner Temple struck the last stroke. Jack Ginger had done every thing to admiration. Nothing could be more splendid than his turn-out. He had superintended the cooking himself of every individual dish with his own eyes—or rather eye—he having but one, the

* This story appeared in *Blackwood*, for April, 1834.—M.

other having been lost in a skirmish when he was midshipman on board a pirate in the Brazilian service. "Ah!" said Jack, often and often, "these were my honest days—Gad—did I ever think when I was a pirate that I was at the end to turn rogue, and study the law."—All was accurate to the utmost degree. The table-cloth, to be sure, was not exactly white, but it had been washed last week, and the collection of the plates was miscellaneous, exhibiting several of the choicest patterns of Delf. We were not of the silver-fork school of poetry, but steel is not to be despised. If the table was somewhat rickety, the inequality in the legs was supplied by clapping a volume of Vesey under the short one. As for the chairs—but why weary about details—chairs being made to be sat upon, it is sufficient to say that they answered their purposes, and whether they had backs or not—whether they were cane-bottomed, or hair bottomed, or rush bottomed, is nothing to the present enquiry.

Jack's habits of discipline made him punctual, and dinner was on the table in less than three minutes after five. Down we sate, hungry as hunters, and eager for the prey.

"Is there a parson in company?" said Jack Ginger, from the head of the table.

"No," responded I, from the foot.

"Then, thank God," said Jack, and proceeded, after this pious grace, to distribute the cod's head and shoulders to the hungry multitude.

CHAP. II.—HOW WE DINED AT JACK GINGER'S.

The history of that cod's head and shoulders would occupy but little space to write. Its flakes, like the snow flakes on a river, were for one moment bright, then gone for ever; it perished unpitiably. "Bring hither," said Jack, with a firm voice, "the leg of pork." It appeared, but soon to disappear again. Not a man of the company but showed his abhorrence of the Judaical practice of abstaining from the flesh of swine. Equally clear in a few moments was it that we were truly British in our devotion to beef. The sirloin was impartially destroyed on both sides, upper and under. Dire was the clatter of the knives, but deep the silence of the guests. Jerry Gallagher, Jack's valetde-chambre, footman, cook, clerk, shoeblack, aid-de-camp, scout, confidant, dun-chaser, bum-defyer, and many other offices *in commendam*, toiled like a hero. He covered himself with glory and gravy every moment. In a short time a vociferation arose for fluid, and the half-and-half—Whitebread quartered upon Chamyton—beautiful heraldry!—was inhaled with the most savage satisfaction.

"The pleasure of a glass of wine with you, Bob Burke," said Joe Macgillicuddy, wiping his mouth with the back of his hand.

"With pleasure, Joe," replied Bob.—"What wine do you choose? You may as well say port, for there is no other; but attention to manners always becomes a gentleman."

"Port, then, if you please," cried Joe, "as the ladies of Limerick say, when a man looks at them across the table."

"Hobnobbing wastes time," said Jack Ginger, laying down the pot out of which he had been drinking for the last few minutes; "and, besides, it is not customary now in genteel society—so pass the bottle about."

[I here pause in my narrative to state, on more accurate recollection, that we had not decanters; we drank from the black bottle, which Jack declared was according to the fashion of the continent.]

So the port was passed round, and declared to be superb. Antony Harrison received the unanimous applause of the company; and, if he did not blush at all the fine things that were said in his favour, it was because his countenance was of that peculiar hue that no addition of red could be visible upon it. A blush on Antony's face would be like gilding refined gold.

Whether cheese is prohibited or not in the higher circles of the West End, I cannot tell; but I know it was not prohibited in the very highest chambers of the Temple.

"It's double Gloucester," said Jack Ginger; "prime, bought at the corner—Heaven pay the cheesemonger, for I shan't—but, as he is a gentleman, I give you his health."

"I don't think," said Joe Macgillicuddy, "that I ought to demean myself to drink the health of a cheesemonger; but I'll not stop the bottle."

And, to do Joe justice, he did not. Then we attacked the

cheese, and in an incredibly short period we battered in a breach of an angle of 45 degrees, in a manner that would have done honour to any engineer that directed the guns at San Sebastian. The cheese, which on its first entry on the table presented the appearance of a plain circle, was soon made to exhibit a very different shape, as may be understood by the subjoined diagram:—

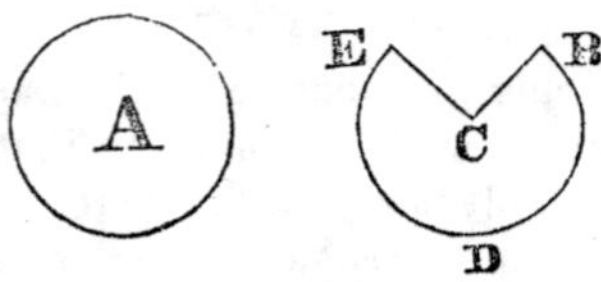

[A, original cheese; EBD, cheese after five minutes standing on the table; EBC, angle of 45°.]

With cheese came, and with cheese went, celery. It is unnecessary to repeat what a number of puns were made on that most pun-provoking of plants.

"Clear the decks," said Jack Ginger to Jerry Gallagher. "Gentlemen, I did not think of getting pastry, or puddings, or desserts, or ices, or jellies, or blancmange, or any think of the sort, for men of sense like you."

We all unanimously expressed our indignation at being supposed even for a moment guilty of any such weakness; but a general suspicion seemed to arise among us that a dram might not be rejected with the same marked scorn. Jack Ginger accordingly uncorked one of Bob Burke's bottles. Whop! went the cork, and the potteen soon was seen meandering round the table.

"For my part," said Antony Harrison, "I take this dram because I ate pork, and fear it might disagree with me."

"I take it," said Bob Burke, "chiefly by reason of the fish."

"I take it," said Joe Macgillicuddy, "because the day was warm, and it is very close in these chambers."

"I take it," said Tom Meggot, "because I have been very chilly all the day."

"I take it," said Humpy Harlow, "because it is such strange weather that one does not know what to do."

"I take it," said Jack Ginger, "because the rest of the company takes it."

"And I take it," said I winding up the conversation, "because I like a dram."

So we all took it for one reason or another—and there was an end of that.

"Be off, Jerry Gallagher," said Jack—"I give to you, your heirs and assigns, all that and those which remains in the pots of half-and-half—item for your own dinners what is left of the solids—and when you have pared the bones clean, you may give them to the poor. Charity covers a multitude of sins. Brush away like a shoeblack—and levant."

"Why, thin, God bless your honour," said Jerry Gallagher, "it's a small liggacy he would have that would dippind for his daily bread for what is left behind any of ye in the way of the drink—and this blessed hour there's not as much as would blind the left eye of a midge in one of them pots—and may it do you all good, if it a'n't the blessing of heaven to see you eating. By my sowl, he that has to pick a bone after you, won't be much troubled with the mate. Howsomever"—

"No more prate," said Jack Ginger. "Here's twopence for you to buy some beer—but, no," he continued, drawing his empty hand from that breeches-pocket into which he had most needlessly put it—"no," said he, "Jerry—get it on credit wherever you can, and bid them score it to me."

"If they will"—said Jerry.

"Shut the door," said Jack Ginger, in a peremptory tone, and Jerry retreated.

"That Jerry," said Jack, "is an uncommonly honest fellow, only he is the damndest rogue in London. But all this is wasting time—and time is life. Dinner is over, and the business of the evening is about to begin. So, bumpers, gentlemen, and get rid of this wine as fast as we can. Mr. Vice, look to your bottles."

And on this, Jack Ginger gave a bumper toast.

CHAP. III.—HOW WE CONVERSED AT JACK GINGER'S.

This being done, every man pulled in his chair close to the table, and prepared for serious action. It was plain, that we all, like Nelson's sailors at Trafalgar, felt called upon to do our duty. The wine circulated with considerable rapidity; and there was no flinching on the part of any individual of the company. It was quite needless for our president to remind us of the necessity of bumpers, or the impropriety of leaving heel-taps. We were all too well trained to require the admonition, or to fall into the error. On the other hand, the chance of any man obtaining more than his share in the round was infinitesimally small. The Sergeant himself, celebrated as he is, could not have succeeded in obtaining a glass more than his neighbours. Just to our friends, we were also just to ourselves; and a more rigid circle of philosophers never surrounded a board.

The wine was really good, and its merits did not appear the less striking from the fact that we were not habitually wine-bibbers, our devotion generally being paid to fluids more potent or more heavy than the juice of the grape, and it soon excited our powers of conversation. Heavens! what a flow of soul! More good things were said in Jack Ginger's chambers that evening, than in the Houses of Lords and Commons in a month. We talked of every thing—politics, literature, the fine arts, drama, high life, low life, the opera, the cockpit—every thing from the heavens above to the bells in St. James's Street. There was not an article in a morning, evening, or weekly paper for the week before, which we did not repeat. It was clear that our knowledge of things in general was drawn in a vast degree from these recondite sources. In politics we were harmonious—we were Tories to a man, and defied the Radicals of all classes, ranks, and conditions. We deplored the ruin of our country, and breathed a sigh over the depression of the agricultural interest. We gave it as our opinion that Don Miguel should be King of Portugal—and that Don Carlos, if he had the pluck of the most nameless of insects, could ascend the throne of Spain. We pitched Louis Philippe to that place which is never mentioned to ears polite, and drank the health of the Duchess of Berri. Opinions differed somewhat about the Emperor of Russia—some thinking that he was too hard on the Poles—others gently blaming him for not squeezing them much tighter. Antony Harrison, who had seen the Grand Duke Constantine, when he was campaigning, spoke with tears in his eyes of that illustrious prince—declaring him, with an oath, to have been a d—d good fellow. As for Leopold, we unanimously voted him to be a scurvy hound; and Joe Macgillicuddy was pleased to say something complimentary of the Prince of Orange, which would have, no doubt, much gratified his Royal Highness, if it had been communicated to him, but I fear it never reached his ears.

Turning to domestic policy—we gave it to the Whigs in high style. If Lord Grey had been within hearing, he must have instantly resigned—he never could have resisted the thunders of our eloquence. All the hundred and one Greys would have been forgotten—he must have sunk before us. Had Brougham been there, he would have been converted to Toryism long before he could have got to the state of tipsyfication in which he sometimes addresses the House of Lords. There was not a topic left undiscussed. With one hand we arranged Ireland—with another put the Colonies in order. Catholic Emancipation was severely condemned, and Bob Burke gave the glorious, pious, and immortal memory. The vote of £20,000,000 to the greasy blacks was much reprobated, and the opening of the China trade declared a humbug. We spoke, in fact, articles that would have made the fortunes of half a hundred magazines, if the editors of those works would have had the perspicacity to insert them—and this we did with such ease to ourselves, that we never for a moment stopped the circulation of the bottle, which kept running on its round rejoicing, while we settled the affairs of the nation.

Then Antony Harrison told us all his campaigns in the Peninsula, and that capital story how he bilked the tavernkeeper in Portsmouth. Jack Ginger entertained us with an account of his transactions in the Brazils; and as Jack's imagination far outruns his attention to matters of fact, we had them considerably improved. Bob Burke gave us all the particulars of his duel with Ensign Brady of the 48th, and how he hit him on the waistcoat pocket, which, fortunately for the Ensign, contained a five shilling piece, (how he got it was never accounted for,) which saved him from grim death. From Joe Macgillicuddy we heard multifarious narrations of steeple-chases in Tipperary, and of his hunting with the Blazers in Galway. Tom Meggot expatiated on his college adventures in Edinburgh, which he maintained to be a far superior city to London, and repeated sundry witty sayings of the advocates in the Parliament House, who seem to be gentlemen of great facetiousness. As for me, I emptied out all Joe Miller on the company; and if old Joe could have burst his cerements in the neighbouring churchyard of St. Clement Danes, he would have been infinitely delighted with the reception which the contents of his agreeable miscellany met with. To tell the truth, my jokes were not more known to my companions than their stories were to me. Harrison's campaigns, Ginger's cruises, Burke's duel, Macgillicuddy's steeple-chases, and Tom Meggot's rows in the High Street, had been told over and over—so often indeed, that the several relators begin to believe that there is some foundation in fact for the wonders which they are continually repeating.

"I perceive this is the last bottle of port," said Jack Ginger; "so I suppose that there cannot be any harm in drinking bad luck to Antony Harrison's wine-merchant, who did not make it the dozen."

"Yes," said Harrison, "the skinflint thief would not stand more than the half, for which he merits the most infinite certainty of non-payment."

(You may depend upon it that Harrison was as good as his word, and treated the man of bottles according to his deserts.)

The port was gathered to its fathers, and potteen reigned in its stead. A most interesting discussion took place as to what was to be done with it. No doubt, indeed, existed as to its final destination; but various opinions were broached as to the manner in which it was to make its way to its appointed end. Some wished that every man should make for himself; but that Jack Ginger strenuously opposed, because he said it would render the drinking unsteady. The company divided into two parties on the great questions of bowl or jug. The Irishmen maintained the cause of the latter. Tom Meggot, who had been reared in Glasgow, and Jack Ginger, who did not forget his sailor propensities, were in favour of the former. Much erudition was displayed on both sides, and I believe I may safely say, that every topic that either learning or experience could suggest, was exhausted. At length we called for a division, when there appeared—

For the jug,	*For the bowl,*
Bob Burke	Jack Ginger
Joe Macgillicuddy	Humpy Harlow
Antony Harrison	Tom Meggot.
Myself.	

Majority 1, in favour of the jug. I was principally moved to vote as I did, because I deferred to the Irishmen, as persons who were best acquainted with the nature of potteen; and Antony Harrison was on the same side from former recollections of his quarterings in Ireland. Humpy Harlow said, that he made it a point always to side with the man of the house.

"It is settled," said Jack Ginger, "and, as we said of Parliamentary Reform, though we opposed it, it is now law, and must be obeyed. I'll clear away these marines, and do you, Bob Burke, make the punch. I think you will find the lemons good—the sugar superb—and the water of the Temple has been famous for centuries."

"And I'll back the potteen against any that ever came from the Island of Saints," said Bob, proceeding to his duty, which all who have the honour of his acquaintance will admit him to be well qualified to perform. He made it in a couple of big blue water-jugs, observing that making punch in small jugs was nearly as great a bother as ladling from a bowl—and as he tossed the steamy fluid from jug to jug to mix it kindly, he sang the pathetic ballad of Hugger-mofane.

"I wish I had a red herring's tail," &c.

It was an agreeable picture of continued use and ornament, and reminded us strongly of the Abyssinian maid of the Platonic poetry of Coleridge.

CHAP. IV.—HOW HUMPY HARLOW BROKE SILENCE AT JACK GINGER'S.

THE punch being made, and the jug revolving, the conversation continued as before. But it may have been observed that I have not taken any notice of the share which one of the party, Humpy Harlow, took in it. The fact is, that he had been silent for almost all the evening, being outblazed and overborne by the brilliancy of the conversation of his companions. We were all acknowledged wits in our respective lines, whereas he had not been endowed with the same talents. How he came among us I forget; nor did any of us know well who or what he was. Some maintained he was a drysalter in the City; others surmised that he might be a pawnbroker at the West End. Certain it is that he had some money, which perhaps might have recommended him to us, for there was not a man in the company who had not occasionally borrowed from him a sum, too trifling, in general, to permit any of us to think of repaying it. He was a broken-backed little fellow, as vain of his person as a peacock, and accordingly we always called him Humpy Harlow, with the spirit of gentlemanlike candour which characterized all our conversation. With a kind feeling towards him, we in general permitted him to pay our bills for us whenever we dined together at tavern or chop-house, merely to gratify the little fellow's vanity, which I have already hinted to be excessive.

He had this evening made many ineffectual attempts to shine, but was at last obliged to content himself with opening his mouth for the admission, not for the utterance, of good things. He was evidently unhappy, and a rightly-constituted mind could not avoid pitying his condition. As jug, however, succeeded jug, he began to recover his self-possession; and it was clear, about eleven o'clock, when the fourth bottle of potteen was converting into punch, that he had a desire to speak. We had been for some time busily employed in smoking cigars, when, all on a sudden, a shrill and sharp voice was heard from the midst of a cloud, exclaiming, in a high treble key,—

"*Humphries told me*"—

We all puffed our Havannahs with the utmost silence, as if we were so many Sachems at a palaver, listening to the narration which issued from the misty tabernacle in which Humpy Harlow was enveloped. He unfolded a tale of wonderous length, which we never interrupted. No sound was heard save that of the voice of Harlow, narrating the story which had to him been confided by the unknown Humphries, or the gentle gliding of the jug, an occasional tingle of a glass, and the soft suspiration of the cigar. On moved the story in its length, breadth, and thickness, for Harlow gave it to us in its full dimensions. He abated it not a jot. The firmness which we displayed was unequalled since the battle of Waterloo. We sat with determined countenances, exhaling smoke and inhaling punch, while the voice still rolled onward. At last Harlow came to an end; and a Babel of conversation burst from lips in which it had been so long imprisoned. Harlow looked proud of his feat, and obtained the thanks of the company, grateful that he had come to a conclusion. How we finished the potteen—converted my bottle of rum into a bowl, (for here Jack Ginger prevailed)—how Jerry Gallagher, by superhuman exertions, succeeded in raising a couple of hundred of oysters for supper—how the company separated each to get to his domicile as he could—how I found, in the morning, my personal liberty outraged by the hands of that unconstitutional band of gens-d'-armes created for the direct purposes of tyranny, and held up to the indignation of all England by the weekly eloquence of the Despatch—how I was introduced to the attention of a magistrate, and recorded in the diurnal page of the newspaper—all this must be left to other historians to narrate.

CHAP. V.—WHAT STORY IT WAS THAT HUMPY HARLOW TOLD AT JACK GINGER'S.

At three o'clock on the day after the dinner, Antony Harrison and I found ourself eating bread and cheese—part of *the* cheese—at Jack Ginger's. We recapitulated the events of the preceding evening, and expressed ourselves highly gratified with the entertainment. Most of the good things we had said were revived, served up again, and laughed at once more. We were perfectly satisfied with the parts which we had respectively played, and talked ourselves into excessive good humour. All on a sudden, Jack Ginger's countenance clouded. He was evidently puzzled; and sat for a moment in thoughtful silence. We asked him, with Oriental simplicity of sense, "Why art thou troubled?" and till a moment he answered—

"What *was* the story which Humpy Harlow told us about eleven o'clock last night, just as Bob Burke was teeming the last jug?"

"It began," said I, "with '*Humphries told me.*'"

"It did," said Antony Harrison, cutting a deep incision into the cheese.

"I know it did," said Jack Ginger; "but what was it that Humphries had told him? I cannot recollect it if I was to be made Lord Chancellor."

Antony Harrison and I mused in silence, and racked our brains, but to no purpose. On the tablet of our memories no trace had been engraved, and the tale of Humphries, as reported by Harlow, was as if it were not, so far as we were concerned.

While we were in this perplexity, Joe Macgillicuddy and Bob Burke entered the room.

"We have been just taking a hair of the same dog," said Joe. "It was a pleasant party we had last night. Do you know what Bob and I have been talking of for the last half hour?"

We professed our inability to conjecture.

"Why, then," continued Joe, "it was about the story that Harlow told last night."

"The story begins with '*Humphries told me,*'" said Bob.

"And," proceeded Joe, "for our lives we cannot recollect what it was."

"Wonderful!" we all exclaimed. "How inscrutable are the movements of the human mind!"

And we proceeded to reflect on the frailty of our memories, moralizing in a strain that would have done honour to Dr. Johnson.

"Perhaps," said I, "Tom Meggot may recollect it."

Idle hope! dispersed to the winds almost as soon as it was formed. For the words had scarcely passed "the bulwark of my teeth," when Tom appeared, looking excessively bloodshot in the eye. On enquiry, it turned out that he, like the rest of us, remembered only the cabalistic words which introduced the tale, but of the tale itself, nothing.

Tom had been educated in Edinburgh, and was strongly attached to what he calls *metapheesicks;* and, accordingly, after rubbing his forehead, he exclaimed—

"This is a psychological curiosity, which deserves to be developed. I happen to have half a sovereign about me," (an assertion, which, I may remark, in passing, excited considerable surprise in his audience,) "and I'll ask Harlow to dine with me at the Rainbow. I'll get the story out of the humpy rascal—and no mistake.

We acquiesced in the propriety of this proceeding; and Antony Harrison, observing that he happened by chance to be disengaged, hooked himself on Tom, who seemed to have a sort of national antipathy to such a ceremony, with a talent and alacrity that proved him to be a veteran warrior, or what, in common parlance, is called an old soldier.

Tom succeeded in getting Harlow to dinner, and Harrison succeeded in making him pay the bill, to the great relief of Meggot's half-sovereign, and they parted at an early hour in the morning. The two Irishmen and myself were at Ginger's shortly after breakfast; we had been part occupied in tossing halfpence to decide which of us was to send out for ale, when —Harrison and Meggot appeared. There was conscious confusion written in their countenances. "Did Humpy Harlow tell you *that* story?" we all exclaimed at once.

"It cannot be denied that he did," said Meggot. "Precisely as the clock struck eleven, he commenced with '*Humphries told me*' "—

"Well—and what then?"

"Why, there it is," said Antony Harrison, "may I be drummed out if I can recollect another word."

"Nor I," said Meggot.

The strangeness of this singular adventure made a deep impression on us all. We were sunk in silence for some minutes, during which Jerry Gallagher made his appearance with the ale, which I omitted to mention had been lost by Joe Macgillicuddy. We sipped that British beverage, much abstracted in deep thought. The thing appeared to us perfectly inscrutable. At last I said "This never will do—we cannot exist much longer in this atmosphere of doubt and uncertainty. We must have it out of Harlow to-night, or there is an end of all the grounds and degrees of belief, opinion, and assent. I have credit," said I, "at the widow's, in St. Martin's Lane. Suppose we all meet there to-night, and get Harlow there if we can?"

"That I can do," said Antony Harrison, "for I quartered myself to dine with him to-day, as I saw him home, poor little fellow, last night. I promise that he figures at the widow's to-night at nine o'clock."

So we separated. At nine every man of the party was in St. Martin's Lane, seated in the little back parlour; and Harrison was as good as his word, for he brought Harlow with him. He ordered a sumptuous supper of mutton kidneys, interspersed with sausages, and set to. At eleven o'clock precisely, the eye of Harlow brightened, and putting his pipe down, he commenced with a shrill voice—

"*Humphries told me*"

"Aye," said we all, with one accord, "here it is—now we shall have it—take care of it this time."

"What do you mean?" said Humpy Harlow, performing that feat, which by the illustrious Mr. John Reeve is called "flaring up."

"Nothing," we replied, "nothing, but we are anxious to hear that story."

"I understand you," said our brokenbacked friend. "I now recollect that I did tell it once or so before in your company, but I shall not be a butt any longer for you or any body else."

"Don't be in a passion, Humpy," said Jack Ginger.

"Sir," replied Harlow, "I hate nicknames—it is a mark of a low mind to use them—and as I see I am brought here only to be insulted, I shall not trouble you any longer with my company."

Saying this, the little man seized his hat and umbrella, and strode out of the room.

"His back is up," said Joe Macgillicuddy, "and there's no use of trying to get it down. I am sorry he is gone, because I should have made him pay for another round."

But he is gone, not to return again—and the story remains unknown. Yes, as undiscoverable as the hieroglyphical writings of the ancient Egyptians. It exists, to be sure, in the breast of Harlow; but there it is buried, never to emerge into the light of day. It is lost to the world—and means of recovering it, there, in my opinion, exist none. The world must go on without it, and states and empires must continue to flourish and to fade without the knowledge of what it was that Humphries told Harlow. Such is the inevitable course of events.

For my part, I shall be satisfied with what I have done in drawing up this accurate and authentic narrative, if I can seriously impress on the minds of my readers the perishable nature of mundane affairs—if I can make them reflect that memory itself, the noblest, perhaps the characteristic, quality of the human mind, will decay, even while other faculties exist—and that in the words of a celebrated Lord of Trade and Plantations, of the name of John Locke, "we may be like the tombs to which we are hastening, where, though the brass and marble remain, yet the imagery is defaced, and the inscription is blotted out for ever."

Bob Burke's Duel with Ensign Brady of the Forty-Eighth.*

CHAP. I.—HOW BOB WAS IN LOVE WITH MISS THEODOSIA MACNAMARA.

"WHEN the 48th were quartered in Mallow,† I was there on a visit to one of the Purcells, who abound in that part of the world, and, being some sixteen or seventeen years younger than I am now, thought I might as well fall in love with Miss Theodora Macnamara. She was a fine grown girl, full of flesh and blood, rose five foot nine at least when shod, had many excellent points, and stepped out slappingly upon her pasterns. She was somewhat of a roarer, it must be admitted, for you could hear her from one end of the Walk‡ to the other; and I am told, that as she has grown somewhat aged, she shows symptoms of vice, but I knew nothing of the latter, and did not mind the former, because I never had a fancy for your nimini-pimini young ladies, with their mouths squeezed into the shape and dimensions of a needle's eye. I always suspect such damsels as having a very portentous design against mankind in general.

"She was at Mallow for the sake of the Spa, it being understood that she was consumptive—though I'll answer for it, her lungs were not touched; and I never saw any signs of consumption about her, except at meal times, when her consumption was undoubtedly great. However, her mother, a very nice middle-aged woman—she was of the O'Regans of the West, and a perfect lady in her manners, with a very remarkable red nose, which she attributed to a cold, which had settled in that part, and which cold she was always endeavoring to cure with various balsamic preparations taken inwardly,—maintained that her poor chicken, as she called her, was very delicate, and required

* This novelette was published in *Blackwood* for May, 1834.—M.

† Mallow is a market-town in the county of Cork, sending one member to Parliament. The population is about 7,000. It formerly was much visited for its mineral spa, believed to be efficacious in consumption.—M.

‡ The Spa-Walk is the principal promenade in Mallow.—M.

the air and water of Mallow to cure her. Theodosia,* (she was so named after some of the Limerick family,) or, as we generally called her, Dosy, was rather of a sanguine complexion, with hair that might be styled auburn, but which usually received another name. Her nose was turned up, as they say was that of Cleopatra; and her mouth, which was never idle, being always employed in eating, drinking, shouting, or laughing, was of considerable dimensions. Her eyes were piercers, with a slight tendency to a cast; and her complexion was equal to a footman's plush breeches, or the first tinge of the bloom of morning bursting through a summer cloud, or what else verse-making men are fond of saying. I remember a young man who was in love with her writing a song about her, in which there was one or other of the similes above mentioned, I forget which. The verses were said to be very clever, as no doubt they were; but I do not recollect them, never being able to remember poetry. Dosy's mother used to say that it was a hectic flush—if so, it was a very permanent flush, for it never left her cheeks for a moment, and, had it not belonged to a young lady in a galloping consumption, would have done honour to a dairy-maid.

"Pardon these details, gentlemen," said Bob Burke, sighing, "but one always thinks of the first loves. Tom Moore says, that 'there's nothing half so sweet in life as young love's dram;' and talking of that, if there's anything left in the brandy bottle, hand it over to me. Here's to the days gone by, they will never come again. Dear Dosy, you and I had some fun together. I see her now with her red hair escaping from under her hat, in a pea-green habit, a stiff cutting whip in her hand, licking it into Tom the Devil, a black horse, that would have carried a sixteen stoner over a six-foot wall, following Will Wrixon's hounds† at the rate of fifteen miles an hour, and singing out, 'Go it, my trumps.' These are the recollections that bring tears in a man's eyes."

* Lady Theodosia Perry, daughter of the late Earl of Limerick, was first wife of Mr. Spring Rice, now Lord Monteagle.—M.

† Mr. Wrixon, an eminent sporting character residing near Mallow, was uncle of Sir W. W. Becher, who married Miss O'Neill, the celebrated Irish actress.—M.

There were none visible in Bob's, but as he here finished his dram, it is perhaps a convenient opportunity for concluding a chapter.

CHAP. II.—HOW ENSIGN BRADY WENT TO DRINK TEA WITH MISS THEODOSIA MACNAMARA.

"THE day of that hunt was the very day that led to my duel with Brady. He was a long, straddling, waddle-mouthed chap, who had no more notion of riding a hunt than a rhinoceros. He was mounted on a showy-enough-looking mare, which had been nerved by Rodolphus Bootiman, the horse doctor,* and though 'a good 'un to look at, was a rum 'un to go;' and before she was nerved, all the work had been taken out of her by long Lanty Philpot, who sold her to Brady after dinner for fifty pounds, she being not worth twenty in her best day, and Brady giving his bill at three months for the fifty. My friend the ensign was no judge of a horse, and the event showed that my cousin Lanty was no judge of a bill—not a cross of the fifty having been paid from that day to this, and it is out of the question now, it being long past the statute of limitations, to say nothing of Brady having since twice taken the benefit of the Act. So both parties jockeyed one another, having that pleasure, which must do them instead of profit.

"She was a bay chestnut, and nothing would do Brady but he must run her at a little gap which Miss Dosy was going to clear, in order to show his gallantry and agility; and certainly I must do to him the credit to say that he did get his mare *on* the gap, which was no small feat, but there she broke down, and off went Brady, neck and crop, into as fine a pool of stagnant green mud as you would ever wish to see. He was ducked regularly in it, and he came out, if not in the jacket, yet in the colours, of the Rifle Brigade,† looking rueful enough at his misfortune, as you may suppose. But he had not much time to

* Bootiman was a veterinary surgeon, who kept livery stables in George's Street, Cork, and was as knowing in horseflesh as if he hailed from Yorkshire.—M.

† The Rifle Brigade, in the British Army, is attired in dark green.—M.

think of the figure he cut, for before he could well get up, who should come right slap over him but Miss Dosy herself upon Tom the Devil, having cleared the gap and a yard beyond the pool in fine style. Brady ducked, and escaped the horse, a little fresh daubing being of less consequence than the knocking out of his brains, if he had any; but he did not escape a smart rap from a stone which one of Tom's heels flung back with such unlucky accuracy, as to hit Brady right in the mouth, knocking out one of his eye teeth, (which, I do not recollect.) Brady clapped his hand to his mouth, and bawled, as any man might do in such a case, so loud, that Miss Dosy checked Tom for a minute, to turn round, and there she saw him making the most horrid faces in the world, his mouth streaming blood, and himself painted green from head to foot, with as pretty a coat of shining slime as was to be found in the province of Munster. 'That's the gentleman you just leapt over, Miss Dosy,' said I, for I had joined her, 'and he seems to be in some confusion.'—'I am sorry,' said she, 'Bob, that I should have in any way offended him or any other gentleman, by leaping over him, but I can't wait now. Take him my compliments, and tell him I should be happy to see him at tea at six o'clock this evening, in a different suit.' Off she went, and I rode back with her message, (by which means I was thrown out,) and would you believe it, he had the ill manners to say 'the h——;' but I shall not repeat what he said. It was impolite to the last degree, not to say profane, but perhaps he may be somewhat excused under his peculiar circumstances. There is no knowing what even Job himself might have said, immediately after having been thrown off his horse into a green pool, with his eye-tooth knocked out, his mouth full of mud and blood, on being asked to a tea-party.

"He—Brady, not Job—went, nevertheless—for, on our return to Miss Dosy's lodgings, we found a triangular note, beautifully perfumed, expressing his gratitude for her kind invitation, and telling her not to think of the slight accident which had occurred. How it happened, he added, he could not conceive, his mare never having broken down with him before—which was true enough, as that was the first day he ever mounted her—and she having been bought by himself at a sale of the Earl of

Darlington's horses last year, for two hundred guineas.* She was a great favourite, he went on to say, with the Earl, who often rode her, and ran at Doncaster by the name of Miss Russell. All this latter part of the note was not quite so true, but then, it must be admitted, that when we talk about horses, we are not tied down to be exact to a letter. If we were, God help Tattersal's !

"To tea, accordingly, the ensign came at six, wiped clean, and in a different set-out altogether from what he appeared in on emerging from the ditch. He was, to make use of a phrase introduced from the ancient Latin into the modern Greek, togged up in the most approved style of his Majesty's forty-eighth foot. Bright was the scarlet of his coat—deep the blue of his facings."

"I beg your pardon," said Antony Harrison, here interrupting the speaker; "the forty-eighth are not royals, and you ought to know that no regiment but those which are royal sport blue facings. I remember, once upon a time, in a coffeeshop, detecting a very smart fellow, who wrote some clever things in a Magazine published in Edinburgh by one Blackwood, under the character of a military man, not to be any thing of the kind, by his talking about ensigns in the fusileers—all the world knowing that in the fusileers there are no ensigns, but in their place second lieutenants. Let me set you right there, Bob; the facings your friend Brady exhibited to the wandering gaze of the Mallow tea-table must have been buff—pale buff."

"Buff, black, blue, brown, yellow, Pompadour, brick-dust, no matter what they were," continued Burke, in no wise pleased by the interruption, "they were as bright as they could be made, and so was all the lace, and other traps which I shall not specify more minutely, as I am in presence of so sharp a critic. He was, in fact, in full dress—as you know is done in country quarters—and being not a bad plan and elevation of a man, looked well enough. Miss Dosy, I perceived, had not been perfectly ignorant of the rank and condition of the gentleman over whom she had leaped, for she was dressed in her purple satin body and white skirt, which she always put on when she wished to

* The Earl of Darlington, much celebrated on the Turf, some thirty years ago, was created Duke of Cleveland in 1833.—M.

be irresistible, and her hair was suffered to flow in long ringlets down her fair neck — and, by Jupiter, it was fair as a swan's, and as majestic too — and no mistake. Yes! Dosy Macnamara looked divine that evening.

"Never mind! Tea was brought in by Mary Keefe, and it was just as all other *teas* have been and will be. Do not, however, confound it with the wafer-sliced and hot-watered abominations which are inflicted, perhaps justly, on the wretched individuals who are guilty of haunting *soirees* and *conversaziones* in this good and bad city of London. The tea was congou or souchong, or some other of these Chinese affairs, for any thing I know to the contrary; for, having dined at the house, I was mixing my fifth tumbler when tea was brought in, and Mrs. Macnamara begged me not to disturb myself; and she being a lady for whom I had a great respect, I complied with her desire; but there was a potato-cake, an inch thick and two feet in diameter, which Mrs. Macnamara informed me in a whisper was made by Dosy after the hunt.

"'Poor chicken,' she said, 'if she had the strength, she has the willingness; but she is so delicate. If you saw her handling the potatoes today.'

"'Madam,' said I, looking tender, and putting my hand on my heart, 'I wish I was a potato!'

CHAP. III. — HOW ENSIGN BRADY ASTONISHED THE NATIVES AT MISS THEODOSIA MACNAMARA'S.

"I THOUGHT this was an uncommonly pathetic wish, after the manner of the Persian poet Hafiz, but it was scarcely out of my mouth, when Ensign Brady, taking a cup of tea from Miss Dosy's hand, looking upon me with an air of infinite condescension, declared that I must be the happiest of men, as my wish was granted before it was made. I was preparing to answer, but Miss Dosy laughed so loud, that I had not time, and my only resource was to swallow what I had just made. The ensign followed up his victory without mercy.

"'Talking of potatoes, Miss Theodosia,' said he, looking at me, 'puts me in mind of truffles. Do you know this most exquisite cake of yours much resembles a *gateau aux truffes?* By

Gad! how Colonel Thornton, Sir Harry Millicent, Lord Mortgageshire, and that desperate fellow, the Honourable and Reverend Dick Sellenger,* and I used to tuck in truffles, when we were quartered in Paris. Mortgageshire—an uncommon droll fellow; I used to call his Lordship Morty—he called me Brad—we were on such terms; and we used to live together in the Rue de la Paix, that beautiful street close by the Place Vendôme, where there's the pillar. You have been at Paris, Miss Macnamara?' asked the ensign, filling his mouth with a half-pound bite of the potato-cake at the same moment.

"Dosy confessed that she had never travelled into any foreign parts except the kingdom of Kerry; and on the same question being repeated to me, I was obliged to admit that I was in a similar predicament. Brady was triumphant.

"'It is a loss to any man,' said he, 'not to have been in Paris. I know that city well, and so I ought; but I did many naughty things there.'

"'O fie!' said Mrs. Macnamara.

"'O, madam,' continued Brady, 'the fact is, that the Paris ladies were rather too fond of us English. When I say English, I mean Scotch and Irish as well; but, nevertheless, I think Irishmen had more good luck than the natives of the other two islands.'

"'In my geography book,' said Miss Dosy, 'it is put down only as one island, consisting of England, capital London, on the Thames, in the south; and Scotland, capital Edinburgh, on the Forth, in the north; population'——

"'Gad! you are right,' said Brady—'perfectly right, Miss Macnamara. I see you are quite a blue. But, as I was saying, it is scarce possible for a good-looking young English officer to escape the French ladies. And then I played rather deep—on the whole, however, I think I may say I won. Mortgageshire and I broke Frascati's one night—we won a hundred thousand francs at rouge, and fifty-four thousand at roulette. You would have thought the croupiers would have fainted; they tore their hair with vexation. The money, however, soon went again—we could

* *Sellenger* is the fashionable pronunciation of St. Leger. Thus, at Oxford, St. Mary's Hall is spoken of as *Simmery 'All*.—M.

not keep it. As for wine, you have it cheap there, and of a quality which you cannot get in England. At Very's, for example, I drank chambertine — it is a kind of claret — for three francs two sous a bottle, which was, beyond all comparison, far superior to what I drank a couple of months ago at the Duke of Devonshire's, though his Grace prides himself on that very wine, and sent to a particular bin for a favourite specimen, when I observed to him I had tasted better in Paris. Out of politeness, I pretended to approve of his Grace's choice; but I give you my honour — only I would not wish it to reach his Grace's ears — it was not to be compared to what I had at Very's for a moment.'

"So flowed on Brady for a couple of hours. The Tooleries, as he thought proper to call them; the Louvre, with its pictures, the removal of which he deplored as a matter of taste, assuring us that he had used all his influence with the Emperor of Russia and the Duke of Wellington to prevent it, but in vain; the Boulevards, the opera, the theatres, the Champs Elysées, the Montagnes Russes — every thing, in short, about Paris, was depicted to the astonished mind of Miss Dosy. Then came London — where he belonged to I do not know how many clubs — and cut a most distinguished figure in the fashionable world. He was of the Prince Regent's set, and assured us, on his hon our, that there was never any thing so ill-founded as the stories afloat to the discredit of that illustrious person. But on what happened at Carlton-house, he felt obliged to keep silence, the Prince being remarkably strict in exacting a promise from every gentleman whom he admitted to his table, not to divulge any thing that occurred there — a violation of which promise was the cause of the exclusion of Brummell. As for the Princess of Wales, he would rather not say any thing.

"And so forth. Now, in those days of my innocence, I believed these stories as gospel, hating the fellow all the while from the bottom of my heart, as I saw that he made a deep impression on Dosy, who sate in open-mouthed wonder, swallowing them down as a common-councilman swallows turtle. But times are changed. I have seen Paris and London since, and I believe I knew both villages as well as most men, and the deuce a word of truth did Brady tell in his whole narrative. In Paris, when not in quarters, (he had joined some six or eight months after Waterloo,) he lived *au cinquantième* in a dog-hole in the Rue Git-le-Cœur, (a street at what I may call the Surrey side of Paris,) among carters and other such folk; and in London I discovered that his principal domicile was in one of the courts now demolished to make room for the fine new gimcrackery at Charing Cross; it was in Round Court, at a pieman's of the name of Dudfield."

"Dick Dudfield?" said Jack Ginger, "I knew the man well—a most particular friend of mine. He was a duffer besides being a pieman, and was transported some years ago. He is now a flourishing merchant in Australasia, and will, I suppose, in due time be grandfather to a member of Congress."

"There it was that Brady lived then," continued Bob Burke, "when he was hob-nobbing with Georgius Quartus, and dancing at Almack's with Lady Elizabeth Conynghame. Faith, the nearest approach he ever made to royalty was when he was put into the King's own Bench, where he sojourned many a long day. What an ass I was to believe a word of such stuff! but, nevertheless, it goes down with the rustics to the present minute. I sometimes sport a duke or so myself, when I find myself among yokels, and I rise vastly in estimation by so doing. What do we come to London or Paris for, but to get some touch of knowing how to do things properly? It would be devilish hard, I think, for Ensign Brady, or Ensign Brady's master, to do me now-a-days by flamming off titles of high life."

The company did no more than justice to Mr. Burke's experience, by unanimously admitting that such a feat was all but impossible.

"I was," he went on, "a good deal annoyed at my inferiority, and I could not help seeing that Miss Dosy was making comparisons that were rather odious, as she glanced from the gay uniform of the Ensign on my habiliments, which having been perpetrated by a Mallow tailor with a hatchet, or pitchfork, or pickaxe, or some such tool, did not stand the scrutiny to advantage. I was, I think, a better-looking fellow than Brady. Well, well—laugh if you like. I am no beauty, I know; but then, consider that what I am talking of was sixteen years ago, and more; and a man does not stand the battering I have gone through for these sixteen years with impunity. Do you call the thirty or forty thousand tumblers of punch, in all its varieties, that I have since imbibed, nothing?"

"Yes," said Jack Ginger, with a sigh, "there was a song we used to sing on board the Brimstone, when cruising about the Spanish main—

"'If Mars leaves his scars, jolly Bacchus as well
Sets his trace on the face, which a toper will tell;
But which a more merry campaign has pursued,
The shedder of wine or the shedder of blood?'

I forget the rest of it. Poor Ned Nixon! It was he who made that song—he was afterwards bit in two by a shark, having tumbled overboard in the cool of the evening, one fine summer day, off Port Royal."

"Well, at all events," said Burke, continuing his narrative, "I thought I was a better-looking fellow than my rival, and was fretted at being sung down. I resolved to outstay him—and, though he sate long enough, I, who was more at home, contrived to remain after him, but it was only to hear him extolled.

"'A very nice young man,' said Mrs. Macnamara.

"'An extreme nice young man,' responded Miss Theodosia.

"'A perfect gentleman in his manners; he puts me quite in mind of my uncle, the late Jerry O'Regan,' observed Mrs. Macnamara.

"'Quite the gentleman in every particular,' ejaculated Miss Theodosia.

"'He has seen a great deal of the world for so young a man,' remarked Mrs. Macnamara.

"'He has mixed in the best society, too,' cried Miss Theodosia.

"'It is a great advantage to a young man to travel,' quoth Mrs. Macnamara.

"'And a very great disadvantage to a young man to be always sticking at home,' chimed in Miss Theodosia, looking at me; 'it shuts them out from all chances of the elegance which we have just seen displayed by Ensign Brady of the 48th foot.'

"'For my part,' said I, 'I do not think him such an elegant fellow at all. Do you remember, Dosy Macnamara, how he looked when he got up out of the green puddle to-day?'"

"'Mr. Burke,' said she, 'that was an accident that might happen any man. You were thrown yourself this day week, on clearing Jack Falvey's wall—so you need not reflect on Mr. Brady.'

"'If I was,' said I, 'it was as fine a leap as ever was made; and I was on my mare in half a shake afterwards. Bob Buller of Ballythomas, or Jack Prendergast, or Fergus O'Connor, could not have rode it better. And you too'—

"'Well,' said she, 'I am not going to dispute with you. I am sleepy, and must get to bed.'

"'Do, poor chicken,' said Mrs. Macnamara, soothingly; 'and, Bob, my dear, I wish it was in your power to go travel, and see the Booleries and the Tooleyvards, and the rest, and then you might be, in course of time, as genteel as Ensign Brady.'

"'Heigho!' said Miss Dosy, ejecting a sigh. 'Travel, Bob, travel.'

"'I will,' said I, at once, and left the house in the most abrupt manner, after consigning Ensign Brady to the particular attention of Tisiphone, Alecto, and Magæra, all compressed into one emphatic monosyllable.

CHAP. IV.—HOW BOB BURKE, AFTER AN INTERVIEW WITH BARNEY PULVERTAFT, ASCERTAINED THAT HE WAS DESPERATELY IN LOVE WITH MISS THEODOSIA MACNAMARA.

"On leaving Dosy's lodgings, I began to consult the state of my heart. Am I really, said I, so much in love, as to lose my temper, if this prating ensign should carry off the lady? I was much puzzled to resolve the question. I walked up and down the Spa-Walk, whiffing a cigar, for a quarter of an hour, without being able to come to a decision. At last, just as the cigar was out, my eye caught a light in the window of Barney Pulvertaft, the attorney—old Six-and-Eightpence, as we used to call him. I knew he was the confidential agent of the Macnamaras; and as he had carried on sixteen lawsuits for my father, I thought I had a claim to learn something about the affairs of Miss Dosy. I understood she was an heiress, but had never, until now, thought of enquiring into the precise amount of her expectances. Seeing that the old fellow was up, I determined to step over, and found him in the middle of law-papers, although it was then rather late, with a pot-bellied jug, of the bee-hive pattern, by his side, full of punch — or rather, I should say, half-full; for Six-and-Eightpence had not been idle. His snuff-coloured wig was cocked on one side of his head — his old velveteen breeches open at the knee — his cravat off — his shirt unbuttoned — his stockings half down his lean legs — his feet in a pair of worsted slippers. The old fellow was, in short, relaxed for the night, but he had his pen in his hand.

"'I am only filling copies of *capiases*, Bob,' said he; 'light and pleasant work, which does not distress one in an evening. There are a few of your friends booked here. What has brought you to me so late to-night? — but your father's son is always welcome. Aye, there were few men like your father — never stagged in a lawsuit in his life — saw it always out to the end — drove it from court to court; — if he was beat, why, so much the worse, but he never fretted — if he won, faith! he squeezed the opposite party well. Aye, he was a good-hearted, honest, straightforward man. I wish I had a hundred such clients. So here's his memory any how.'

"Six-and-Eightpence had a good right to give the toast, as what constituted the excellence of my father in his eyes had moved most of the good acres of Ballyburke out of the family into the hands of the lawyers; but from filial duty I complied with the attorney's request — the more readily, because I well knew, from long experience, that his skill in punch-making was unimpeachable. So we talked about my father's old lawsuits, and I got Barney into excellent humour, by letting him tell me of the great skill and infinite adroitness which he had displayed upon a multiplicity of occasions. It was not, however, until we were deep in the second jug, and Six-and-Eightpence was beginning to show symptoms of being *cut*, that I ventured to introduce the subject of my visit. I did it as cautiously as I could, but the old fellow soon found out my drift.

"'No,' hiccuped he—'Bob—'twont—'twont do. Close as green—green wax. Never te-tell profess-profess-professional secrets. Know her expec—hiccup—tances to a ten-ten-penny. So you are after—after—her? Ah, Bo-bob? She'll be a ca-catch—let not a wo-word from me. No—never. Bar-ney Pepulverta-taft is game to the last. Never be-betrayed ye-your father. God rest his soul—he was a wo-worthy man.'

"On this recollection of the merits of my sainted sire, the at torney wept; and in spite of all his professional determinations, whether the potency of the fluid or the memory of the deceased acted upon him, I got at the facts. Dosy had not more than a couple of hundred pounds in the world—her mother's property was an annuity which expired with herself; but her uncle, by the father's side, Mick Macnamara of Kawleash, had an estate of at least five hundred a-year, which, in case of his dying without issue, was to come to her—besides a power of money saved; Mick being one who, to use the elegant phraseology of my friend the attorney, would skin a flea for the sake of selling the hide. All this money, ten thousand pounds, or something equally musical, would in all probability go to Miss Dosy—the £500 a-year was hers by entail. Now, as her uncle was eighty-four years old, unmarried, and in the last stage of the palsy, it was a thing so sure as the bank, that Miss Dosy was a very rich heiress indeed.

"'So—so,' said Six-and-Eightpence—'this—this—is strictly confidle-confid-con-fiddledential. Do—do not say a word about it. I ought not to have to-told it—but, you do-dog, you wheedled it out of me. Da-dang it, I co-could not ref-fuse your father's so-son. You are very like him—as I sa-saw him sitting many a ti-time in that cha-chair. But you nev-never will have his spu-spunk in a sho-shoot (suit). There, the lands of Arry-arry-arry-bally-bally-be-beg-clock-clough-macde-de-duagh—confound the wo-word—of Arryballybegcloughmacduagh, the finest be-bog in the co-country—are ye-yours—but you haven't spu-spunk to go into Cha-chancery for it, like your worthy fa-father, Go-god rest his soul. Blow out that se-sec-ond ca-candle, Bo-bob, for I hate waste.'

"'There's but one in the room, Barney,' said I.

"'You mean to say,' hiccuped he, 'that I am te-te-tipsy? Well, well, ye-young fe-fellows, well, I am their je-joke. However, as the je-jug is out, you most be je-jogging. Early to bed, and early to rise, is the way to be——. However, le-lend me your arm up the sta-stairs, for they are very slip-slippery to-night.'

"I conducted the attorney to his bedchamber, and safely stowed him into bed, while he kept stammering forth praises on my worthy father, and upbraiding me with want of spunk in not carrying on a Chancery-suit began by him some twelve years before, for a couple of hundred acres of bog, the value of which would scarcely have amounted to the price of the parchment expended on it. Having performed this duty, I proceeded homewards, labouring under a variety of sensations.

"How delicious is the feeling of love, when it first takes full possession of a youthful bosom! Before its balmy influence vanish all selfish thoughts—all grovelling notions. Pure and sublimated, the soul looks forward to objects beyond self, and merges all ideas of personal identity in aspirations of the felicity to be derived from the being adored. A thrill of rapture pervades the breast—an intense but bland flame permeates every vein—throbs in every pulse. Oh, blissful period! brief in duration, but crowded with thoughts of happiness never to recur again! As I gained the Walk, the moon was high and bright in heaven, pouring a flood of mild light over the trees. The stars shone with sapphire lustre in the cloudless sky—not a breeze disturbed the deep serene. I was alone. I thought of my love—of what else could I think? What I had just heard had kindled my passion for the divine Theodosia into a quenchless blaze. Yes, I exclaimed aloud, I *do* love her. Such an angel does not exist on the earth. What charms! What innocence! What horsewomanship! Five hundred a-year certain! Ten thousand pounds in perspective! I'll repurchase the lands of Ballyburke—I'll rebuild the hunting-lodge in the Galtees—I'll keep a pack of hounds, and live a sporting life. Oh, dear, divine Theodosia, how I *do* adore you! I'll shoot that Brady, and no mistake. How dare he interfere where my affections are so irrevocably fixed?

"Such were my musings. Alas! how we are changed as we progress through the world! That breast becomes arid, which once was open to every impression of the tender passion. The rattle of the dice-box beats out of the head the rattle of the quiver of Cupid—and the shuffling of the cards renders the rustling of his wings inaudible. The necessity of looking after a tablecloth supersedes that of looking after a petticoat, and we more willingly make an assignation with a mutton-chop, than with an angel in female form. The bonds of love are exchanged for those of the conveyancer—bills take the place of billets, and we do not protest, but are protested against, by a three-and-sixpenny notary. Such are the melancholy effects of age. I knew them not then. I continued to muse full of sweet thoughts, until gradually the moon faded from the sky—the stars went out—and all was darkness. Morning succeeded to night, and, on awaking, I found, that owing to the forgetfulness in which the thoughts of the fair Theodosia had plunged me, I had selected the bottom step of old Barney Pulvertaft's door as my couch, and was awakened from repose in consequence of his servant-maid (one Norry Mulcaky) having emptied the contents of her—washing tub, over my slumbering person.

CHAP. V.—HOW BOB BURKE, AFTER CONSULTATION WITH WOODEN LEG WADDY, FOUGHT THE DUEL WITH ENSIGN BRADY FOR THE SAKE OF MISS THEODOSIA MACNAMARA.

"At night I had fallen asleep fierce in the determination of exterminating Brady; but with the morrow, cool reflection came—made probably cooler by the aspersion I had suffered. How could I fight him, when he had never given me the slightest affront? To be sure, picking a quarrel is not hard, thank God, in any part of Ireland; but unless I was quick about it, he might get so deep into the good graces of Dosy, who was as flammable as tinder, that even my shooting him might not be of any practical advantage to myself. Then, besides, he might shoot me; and, in fact, I was not by any means so determined in the affair at seven o'clock in the morning as I was at twelve o'clock at night. I got home, however, dressed, shaved, &c. and turned out. 'I think,' said I to myself, 'the best thing I can do, is to go and consult Wooden-leg Waddy; and, as he is an early man, I shall catch him now.' The thought was no sooner formed than executed; and in less than five minutes I was walking with Wooden-leg Waddy in his garden, at the back of his house, by the banks of the Blackwater.

"Waddy had been in the Hundred-and-First, and had seen much service in that distinguished corps."

"I remember it well during the war," said Antony Harrison; "we used to call it the Hungry-and-Worst;—but it did its duty on a pinch nevertheless."

"No matter," continued Burke; "Waddy had served a good deal, and lost his leg somehow, for which he had a pension besides his half pay, and he lived in ease and affluence among the Bucks of Mallow. He was a great hand at settling and arranging duels, being what we generally call in Ireland a *judgmatical* sort of man—a word which, I think, might be introduced with advantage into the English vocabulary. When I called on him, he was smoking his meershaum, as he walked up and down his garden in an old undress coat, and a fur cap on his head. I bade him good morning; to which salutation he answered by a nod, and a more prolonged whiff.

"'I want to speak to you, Wooden-leg,' said I, 'on a matter which nearly concerns me.' On which, I received another nod, and another whiff in reply.

"'The fact is,' said I, 'that there is an Ensign Brady of the 48th quartered here, with whom I have some reason to be angry, and I am thinking of calling him out. I have come to ask your advice whether I should do so or not. He has deeply injured me, by interfering between me and the girl of my affections. What ought I to do in such a case?'

"'Fight him—by all means,' said Wooden-leg Waddy.

"'But the difficulty is this—he has offered me no affront, direct or indirect—we have no quarrel whatever—and he has not paid any addresses to the lady. He and I have scarcely been in contact at all. I do not see how I can manage it immediately with any propriety. What then can I do now?'

"'Do not fight him, by any means,' said Wooden-leg Waddy.

"'Still these are the facts of the case. He, whether intentionally or not, is coming between me and my mistress, which is doing me an injury perfectly equal to the grossest insult. How should I act?'

"'Fight him, by all means,' said Wooden-leg Waddy.

"'But then I fear if I were to call him out on a groundless quarrel, or one which would appear to be such, that I should lose the good graces of the lady, and be laughed at by my friends, or set down as a quarrelsome and dangerous companion.'

"'Do not fight him then, by any means,' said Wooden-leg Waddy.

"'Yet as he is a military man, he must know enough of the etiquette of these affairs to feel perfectly confident that he has affronted me; and the opinion of a military man, standing, as of course he does, in the rank and position of a gentleman, could not, I think, be overlooked without disgrace.'

"'Fight him by all means,' said Wooden-leg Waddy.

"'But then, talking of gentlemen, I own he is in an officer of the 48th, but his father is a fish-tackle seller in John Street, Kilkenny, who keeps a three-halfpenny shop, where you may buy every thing, from a cheese to a cheese-toaster, from a felt hat to a pair of brogues, from a pound of brown soap to a yard of huckaback towels. He got his commission by his father's retiring from the Ormonde interest,* and acting as whipper-in to the sham freeholders from Castlecomer; and I am, as you know, of the best blood of the Burkes—straight from the De Burgos † themselves—and when I think of that, I really do not like to meet this Mr. Brady.'

"'Do not fight him, by any means,' said Wooden-leg Waddy.

"This advice of your friend Waddy to you," said Tom Meggot, interrupting Burke, "much resembles that which Pantagruel gave Panurge on the subject of his marriage, as I heard a friend of mine, Percy, of Gray's Inn, reading to me the other day."

"I do not know the people you speak of," continued Bob, "but such was the advice which Waddy gave me.

* The Marquis of Ormonde resided at the Castle, Kilkenny, and had considerable interest in the parliamentary borough.—M.

† Ulick John de Burgh (*alias* Burke), Marquis of Clenricarde, claims to be representative of the De Burgo family, of the county of Galway.—M.

"'Why," said I, 'Wooden-leg, my friend, this is like playing battledore and shuttlecock; what is knocked forward with one hand is knocked back with the other. Come, tell me what I ought to do."

"'Well,' said Wooden-leg, taking the meershaum out of his mouth, '*in dubiis suspice*, &c. Let us decide it by tossing a halfpenny. If it comes down *head*, you fight—if *harp*, you do not. Nothing can be fairer.'

"I assented.

"'Which,' said he, 'is it to be—two out of three, as at Newmarket, or the first toss to decide?'

"'Sudden death,' said I, 'and there will soon be an end of it.'

"'Up went the halfpenny, and we looked with anxious eyes for its descent, when, unluckily, it stuck in a gooseberry bush.

"'I don't like that,' said Wooden-leg Waddy; 'for it's a token of bad luck. But here goes again.'

"Again the copper soared to the sky, and down it came—*head.*

"'I wish you joy, my friend,' said Waddy; 'you are to fight. That was my opinion all along, though I did not like to commit myself. I can lend you a pair of the most beautiful duelling pistols ever put into a man's hand—Wogden's, I swear. The last time they were out, they shot Joe Brown of Mount Badger as dead as Harry the Eighth.'

"'Will you be my second?' said I.

"'Why, no,' replied Wooden-leg, 'I cannot; for I am bound over by a rascally magistrate to keep the peace, because I barely broke the head of a blackguard bailiff, who came here to serve a writ on a friend of mine, with one of my spare legs. But I can get you a second at once. My nephew, Major Mug, has just come to me on a few days' visit, and, as he is quite idle, it will give him some amusement to be your second. Look up at his bedroom—you see he is shaving himself.'

"In a short time the Major made his appearance, dressed with a most military accuracy of costume. There was not a speck of dust on his well-brushed blue surtout—not a vestige of hair, except the regulation whiskers, on his closely-shaven countenance. His hat was brushed to the most glossy perfection—his boots shone in the jetty glow of Day and Martin. There was scarcely an ounce of flesh on his hard and weather-beaten face, and, as he stood rigidly upright, you would have sworn that every sinew and muscle of his body was as stiff as whipcord. He saluted us in military style, and was soon put in possession of the case. Wooden-leg Waddy insinuated that there were hardly as yet grounds for a duel.

"'I differ,' said Major Mug, 'decidedly—the grounds are ample. I never saw a clearer case in my life, and I have been principal or second in seven-and-twenty. If I collect your story rightly, Mr. Burke, he gave you an abrupt answer in the field, which was highly derogatory to the lady in question, and impertinently rude to yourself?'

"'He certainly,' said I, 'gave me what we call a short answer; but I did not notice it at the time, and he has since made friends with the young lady.'

"'It matters nothing,' observed Major Mug, 'what you may think, or she may think. The business is now in *my* hands, and I must see you through it. The first thing to be done is to write him a letter. Send out for paper—let it be gilt-edged, Waddy—that we may do the thing genteelly. I'll dictate, Mr. Burke, if you please.'

"And so he did. As well as I can recollect, the note was as follows:—

"'Spa Walk, Mallow, June 3, 18—

"'Eight o'clock in the morning.

"'SIR,—A desire for harmony and peace, which has at all times actuated my conduct, prevented me, yesterday, from asking you the meaning of the short and contemptuous message which you commissioned me to deliver to a certain young lady of our acquaintance, whose name I do not choose to drag into a correspondence. But now that there is no danger of its disturbing any one, I must say that in your desiring me to tell that young lady she might consider herself as d—d, you were guilty of conduct highly unbecoming of an officer and a gentleman, and subversive of the discipline of the hunt. I have the honour to be, sir, your most obedient humble servant,

"'ROBERT BURKE.

"'P. S.—This note will be delivered to you by my friend, Major Mug, of the 3d West Indian; and you will, I trust, see the propriety of referring him to another gentleman without further delay.'

"'That, I think, is neat,' said the Major. 'Now, seal it with wax, Mr. Burke, with wax—and let the seal be your arms. That's right. Now, direct it.'

"'Ensign Brady?'

"'No—no—the right thing would be, "Mr. Brady, Ensign, 48th foot," but custom allows "Esquire." That will do.—"Thady Brady, Esq., Ensign, 48th Foot, Barracks, Mallow." He shall have it in less than a quarter of an hour.'

"The Major was as good as his word, and in about half an hour he brought back the result of his mission. The Ensign, he told us, was extremely reluctant to fight, and wanted to be off, on the ground that he had meant no offence, did not even remember having used the expression, and offered to ask the lady if she conceived for a moment he had any idea of saying any thing but what was complimentary to her.

"'In fact,' said the Major, 'he at first plumply refused to fight; but I soon brought him to reason. 'Sir,' said I, 'you either consent to fight, or refuse to fight. In the first case, the thing is settled to hand, and we are not called upon to enquire if there was an affront or not—in the second case, your refusal to comply with a gentleman's request is, of itself, an offence for which he has a right to call you out. Put it, then, on any grounds, you must fight him. It is perfectly indifferent to me what the grounds may be; and I have only to request the name of your friend, as I too much respect the coat you wear, to think that there can be any other alternative.' This brought the chap to his senses, and he referred me to Captain Codd, of his own regiment, at which I felt much pleased, because Codd is an intimate friend of my own, he and I having fought a duel three years ago in Falmouth, in which I lost the top of this little finger, and he his left whisker. It was a near touch. He is as honourable a man as ever paced a ground; and I am sure that he will no more let his man off the field until business is done, than I would myself.'

"'I own,' continued Burke, 'I did not half relish this announcement of the firm purpose of our seconds; but I was in for it, and could not get back. I sometimes thought Dosy a dear purchase at such an expense; but it was no use to grumble. Major Mug was sorry to say that there was a review to take place immediately, at which the Ensign must attend, and it was impossible for him to meet me until the evening; 'but,' added he, 'at this time of the year it can be of no great consequence. There will be plenty of light till nine, but I have fixed *seven*. In the meantime, you may as well divert yourself with a little pistol practice, but do it on the sly, as, if they were shabby enough to have a trial, it would not tell well before the jury.

"Promising to take a quiet chop with me at five, the Major retired, leaving me not quite contented with the state of affairs. I sat down, and wrote a letter to my cousin, Phil Purdon of Kanturk, telling him what I was about, and giving directions what was to be done in the case of any fatal event. I communicated to him the whole story — deplored my unhappy fate in being thus cut off in the flower of my youth — left him three pair of buckskin breeches — and repented my sins. This letter I immediately packed off by a special messenger, and then began half-a-dozen others, of various styles of tenderness and sentimentality, to be delivered after my melancholy decease. The day went off fast enough, I assure you; and at five the Major, and Wooden-leg Waddy, arrived in high spirits.

"'Here, my boy,' said Waddy, handing me the pistols, 'here are the flutes; and pretty music, I can tell you, they make.'

"'As for dinner,' said Major Mug, 'I do not much care; but, Mr. Burke, I hope it is ready, as I am rather hungry. We must dine lightly, however, and drink not much. If we come off with flying colours, we may crack a bottle together by and by; in case you shoot Brady, I have every thing arranged for our keeping out of the way until the thing blows over — if he shoot you, I'll see you buried. Of course, you would not recommend any thing so ungenteel as a prosecution. No. I'll take care it shall all appear in the papers, and announce that Robert Burke, Esq., met his death with becoming fortitude, assuring the unhappy survivor that he heartily forgave him, and wished him health and happiness.'

"'I must tell you,' said Wooden-leg Waddy, 'it's all over Mallow, and the whole town will be on the ground to see it. Miss Dosy knows of it, and is quite delighted—she says she will certainly marry the survivor. I spoke to the magistrate to keep out of the way, and he promised, that though it deprived him of a great pleasure, he would go and dine five miles off—and know nothing about it. But here comes dinner. Let us be jolly.'

"I cannot say that I played on that day as brilliant a part with the knife and fork as I usually do, and did not sympathize much in the speculations of my guests, who pushed the bottle about with great energy, recommending me, however, to refrain. At last, the Major looked at his watch, which he had kept lying on the table before him from the beginning of dinner—started up—clapped me on the shoulder, and declaring it only wanted six minutes and thirty-five seconds of the time, hurried me off to the scene of action—a field close by the Castle.*

"There certainly was a miscellaneous assemblage of the inhabitants of Mallow, all anxious to see the duel. They had pitted us like game-cocks, and bets were freely taken as to the chances of our killing one another, and the particular spots. One betted on my being hit in the jaw, another was so kind as to lay the odds on my knee. A tolerably general opinion appeared to prevail that one or other of us was to be killed; and much good-humoured joking took place among them, while they were deciding which. As I was double the thickness of my antagonist, I was clearly the favorite for being shot; and I heard one fellow near me say, 'Three to two on Burke, that he's shot first—I bet in ten-pennies.'

"Brady and Codd soon appeared, and the preliminaries were arranged with much punctilio between our seconds, who mutually

* The Castle is the residence of Sir C. D. O. Jephson Norreys, M. P. for the town of Mallow. The family name is Jephson, (changed to Norreys in 1838,) and the family who own the Manor of Mallow, are descendants from Sir John Jephson who, in the time of James I., married the heiress of Sir John Norreys, President of Munster.—M.

and loudly extolled each other's gentlemanlike mode of doing business. Brady could scarcely stand with fright, and I confess that I did not feel quite as Hector of Troy, or the Seven Champions of Christendom, are reported to have done on similar occasions. At last the ground was measured—the pistols handed to the principals—the handkerchief dropped—whiz! went the bullet within an inch of my ear—and crack! went mine exactly on Ensign Brady's waistcoat pocket. By an unaccountable accident, there was a five-shilling piece in that very pocket, and the ball glanced away, while Brady doubled himself down, uttering a loud howl that might be heard half a mile off. The crowd was so attentive as to give a huzza for my success.

"Codd ran up to his principal, who was writhing as if he had ten thousand colics, and soon ascertained that no harm was done.

"'What do you propose,' said he to my second—'What do you propose to do, Major?'

"'As there is neither blood drawn nor bone broken,' said the Major, 'I think that shot goes for nothing.'

"'I agree with you,' said Captain Codd.

"'If your party will apologize,' said Major Mug, I'll take my man off the ground.'

"'Certainly,' said Captain Codd, 'you are quite right, Major, in asking the apology, but you know that it is my duty to refuse it.'

"'You are correct, Captain,' said the Major; 'I then formally require that Ensign Brady apologize to Mr. Burke.'

"'I as formally refuse it,' said Captain Codd.

"'We must have another shot, then,' said the Major.

"'Another shot, by all means,' said the Captain.

"'Captain Codd,' said the Major, 'you have shown yourself in this, as in every transaction of your life, a perfect gentleman.'

"'He who would dare to say,' replied the Captain, 'that Major Mug is not among the most gentlemanlike men in the service, would speak what is untrue.'

"Our seconds bowed, took a pinch of snuff together, and proceeded to load the pistols. Neither Brady nor I was particularly pleased at these complimentary speeches of the gentlemen, and, I am sure, had we been left to ourselves, would have declined the second shot. As it was, it appeared inevitable.

"Just, however, as the process of loading was completing, there appeared on the ground my cousin Phil Purdon, rattling in on his black mare as hard as he could lick. When he came in sight he bawled out,—

"'I want to speak to the plaintiff in this action—I mean, to one of the parties in this duel. I want to speak to you, Bob Burke.'

"'The thing is impossible, sir,' said Major Mug.

"'Perfectly impossible, sir,' said Captain Codd.

"'Possible or impossible is nothing to the question,' shouted Purdon; 'Bob, I *must* speak to you.'

"'It is contrary to all regulation,' said the Major.

"'Quite contrary,' said the Captain.

"Phil, however, persisted, and approached me. 'Are you fighting about Dosy Mac?' said he to me in a whisper.

"'Yes,' I replied.

"'And she is to marry the survivor, I understand?'

"'So I am told,' said I.

"'Back out, Bob, then; back out, at the risk of a hunt. Old Mick Macnamara is married.'

"'Married!' I exclaimed.

"'Poz,' said he. 'I drew the articles myself. He married his housemaid, a girl of eighteen; and,'—here he whispered.

"'What,' I cried, 'six months!'

"'Six months,' said he, 'and no mistake.'

"'Ensign Brady,' said I, immediately coming forward, 'there has been a strange misconception in this business. I here declare, in presence of this honourable company, that you have acted throughout like a man of honour, and a gentleman; and you leave the ground without a stain on your character.'

"Brady hopped three feet off the ground with joy at the unexpected deliverance. He forgot all etiquette, and came forward to shake me by the hand.

"'My dear Burke,' said he 'it must have been a mistake: let us swear eternal friendship.'

"'For ever,' said, 'I resign you Miss Theodosia.'

"'You are too generous,' he said, 'but I cannot abuse your generosity.'

"'It is unprecedented conduct,' growled Major Mug. 'I'll never be second to a *Pekin* again.'

"'*My* principal leaves the ground with honour,' said Captain Codd, looking melancholy nevertheless.

"'Humph!' grunted Wooden-leg Waddy, lighting his meerschaum.

"The crowd dispersed much displeased, and I fear my reputation for valour did not rise among them. I went off with Purdon to finish a jug at Carmichael's, and Brady swaggered off to Miss Dosy's. His renown for valour won her heart. It cannot be denied that I sunk deeply in her opinion. On that very evening Brady broke his love, and was accepted. Mrs. Mac. opposed, but the red-coat prevailed.

"'He may rise to be a general,' said Dosy, 'and be a knight, and then I will be Lady Brady.'

"'Or if my father should be made an earl, angelic Theodosia, you would be Lady Thady Brady,' said the ensign.

"'Beautiful prospect!' cried Dosy; 'Lady Thady Brady! What a harmonious sound!'

"But why dally over the detail of my unfortunate loves? Dosy and the ensign were married before the accident which had befallen her uncle was discovered; and, if they were not happy, why, then you and I may. They have had eleven children, and, I understand, he now keeps a comfortable eating-house close by Cumberland basin in Bristol. Such was my duel with ensign Brady of the 48th."

"Your fighting with Brady puts me in mind, that the finest duel I ever saw," said Joe MacGillycuddy, "was between a butcher and bulldog, in the Diamond of Derry."

"I am obliged to you for your comparison," said Burke, "but I think it is now high time for dinner, and your beautiful story will keep. Has any body the least idea where dinner is to be raised?"

To this no answer was returned, and we all began to reflect with the utmost intensity.

Drink.

WHEN Panurge and his fellows, as Rab'lais will tell us,*
Set out on a sail to the ends of the earth,
And jollily cruising, carousing, and boozing,
To the oracle came in a full tide of mirth,
Pray what was its answer? come tell if you can, sir;
'Twas an answer most splendid and sage, as I think;
For sans any delaying, it summ'd up by saying,
The whole duty of man is one syllable — "DRINK."

O bottle mirific! advice beatific!
A response more celestial sure never was known;
I speak for myself, I prefer it to Delphi,
Though Apollo himself on that rock fixed his throne;
The foplings of fashion may still talk their trash on,
And declare that the custom of toping should sink;
A fig for such asses, I stick to my glasses,
And swear that no fashion shall stint me in drink.

And now in full measure I toast you with pleasure,
The warrior — †
— the poet — ‡
— the statesman — §
— and sage; ||
Whose benign constellation illumines the nation,
And sheds lively lustre all over the age;

* See Rabelais' Pantagruel, Livre V. chap, xliv. After arriving at the oracle of the holy bottle, and asking its advice, "de la sacrée bouteille yssit ung bruit tel que font les abeilles naissantes de la chair dung jeune taureau occiz et accoustre selon l'art et invention d'Aristeus; ou tel que faict une guarot desbandant l'arbaleste, ou, en esté, une forte pluye soubdainement tumblant. Lors feut ouy ce mot, TRINQ," which Bacbue the priestess' son interprets to be a panomphean, signifying Drink. — C. N. [Maginn was very fond of Rabelais, and once said that he thought the stories he told in Pantagruel were repeated in his early life to boon companions, and written down by him, in advanced years, rather to amuse himself than for fame. He (Maginn) had found that all the authorities cited in the trial chamber were correct and genuine. He believed, also, that Shakspere must have been a close student of Rabelais, and that the first scene in "The Tempest" proved this; also, that Father John was Rabelais' pet character, and that with which he took most pains. There was no imitating Rabelais. — M.]

† Odoherty. ‡ Hogg. § Timothy Tickler. || North

Long, long may its brightness, in glory and lightness,
Shine clear as the day-star on morning's sweet brink!
May their sway ne'er diminish! and therefore I finish,
By proposing the health of the four whom I drink.*

Crambambulee.†

CRAMBAMBULEE!—all the world over,
Thou'rt mother's milk to Germans true—Tra li ra.
No cure like thee can sage discover
For colic, love, or devils blue—Tra li ra.
Blow hot or cold, from morn to night,
My dream is still my soul's delight,
Cram-bam-bim-bam-bu-lee!—Crambambulee!

Hungry and chill'd with bivouacking,
We rise ere song of earliest bird—Tra li ra.
Cannon and drums our ears are cracking,
And saddle, boot, and blade's the word—Tra li ra.
"Vite en l'avant," our bugle blows,
A flying gulp and off it goes,
Cram-bam-bim-bam-bu-lee!—Crambambulee!

Victory's ours, off speed despatches,
Hourra! The luck for once is mine—Tra li ra.
Food comes by morsels, sleep by snatches,
No time, by Jove, to wash or dine—Tra li ra.
From post to post my pipe I cram,
Full gallop smoke, and suck my dram.
Cram-bam-bim-bam-bu-lee!—Crambambulee

When I'm the peer of kings and kaisers,
An order of my own I'll found—Tra li ra.
Down goes our gage to all despisers,
Our motto through the world shall sound—Tra li ra.
"Toujours fidele et sans souci,
C'est l'ordre de Crambambulee!"
Cram-bam-bim-bam-bu-lee!—Crambambulee!

---

* From *Blackwood* for September, 1825, sang at THE NOCTES.—M.
† From *Blackwood* for December, 1825, sang at THE NOCTES.—M.

Twenty-one Maxims to Marry by.*

> "To be thus, is nothing;
> But to be *safely* thus—!"
>
> SHAKSPERE.

I NEVER knew a good fellow, in all my life, that was not, some way or other, the dupe of women. One man is an ass unconsciously; another, with his eyes open: but all, that are good for any thing, are saddled and bridled in some way, and at some time or other.

If a good fellow drinks—your best perhaps won't drink very much now—but, if he does drink, ten to one, it is because he is out of humour with some woman. If he writes, what can he write about, but woman? If he games, why is it, but to get money to lavish upon her? For all his courage, ardour, wit, vanity, good-temper, and all other good qualities that he possesses, woman keeps an open market, and can engross them wholly! Why, then, after we have abused women—which we all of us do—and found out that they are no more to be trusted than fresh-caught monkeys—which the best of us are very likely to do;—after all, what does it come to but this—that they are the devil's plagues of our lives—and we *must* have them?

For, if you are "five-and-twenty, or thereabouts," and good for any thing, you'll certainly become *attached* to some woman; and—you'll find I'm right, so take warning in time—depend upon it, it had better be to an honest one. It's Cockney taste, lads, nasty, paltry, Bond-street stuff—to be seen driving about in a cabriolet with the mistress of half the town. And, for the attachment, never flatter yourselves that you are certain to get "tired" of any woman with whom you constantly associate. Depend upon it, you are a great deal more likely to become very inextricably fond of her. Kick it all out of doors, the stale trash, that men are naturally "indifferent" to their wives. How

* The Maxims to Marry by, which contain good sense, close observation, and sharp truth, appeared in *Blackwood* for May, 1826. They were particularly "Addressed to single gentlemen."—M.

the deuce should a fine woman be the worse for being one's wife? And are there not five hundred good reasons—to every body but a puppy—why she must be the better? Then, as you must all of you be martyred, suffer in respectable company. MARRY! boys—it's a danger; but, though it is a danger, it is the best. It is a danger! I always feel thankful when a man is hanged for killing his wife; because I should not choose to kill a wife of my own—and yet the crying of the "dying speech"—"for the barbarous and inhuman murder!" &c. &c.—is a sort of warning to her—as one rat, losing his tail in the rat-trap, frightens the whole granary-full that are left. But, though marriage is a danger, nevertheless, hazard it. Between evils, boys!—you know the proverb?—choose the least. Marry, I say, all and each of you! Take wives; and take them in good time, that "your names may be long in the land." And then, seeing that you could, one and all of you, have wives—comes the question, how you should go about to get them?

Then, in the first place, I shall assume, that he who reads this paper and marries, marries for a wife. Because, if he wants a "fortune" to boot, or a "place," or to be allied (being plebeian) to a "titled family," the case is out of my *métier;* he had better apply to an attorney at once. Don't make these things indispensable, any of you, if you can help it.. For the fortune, a hundred to one—when you get it—if it does not over-ride you with "settlements," and "trusts," and whole oceans of that sort of impertinence, which every proper man should keep clear of. No woman ought to be *able* to hold property independent of her husband. And, if that is not the law, all I can say is, that it ought to be so. Then, for the "Place—it's very well to have a place, where you can get one—but it must be the very devil to have the donor eternally, all your life afterwards, reminding you how you came by it. And, for the "Titled family," why, shut the book this minute, and don't have the impudence to read another line that I write, if you wouldn't quoit a brother-in-law that was "right honourable," with one impetus from Charing-Cross to Whitechapel, just as soon as a kinsman that was a clerk in the Victualling-office—provided he deserved it, or you took it into your head that it was convenient to do it! Besides, a nice woman is worth all the money in the Bank. What would would you do with it, after you had it, but give it all for one? Please your taste, my children; and so that you get an honest woman, and a pleasing one, to the devil send the remainder. And then to guide your choice, take the following maxims: Those who have brains, will perceive their value at a glance; and such as are thick-headed can read them three or four times over. And let such not be too hastily disheartened; for it is part of wit; (and of this Magazine,) to bear with dulness; and one comfort is, when you have at least beaten anything into a skull of density, the very devil himself can hardly ever get it out again. "We write on brass," as somebody or other observes, and somewhere, "less easily than in water; but the impression, once made, endures for ever."

Maxim First.

Now, in making marriage, as in making love—and indeed in making most other things—the beginning it is that is the difficulty. But the French proverb about beginnings—"C'est le premier pas qui *coute*"—goes more literally to the arrangement of marriage; as our English well illustrates the condition of love,—"The first step over, the rest is easy." Because, in the marrying affair, it is particularly, the "first step" that "costs"—as to your cost you will find, if that step happens to go the wrong way. And most men, when they go about the business of wedlock, owing to some strange delusion, begin the affair at the wrong end. They take a fancy to the white arms—(sometimes only to the kid gloves)—or to the neat ancles of a peculiar school girl; and conclude, from these premises, that she is just the very woman of the world to scold a houseful of servants, and to bring up a dozen children! This is a convenient deduction, but not always a safe one. Pleasant—like Dr. Maculloch's deductions in his Political Economy—but generally wrong. "Let not the creaking of shoes, nor the rustling of silk, betray thy poor heart," as Shakspere says, &c. &c. "to woman!"—Implying thereby, that red sashes and lace flounces are but as things transitory; and that she who puts ornaments of gold and silver upon her own head, may be a "crown to her husband"

—and yet not exactly such a "crown" as King Solomon meant a virtuous woman should be. He that has ears to hear—(while he has nothing worse than ears)—let him hear! A word to the wise should be enough.—There are some particular qualities now and then very likely to lead a gentleman on the sudden to make a lady his wife; and, after she has become so, very likely again to make him wish that they had made her anybody else's.

Maxim Second.

White arms, and neat ancles, bring me, naturally, at once, to the very important consideration of beauty. For, don't suppose, because I caution you against all day dishabilles, that I want to fix you with a worthy creature, whom it will make you extremely ill every time you look at. No! leave these to apothecaries—lawyers—and such, generally, as mean to leave money behind them when they die. You have health—a competence—a handy pull at a nose, or at a trigger:—let them grovel. For the style of attraction, please yourselves, my friends. I should say a handsome figure—if you don't get both advantages—is better than a merely pretty face. I don't mean, by "handsome figure," forty cubits high, and as big round as the chief drayman at Meux's brew-house. But finely formed and set. Good eyes are a point never to be overlooked. Fine teeth—full, well-proportioned limbs—don't cast these away for the sake of a single touch of the smallpox; a mouth something too wide; or dimples rather deeper on one side than the other.

Maxim Third.

It may, at some time, be a matter of consideration, whether you shall marry a maid or a widow. As to the taste, I myself will give no opinion—I like both; and there are advantages and disadvantages peculiar to either. If you marry a widow, I think it should be one whom you have known in the lifetime of her husband; because, then—*ab actu ad posse*—from the sufferings of the defunct, you may form some notion of what your own will be. If her husband is dead before you see her, you had better be off at once; because she knows (the jade!) what you will like, though she never means to do it; and, depend upon it, if you have only an inch of *penchant*, and trust yourself to look at her three times, you are tickled to a certainty.

Maxim Fourth.

Marrying girls is a nice matter always; for they are as cautious as crows plundering a corn-field. You may "stalk" for a week, and never get near them unperceived. You hear the caterwauling, as you go up stairs, into the drawing-room, louder than thunder; but it stops—as if by magic! the moment a (marriageable) man puts his ear to the keyhole. I don't myself, I profess, upon principle, see any objection to marrying a widow. If she upbraids you at any time with the virtues of her former husband, you only reply—that you wish he had her with him, with all your soul. If a woman, however, has had more than three husbands, she poisons them; avoid her.

Maxim Fifth.

In widow-wiving, it may be a question whether you should marry the widow of an honest man, or of a rascal. Against the danger, that the last have learned ill tricks, they set the advantage—she will be more sensible (from the contrast) to the kindness of a gentleman and a man of honour. I think you should marry the honest man's widow; because, with women, habit is always stronger than reason.

Maxim Sixth.

But the greatest point, perhaps, to be aimed at in marrying, is to know, before marriage, what it is that you have to deal with. You are quite sure to know this, fast enough, afterwards. Be sure, therefore, that you commence the necessary perquisitions before you have made up your mind, and not as people generally do, *after*. Remember there is no use in watching a woman that you *love;* because she can't do anything—do what she will—that will be disagreeable to you. And still less, in examining a woman that loves *you;* because for the time, she will be quite sure not to do anything that ought to be disagreeable to you. I have known a hundred perfect tigresses as playful as kittens—quite more obliging than need be—under such circumstances. It is not a bad way—maid or widow—when you find yourself fancying a woman, to make her believe that you have an aversion to her. If she has any concealed good qualities, they are pretty sure to come out upon such an occasion.

N.B. Take care, nevertheless, how you make use of this suggestion; because, right or wrong, it is the very way to make the poor soul fall furiously and fatally in love with you. *Vulnus alit venis, et cæco carpitur igni!*

Maxim Seventh.

In judging *where* to look for a wife—that is, for the lady who is to form the "raw material" of one—very great caution is necessary. And you can't take any thing better with you, in looking about, as a general principle, than that good mothers commonly make tolerably good daughters. Of course, therefore, you won't go, of consideration prepense, into any house where parents are badly connected, or have been badly conducted. Nor, upon any account at all, into any house where you don't quite feel, that if you don't conduct yourself properly, you'll immediately be kicked out of it. This assurance may be troublesome while you are only a visitor; but when you come to be one of the family, you'll find it mighty convenient. If you can find any place where vice and folly have been used to be called by their right names, stick to that by all means—there are seldom more than two such in one parish; and if you see any common rascal let into a house where you visit as readily as yourself, go out of it immediately.

Maxim Eighth.

Mind—but I need hardly caution you of this,—that you are not taken in with that paltry, bygone nonsense about—"If you marry—marrying a fool." Recollect that the greatest fool must be sometimes out of your sight; and that she will yet carry you (for all purposes of mischief) along with her. A shrew may want her nails kept short; but if you keep a strait waistcoat in the house, you may always do this yourself. And she is not, of necessity, like your "bleating innocent," a prey to the first wolf who chooses to devour her.

Maxim Ninth.

At the same time, while you avoid a fool, fly—as you fly from sin and death—fly from a philosopher! It is very dangerous to weak minds, examining (farther than is duly delivered to them) what is right or wrong.—I never found any body yet who could distinctly explain what murder is, if put to a definition.

All who find their minds superior to common rule and received opinion; value themselves on original thinking; talk politics; read Mary Wolstonecraft; or meddle with the mathematics: these are unclean birds upon whom the protecting genius of honest men has set his mark that all may know; and pray do you avoid them.

Maxim Tenth.

If you marry an actress, don't let her be a tragedy one. Habits of ranting and whisking up and down with a long train before a row of "footlamps," are apt to cast an undue ludicrousness (when transplanted) over the serious business of life. Only imagine a castigation delivered to the cook, in "King Cambyses' vein," upon the event of an underdone leg of mutton at dinner; or an incarnation of Helen M'Gregor, ordering the cat to be thrown alive into the cistern, if a piece of muffin was abstracted, without leave, at breakfast!

Maxim Eleventh.

If you do marry an actress, the singing girls perhaps are best; Miss Paton, I think, seems very soft, and coaxing, and desirable. I myself should prefer Kitty Stephens to any of them.* Though she is a sad lazy slut—won't learn a line, and sleeps all day upon the sofa! But I'm a teacher; and therefore the less I parade my own practice—at least so the belief goes—the better.

* Miss Paton, well known in America as Mrs. Joseph Wood. Miss Stephens, by her marriage with an aged peer (now dead) is Dowager-Countess of Essex.—M.

Maxim Twelfth.

Be sure, wherever you choose, choose a proud woman. All honesty is a kind of pride; or at least three-fourths of it. No people do wrong, but in spite of themselves they feel a certain quantity of descent and self-degradation: the more a woman has to forfeit, the less likely she is to forfeit anything at all. Take the pride, although you have the virtue; the more indorsements you get, even on a good bill, the better.

Maxim Thirteenth.

I don't think the Saints — after all is said and done — are the worst people in the world to match among. Nine-tenths of the mischief that women do arise less from ill design than from idle, careless, vagabond levity. It falls out commonly among the great card-players, and play-hunters; very little among the Methodists and Presbyterians. Of course, you won't contract for anything beyond going to church three times a-day; and such like public professions of faith and feeling. But for the rest, I don't see why you should embarrass yourself about any system of belief, so long as it offends only against reason, and tends to the believer's temporal advantage.

Maxim Fourteenth.

At the same time, after the last sentence of the above exhortation, I need hardly tell you that you must not marry a Roman Catholic. Indeed I suppose it would be a little too much for any of you, who read *me*, to fancy a pleasant gentleman claiming the right to catechise your wives in private? For my part, God help any rascal who presumed to talk of law, human or divine, in my family; except the law, which, like Jack Cade's law, came "out of my mouth!" I know something of these matters, having once contemplated being a monk myself — in fact, I had stolen a dress for the purpose. On the same principle — I rather think I mentioned this before — suffer no "guardianships," or "trusteeships," in your family, to disturb your reign, or fret your quiet. I knew a very worthy fellow, who, having only a marriage settlement brought to him, broke the solicitor's clerk's neck down stairs that brought it; and it was brought in "Justifiable Homicide." If a dog dares but to hint that there *is* such a thing as "parchment" in your presence, plump, and rib him.

Maxim Fifteenth.

I don't think, by the way, that there *ought* to be any parchment, except the petitions to the House of Commons, which are cut up to supply the tailors with measures. This is useful. Messrs. Sheil and O'Connell's work takes the dimensions of my person once a month very accurately. I mention this, because it has been said that no *measures*, in which the work of those gentlemen was concerned, ever could be taken accurately.

Maxim Sixteenth.

Talking of accuracy leads me to observe:—Don't marry any woman hastily at Brighton or Brussels, without knowing who she is and where she lived before she came there. And whenever you get a reference upon this, or any other subject, always be sure and get another reference about the person referred to.

Maxim Seventeenth.

Don't marry any woman under twenty—she is not come to her wickedness before that time. Nor any woman who has a red nose at any age; because people make observations as you go along the street. A "cast of the eye,"—as the lady casts it upon you—may pass muster under some circumstances—and I have even known those who thought it desirable; but absolute squinting is a monopoly of vision which ought not to be tolerated.

Maxim Eighteenth.

Talking of "vision," reminds me of an absurd saying,—That such or such a one can "see as far through a mill-stone as those that picked it." I don't believe that any man ever saw through a mill-stone but Jeremy Bentham; and he looked through the hole.

Maxim Nineteenth.

One hears a great deal about "City taste;" I must say, I don't think an Alderman's daughter by any means (*qua* Cornhill merely) objectionable. A fine girl may be charming, even though her father should be a Common Councilman — Recollect this.

Maxim Twentieth.

On the question of getting an insight into matters before marriage, if possible, I have dropped a word already. It is a point of very great importance, and there are two or three modes in which you may take your chance for accomplishing it. If you are *up to* hiring yourself into any house as a chambermaid — it requires tact, and close shaving; but it would put you into the way of finding out a thing or two. I "took up my livery" once as a footman, and I protest I learned so much in three weeks, that I would not have married any female in the family. An old maiden aunt, or sister, if you have one, is capable of great service. She will see more of a tomboy in five minutes than you would in six months; because, having been in the oven herself, she knows the way. On the other hand, there is the danger that she may sell you to some estate that she thinks lies convenient; or even job you off to some personal favourite, without the consideration of any estate at all. The Punic faith of all agents — especially one's own relatives — is notorious.

Maxim Twenty-first.

On the subject of accomplishment, it is hardly my business to advise. I leave a great part — the chief part — upon this point, to your own fancy. Only don't have any waltzing, nor too much determined singing of Moore's songs; there is bad taste, to say the best of it, in all such publicities. For music, I don't think there is a great deal gained by a woman's being able to make an alarming jangle on the piano-forte, particularly under that unmerciful scheme of "Duets," in which two tyrants are enabled to belabour the machine at the same time. Dancing, a girl ought to be able to execute well; but don't go anywhere, where a *Monsieur* has been employed to give the instruction. As dancing is an art to be acquired merely from imitation, a graceful female — being the precise thing to be imitated — must be a far more efficient teacher than even Mr. Kick-the-Moon himself can be. Besides, I don't like the notion of a d—d scraper putting a girl of thirteen into attitudes. If I were to catch a balletmaster capering in my house, I'd qualify the dog to lead in the opera before he departed.

N. B.—Now we are on the subject of dancing, don't on any account marry a "lively" young lady. That is, in other words, a "romp." That is, in other words, a woman who has been hauled about by half your acquaintance.

And now, my friends, my first twenty-one rules—just beginning your instruction, each of you, how to get a wife—are spoken out. And any directions how to manage one, if they come at all, must come at some future opportunity. Just two words, however, even upon this head; for I would not leave you, upon any subject, too much unprovided.

In the first place, on the very day after your marriage, whenever you do marry, take one precaution—be cursed with no more troubles for life than you have bargained for. Call the roll of all your wife's even speaking acquaintance; and strike out every soul that you have—or fancy you ought to have—or fancy you ever shall have—a glimpse of dislike to.

Upon this point be merciless; your wife won't hesitate—a hundred to one—between a husband and a gossip; and—if she does—don't you. Be particularly sharp upon the list of women; of course, men—you would frankly kick any one from Pall-Mall to Pimlico, who presumed only to recollect ever having seen her.

And don't be manœuvred out of what you mean, by cards, or morning calls, or any notion of what people call "good breeding." Do you be content to show your ill breeding by shutting the door, and the visitors can show their good breeding by not coming again.

One syllable more to part—if you wish to be happy yourself, be sure that you must make your wife so. Never dispute with her where the question is of no importance; nor, where it is of the least consequence, let any earthly consideration ever once induce you to give way. Be at home as much as you can; be as strict as you will, but never *speak* unkindly; and never have a friend upon such terms in your house, as to be able to enter it without ceremony. Above all, remember that these maxims are intrusted to all of you, as to persons of reason and discretion. A naked sword only cuts the fingers of a madman; and the rudder with which the pilot saves the ship, in the hands of the powder monkey, would only probably force her upon the rocks. Recollect, that your inquest as to matrimony is a matter of the greatest nicety; because, either an excess of vigilance, or a deficiency, will alike compromise its success. If you don't question far enough, the odds are ten to one that you get a wife who will disappoint you. If you question a jot too far, you will never get a wife at all,

END OF VOL. I.

www.ingramcontent.com/pod-product-compliance
Lightning Source LLC
LaVergne TN
LVHW020123110826
845151LV00001B/257